THE
NAVAJO-HOPI LAND DISPUTE

....

THE
NAVAJO-HOPI LAND DISPUTE

·················

An American Tragedy

DAVID M. BRUGGE

UNIVERSITY OF NEW MEXICO PRESS

ALBUQUERQUE

Library of Congress Cataloging-in-Publication Data
Brugge, David M.
　　The Navajo-Hopi land dispute : an American tragedy / David M. Brugge.—1st ed.
　　　p.　cm.
　　Includes bibliographical references and index.
　　Contents: Friends and enemies, the history of an ambiguous relationship—Peace
and strife—Preparation, the road to Prescott—Prescott—The long wait—Progress (of
sorts)—False hopes—Confrontation—The end of line—Final thoughts.
　　　ISBN 0–8263–1513–5
　　1. Navajo Indians—Land tenure.　2. Navajo Indians—Land transfers.　3. Hopi
Indians—Land tenure.　4. Indians of North America—Arizona—Land transfers.
5. Indians of North America—Government relations—1934–　I. Title.
E99.N3B757　1994
979.1′3′0047972—dc20
93-46954

Frontispiece by Tony Hood.

To Ruth

CONTENTS

MAPS

....

INTRODUCTION

WHEN I FIRST went to work for the Navajo Tribe in 1958 to assist in research for their land claim case against the U.S. government and eventually for other land disputes, I already had many Navajo friends whom I could easily accept as people, each with his or her own unique personality. I entered into the work with a firm belief that our system of courts was also a system of justice and that if we could demonstrate fairly that Navajos had long occupied certain tracts of land, their claims would be upheld.

When I was assigned to work on *Healing* v. *Jones* (the by-now infamous Navajo-Hopi land dispute case), I believed there was some small risk that the tribe might lose, but as the work progressed and I came to know the Navajo people living in the 1882 Executive Order Reservation, to learn their history as revealed by their traditions, by our archeological investigations, and by the archival accounts written by white observers, I found that I could fully sympathize with their cause. I could not believe that my own government, which I had been raised to trust, would ever dispossess so many poverty-stricken and thoroughly traditional people from a land upon which their lives and well-being were so completely dependent. I was aware of the bias against the Navajos that was, and still is, widespread in the Southwest, but again I had been so convinced of the basic fairness of our society that I could not conceive of such prejudice influencing official government decisions. I even prided myself that I was helping the Navajos find a way within the legal system of the United States to settle peacefully a boundary problem that would be a proper fence to make good neighbors for a long a time to come.

I was still in many ways the naive young man who, as a draftee in the army not too many years before, had given up my seat on a bus in Georgia to an elderly African American. Rosa Parks and the civil rights movement were still well in the future. Perhaps my army uniform and Yankee accent had spared me, and her, certain disaster then, but I went away retaining an unreal and idealistic view of how our society worked.

Then I met John Boyden in a courtroom in Prescott, Arizona. His vivid black-versus-white portrayal of Navajos and Hopis made my former misgivings of Navajo loss return as an all-too-real possibility. I found his melodramatic bluster banal, and I still could not believe the Navajos could lose their homes unless we failed to do an adequate job of presenting the case, but his approach to the contest left me with a feeling of foreboding.

In the years since, I have tried to understand why *Healing* v. *Jones* led ultimately to a result that I had not thought possible. Jerry Kammer's book, *The Second Long Walk: The Navajo-Hopi Land Dispute*,[1] skimmed so lightly over the years that I knew about from personal experience that I could not be comfortable with it. He appeared to relate the story in too facile a manner. This may have been largely a result of his journalistic style, but I felt a need to take another look at what had happened.

What I have written here is intended to present not merely yet another view of the Navajo-Hopi dispute, one that I feel I owe the Navajo people, but in addition such insight as I have been able to gain after years of thought and a restudy of the events that led up to the lawsuit, what happened in court, and what transpired in the wake of the judges' decision.

I have made a studied effort to be fair to both sides, but my view is necessarily from the Navajo side of the fence. I expect to be accused of bias, but I feel confident that my views are justified. In a single book it is not possible to include everything. I have chosen to present those facts that bear on my ultimate thesis—that prejudice and stereotyping were decisive in the outcome of the case. Even if I am wrong, I suspect that John Boyden would have agreed that these were of major importance at the very least, for his eloquent rhetoric was designed to reinforce any latent bias in those who listened and he used it in a well-planned campaign that resulted in the outcome he sought. I have too much respect for his intelligence to believe that he did not know what he was doing.

While in the midst of this writing the issue of "political correctness," or "PC," suddenly appeared in the press and even at my own alma mater. I explicitly do not agree with the extremists on either side of this debate, finding too many of those who attack what they call "PC" to be promoters of bias in one direction and some of those who promote it to exhibit bias in the opposite direction. It is vital that we all stand up for the rights of everyone else, but also that we not assert as truth what we know to be otherwise, no matter how good the cause.

Under our constitution, bigots have as much right to speak and write as anyone else, as long as they do not trample the rights of others. Only where this right to free expression exists can we know who is the enemy. Only when bigotry is staunchly opposed can any of us be safe. Opposition to bigotry must be firm, yet restrained, and it is up to private citizens to provide that opposition in all instances where the law cannot do so, for what is legal does not define all that is right, nor does what is illegal define all that is wrong. Some things lie beyond the purview of government in a true democracy. Only our eternal vigilance can keep them in check. This book is, among other things, my effort to provide some of that opposition. Too many of us who were most intimately involved in *Healing* v. *Jones* are no longer able to do so.

Healing v. *Jones* and the events that followed do raise some serious questions as to the limits that should or might be placed on resort to ethnic hatreds in order to achieve one's goals, as well as to how those limits might be maintained without infringing on important freedoms. I am better at raising the questions, or at least at placing an old question in another context, than I am at finding an answer. I feel that the responsibility lay in part with those of us who defended the Navajo claim. We may have failed to meet the need in some very basic way, whether due to an overriding concern for fairness, to an overemphasis of the Navajo desire to avoid conflict, to an inability to define just what was really at stake, or to some other, less obvious factor. We were not alone, however. The courts, the Congress, and the Bureau of Indian Affairs (if not the Department of Interior itself) also failed to exclude ethnic bias from their thinking or to recognize and oppose it in others. We still have things to learn that would help us better deal with such situations, particularly where one party to a dispute is aggressively set upon raising ethnic issues in ways that play on the emotions.

At this point, a note on my usages in writing is required. I have consistently used the term *Navajo Tribe* for the political entity that today calls itself the Navajo Nation, as that was the official usage during the times with which I am dealing. The term refers to the Navajo people as a whole or as a corporate entity, one that has had a changing formal structure during the years covered by my account. At times the use of the term *tribe* has depended almost solely on the people's own sense of themselves as a unit, at other times on a formal religious sanction, and during most of this century on a developing political structure modeled on modern usages among Anglo-Americans. The word *Navajos* has also frequently been used with the same meaning.

In a like manner, the term *Hopi Tribe* has been used to mean the Hopi people as a whole and as a corporate entity. I have, however, had to face the reality of the extreme divisiveness of modern Hopi politics. For the period since the 1930s, the formal political structure provided by the Bureau of Indian Affairs has been accepted as the "Hopi Tribe" by the United States government, except for several years when it lapsed due to internal opposition. Despite this, there has continued to be a significant portion of traditional Hopi people who refuse to recognize any legitimacy of this structure. I have, nonetheless, used the term *Hopi Tribe* to refer to this formal political organization where I feel I will not be misunderstood, and the term *Hopi council* or *Hopi council faction* where the distinction between the political entity and more traditional groups might need to be emphasized. I have sometimes resorted to use of the term *Hopis* to signify this same political entity in order to avoid excessively cumbersome prose. This does not mean that I am thereby discounting the "traditional" Hopi faction. I usually specify them by their preferred descriptor ("traditional"), despite the fact that the council faction disputes their right to that title. My justification for using the term *Hopis* to describe the council faction lies in the fact that all actions taken by the federal government in its relations with that faction are deemed by law to apply to all Hopis, whether or not they recognize the Hopi tribal government.

In the final stages of preparation, I must acknowledge my gratitude to Beth Hadas, but for whose interest I might never have persevered; to Larry Ball for sage editorial advice; to Ruth Steinberg for expert copy-editing; to Emmy Ezzell for aid with art and illustrations; to Donald L. Parman for a final critical review; to Martin A. Link for finding an artist and to Tony Hood for being that artist; to Jerry Livingston for his careful drafting of maps; to Octavia Fellin, Marshal Plummer, Clarenda Begay, Irving Nelson, Patricia D. Begay, Richard Rudisill, Arthur L. Olivas for assistance in locating historic photographs and/or permissions for their use; Tom Arviso for permissions to use illustrations from *The Navajo Times*; Kenji Kawano for photocopying; and David F. Aberle for permission to use an extensive quote from his report to Congress.

I must express my thanks to the many who suffered through the toil, trials, and tribulations that left us wondering about ourselves and our fellow *Homo sapiens.* To those who worked in the research I owe a great debt, including Richard F. Van Valkenburgh, Edward O. Plummer, J. Lee Correll, Dr. George P. Hammond, Joseph Colgan, Bernadine Whitegoat, Maxwell Yazzie, Clyde Peshlakai, Dr. Clyde Kluckhohn, Dr. Roscoe Wilmeth, Stanley Stubbs, Dr. Aubrey W. Williams, Jr., Helena Yazhe, Martin A. Link, and Dr. David L. DeHarport. In addition, we were assisted by a great many people, far too many to acknowledge individually here—those in the local communities who served as guides, interpreters, and helpers, and those in the tribal offices working as clerks, typists, draftsmen, and in a multitude of other roles. The names of some appear in the account that follows, but to all, whether identified or not, I express my appreciation.

Several Bureau of Indian Affairs employees deserve special mention here, including Dr. Robert W. Young, Graham Holmes, Wilbur Morgan, Howard Zutzius, and Arthur Hubbard.

Despite my differences of opinion with some of the tribal attorneys, I must acknowledge their importance in my journey to knowledge and perplexity and note that by the standards of their profession they served their clients well, even if the legal mind is not attuned to an anthropologist's way of thinking. So, to Norman M. Littell, Joseph F. McPherson, Walter Wolf, James Thomson, Theodore Mitchell, William McPherson, William Lavell, Leland O. Graham, Harold Mott, and others whose names I may have omitted, *muchas gracias.*

Some of the people working for opposing attorneys were also colleagues in terms of research interests, and I owe them a debt for intellectual stimulation. For a better appreciation of the historian's role in ethnohistory, I owe most to Dr. Myra Ellen Jenkins. Others who deserve credit, but no blame, for my progress include Dr. Florence H. Ellis, Albert H. Schroeder, Dr. Shuichi Nagata, and Dr. Fred Eggan, who raised questions that I found worth pursuing. Other colleagues who through the years have contributed to my fund of fact and theory and who should be mentioned here include Frank McNitt, Dr. John P. Wilson, Dr. Leland C. Wyman, Dr. Charlotte J. Frisbie, and Dr.

Stephen C. Jett. To W. W. (Nibs) Hill, I owe most of all, but especially for his advice, "Never work for the BIA."

I wish to thank the staff at Brown and Bain, in particular Dolph Barnhouse, Terry Fenzyl, Craig Soland, Scott Russell, John Rogers, Sharon Debowski and Marilyn Mills; and for assistance in locating and access to sources, those at the Coronado Room, Zimmerman Library, University of New Mexico and at the Laboratory of Anthropology, Museum of New Mexico.

Dr. Charlotte J. Frisbie and Dr. Dorothy Parker read the initial version of my text and offered many valuable suggestions. Dr. Donald L. Parman, as peer reviewer, has provided equally insightful comments. Lauren H. Rimbert typed the manuscript. For assistance with computers and word processing, I owe gratitude to Michael F. Rimbert, James K. Hesch, and Donald E. Johnson.

For all errors, overly rash opinions, and any other sins of commission or omission, I take full responsibility. Royalties, if any, will go to Navajo Community College.

THE
NAVAJO-HOPI LAND DISPUTE

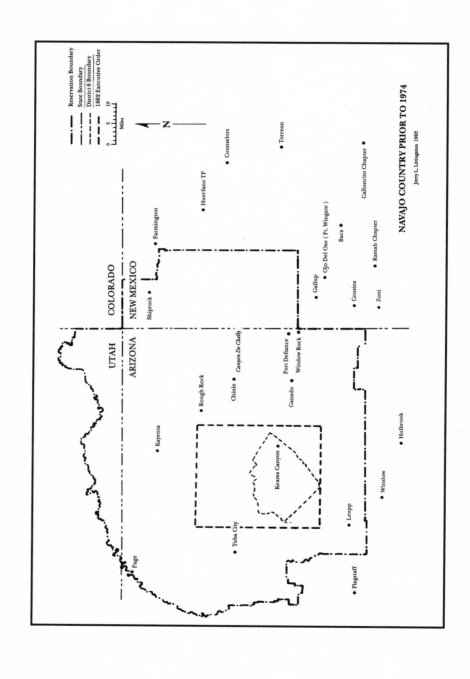

NAVAJO COUNTRY PRIOR TO 1974

Jerry L. Livingston 1992

Reservation Boundary
State Boundary
District 6 Boundary
1882 Executive Order

Miles
0   5   10

N

UTAH
COLORADO
ARIZONA
NEW MEXICO

Page
Kayenta
Rough Rock
Chinle
Canyon De Chelly
Shiprock
Farmington
Huerfano TP
Counselors
Torreon
Ganado
Fort Defiance
Window Rock
Tuba City
Keams Canyon
Leupp
Winslow
Holbrook
Flagstaff
Gallup
Ojo Del Oso (Ft. Wingate)
Baca
Cousins
Zuni
Ramah Chapter
Cañoncito Chapter

FRIENDS AND ENEMIES

The History of an Ambiguous Relationship

SOMEWHERE IN THE semiarid Southwest an uncounted number of centuries ago, small bands of Athabaskan hunters and gatherers dressed in tailored skin clothing met Pueblo farmers who wore woven textiles. We can only speculate about those initial encounters as people from the far northern boreal forests penetrated country once the domain of sedentary agriculturists.

The Pueblo people were in retreat. They were abandoning, or had already deserted, many small settlements throughout the Colorado Plateau to gather in growing centers of population. Rains had failed for too many years in succession; usually plentiful staple crops of corn, beans, and squash now produced too little food; laboriously gathered wild crops did not suffice to make up the difference. Favored areas attracted those who survived. Hamlets and villages gave way to towns, often of a few thousand inhabitants—populations large enough to resist the inroads of neighbors who might envy and covet a good harvest.

One center of Puebloan concentration was at the southern edge of Black Mesa, where stable dunes held moisture, and water courses that drained extensive highland areas emerged and spread out to water valley bottoms. Diverse groups sought refuge in this unlikely oasis, but the Hopi language became dominant.

Athabaskan migrants from the north probably did not arrive until the land had begun to recover from the drought. We do not know what forces drove them to leave their homes, although famine, volcanic eruptions and ashfalls, and simple population growth as wild herds of game animals expanded are all possibilities. They filled the vacant lands and adapted to life in their new environment, living in scattered campsites, much like the remote ancestors of the Puebloan peoples had lived much earlier. As time passed, a group of Athabaskans known as Apaches de Navajo became the northern and eastern neighbors of the Hopi pueblos.

APACHE-PUEBLO DYNAMICS

The Apache and Pueblo peoples of the American Southwest have been neighbors for a long time. Records of the nature of their relationship go back to the earliest Spanish accounts, which describe both enmities and friendly interactions. For precontact times, we cannot be certain of the reasons for these differences. The most probable explanation may be that individual Apachean bands or tribes had alliances and trade relations with individual pueblos, even as they were at odds with other pueblos that were also enemies of their Pueblo trading partners. Interpueblo warfare is amply documented during the period of Spanish explorations, 1540–1598.[1]

As long as interpueblo hostilities remained and trade between Pueblos and Apaches maintained a stable balance in a system that might even be characterized as symbiotic to some degree,[2] any system of alliances and enmities would also likely remain stable. The arrival of the Spaniards as colonizers disrupted the trade in many ways as the conquerors began first to claim the profits of the exchanges and then take them over altogether. New social dynamics arose that changed the nature of Puebloan-Apachean relationships dramatically.

The Pueblo peoples are believed to have long been subject to strong intrapueblo factionalism. Even if there were only a mild factionalism, however, unity of a pueblo would be subject to severe strains under the conditions of foreign rule. It seems almost inevitable that one faction would ally itself with the invaders while the other would oppose them. This is indeed what took place at many pueblos, a good example being Pecos.[3] Similar divided alliances existed at Jemez, Isleta, Alameda, San Felipe, Cochiti, Acoma, Laguna, the Tewa and Piro villages, Zuni, and even among the Hopis. The natural allies for the anti-white faction at most pueblos were their old Apachean trading partners, who remained free of European domination.[4]

SPANISH EXPLORATION

As early as 1583 when Antonio de Espejo led a small party on a visit to the Hopi country, the Hopis called on Querechos (probably neighboring Athabaskan-speaking Apacheans) to help defend their land, doubtless remembering well the destruction of Pueblo towns by Coronado's army in 1540. They sent their women and children, along with their flocks of turkeys, to hiding places in the mountains. When Espejo convinced them that he had come in peace, they sent the Querechos away.[5]

There was another aspect to the small party's dealings with the Hopis, however. One or more Querecho women who were held as captives by the Hopis were traded to individual white soldiers. This fact would have gone unrecorded had it not been that one of these women escaped. The woman joined a band of Querechos among whom she had relatives after the explorers reached an area north of Acoma occupied by people who were trading partners and allies of the Acomas. This helped precipitate hostilities, which hastened the Spaniards' retreat back to Mexico.[6]

SPANISH COLONIAL PERIOD

In 1604–1605 Don Juan de Oñate, having established a colony at San Gabriel on the upper Rio Grande, visited Hopi both going to and returning from an exploring expedition to the Gulf of California. A journal of the expedition notes encounters with Yavapais and, somewhat inferentially, Apacheans at the Hopi villages. No explanation is given as to why these people were at Hopi, but trade seems a likely reason.[7]

In 1629 Franciscan missionaries were finally sent to Hopi as the Spanish effort to convert the Pueblo Indians was increased. Fray Francisco de Porras and Fray Andres Gutiérrez, both priests, and a lay brother, Fray Cristóbal de la Concepción, arrived via Zuni with an escort of twelve soldiers. An apostate from one of the Christian pueblos had preceded them and warned the Hopis that the Spaniards were coming to burn their towns, take their property, and kill their children. He said the missionaries were impostors who would cause them to die by sprinkling water on their heads.

This news caused the Hopis to call on their Apache neighbors, with whom they "had a truce." The second night at Awatovi, the easternmost

Hopi town at the time, "enemy captains" came to attack the Spaniards, but the guard was alert and the soldiers were up and mounted by the time they arrived. This happened on another night as well, and the visitors felt it necessary to threaten the Hopis with the vengeance of a Spanish army if they should be harmed.

During this initial period, the missionaries spent their days preaching in the streets, attracting not only the people of the pueblo, but others who came "from near-by valleys and neighboring forests." They offered gifts such as "rattles, beads, hatchets and knives," but the Indians refused them, fearing that anything given them by the friars might bring death.[8]

Whether the Apaches were asked to help in the attempted killing of the Spaniards, and whether the people from outside the pueblo who came to hear the priests were Apaches, is not entirely clear in the account, but in each case it seems likely that they were. In any case, the Navajo Apaches were not far distant.

It was reported that Fray Francisco miraculously restored sight to a blind boy, thereby winning the trust of the majority of the Hopis of Awatovi. Sometime between 1626 and 1639 Fray Martín de Arvide, then missionary at Jemez, made a trip to the west to preach to the Navajos, which he did "in the same region, on the western border of New Mexico, where the blessed father, Fray Francisco de Porras, performed the miracle of giving sight to the blind boy. . . ."[9]

Thus it seems that up until actual missionization both the Hopis and their neighboring Apaches, perhaps including both Navajos and Western Apaches, were divided as to the wisdom of receiving missionaries. Their views, as filtered through Spanish understanding, were not based on any doubt as to the validity of the invaders' religion. There was abundant material evidence in the horses and other livestock, metal arms and armor, firearms, metal tools, the mystery of writing, the Spaniards' dramatic music, and the imposing architecture that they introduced to convince all that these newcomers had great supernatural power. The real question for the native peoples was how the Spaniards would use that power. Some felt there were advantages in allying with them, and others feared them and tried to resist or avoid them. The split was not only along tribal lines, but also within tribes and communities, aggravating any dissentions which may have existed prior to the Spanish arrival.

Once the missionaries had established themselves in the Hopi pueblos, the logical outcome would have been for any faction that continued to oppose Spanish rule to seek the support of neighboring peoples, as had happened at other pueblos to the east.[10] This is probably what did happen. Some hint that this was the case appears in the fact that the trail from Hawikuh in the Zuni country to Awatovi came to be considered by the Spaniards "the most dangerous part of this kingdom" by 1664.[11] That anti-Spanish Hopi leaders encouraged Navajos to harass Spanish travelers can be no more than a guess, but one that would not be contrary to later patterns. That there were also Hopis who were friendly with the Spaniards and willing to initiate hostilities against the Apacheans is clear from the account of the people of Walpi, who took nine Apacheans captive in 1661, presenting two to the whites as gifts and offering the other seven for sale.[12] Unfortunately, little else is known of the relations between the Hopis and the Apacheans during the mission period in the *Provincia de Moqui.*

The Pueblo Revolt of 1680 ended Spanish rule of the Hopis. The Hopis killed the four or five priests then in their villages and moved to the mesa tops for protection from Spanish retaliation.[13]

The Hopis remained secure from Spanish intrusion until 1692 when Diego de Vargas made his first expedition into Pueblo country. As Vargas invaded the upper Rio Grande region, Hopis, Jemez, Keres, Pecos, Zunis, Faraón Apaches, Coninas, and others met near Acoma to plan their resistance.[14] By the judicious use of diplomacy and threat, Vargas was able to undermine this alliance and to visit most of the villages of the Pueblo peoples said to have been represented at the meeting. The Faraón Apaches had told the Hopis that Vargas intended to come under the pretense of peace and then kill them. The Hopis fled to the mountains, taking their livestock with them and sending scouts to observe what the whites did at Zuni. Having seen that they did no harm at the other pueblos, the scouts calmed the fears of their people, who nonetheless greeted the Spaniards with a strong show of opposition when they first arrived at Awatovi. Vargas was able to gain the nominal submission of all Hopi villages except Oraibi before he turned back at Second Mesa. Factional divisions among the Hopis were influential in his success, for some had wished to attack and destroy the small party of soldiers led by Vargas from Zuni, where the greater part of his army rested. Others had advocated receiving him peacefully, and one leader at Awatovi had even threatened to help the Spaniards defend themselves should they be attacked.[15] Upon Vargas's return to New Mexico in 1693, resistance developed among the eastern pueblos, which prevented him from giving any attention to the Hopis or the Apachean tribes. The Hopi country became a refuge for many of the Pueblo people fleeing defeat in the east. Their accounts of battles with the Spaniards and their determination to remain free undoubtedly reinforced the Hopi factions that favored defending their country from foreign rule.[16]

The Revolt of 1696, which erupted a scant two years after Vargas had enforced his "bloodless" reconquest of 1692 with a far from bloodless sequel, was reported to have the support of the Hopis, but again the action was far from their country and their towns remained undisturbed.[17] It is probable that an additional influx of refugees helped swell Hopi forces and strengthen Hopi resolve.

The final Spanish foothold among the Hopis came at Awatovi in 1700 and it was a tenuous one. One or two Franciscan priests visited the town in the spring of that year after receiving an invitation from some of the residents who had refurbished the *convento* of the mission complex. The priests were able to baptize many of the people, but were discouraged from going on to the other Hopi towns. After they left, sometime in the fall of 1700 or early in 1701, Hopis from the other towns destroyed Awatovi in a frenzy of brutality that exceeded even the early Spanish treatment of defeated pueblos, if the traditions may be trusted. Not only were many of the men trapped in the kivas that were burned, but chile peppers were thrown into the fires to make their suffering greater. Many of the captives taken in the attack on Awatovi were killed at a place called Skeleton Mound, or Skull Mound. According to one Navajo tradition, the captives were dismembered while still living. An archeological find of thirty or more skeletons which had been dismembered, cooked, and probably cannibalized has been dated at about the time of the massacre. Women and children taken captive and not killed were distributed to the various villages that took part in the attack.[18]

The various traditional accounts are consistent in telling that the chief of Awatovi asked the leaders of the other Hopi towns to destroy his town and that he assisted them in doing so.[19] One source notes that this theme appears in the traditions of the demise of other former Hopi settlements.[20] Courlander suggests that this feature is merely a "literary" device of Hopi story-telling.[21] Whether destruction of a corrupt village at the behest of its chief has actually been a pattern in Hopi affairs is a matter of some consequence for an understanding of the event. There were survivors of the killing other than the captives, and it may be assumed that they were members of an anti-Spanish faction.

At least some of these survivors joined the Navajos. They are said to be the descendants of people who settled at Awatovi when it was already a thriving Hopi town, coming from the vicinity of the San Francisco Peaks and forming a distinct population within the pueblo. Having survived the attack at Awatovi, many, if not all, of them became members of the Navajo *Táchii'nii* Clan, forming several branches of that clan which retained Hopi clan names. Most prominent is the group known as the *Nát'oh Dine'é Táchii'nii*, or Tobacco People *Táchii'nii*. Others include the *Biih Dine'é Táchii'nii*, or Deer People *Táchii'nii*; the *Gah Dine'é Táchii'nii*, or Rabbit People *Táchii'nii*; the *Ostse' Dine'é Táchii'nii*, or Tansy Mustard People *Táchii'nii*; and the *Yé'ii Dine'é Táchii'nii*, perhaps best translated as the Kachina People *Táchii'nii*. There are said to be seven such subclans, but I have learned the names for only these five and have actually met only members of the Tobacco People *Táchii'nii*. A Zuni People *Táchii'nii* subclan appears in the published literature,[22] but it seems unlikely that this was one of the seven believed to originate from Awatovi.

Having evaded death when the other Hopis overwhelmed their village, these people moved first toward the south, thence to Canyon de Chelly where they were absorbed into the Navajo population, and subsequently to *Táchii'* near Blue Gap. Some eventually found their way back to the Jeddito Valley where they began again to farm the lands that had once been those of their Pueblo ancestors.[23]

The early eighteenth century saw continuing close relations between the Hopis and some of the Navajos. Early in 1704 Navajos hosted a meeting with Hopis and Tewas at Piedra Alumbre in the Chama Valley.[24] By the end of the year the Navajos were staging raids against the Spanish colony. Among other reasons, they had been encouraged by the Hopis, who had offered friendship if the Navajos would deliver the scalps of Domingo Romero of Tesuque, of the lieutenant of San Ildefonso, and of the Tiwas.[25] Again in 1707 Hopis provided the initiative for additional attacks, making gifts of blankets to the Navajos and other Apaches to induce them to fight the Spaniards, perhaps to offset the gifts given Navajo headmen by the governor of New Mexico. The Navajos fulfilled their obligation by capturing two herds of the Spaniards' horses. There followed Navajo attacks in the El Paso area, perhaps aimed at the Tiwa loyalists who had gone south during the Pueblo Revolt.[26] The Hopis themselves were not idle in this warfare. In 1707 they killed seven Zunis in a surprise attack near Zuni,[27] and there are hints of other Hopi attacks in the same vicinity.

Hopi attacks on Spanish territory are said to have ended about 1717 or 1718.[28] Through the mid-portion of the eighteenth century, from about 1717 until 1773, the Navajos were also at peace with the Christians. Most Hopi contacts reported in Spanish sources during this period involved only the Franciscans (who visited the mesa-top villages in hopes of making converts) and Hopi traders visiting New Mexico. They tell little of Navajo-Hopi relations, but do provide insights into conditions at Hopi.

A return of refugee populations from Hopi to their former homes in the Rio Grande area began in earnest in the 1740s. It had been two generations since they fled Vargas's reconquest; memories of the revolt had faded. In 1742 Fathers Carlos Delgado and Ignacio Pino brought back 441 people, apparently mostly Southern Tiwas, for the only original pueblos mentioned were Pajarito, Alameda, and Sandia.[29] The conversion of this group began with baptisms of the children, several in the fall of that year at Isleta and Santa Clara, and a few later at Jemez.[30]

In 1745 the Hopis were reported to be embroiled in civil war. As a result, the two priests, Delgado and Pino, with the assistance of a few soldiers and settlers, were able as a result to bring back some 500 people to settle at Jemez and Isleta.[31] Escalante wrote much later that a factional split at Oraibi over the election of a chief brought a violent clash between the opposing parties. The losers took refuge at a Tiwa village which was already at odds with the rest of the inhabitants of Hopi country.[32] The priests were able to bring both the Tiwas and the Oraibi dissidents to New Mexico to refound Sandia. Another dispute involving the Tanos caused another eight families, all Tanos, to leave Hopi at about the same time. As a result, the Hopi leaders were said to have imposed very severe restrictions on their people to prevent additional defections.[33]

A major expedition, including troops from the Janos Presidio, reached Zuni in 1747 with sufficient force to overcome the Hopis. They reported Piros, Tanos, and Tiwas as well as Hopis in the Hopi Province. Hopi leaders hurried to Zuni to assure the Spaniards that they were loyal vassals of the king, and some fifty families of "fugitives" left Hopi to return to mission life, for they were "vexed" and "oppressed" at Hopi. Once the troops turned back, the Hopis ignored their pledges of obedience.[34]

The Hopis were said to number over 10,000 people in the 1740s. Overcrowding of a limited land base and a few dry years were probably at the heart of both the friction and the willingness of refugee populations to depart. Navajos were also seriously considering settling in missions at this time, but only two very abortive missions were ever established.[35] The correspondence in time between the return of refugee populations from Hopi and the brief establishment of Navajo missions may be due largely to the effects of the drought and the zeal of certain Franciscans present in the New Mexico missions, but there were undoubtedly contacts between the Hopis and Navajos that influenced the course of events as well, for neighboring tribal societies did not live in isolation from each other.

The next well-documented period in Hopi history comes some three decades later, and it also pairs drought and the return of refugee peoples, but Navajo contacts are much clearer and of a very different sort.

Detailed accounts of visits to Hopi begin again in 1775. In that year Fray Silvestre Vélez de Escalante, then stationed as missionary at Zuni, made a trip to Hopi with a Zuni escort. At the same time that he was at Walpi, there were more than a hundred Navajos there. He was warned that the Navajos had been overheard planning to ambush his party on its return.[36] He began the return journey about a week later. His Hopi friends at Walpi sent out a party of forty armed men to scout the trail, a different and more southerly route than that by which he had come, and he did encounter "a well-known Navajo" (or at least some of his horses) on the trail, but experienced no problems.[37]

In July of the following year, 1776, Fray Francisco Garcés visited Oraibi, where he was most inhospitably received. He noted that the Hopis and Navajos were on friendly terms at that time.[38] In November of the same year Escalante, along with a number of other Spaniards, arrived at Oraibi from the west on their return from an unsuccessful effort to blaze a trail through the Ute country to California. They were unable to communicate with the Hopis until it was discovered that there were people in each group with some knowledge of the Navajo language. In Shongopavi, again, the travelers

found it necessary to communicate with the Second Mesa people by the use
of Navajo, supplemented by signs. When they reached First Mesa, they were
told that the Hopis were at war with the Navajos, who had killed and captured many Hopis, and that the Hopis wished to form an alliance with the
Spaniards. At a meeting in a kiva with representatives of the various villages,
the Hopi leaders decided to send an emissary to Santa Fe to meet with the
governor in order to formalize the desired alliance. The priests, Escalante
and Fray Francisco Atanacio Domínguez, urged the Hopis to become Christians, for then they would receive the protection they sought. The Hopis
made various arguments against this and at last concluded that they should
not dispatch an ambassador, reciting their traditions and deciding that their
current sufferings were preferable to submitting to Spanish rule. This outcome leaves doubt as to the severity of the alleged Navajo hostilities, especially in view of the Hopi reasoning that since there were more gentiles than
Christians, they preferred to be on the side of the majority.[39]

The Hopi complaints appear even less sincere when Father Juan Agustín
de Morfí's remarks of 1778 are considered, for he described the Hopis as the
best supplied with livestock and goods of all kinds, often being the providers
of animals and seeds for the colonists.[40] Indeed, the Hopis were said to be
great traders with tribes as distant as the Colorado River and the Gulf of
California. Morfí was apparently already a bit behind the times. A severe
drought began in 1777 in the Hopi Province that would lead to renewed
Spanish efforts to overcome the Hopis' determination to preserve their independence.[41]

Perhaps a factional split similar to that at Pecos had developed at Hopi,
whereby one faction was more involved in trade and thus had differing interests from another, more agriculturally inclined faction.[42] This would certainly be congruent with historical events. One Hopi faction, apparently
strongest in the more eastern villages, was obviously eager to maintain good
relations with the Spaniards, their ultimate source for European goods—at
least so long as submission to God and King could be avoided. This faction
tended to emphasize conflicts with the Navajos. A more conservative faction
of priests and farmers, however, stronger in the more westerly villages, gave
every indication of being on speaking terms, if not more closely associated,
with the Navajos.

A most revealing series of incidents is associated with the attempt by

Governor Juan Bautista de Anza to convert the Hopis through peaceful means. In 1779, the third year of the drought, the Hopis were growing desperate. Many had scattered to the hinterland, where they had to resort to gathering wild plants, laboring for the nations with whom they had formerly traded, and even selling their children to obtain food. Anza asked the missionary at Sandia to assist the Hopis by assembling migrants at Zuni, but the priest "completely forgot it" and nothing came of the plan.

Anza was especially concerned because of information he had that the Navajos were impeding those who wanted to move to New Mexico.[43] When the failure of this absent-minded priest came to Anza's attention, he delegated the job to Fray Andrés García, the missionary at Zuni. In October 1779, García set out to assist Hopis who were residing among the Navajos but who were reportedly willing to remove to New Mexico. Just as he was leaving Zuni, emissaries who had been sent ahead returned with thirty-three "pagans" whom the local alcalde then conducted to Sandia.[44] García may have accompanied them as far as Laguna, for he is known to have left from there in the company of a Christian Hopi from Sandia. At "el Joso" (apparently Ojo del Oso, near present-day Fort Wingate), the Christian Hopi went ahead, along with his "infidel" brother, in order to bring back their mother and sister. After waiting six days for the Christian Hopi and his family to reappear, Fray Andrés was informed by a Navajo that they had been delayed because they needed horses. The Franciscan felt obliged then to return to his own mission at Zuni. He had by then learned that those Hopis who had been among the Navajos had already returned to their villages and that pastures and water were insufficient along the trail to Hopi for him to proceed in that direction, anyway.

There can be little doubt that the drought was real, for Fray Andrés asked that Anza send him trade goods that he might barter with the Navajos for fat sheep, those at Zuni being lean as a result of poor pastures. The implication that the range was better in Navajo country suggests that travel to Hopi, at least by a small party, should not have been totally impossible. In any case, there was the prospect that many Hopis would come down in the spring if the rains did not come.[45]

In March of 1780 García set out again at Anza's request and brought back from Hopi seventy-seven people who had let it be known that they would move to the New Mexico colony. He might have brought more had not the

Navajos persuaded the Hopis not to trust the Spaniards.[46] The competition for alliance was no longer between Pueblo patriots and the Spaniards for Navajo friendship, but between the Navajos and the Spaniards for Hopi favor, or so it would seem.

Anza was worried that an alliance of Hopis, Utes, Apaches, and Navajos would confront New Mexico with a formidable enemy. He decided to follow up García's visit with a full-scale expedition after another forty families were said to be willing to migrate into Spanish territory. The Hopis were reportedly suffering not only from drought and famine, but also from an epidemic of an unspecified disease and from wars with neighboring tribes. When Anza reached the Hopi mesas in late September, he was told that the forty families had gone to stay with the Navajos until he should arrive. The Navajos, however, were said to have killed all the men, except two who escaped to tell the story, and to have enslaved the women and children. Anza counted the number of Hopi families remaining, multiplied by six, and concluded that there were only 798 Hopis left of the 7,494 reported by Escalante three years earlier. He believed that the others had died "if some are not concealed from us."[47]

Brew provides a critical assessment of the Hopis' plight as reported by Anza and concludes that it was not as bad as it seemed. First, he notes that Anza arrived during the harvest season, when most Hopis would have been away from the villages at their fields, some up to ten or fifteen miles distant. Anza was also unfamiliar with Hopi agriculture. The sand dune fields that he saw near the villages, along with the short corn stalks, convinced him that they were in dire circumstances. In actuality, the dune fields usually provided ample moisture for crops and Hopi corn had long been adapted for deep planting (to ensure that the roots reached the depth of such soil moisture as is held by the sand at planting time). When planted at this customary depth, the stalks above the ground are naturally short. Brew concludes that the litany of misfortunes was little more than a standard Hopi lament, such as could still be heard in the 1940s.[48]

To a degree, Brew was right. We can reasonably doubt the extreme pessimism of the Hopi leaders in view of their ultimate decision to take no action to alleviate their distress. Still, there was a drought in northeastern Arizona in the 1770s and 1780s.[49] Anza found similar, if less extreme, conditions at

Zuni, where many families were staying at outlying ranches and others had gone for relief to the more easterly pueblos.[50] The high population density shown in Escalante's census was brought about by refugees still in Hopi country at the time and undoubtedly exceeded the long-term carrying capacity of the land. Many of the people who left Hopi to settle in the Christian pueblos of New Mexico were, in fact, the descendants of refugees.[51] It is probable that their ancestors, as late arrivals in the west, had been forced to cultivate marginal fields, where the risks due to drought would have been greatest. Thus, less well integrated into Hopi society, perhaps subject to ethnic prejudice when harvests were slight, with sickness rampant and raiding frequent, these latecomers would have been among the first to leave, even when that meant a return to the foreign rule that their forebears had fled eight or nine decades earlier. Most of the descendents of the earliest Hopi settlers, however, could still afford to hold firm in their resolve to remain in their homes.

The Hopi effort to arouse Spanish sympathy may have been further stimulated by a belief that the drought and pestilence were the result of evil magic by the Spaniards. Garcés had predicted these troubles when he was so ill received at Oraibi in 1776. While the Spaniards saw these misfortunes as God's just punishment, the Indians undoubtedly blamed all on witchcraft by the Christians.[52]

It is beyond knowing today how many of the people at Hopi, whether Hopis proper or members of other Puebloan peoples, joined the Navajos on a permanent basis at this time. The unstable, on-again, off-again relations that characterized Navajo-Spanish interaction for the next four decades must have had an unsettling effect on any kind of Navajo-Hopi integration. There is little mention of Navajos and Hopis together in the Spanish records in this period. The well-known 1805 incursion of Antonio Narbona at Canyon de Chelly resulted in the capture of one Hopi Indian, but whether he was visiting the Navajos or living among them is not apparent.[53]

It was only after warfare between the Navajos and the whites again became so frequent as to permit little confusion regarding the overall tenor of that relationship that the Hopis were once again noted more frequently in the context of Navajo affairs.

War between the Navajos and Spaniards broke out in 1818, apparently a result of conflicts over grazing lands, Navajo suspicion of Spanish complicity in Comanche raids, and possibly other problems. Governor Facundo Melgares led an indecisive campaign in the fall of that year.[54] Despite the less-than-spectacular outcome of this campaign, some Navajos had moved close to the Hopi villages for security. In February 1819 a delegation of Hopi chiefs visited Zuni to ask for assistance against Navajos who had settled about two leagues from First Mesa. Melgares concluded that this represented another opportunity to convert the Hopis. He wrote to the head of the missions requesting prayers for the success of a second expedition. The new campaign was said to have put the Navajos to flight, one of three engagements being fought near First Mesa. Following this, Melgares sent five Indians from Sandia to Hopi to prepare the Hopis to receive the Spanish priests.[55]

In August Melgares included in a peace treaty with the Navajos the provision that, "They will respect the persons and property of the Moqui [Hopi] Pueblos, because this government takes them under the protection of its amiable sovereign, in whose shadow they have been placed."[56] The Hopis seem not to have remained long, if at all, in the king's shadow, for nothing further was reported of a Hopi mission and Mexico soon gained her independence from Spain.

MEXICAN INDEPENDENCE

A campaign against the Navajos led by José Antonio Vizcarra in 1823 marched to Hopi where events were recorded which shed some light on earlier affairs. The army arrived at First Mesa on July 17, expecting to find Navajos or their herds there. The Hopi war captain offered to guide the troops to a refuge where the Navajos were said to be with their stock, but Vizcarra declined his assistance. On the nineteenth Vizcarra led a detachment to scout as far as Oraibi. On the return they sighted three Navajos and pursued them unsuccessfully. On the twenty-fourth a party of four soldiers and a Navajo named Francisco encountered two Navajos, killing one and capturing the other. The captive informed the Spaniards that livestock belonging to the Navajo headman Segundo had been mixed in with the Hopi stock to hide it from the Spaniards. Two hundred and thirty-nine head of

Navajo sheep and goats were confiscated. Two of the Hopis among whose herds the Navajo stock had been allowed to be hidden were detained as guides on the twenty-fifth. An additional forty-eight head were taken the next day from among the Hopi flocks. Detachments then marched from the camp near Hopi, but with only minimal success. It was not until a Paiute was captured and used as a guide that a large Navajo party was overtaken, and this after such an arduous pursuit that the worn-out troops could only capture a little livestock and skirmish briefly with the Navajo rearguard. If the Hopis who had hidden Navajo stock were relied upon for guiding, as seems to have been the case, Vizcarra obviously was selecting people who were friends of the Navajos and he might have had greater success had he accepted the freely offered services of the war captain.[57]

In any case, there were Hopis willing to take considerable risks to help the Navajos, as well as others who would call on aid from the New Mexicans to attack them. The implication that factional divisions continued to split the Hopis in regard to their relations with both the Navajos and the whites cannot be ignored in these seemingly inconsistent Hopi actions.

During this period of renewed warfare there were several years of drought in Navajo country, beginning about 1818 and extending through 1824.[58] It was during this drought that the headman Narbona led his followers westward from the Tunicha Valley to the banks of the Dinnebito Wash west of Oraibi. They stayed there several years until the rains returned. Three of his children married Hopis, one daughter bringing her Hopi spouse to join the band and two sons remaining at Hopi with their wives.[59]

In the 1830s, during the boyhood of the Hopi Djasjini, an informant of an early ethnographer, Navajos lived on the mesas all around the Hopi country. The two tribes were friends, and Navajos visited the Hopi villages frequently. Djasjini learned to speak Navajo as a result.[60]

Despite these friendly relations, oral tradition tells of a devastating Navajo attack on Oraibi about 1837 to avenge the death of Navajo visitors at Hopi.[61] It may well be that the accounts exaggerate the extent of Navajo success in this raid; the James account, in particular, seems to go beyond what is reasonably probable.[62] A Hopi story reported by Waters corresponds in several details with the Navajo accounts, but is placed at a much earlier date and describes the Hopis as the victors.[63] This account seems to incorporate motifs from two different stories into one telling. Regardless of the details, Hopi factionalism, especially regarding their attitudes toward the Navajos, continues to appear in Hopi traditions in this time period.

SUMMARY OF HISPANIC TIMES

It would seem that during the last century and a quarter of Hispanic rule in New Mexico, the dynamics of Navajo-Hopi relations were governed largely by pragmatic adaptations to the power of the whites, disrupted perhaps when interpersonal disputes became issues at the tribal level. At Hopi two factions contended for power. One was a conservative faction, whose members probably relied almost entirely on farming, and who were anti-white, anti-Christian, and pro-independence. This faction seems to have regarded the Navajos as a valuable buffer between themselves and the whites. The other faction relied to some degree on trading and favored good relations with the whites, the source of many trade goods, as long as this did not require that they give up their independence and religion. This faction was less friendly with the Navajos, perhaps finding them to be competitors in trade. Perhaps an enmity with the Navajos also provided one avenue to better relations with the whites during those periods when this would provide a coincidence of interests. As long as the whites were seen as a threat to Hopi lifeways, however, Hopi attitudes toward the Navajos may have been rather ambiguous and situational.

Both tribes had learned painfully the ideals of tribal freedom and of preservation of their culture and religion. Those ideals helped shape their relations with each other, as each tried to influence the other in ways that would improve its position in dealing with the economic and military power of the Hispanics. In the first two decades following the Reconquest, the Navajos and Hopis were generally allied against the Spaniards and both hosted significant numbers of refugees from peoples who had been forced to submit to foreign rule. Following this period, as peaceful relations with the whites developed at about the same time for both tribes, economic factors replaced military ones.

Spanish ideology made acceptance of Indian nations as sovereign powers difficult, and this was especially true with regard to the Hopis, who had once been subject to God and King and who had subsequently regained their independence. The importance to the Spaniards of maintaining peace did eventually overcome their ideological considerations to some degree, but the hope of bringing the Hopis back into the Church was still alive at the end of Spanish rule in Mexico. Anza was under orders to treat the Hopis kindly and not to try to remove them from their own country. Despite this, both he and the missionaries argued that armed force would be necessary to assert Spanish rule over them, and that the resources of the colony were sufficient to the task only if the Hopis were resettled on the Rio Grande. Navajo efforts to prevent the Hopis from joining the Spaniards, and Spanish fears of an alliance between the Hopis and the Navajos, indicate that the Hopis were considered important in the regional balance of power.

The Hopis soon found that an evasive policy worked best to parry Spanish thrusts. At first they claimed that they really were loyal Spanish vassals, a claim forgotten as soon as the threat of Spanish attack receded. As the Spanish peace policy became evident, they discovered that they had only to expound on their troubles, real or imagined, to arouse Spanish sympathy and be left alone. As long as they could represent themselves as an impoverished remnant sliding quietly into oblivion, they were safe. With the Navajos controlling the territory intervening between New Mexico and Hopi, the New Mexicans did not consider the Hopi towns worthy of conquest, but the Hispanics could be manipulated to avenge Hopi grievances against the Navajos.

ANGLO RULE

When the Anglo-Americans arrived in the Southwest, they inherited a long and complex history of Hispanic dealings with the Hopis, a history that they but dimly perceived. The complications of Navajo-Hopi relations were glossed over with the "traditional enemy" stereotype by which so many intertribal relations were characterized. As the limited chronicle provided by Spanish and Mexican records and Navajo and Hopi tradition makes clear, this was very much an oversimplification. It was, however, a view that one Hopi faction could cultivate to its own advantage, as they had also cultivated the vain Spanish hope that due to their sufferings, the Hopis would soon submit voluntarily to mission life.

Hopi experience with Anglo-Americans during the Mexican period was apparently limited to an incursion of some two hundred trappers who destroyed their crops and killed fifteen to twenty Hopis.[64] The Navajos, having good contacts further to the east, realized the value of friendship and trade with a people who could supply firearms in quantity,[65] but could not attract the Anglos in any numbers to their western lands when there were profits to be made further east among the Utes and the New Mexicans.

As early as 1846 the first United States governor of New Mexico, Charles Bent, reported that the Hopis "were formerly a very numerous tribe—but have been reduced in numbers and possessions by their more warlike neighbors and enemies the Navajoes."[66]

Not long after his arrival in Santa Fe in 1849, James S. Calhoun, then Indian agent for the territory, wrote that the Hopis were "opposed to all wars" and that they had once abandoned a town because its soil was "stained with the blood of a human being."[67] In October of the following year, Calhoun was visited by a delegation from the Hopi country consisting of the cacique of the entire tribe, the chief of the largest pueblo, which would have been Oraibi, and two others. Their main purpose was to learn what view the United States government took of their people. They did not fail to complain "bitterly" of the Navajos.[68] By April 1851, however, the Zuni governor reported that the Hopis were friendly with the Navajos and that they frequently asked about the Americans' plans with regard to the Navajos, apparently in an attempt to secure information for that tribe.[69]

Hopi friendship with the Navajos involved a lively trade. According to one report, "the Navajos came daily to their pueblos, traded them mules, horses and sheep for corn bread, red flannel, indigo etc." The Hopis were reputed to have more than sixty government mules, which they had purchased from the Navajos. Henry L. Dodge bought two of these mules at Zuni and proposed that he be commissioned to go to Hopi to buy the rest, believing that he could get them for ten dollars each in trade goods.[70]

It is just possible that Dodge created a booming market for government mules at Hopi, for the Navajos and Apaches soon began to run off mules from the army and the U.S. Boundary Commission south of the Gila River.[71]

Another Hopi delegation visited Calhoun in Santa Fe in August 1851. Again they complained, saying that the Navajos robbed them until they were reduced to poverty and, since they had nothing left to steal, were now at peace. When they once again had something worth taking, they expected the Navajos to resume their thefts.[72]

Curiously, in October Hopi emissaries visited Fort Defiance on behalf of the Navajos in order to help begin negotiations to re-establish peace following Colonel Edwin Vose Sumner's invasion of Canyon de Chelly.[73]

Early in 1854 there were again hostilities between the Navajos and the Hopis, which led to the death of one Navajo and five Hopis.[74] Some two years later the commanding officer at Fort Defiance visited the Hopis. His evaluation of their prospects was as pessimistic as had been Anza's. He reported that they were decreasing in number and that "unless something can be done for them, they are doomed to utter extinction." He added:

> Their viscious [sic] system of intermarriage has deprived them of all manliness, and the Navajos ride over them rough shod. It will be very difficult to puebloize the latter while the Moquis give so unfavorable an example of that system; for this reason, if none other, it would be well to resuscitate those Pueblos.[75]

In 1857 the village of Mishongnovi lost livestock to both the Navajos and the Comanches. There was also some contention over land use between the Navajos and Oraibi.[76]

In 1858, however, when war between the United States and the Navajos broke out, it was reported that the division among the Hopis as to which side they should support was so strong that those opposed to allying themselves with the Navajos sent a representative to Zuni to find out if they could take refuge there.[77] Lieutenant Colonel D. S. Miles, commander of the campaign against the Navajos, threatened to "attack and destroy" the Hopis if they should join with the Navajos.[78] The Navajo war was over shortly and the Hopis were not directly involved on either side.

There followed only a brief period of peace before Lieutenant Colonel Edward R. S. Canby led another campaign in 1860. He reported that the Navajos were fleeing, some going toward the Hopi villages. An unofficial battalion of five volunteer companies under the command of Manuel Chaves took part in the campaign, and this appears to have been the only force to visit the Hopi villages, which it reached about the first week in November. The volunteers returned with a large number of captured livestock and captives, but no contemporary report of their activities at Hopi has come to light.[79] John Ward, Pueblo agent, later wrote that during the war both the

Navajos and "the independent campaigns" had robbed the Hopis, the latter taking their corn on the pretext that they were allied with the Navajos.[80] There can be little doubt that Ward got his information from those Hopis who had taken the side of the army in the war and who appear to have been put upon by both sides. In March 1861, following the conclusion of a treaty between the Navajos and the United States, a delegation of eighty-eight Hopis visited Fort Defiance, where they "were informed of the conditions of the treaty, that they were included in its provisions and that any infractions on their part would be followed by prompt punishment."[81]

Mormon relations with the Hopis followed a somewhat separate course, but their reports add to the sparse documentary record. A Mormon party visited Oraibi in December 1862. They found the Hopis prepared for war, saying they thought the visitors were Navajos who had recently stolen many flocks of sheep and goats from them.[82]

The next, and last, Navajo campaign was that led by Kit Carson, and again the inconsistent actions of the Hopis indicate a continuing difference of opinion as to how they should regard the Navajos and the whites. In August 1863 Carson captured five Hopis on the trail between Hopi and Zuni. The captives informed Carson that there were Navajos with their livestock near the Hopi villages. Carson immediately set out for the Hopi country where he encountered a number of parties of Navajos, killing and capturing some and taking some horses, mules, sheep, and goats. The Hopis gave every indication of cooperating with the army by providing information on Navajo movements. The Navajos did not disperse at once, however, but managed to take some mules from Carson's command and even to make an effort to drive off his entire horse herd.[83]

In November 1863 Carson again led his troops to Hopi. He found all the villages except Oraibi willing to assist him by participating in his operations. He was told that Oraibi was in league with the Navajos. He made two of the Oraibi chiefs prisoners and took them with him, as he wanted Hopis to be seen among his men so that they could not easily realign themselves with the Navajos.[84] As late as October 1864 there were Hopis who were still opposing the government and telling Navajos that they should not surrender.[85] Sometime during this period, when the Navajos were extremely hard-pressed, Hopis took advantage of their weakened condition, killing many and selling captive women and children to New Mexican slave traders.[86] By

1866 some Hopis had turned on those Navajos who had managed to elude Carson's net and were still free. One Hopi party attacked the remnants of Manuelito's band, wounding the headman himself.[87] Hopis also joined with New Mexican raiders to attack the Navajos on Gray Mountain. In addition, Hopis decoyed Navajos to their villages, disarmed them, and then threw them off the cliffs.[88]

The Navajos were driven into exile at Fort Sumner in eastern New Mexico, where they lived in abject misery until the negotiation of their final treaty in 1868.[89]

Thus, the Indian wars in the Navajo and Hopi countries ended with fully as much brutality and violence as ever. On the other hand, peoples who are neighbors must of necessity get along peacefully most of the time. Navajos and Hopis had been friends as individuals throughout this period, and there had often been alliances against a common enemy, the whites who threatened the independence of both tribes. Hopi factionalism had clearly played a role in this unsteady relationship, and it is not unlikely that differing interest groups among the Navajos played a similar role on their side. Navajo factions were less well defined, however, and the evidence for them is far less clear.

The Hopi ideal of pacifism appears to have been something less than a standard by which to live, but perhaps still something more than mere self-righteous propaganda to help fend off more powerful foes. The seed from which the ideal grew was probably the simple appreciation of peace common to all societies. It is quite clear that its origins lie in the Hopi maneuvering to avoid attack by superior Spanish military forces. It lacked the strength to restrain violent action when strong motivations for vengeance, material gain, or a position of dominance were coupled with little perceived risk. It may never have been thought to apply in dealings among Indians. The pacifistic stance was successful beyond any expectations that its innovators might have imagined, for it led to a very favorable stereotype among the most demanding intruders into Hopi country—the Spaniards, Mexicans, and Anglo-Americans.

PEACE AND STRIFE

T HE TREATY OF June 1, 1868, ended the Navajo wars. The Navajos were clearly no longer an independent people, but foreign rule, once they returned to their own country from their exile at Fort Sumner, was rather tenuous. For better or worse, a parsimonious Congress refused to provide the means to administer the affairs of the tribe with any close attention to detail. A single agent with a few helpers was expected to attend to the affairs of a tribe of thousands of people spread over millions of acres of semiarid terrain, even in theory a very difficult task and in actuality an impossible assignment. Good men left after a short period of service out of a sense of frustration and hopelessness, while incompetents were regularly driven away by the Navajos' effectively voiced complaints. All tribal structure had been shattered by the wars.[1] For nearly three decades the responsibility for most political control fell to the individual headmen. Despite many problems, the headmen were able to shepherd their people safely into a future that they themselves could never quite comprehend.

The Navajo Agency was located in the crumbling buildings of Fort Defiance, far from the Hopi country. Confrontations between U.S. citizens and Navajos were of far more urgent concern for the agents, but reports of events in the west got at least passing notice. On rare occasions the agents were able to take some action to settle disputes.

Even under these light restraints, the option of warfare for the Navajos was virtually eliminated. Although the terms "raid" and "depredation" continued in use, and at times troops were even sent to help settle differences, individual rather than tribal liability came more frequently to be the basis for resolution of wrongs.

In 1869 old stereotypes were resurrected when it was asserted that the

Navajos "plundered" the Hopis, as did the Apaches, whereas the Hopis were described as "not a warlike race, but [they] claim they can defend themselves."[2] In 1870 a Mormon missionary helped a Navajo recover a sheep stolen by a Hopi.[3]

The annual report of the Hopi agent for 1871 described the six easternmost Hopi villages as friendly toward the government, while Oraibi was described as hostile. This division mirrored a factional split within the tribe, and Oraibi continued to maintain close relations with the Apaches. Most significant here is the agent's description of matters with regard to the Navajos.

> I also found an unfriendly relation existing between the Moquis and the Navajo Indians, growing out of the Navajo War; but, by the assistance of J. H. Miller, agent for Navajo matters, have been amicably settled, and I take pleasure in saying the two tribes are living on terms of perfect friendship.[4]

Earlier the Hopis were said to have killed six Navajos,[5] but this may have been a reference to deaths in the previous war, if the Hopi agent's report can be considered an accurate summation of the situation.

In the mid-1870s the agents encouraged the Hopis to expand their area of land use, issuing them sheep and inducing them to plant at a greater distance from their villages. By the end of the decade land conflicts between Hopis and Navajos were apparent, as the two tribes were in close contact at places such as Keams Canyon, Awatovi, and Tuba City.[6]

The earliest specific recommendation for a Hopi reservation of some fifty square miles seems to have been made in 1876.[7] Another proposal suggested that three tracts in the shape of parallelograms six to eight miles long and three or four miles wide, and centered on the three mesas, be set aside for the Hopis, along with an area for wood-gathering six to eight miles square at a distance of ten miles. Still another suggestion was for a rectangle, with the northeast corner at the intersection of 36° latitude with 110° of longitude and measuring forty-eight miles east-to-west by twenty-four miles north-to-south.[8]

In 1880 Thomas Keam took a delegation of Hopi leaders to visit Washington. In response to their complaints of Navajo trespass, they were told to

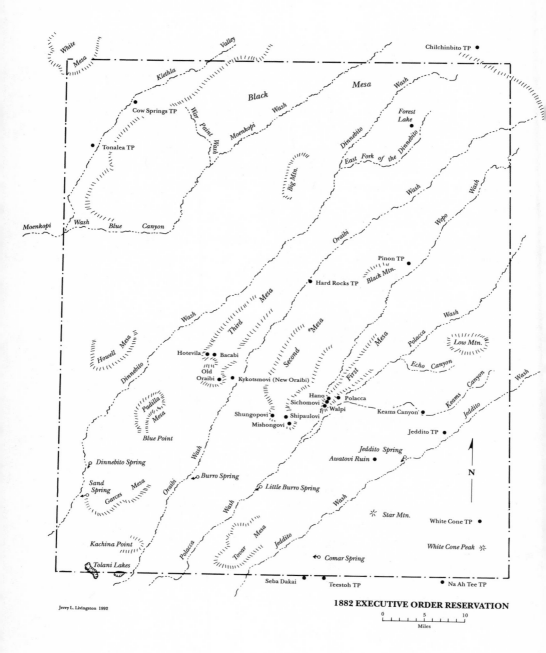

White Mesa

Valley

Chilchinbito TP •

Klethla

Black   Mesa   Wash

Cow Springs TP •

War Paint Wash

Moenkopi Wash

Forest Lake •

• Tonalea TP

Dinnebito

East Fork of the Dinnebito

Big Mtn.

Wash

Wash

Moenkopi   Wash   Blue   Canyon

Oraibi

Wepo

Pinon TP •

• Hard Rocks TP

Black Mtn.

Wash

Third   Mesa

Howell   Mesa

Wash

Mesa

Polacca

Low Mtn.

Dinnebito

Second

Echo   Canyon

Hotevila • • Bacabi

Mesa

First

Keams   Canyon

Wash

Old Oraibi

Padilla Mesa

• Kykotsmovi (New Oraibi)

Hano

• Polacca

Keams Canyon •

Jeddito

Blue Point

Shungopovi •

Sichomovi

• Walpi

Mishongovi

• Shipaulovi

Keams Canyon

Jeddito TP •

• Dinnebito Spring

Jeddito   Spring

Sand Spring

Garces   Mesa

Oraibi   Wash

← Burro Spring

Awatovi Ruin •

N

☼ Star Mtn.

White Cone TP •

Kachina Point

← Little Burro Spring

Wash

Polacca

Tovar   Mesa

Jeddito   Wash

White Cone Peak ☼

Tolani Lakes

←○ Comar Spring

Seba Dakai

Teestoh TP •

• Na Ah Tee TP

Jerry L. Livingston 1992

1882 EXECUTIVE ORDER RESERVATION

0   5   10

Miles

establish villages at springs near their fields, a proposal that they felt was not practical.[9] In 1882 Indian Inspector C. H. Howard recommended a single reservation for both the Hopis and the western Navajos.[10]

In the meantime, Hopi Agent J. H. Fleming asked that a reservation be established for the Hopis in order to protect them from the intrusions of white men. He described the boundaries of what soon became the Executive Order Reservation of December 16, 1882. This included the lands between 110° longitude on the east and 111° longitude on the west, and from 35°30′ latitude on the south to 36°30′ on the north.[11] This area encompassed about 2 1/2 million acres, or some 3,900 square miles. The reservation was set aside for the Moquis (Hopis) and "such other Indians as the Secretary of the Interior may see fit to settle thereon."[12] While it has been asserted by the Hopi Tribal Council that this reservation area was intended to exclude the Navajos, it would seem more likely that it was meant to help regulate Navajo as well as Hopi land use.

In 1884 the Navajo agent noted that despite quarrels when Navajo herds overran outlying Hopi gardens, there existed "the best of good feelings" between the two tribes and they "constantly mingle together at festivals, dances, feasts, etc. . . ."[13]

Navajo Agent S. S. Patterson reported a similar situation in September 1888, asserting that although he had to attend to some cases of horse theft and other problems, relations between the two peoples were generally friendly. More adamant Hopi complaints of trespass and theft by Navajos were made later that month, however, and these led to official action in Washington. Troops were ordered from Fort Wingate to control Navajo trespass by permanently removing the Navajos from the Executive Order Reservation. Henry Chee Dodge, the Navajo interpreter for the army, pointed out that to evict some one hundred families in the winter weather would neither benefit the Hopis nor be just treatment of the Navajos. As a result, the orders were modified to allow the army officers to adapt their actions to the situation. Ultimately, their decision was that the Navajos would be required to stay "at least twelve miles from the Moquis." Responsibility for enforcing this rule was delegated to the Navajo headman, Sam Begody.[14]

Apparently Begody was not entirely successful, for in July 1889 there were complaints of Navajos watering their flocks only five or six miles from the Hopi villages. The suggestion was made that natural boundaries be designated to separate the two tribes, but no action seems to have been taken.[15]

In 1890 the Hopis managed to link the issue of Navajo encroachment to the issue of Indian education by refusing to send more children to school unless the Navajos were controlled. A serious encounter, in which some Navajos were accused of attacking Hopis in a cornfield and beating them, may have been the impetus for the Hopi stance. The two issues did at least provide common ground to unite the two Hopi factions and may have contributed to a degree of tribal unity, at least in their dealings with the whites. With regard to Navajo encroachment, the agent had set "certain specified limits" for Navajo herds, perhaps adopting the "twelve-mile" proposal of the previous year. This did not, however, solve the second problem. Finally, in December of 1890, troops were sent to Oraibi, where they took more than 100 children for school. The troops stayed on into January surveying and marking a boundary with a radius of sixteen miles centered on the town of Mishongnovi. Both the Navajos and the Hopis appeared satisfied with the line. In March it was reported that the Navajos were honoring the new boundary and that some 150 hogans within the area had been abandoned.[16]

In 1892 the government began an allotment program at Hopi, sending John S. Mayhugh to survey allotments of 160 acres each. In August Mayhugh observed that the 1891 boundary was still in effect. By the next year, however, Mayhugh himself seems to have overridden the sixteen-mile rule, first by surveying an allotment inside the line for a Navajo and later by surveying Hopi allotments outside the line and ordering the Navajos at the latter place, Jeddito Springs, to move. Mayhugh's lack of concern for the boundary may have led to a similar attitude on the part of the Indians. In any case, in 1893 Hopi complaints of Navajo trespass were once again being heard, but whether these involved lands inside or outside the sixteen-mile limit is not clear. The allotment program was discontinued in 1894 and approval of the surveyed tracts withheld as a result of a report that neither the land nor the customs of the Hopis were amenable to individual title to farmlands.[17]

In the 1890s young children of the Hopi faction friendly to the government were taught that the Navajos were evil people. For example Don Talayesva, born in 1890, wrote concerning his early childhood that he was told repeatedly that Navajos "could not be trusted, that they were thieves and raiders who even taught their children to steal." He was warned that they stole livestock, fruit and other crops, water, and children.[18]

A new Hopi agent in 1899 wrote that Navajos had settled close to Hopis and that Hopi stock damaged Navajo crops. He wanted "to return the Navajos to their own reservation," but was advised from Washington that "the Navajos have always trespassed on the Moqui" reservation. He repeated his complaint of Navajo occupation in 1900 and suggested controlling this by registering all Navajos. Again the Washington office rejected his suggestion.[19]

Use of Navajo police in 1903 to enforce school attendance at Oraibi further complicated intertribal relations.[20] This use of force also probably helped precipitate the breakup of Oraibi in 1906. Under the leadership of Youkeoma, the conservative Hopis expelled from Oraibi settled at Hotevilla, where they experienced a difficult winter.[21] According to Navajo tradition, neighboring Navajos aided them with food.[22]

A new allotment program was undertaken in 1908, Matthew W. Murphy being sent to do the work. Murphy complained shortly after his arrival that Navajos had taken possession of many of the springs and that it would be necessary to evict them. He later concluded that only two or three Navajo families would have to be moved. He soon received instructions to allot land to Navajos as well as to Hopis. In 1910 about fifty Hopi families proposed that they be given allotments together at Little Burro Spring, where they planned to found a new village. Three Navajo families were already living at the spring; they were probably the same families from whom the Navajo police were recruited to help with the government raid for Hopi school children in 1903. In 1911 the second allotment program was cancelled for the same reasons that the previous allotment effort had been given up. By this time, Murphy had surveyed allotments for some 300 Navajos.[23]

One possible benefit of an allotment program was that it might have settled the disputes over land use between the Navajos and Hopis. With the final abandonment of this approach, new suggestions had to be made for a boundary. In 1912 the problem of damage to Navajo and Hopi crops by livestock of the other tribe had become a continuing problem. The former sixteen-mile limit was no longer recognized. The success of the government in encouraging stock raising by the Hopis had generated new conflicts with the Navajos. In 1914 the Navajos were well established on their 300 allotments, and these tracts blocked further Hopi expansion. One proposal was that additional land be acquired for the Navajos so that they could be moved from the 1882 Reservation. But since the government had already given tacit approval to the Navajo occupation of land within the boundary of the 1882 Reservation, such a move would have been difficult to justify. In 1915 Hopi Superintendent Leo Crane revived the idea of dividing the reservation. In the following year Congressman Carl Hayden made the same suggestion.[24]

The first specific description of an area to be set aside exclusively for the Hopis as a result of this ferment from the termination of allotments was made by Inspector H. S. Traylor in 1916. He described a reservation extending from Keams Canyon to fifteen miles west of Oraibi, and from twenty miles south of First Mesa to twenty miles north—a tract which would have included about half of the 1882 Reservation.[25]

In 1918 Superintendent Leo Crane reported in detail on land use on the reservation. He estimated that the Hopis made use of only some 600 square miles and the Navajos about 2,200 square miles, an additional 1,600 square miles being worthless. He then reiterated Traylor's proposal that about half of the reservation be set aside for the Hopis, but no action was taken.[26] It is obvious from his figures that the Traylor proposal would have dispossessed a great many Navajos, a factor that may explain why it was not given serious consideration.

The next Hopi superintendent, Robert E. L. Daniel, estimated in his annual reports of 1920, 1921, and 1922 that Hopi land use was restricted to 600 square miles or less. In the 1922 report Daniel suggested that 1,200 square miles be assigned to the Hopis and the remaining 2,663 square miles to the Navajos. In 1924 former inspector A. L. Dorrington submitted a report echoing Daniel's recommendations.[27]

Daniel's successor, Edgar J. Miller, commented on Dorrington's report in 1925. He observed that the dynamic of encroachment had reversed, with the Hopis now expanding at the expense of the Navajos, but he thought that in general the two peoples got along well together. He opposed any partition, as this would cause some families of both tribes to be displaced from their homes. A year later, however, he had changed his mind and wanted a definite boundary laid out. Hopi expansion was creating more conflicts, and by 1927 a division somewhat like that proposed by Dorrington now had his favorable recommendation.[28]

In 1926 some Hopis had asked Arizona Senator Ralph H. Cameron to make the 1882 Reservation an exclusive Hopi reservation and to have the Navajos expelled. The senator asked the Commissioner of Indian Affairs about the situation and was informed that Navajos had long lived there and that their rights needed to be taken into account.[29]

In 1928 an Assistant Commissioner of Indian Affairs assigned Chester E. Faris, superintendent of the Southern Pueblo Agency, the task of investigating the proposal to divide the 1882 Reservation. Faris concluded that a division of the land would bring about more troubles rather than solve those then existing.[30]

In 1930 the Commissioner asked several people to look at the problem, including Faris, H. J. Hagerman, A. G. Hutton, and H. H. Fiske. The first to submit a report was Hutton, who noted serious overgrazing of the land, but who reinforced the observations of the others that the conflict was not now one of Navajo encroachment but of Hopi expansion. He suggested that the land not be partitioned, but that the name of the reservation be changed in view of the fact that the Hopis were not the sole occupants, and that steps be taken to upgrade the Indians' livestock.[31]

In the same month, June 1930, Superintendent Miller reiterated his 1926 position urging that the reservation be divided. He also forwarded a petition from the Hopis in which they claimed a major portion of northeastern Arizona on the basis of the locations of places sacred in their religion.[32]

Fiske's report was completed the following month. He favored segregation of the two tribes, but in his proposal he modified Miller's projected boundary in order not to displace so many people. He felt that Miller's ideas would disproportionately harm the Navajos, who were already losing land to Hopi expansion.[33]

November 6, 1930, was the date of the first formal negotiation between Navajo and Hopi leaders to discuss the land question. Hagerman and Fiske directed the negotiation. The Hopis in attendance said that they had no authority in the matter, but Tom Pavatea and Kotku opposed a division of the land. On the other side, Billy Pete, a Navajo, thought the Fiske boundary a reasonable suggestion.[34]

Hagerman and Faris wrote a joint report in which they commented on the negotiating session, which had been held in Flagstaff. On the basis of that meeting, they believed that the Hopis would never favor a division of the land. They stated that if the government did not unilaterally impose a solution, "the situation would constantly grow worse," and that a settlement should be based on existing land use. They outlined two tracts for exclusive Hopi use, one of about 438,000 acres around the main Hopi villages, and the other of about 23,000 acres around Moenkopi. They recognized that a more detailed study of land use would be necessary in order to set precise boundaries that were equitable. They emphasized, however, that their boundaries encompassed all, or even more than all, of "the land which has been within the memory of living man used by the Hopi Indians for grazing purposes in this vicinity." Both the Commissioner of Indian Affairs and the Secretary of the Interior approved the proposed boundaries. Funds were lacking to fence the area, but precise lines were yet to be delineated.[35]

At a hearing of the Senate Committee on Indian Affairs held at Keams Canyon in May 1931, the Navajo leaders favored splitting the land, while the Hopis argued for the expulsion of all Navajos from the 1882 Reservation. One Hopi, Otto Lomavitu, proposed a survey of land use as a basis for a boundary. Since he also favored the Hopi claim to the entire 1882 Reservation, it seems likely that his ideas did not come through with full clarity in his testimony.[36]

In 1932 Hagerman included his suggestions for new boundaries in the disputed lands of the 1882 Reservation as part of a separate proposal to re-draw the boundaries of the entire Navajo Reservation. Later in the same year, it was suggested that certain outlying Hopi shrines be surveyed and also made a part of the exclusive Hopi area.[37]

The initial version of a bill to establish the exterior boundaries of the Navajo Reservation was sent to Congress in 1932. This first draft followed the Hagerman lines for an exclusive Hopi Reservation. Hopi objections were soon heard. The Hopis were not united on the issue, however. The First Mesa people wanted the situation left as it was, while those on Second Mesa and many of the Third Mesa people advocated a much larger Hopi claim. Ultimately, the question was left unresolved, and the bill that became law in 1934 merely stated that the "existing status" of the 1882 Reservation was not affected.[38]

The government began work to control the heavy grazing of the range on both reservations in the 1930s. In the process, grazing districts were defined in 1936. District 6 included territory around the Hopi villages and was intended to include all Hopi land except that used by the Moenkopi people.[39]

Although District 6 was "reserved specifically for Hopi use," the new boundary was supposedly established merely for administrative efficiency. It was recognized that there were Hopis outside the new boundary line and Navajos within it. Although it was initially understood that these people would retain their original rights no matter where they were located, in 1938 the Navajo general superintendent, E. R. Fryer, decided that Navajo rights within the District 6 boundary should not be equal to Hopi rights.[40] This decision apparently only confirmed what was already the case, for several Navajo families still claim compensation for losses they suffered when evicted from their District 6 homes in 1937.

In response to Hopi protests concerning the status of District 6, Commissioner of Indian Affairs John Collier suggested that the two tribal councils appoint negotiating committees to work out a solution to the problem. The Hopi Tribal Council refused to participate in this plan, being unwilling to concede any Navajo rights.[41]

A more intensive survey of land occupation and use was initiated in 1938 as part of a broader study called the Human Dependency Survey.[42] The final report on these studies was not made until December 1939, and recommendations based on them were reported in March 1940 by C. E. Rachford, who headed a commission to study the matter. He proposed a number of boundary changes that would increase the size of District 6 by over 29,000 acres. He suggested that people living near the line, but on the wrong side, be moved as soon as possible, and that those isolated within the territory of the other tribe be moved within a year. The superintendents of the two tribes wanted some changes. Additional legal complications and another study by Willard R. Centerwall in 1942 resulted in additional increases in the recommended size of District 6 of about 113,000 acres. A later agreement between the two superintendents reduced Centerwall's total addition by nearly 10,000 acres, and in April 1943 these expanded District 6 boundaries were made official by the Commissioner of Indian Affairs.[43]

Again, many Navajo families, probably more than 100, and a few Hopi families were forced to move.[44] The oft-noted expansion of Hopi territory continued with official sanction. There continued to be assurances to the Hopis that District 6 did not constitute a reservation, and Hopis continued to claim the entire 1882 Executive Order Reservation as theirs exclusively.

By this time the public stereotypes of the Navajos and Hopis had crystal-lized into a rather negative image for Navajos, especially when contrasted to Pueblos, and a very positive, romanticized image for the Hopis. Edward Everett Dale's book, *The Indians of the Southwest*, perpetuated the "traditional enemy" concept with regard to the two peoples, as have other books before and since.[45] He described the Hopis as very poor and of necessity extremely frugal, as well as peaceful and not inclined "to liquor, crimes, or the wasting of food or other resources," but having great difficulty in working together.[46] He also asserted that the Hopis had "developed an intense dislike" for the Navajos, noting that they maintained that "the Navajo was a natural thief and robber and insisted that the Hopi reservation should be given to the Hopi alone and the Navajo forced to move from it."[47] His description of the Navajos was rather cursory and did nothing to counterbalance the Hopi view. He contrasted the "peaceful, sedentary" Pueblos with the "wilder and more warlike" Apaches, Navajos, Utes, Shoshones and Coman-ches.[48] Other terms he used to characterize the Pueblo people generally were kindly, hospitable, clean, industrious, and thrifty. The Hopis spe-cifically he found devoted to work and prayer. They were gay, kindly, hospitable, cheerful, happy, contented, and peaceful, but lived in fear of Navajo attacks.[49] The Navajos, a wilder people, had "acquired large herds" as a result of raiding. "Predatory, warlike and restless," in his view, "they were a perpetual source of trouble to Spanish and Mexican settlers farther south and to peaceful pueblo dwellers." He did note that the Mexi-cans and Pueblos also had raided the Navajos to take livestock and captives to be held as slaves.[50] Still, the overall picture was clearly one of the Navajos as an inherently villainous people who preyed on virtuous and unoffending Hopis.

Little attention was paid to the boundary issue during World War II. The immediate postwar period of the late 1940s and early 1950s were years of crisis marked by extreme poverty on the reservations, as veterans and war workers returned to their homes on lands already strained to the limit to support a burgeoning population. There continued to be dealings between Navajos and Hopis, but official recognition of either disputes or cooperation seems to be sparse in government archives. The minutes of the Navajo Tribal Council do provide some insights for the 1950s.

At the January 1953 meeting of the council, for instance, the issue was raised when Oscar Yonnie, a councilman from the Pinon area, in discussing medical care for his constituents, noted:

> We have a hospital in Keams Canyon, but that is in Hopi country and the Hopies [sic] tell us that hospital is for Hopis and they want us to keep out . . .[51]

Another councilman, Kenneth Yazzie from the Tolani Lake area, complained of the lack of a fence between Navajo District 5 and the Hopi District 6:

> The Hopis have no mercy on Navajo people. When our cattle go into their precinct, we must pay a fine. On the other hand, their cattle get into District No. 5 and we do not ask them to pay a fine or corral their stock. That is causing great trouble between the Navajos and the Hopis. The people I met with say that the portion that is not fenced on the border should be taken care of and if it can be built, we would like to have it built so that there will not be any trespassing going on back and forth.[52]

It was later revealed that the fencing was not done because of objections by Hopis at Oraibi.[53]

Then Navajo Tribal Chairman Sam Ahkeah announced that he had recently met with the U.S. senator-elect for Arizona, Barry Goldwater, who told him that the Hopis did not want to continue to be under the administration of the same area director as the Navajos. Ahkeah thought this a good idea, but he wanted to hear the area director's opinions.

Allan G. Harper, then Gallup Area Director, replied that he thought such a change would cause increased problems. He noted friction over the gathering of wood and the need for continuity in road programs between the Navajo and Hopi areas. He felt that the real problem was the failure of the Hopis themselves to form a tribal council.[54]

Earl Johnson, another Navajo councilman from the country southwest of Hopi, following a discussion of the Leupp School, brought up the grazing trespass issue a second time:

> Again about the Hopis over there. It is true that these Hopis corral our horses when they enter their country and last year they had to corral horses and they finally phoned us that they had corralled them over there. In the case of the Hopis, if you pick up a stick in their territory, they follow you home and try to get that stick back. We feel that we would be grateful if that fence was made complete all around the Hopi area from our side to avoid any trespassing.[55]

Johnson also complained that Hopis were bootlegging liquor in his district.[56]

In 1956 Norman M. Littell, chief attorney for the Navajo Tribe, reported to the Navajo council that the Hopis, who once again had a functioning tribal council of their own, had filed a brief with the Department of the Interior, claiming exclusive rights to all minerals in the 1882 Executive Order Reservation. Littell predicted that the question would have to go to Congress, and he recommended that the tribe should oppose the Hopi claim in the courts, if necessary. He then summarized the archeological data acquired by Richard F. Van Valkenburgh showing Navajo occupancy in the 1882 Reservation over a long period of time. Van Valkenburgh and Maxwell Yazzie appeared before the council to exhibit and explain a map of the locations of their archeological sites. Over 350 hogan groups, or sites, had been recorded, and tree-ring dates as early as 1622 had been obtained from wood from hogans within the Executive Order Reservation boundaries. It is probable that the total number of sites recorded at this time was not limited to land within the 1882 Reservation, but represented all those identified in the course of research for the Navajo land claims case to be heard by the Indian Claims Commission.[57]

Littell also mentioned archival research for historical documentation. Again, he called on Van Valkenburgh to explain maps of the various boundaries for the Hopis which had been proposed by government officials from 1880 on. Some of this documentation had been found in the National Ar-

chives in Washington, but Robert W. Young, a Bureau of Indian Affairs employee in Window Rock, had located a great deal of it in the agency files
and library. The archival research in Washington was accomplished under
the direction of Dr. George P. Hammond of the Bancroft Library at the University of California in Berkeley. Littell described how the work was done to
document the history of the dispute.[58]

As a result of the need for additional research to counter the Hopi claim,
Littell asked the council for an appropriation of $10,000 to fund research
under Hammond's supervision. He mentioned the possibility of mineral
wealth in the area in his urging that the money be provided, suggesting that
it might be a wise investment.[59]

The Navajo vice-chairman, Scott Preston, who was chairing the session,
also supported the expenditure, not in terms of mineral wealth, however, but
because he feared that if the Hopis won the land they would demand that
the Navajos be evicted. The motion to spend the money was passed by a
vote of sixty-nine in favor and none opposed.[60]

Not long after this session, a Hopi Boundary Bill that would have set up
a special three-judge court to settle the Navajo-Hopi boundary question was
introduced in Congress. Littell and Hopi attorney John Boyden had worked
out the details of the Hopi Boundary Bill so that it would not only set up a
court to hear the case, but would provide the needed congressional authorization for the division of the land by court action to establish reservation
lines between the two tribes. On July 20, 1956, the Navajo tribal legal office
reported to the council that the bill had passed the Senate. It was held up in
committee in the House of Representatives, however, due to objections from
the Justice Department that were relayed to the other committee members
through John Rhodes, the representative from Phoenix. Navajo Chairman
Paul Jones telegraphed Rhodes to protest the delay. Littell had contacted
Rhodes personally to press for committee approval, which was finally forthcoming on July 19.[61] The bill did not fare well on the floor of the House,
however. On the basis of objections from Hopi traditionalists, the Justice
Department was able to force the bill back to committee so that there might
be hearings on it.[62]

Anticipating that authority to settle the boundary issue in court would
make an administrative decision on mineral rights unnecessary, both Littell

and the solicitor for the Department of the Interior agreed to postpone any brief answering the Hopi claim, at least while the bill was pending in Congress. When the bill failed to pass, Boyden asked the solicitor to require a brief of the Navajo attorney. This the solicitor did, setting a due date of 1 March 1957.

Meanwhile, the bill to authorize a court hearing was re-introduced after the first of the year in the new Congress. Senators Clinton P. Anderson of New Mexico and Carl Hayden of Arizona sponsored the bill. On the House side, Representative Stewart Udall of Arizona took the initiative.

When Littell reported these developments to the Tribal Council in February 1957, the problem of livestock trespass was again raised, this time by Councilman Clifford Beck from Pinon. The Navajos had concluded that if the Hopis were gong to continue to impound their trespass stock, they might accord the Hopis the same kind of treatment, and the Bureau of Indian Affairs officials at Window Rock backed them up in that decision.

It also developed that the Hopis had been pressuring Navajo tribal officials to insist that Littell submit his brief to Interior, the implication being that Littell was not doing his job. Littell explained that the brief was not overdue and that he did not want to file it until the due date, so as not to reveal too much of the Navajo case to the opposing litigants sooner than was absolutely necessary. While he was able to explain the situation to the council's satisfaction, some hard feelings caused by the Hopi meddling in Navajo affairs had to be smoothed over.[63]

At the May 1957 meeting, the Navajo Tribal Council was asked to pass a resolution favoring the House version of the new bill before Congress. Among other things, the resolution supported a provision that the federal government loan the Hopi tribe the funds needed to prepare their case, a suggestion which the Navajo Council approved in the interest of assuring fairness in the contest, for the Hopi tribe lacked the resources. The council also authorized the "officers of the tribe and the General Counsel" to decide on whether or not to support any amendments that might be made to the bill. The opposition to the bill of Hopi traditionalists was apparently the critical factor in drafting the resolution.

In urging the resolution's passage, Littell again raised the possibility of mineral wealth in the disputed area. Chairman Jones, however, stressed the importance of establishing the rights of the Navajos then living on the land.

Jones had served as district supervisor in District 4 during World War II and had actually had to place himself physically between armed parties to keep the peace at that time. He was well aware of the potential for tragedy in the intertribal rivalry and believed that litigation was the means of settling the matter peacefully. The resolution passed on a vote of sixty-six in favor, none opposed, and five abstaining.[64]

There continued to be uncertainty in Congress concerning the merits of the bill, and once again it failed to pass. The attorneys for both tribes continued their support for the legislation, however.[65]

The bill finally become law in the following year as the Act of July 22, 1958. It authorized the two tribes to sue each other in the U.S. District Court for the District of Arizona

> . . . for the purpose of determining the rights and interests of said parties in and to said lands and quieting title thereto in the tribes of Indians establishing such claims pursuant to such Executive Order [of December 16, 1882] as may be just and fair in law and equity . . . .[66]

The court was authorized to define tribal, village, clan and individual rights for both Hopis and Navajos.[67]

Preparations for representing the interests of both tribes were already under way.

PREPARATION

The Road to Prescott

T HAT PROOF OF occupancy would become important in the dispute over the land was apparent long before a bill to settle the issue in court was passed. The first archeological field work in Navajo sites in the 1882 Executive Order Reservation came in the summer of 1953. It was probably intended not to help resolve the question of land ownership, but to provide evidence of aboriginal occupancy in the Navajo Land Claim case before the Indian Claims Commission, a lawsuit for payment for lands already lost. The Land Claim case required proof not only of prior occupancy on land lost, but similar proof on lands then held if the current tribal acreages were not to be subtracted as offsets from those for which an award might be made. Research in that case had already begun, first under the direction of Malcolm F. Farmer and later under the leadership of Richard F. Van Valkenburgh.

Van Valkenburgh had a crew of Navajo assistants that included Maxwell Yazzie, one of the few Navajo college graduates of his generation. A short, slender man, Yazzie had a quick, energetic manner that was uncharacteristically Navajo, but a very Navajo sense of humor. He was relatively well-off by Navajo standards. Although he and his wife had only one child of their own, they had raised several adoptive children. He served several terms on the tribal council and was influential in tribal politics. He was highly intelligent and had a fund of traditional knowledge well beyond the ordinary. Van Valkenburgh had also given him training in the recording of Navajo archeological sites.

Yazzie lived near Cameron, Arizona, and relied on Clyde Peshlakai of Wupatki for traditional knowledge beyond that which he himself possessed. Peshlakai was a son of a well-known western Navajo headman, Peshlakai Etsedi who was a singer, or medicine man as they are called in English, as well as a leader.[1] Peshlakai himself was an herbalist and a traditionalist who

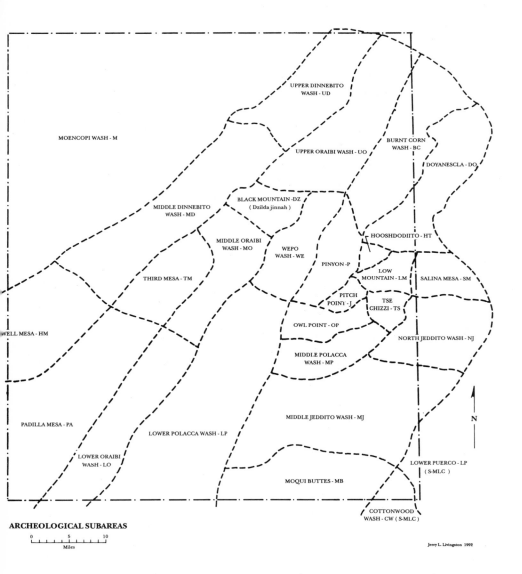

MOENCOPI WASH - M

UPPER DINNEBITO
WASH - UD

UPPER ORAIBI WASH - UO

BURNT CORN
WASH - BC

DOYANESCLA - DO

MIDDLE DINNEBITO
WASH - MD

BLACK MOUNTAIN -DZ
(Dzilda jinnah)

MIDDLE ORAIBI
WASH - MO

WEPO
WASH - WE

PINYON -P

HOOSHDODIITO - HT

LOW
MOUNTAIN - LM

SALINA MESA - SM

THIRD MESA - TM

PITCH
POINT - J

TSE
CHIZZI - TS

OWL POINT - OP

WELL MESA - HM

NORTH JEDDITO WASH - NJ

MIDDLE POLACCA
WASH - MP

PADILLA MESA - PA

MIDDLE JEDDITO WASH - MJ

N

LOWER POLACCA WASH - LP

LOWER ORAIBI
WASH - LO

LOWER PUERCO - LP
(S-MLC)

MOQUI BUTTES - MB

COTTONWOOD
WASH - CW (S-MLC)

ARCHEOLOGICAL SUBAREAS

0   5   10
Miles

Jerry L. Livingston 1992

knew in great detail the histories of both his father's and his mother's families. He knew very little English, which he had picked up during wage work, so that his command of English grammar and idioms was rudimentary. He was an expressive speaker in Navajo, however, and had the strong concern for accuracy that characterizes those who must depend on memory for the preservation of information. Thus he was not inclined toward careless discourse merely for the pleasure of an audience. Tall and slender, with a prominent nose, receding chin, and untamed hair, he was not handsome, but I never considered him really ugly as did some who knew him. He was a gentle man and serious in most circumstances, solicitous to pass on his lore to younger Navajos, and sufficiently offended by excessive drinking that if the crew should overindulge, he did not hesitate to let his displeasure be known. Even into his seventies he retained his youthful attraction to pretty women. He lived according to the traditional Navajo values of harmony, moderation, truthfulness, frugality, and respect with which he had been raised far better than most men I have known of any culture.

In August 1953 Yazzie and Peshlakai began to locate early Navajo sites in the eastern part of the 1882 Executive Order Reservation, working in the vicinity of Owl Point, Tse Chizzi, and Pinon. By the end of September they had extended their surveys into the upper Jeddito drainage and onto Balukai Mesa, as well as into the country just south of Jeddito Wash. They continued their explorations in October on Balukai Mesa and in the Pinon area. In November they located a few sites in the upper Oraibi drainage. All of these sites were north or east of the Hopi villages, and a few, such as those on Balukai Mesa, were actually east of the 1882 Reservation line. In February of the following year, they noted a few sites to the southwest of the Hopi villages in the region of Padilla Mesa.[2]

The archeological team collected samples of structural wood from many of these sites. At that time the only dating procedure independent of oral tradition and typology for historic-period Navajo sites was dendrochronology.[3] In the semiarid Southwest, the limiting factor on tree growth is soil moisture, which is dependent on rainfall, except in places with permanent surface water such as running streams or locations with a very shallow water table. Thus, the annual growth of many trees varies according to the amount of precipitation during the year. Not all trees can be dated easily. The techniques available in the 1950s allowed dating only of piñon pine, ponderosa (or western yellow) pine, Douglas fir, and the various spruce and true fir species of very high elevations. Cottonwood and willow grow in wet areas where annual variations in rainfall have little effect on their growth patterns. The junipers grow in a rather erratic manner that has been understood well enough for dating only recently. The vast majority of hogan dates were obtained from piñon pine, one of the more commonly used trees in Navajo structures.

Wet years produce wide growth rings in the wood, dry years narrow rings, and average years rings of intermediate width. The patterns of wide and narrow rings are unique to any time span of thirty years or more and can be matched with established chronologies for different areas. The dating of the Navajo specimens was done at the Laboratory of Tree-Ring Research at the University of Arizona in Tucson. Terah L. Smiley was overall director of the dating project, and the work was done under the direct supervision of Marvin A. Stokes.

When the dates for Yazzie's western sites were reported, there were many eighteenth century and early to mid-nineteenth century dates. All were from the region north and east of the Hopi villages. The list included one date from the 1600s, twenty-four from the 1700s, eighteen from the 1800s prior to the final Navajo treaty of 1868, two postdating the treaty, and one from the 1900s.[4]

These dates were so encouraging that further work was done in the same region in 1955. By this time, Van Valkenburgh had added to his staff. Clifford Gedekoh was hired as photographer, and J. Lee Correll, a graduate student in anthropology at the University of New Mexico, led the field crews. A second graduate student, Roscoe Wilmeth, was also hired, but he worked on the project only one season and only on the Navajo Land Claim case.

I never had the opportunity to know Gedekoh well, for he was no longer our photographer during the period that I was in the field, 1958 and later, but I worked with Lee Correll for almost ten years. He was a stocky but nervous man with a driving, compulsive personality that led him to do nothing in a tentative fashion. While this had its disadvantages in terms of the speed at which he drove, how much he drank, and how he used spices and medication, it also made him a workaholic whose attention to detail was unparalleled in my experience. Whether describing phenomena, compiling and organizing data, or indexing a text, he worked with determination and precision. Lee's original ambitions were in music, but the frantic competition in that field drove him to look for another career. I believe that his experiences in North Africa, Italy, and Germany during World War II led him into anthropology, for he saw not only the native cultures of the Mediterranean and the ruins of Pompeii, but the death camps of the Holocaust while they were still filled with emaciated bodies. His typing speed and ability at shorthand stood him in good stead in meetings, court hearings, and even in the field when interviewing tribal elders. From his constant probing for more details came one of his Navajo names, "The Questioner."

Bernadine Whitegoat, a Navajo from Hunter's Point, was also hired about 1955. He had received training at Saint Michael's Mission as an interpreter, and he was exceptionally skilled in establishing rapport with the older Navajos who worked with us as guides. His knowledge of the polite forms of address in Navajo and attention to the finer points of the Navajo system of kin and clan facilitated this process, but it was perhaps his almost inexhaustible patience that was the deciding factor when trying to persuade a reluctant elder to help the tribal cause. Heavy-set and diabetic, he was slow moving and sometimes moody. His humor could be cutting, but this was seldom without reason. Humor often functions as a means of social control in Navajo society, and he knew how to use it to good effect for his own purposes, often in ways that readers of the comic artist, Gary Larson, author of *The Far Side*, would appreciate. While his English was far inferior to his Navajo, he was seldom at a loss for some expressive manner of communicating what he had to say. Younger Navajos in the office often ridiculed his antiquated ways, but in the field with the old people he was fully at home in a world modern youth did not entirely comprehend, capable, sure of himself, and almost invariably successful in whatever he undertook. His son Willie, still quite young and not yet married, sometimes worked on the project as well, usually as a helper with camp chores and driving, but as an interpreter when this was needed.

The pace of field work accelerated with the increased staffing, making possible more investigation of new questions. The personnel at the Laboratory of Tree-Ring Research found the growth patterns of the trees of the region sufficiently interesting that they felt the definition of a chronology specifically for that area would be worthwhile. Among other reasons for doing so, they believed that they would be able to increase the proportion of specimens successfully dated with a localized chronology.

In June 1955 Correll led a field party that included Peshlakai and Johnny Begay as guides. Stokes accompanied them to take cores from living trees close to the sites where archeological specimens were collected. A number of the sites recorded by Yazzie were revisited, and several newly discovered sites were investigated. The crew worked in the upper Jeddito drainage, the Tse Chizzi and Pinon areas, and along the upper Oraibi Wash. The same crew returned in September to record additional sites in the upper Jeddito area.

In October Van Valkenburgh himself visited some of the upper Oraibi sites with Correll. By early November virtually the full staff was in the field, recording sites throughout much of the Jeddito drainage as well as south of the Polacca Wash and in the Tse Chizzi area. Local guides employed during this effort included John Tsosie Nez of Jeddito, Don Grayhair, and Noisy's Grandson, all older men who knew the country well.

Wood collected from twenty-two structures in seventeen sites proved to be datable. Although only two seventeenth-century dates were obtained, there were five from the eighteenth century and fifteen from the nineteenth century prior to 1868. There were eight later dates, all but one being from the nineteenth century. In terms of structures dated, there were one sweathouse possibly from the 1600s, three hogans that may have dated from the 1700s, two corrals and nine hogans from the early (pre-1868) portion of the 1800s, and one sweathouse and five hogans from later years.

The Hopi boundary dispute was not the only case being researched. Other areas received priority during the next three years. Only limited work was accomplished within the 1882 reservation. Instead, efforts were concentrated on the exterior boundaries of the land claims, on land disputes in Utah where the discovery of oil gave urgency to the assertion of Navajo tribal rights against claims by the state of Utah and local white ranchers, and on preparation of the great mass of data into an organized set of reports for presentation in court. Van Valkenburgh prepared a report on the archeological work in the country around the Hopi area, a report concerned not with current land use, but with the issues of historic occupancy before the Indian Claims Commission.[5]

In the midst of this activity, in 1957, Van Valkenburgh died. Correll assumed his duties as head of the research effort and soon found himself badly overloaded in his attempt to administer the program and at the same time continue all the anthropological research that was required.

In addition to the archeological work, a major effort was under way to assemble all the historical documentation that pertained to Navajo history for the periods considered relevant in a legal sense to the various law suits then under way. For the Navajo Land Claim the date that the United States first entered the Southwest, 1846, or that of the Treaty of Guadalupe Hidalgo which ended the Mexican War in 1848, was the beginning of the critical period, for the Indian Claims Commission assumed no jurisdiction over losses suffered by Indian tribes prior to the beginning of United States sovereignty in any area. The date for the official loss of Navajo lands was that of the final treaty with the Navajo Nation, 1 June 1868. Historical documents can be dated with far greater accuracy than can archeological remains. In order to keep the expense of research within reasonable limits, only documents that fell within the broader of these temporal limits, 1846 to 1868 inclusive, and a few later documents that referred back in time to that period, were selected for use as exhibits.

The archival search in the National Archives was conducted by Joseph G. Colgan, while Dr. Dale Morgan did searches in the archives in Utah. Dr. George P. Hammond of Berkeley headed the research, and microfilmed copies of all documents that might be useful were sent to him. His staff produced typescript copies of those that he judged significant, and mimeographed copies were prepared for use as exhibits in court. The crew in Window Rock received copies of these, both for use as aids in planning the archeological survey and so that Correll could organize the overall series of exhibits for courtroom use.

These documents contained a great deal of cultural information, including detail on land use that might be especially valuable for demonstrating the nature of Navajo occupancy. Correll had undertaken a detailed study of Navajo agriculture, combining the information from these historic documents with what had been reported in the published literature on Navajo crops, methods of farming, and uses made of the harvest of grains, fruits, and fibers.

By October 1958 he had become so overworked that he hired me to revise and complete his manuscript on Navajo agriculture. I had, by this stage of my career, considerable experience working with Navajos and even some in recording Navajo archeological sites along the route of the Four Corners pipeline and in Glen Canyon. I spent October in Albuquerque, making use of the resources of the Zimmermann Library at the University of New Mexico and the documentary record which Hammond's research provided. The result was a jointly authored monograph.[6] Van Valkenburgh, in collaboration with Dr. Clyde Kluckhohn, had earlier produced a similar report on Navajo sacred places.[7]

As soon as I had completed the agriculture study, Correll asked me to begin field work on the survey for the Land Claim case. I spent most of the remainder of the year investigating Navajo archeological sites in the eastern and northern sectors of the claim. This work continued during the early months of 1959.

Then, in the middle of the year, another lawsuit was commenced. Public Law 85-547, approved 22 July 1958, authorized the Navajo and Hopi tribes to file suit against each other to settle the boundary question. The Hopi Tribe began action against the Navajo Tribe under this authority on 1 August 1958.[8]

Our initial belief was that the same critical period that applied to the Navajo Land Claim would be significant in the boundary dispute. Because the lands concerned in the litigation were set aside in 1882, we assumed that sites dating as late as that year would probably be pertinent to the issues. We therefore asked our guides to take us to hogans and other structures used or occupied by their ancestors prior to the Fort Sumner exile and up to about fourteen years after the return from exile.

Maxwell Yazzie and Clyde Peshlakai began field work on their own in the Moenkopi Wash region in late winter. By the second week in March, I was in the field with Bernadine Whitegoat. We established our headquarters in Pinon, where the local chapter officers allowed us to camp in the chapter house. We hired a young Navajo man, Ben Silver, as an aide and guide to the homes of older men who might be knowledgeable guides to archeological remains. Our first contact, Hastiin Késhgolii Biye' Adika'í of Forest Lake, was a singer of Blessingway who had lived his entire life on Black Mesa. He was an unusually active and intelligent man in his seventies, and proved to be an especially competent guide to whom I was to return many times for help. In sharp contrast to the guides who worked with us in lands no longer their own, Mr. Adikai, as we came to call him, knew every small ridge and arroyo in lands that had been his home since childhood. He could not only recall sites occupied by his ancestors or their kin, he could unerringly plot the best way to drive our jeep to within easy walking distance, even for sites that had been situated originally for concealment from enemies. There was none of the casting about in vaguely familiar territory to return to a site seen in passing while pursuing a wounded deer or while working for a white rancher that we so often experienced on the claims work. Other guides were to be similarly skilled. Here, they took us to sites that they had seen numerous times while engaged in more prosaic activities on home ground. This was especially valuable when Bernadine was my interpreter, for he had a bad leg and found it difficult to hike in rough terrain.

Adikai was a small and quiet man with an overwhelming fund of facts, from the trivial to the profound, and a sly sense of humor. He was the first Navajo I had ever met who raised pigs, but I later found that others in that area kept pigs as well. He had affairs of his own to look after, yet he was willing to work with us more frequently than most, in part I am sure because he and Bernadine became good friends. His assistance was very important to our success.

Beginning March 8 I worked with Bernadine, Ben, and Mr. Adikai in the Upper Dinnebito, Moenkopi, and nearby subareas as defined by Van Valkenburgh's system for identifying sites. The entire claim was divided into four sections: Eastern, Southern, Western, and Northern. With the exception of the extreme northeastern and southeastern corners, the 1882 Reservation lay within the Western Sector and within the Lower Little Colorado area, W-LLC in the site designations. Added to this were the initials of the subareas:

Burnt Corn Wash	*BC*
Doyanescla Mesa	*DO*
Black Mountain	*DZ*
Hooshdodiito Mesa	*HT*
Pitch Point	*J*
Low Mountain	*LM*
Lower Oraibi Wash	*LO*

Lower Polacca Wash	LP
Moenkopi Wash	M
Moqui Buttes	MB
Middle Dinnebito Wash	MD
Middle Jeddito Wash	MJ
Middle Oraibi Wash	MO
Middle Polacca Wash	MP
North Jeddito Wash	NJ
Owl Point	OP
Pinon	P
Salinas Mesa	SM
Tse Chizzi	TS
Upper Dinnebito Wash	UC or UD
Upper Oraibi Wash	UO
Wepo Wash	WE

Each site within a subarea received a sequential alpha-numeric label, beginning with "A" and progressing through the alphabet, then through multiple-letter series in alphabetical sequence, and finally, in subareas where numerous sites were recorded, letters combined with numbers. Thus, the first recorded site in the Moenkopi subarea was W-LLC-M-A, and the last recorded site received the designation W-LLC-M-A23.

The advantages of working with sites in the 1882 Reservation were not limited to the fact that the guides knew the country intimately. They could also usually identify the former occupants, often people ancestral to their own families, and sometimes provide additional details relating to a site or to the people who had lived there. More significant for our archeological investigations, the sites had had little disturbance since abandonment, so we were able to produce increasingly better descriptions. We learned enough about Navajo archeological remains that we were soon led to revise our field form to aid in recording our more thorough observations. We heard reports later that Hopis, having learned of our research, were looking for early Navajo sites while gathering firewood, so that they could haul away the wood. If true, there were still so many sites that their attempt to destroy the evidence had no effect on our own efforts to make a record of it.

On that first day with Mr. Adikai as guide I recorded six sites. The first,

W-LLC-UD-A, was only a mile and a half from his winter home and con-sisted of a forked-pole hogan, a cribbed-log hogan, and a corral. Preserva-tion was quite good, and I was able to write detailed descriptions of all three structures. Mr. Adikai believed that the site had been occupied prior to the Fort Sumner exile, and he could name several people who had lived there. We collected twenty-two sherds of Navajo pottery, a metal pan, and three wood specimens for dating. I tried to select large, well-preserved timbers for sampling, preferably those that retained some bark in order to have dates that would clearly relate to the last year of the tree's growth. Only one of the three specimens was datable. It produced a date of 1843+incG, a prob-able outside ring date as indicated by the "inc" suffix (for incomplete growth of the exterior ring) and the "G" (for beetle galleries, which appear only on the surface of a tree trunk or limb). I did not know at the time the tree-ring date, but I was already beginning in my mind to associate certain features with possible pre–Fort Sumner dates. We used a rather loose definition of "pre Fort Sumner" as indicative of sites occupied up to about 1868. This date had functional significance, for warfare generally tapered off rapidly following the final Navajo treaty. Mr. Adikai told us that according to Nav-ajo tradition, U.S. troops did not penetrate Black Mesa during the final war, but that the Utes did raid there, an assertion that was corroborated by the documentation of that era.

The second site to which we were taken, W-LLC-UD-B, consisted of a forked-pole hogan, a corral, and a storage platform in a juniper tree. Our guide did not know who had occupied the site, but claimed it to be over 100 years old. We cut only one wood specimen, which dated to 1849+incG.

The third site consisted of only one very old and poorly preserved sweathouse. Again Mr. Adikai did not know the site history, but thought it to be 150 years old. Unfortunately, no wood worth collecting for dating was present, and we found no other materials of value for independent confirma-tion of Mr. Adikai's estimate. While here, he observed that at a nearby spring Ute raiders had killed several Navajos and that more Navajos were killed by Utes at a cave about a mile distant.

The next site had been occupied after Fort Sumner and had not been finally abandoned until about thirty years prior to our visit. There was a single hogan and a corral. The presence of trash that included tin cans, glass, crockery, and round nails was compatible with the date claimed. We cut only one tree-ring specimen from which no date was obtained. A large number of the specimens that we sent to the tree-ring lab were never processed because the work progressed too slowly there to keep up with the quantity that we were sending. As time grew short before the hearings, we identified for the laboratory staff the more important sites for which we needed dates. This one, Site W-LLC-UD-E, would obviously not have been given high priority.

Mr. Adikai next took us to a site where his father and grandfather had lived. It included a cribbed-log hogan, a log cabin, and a corral. It was here, at W-LLC-M-C, that I first collected sherds of a distinctive kind of Navajo pottery that I had not seen previously. I was later to give it a name, Pinyon Utility or Pinyon Gray.[9] Two wood specimens from the site were never dated.

The last site located that day was close to Forest Lake. It included four cribbed-log hogans and a corral, requiring a long time to record fully. By the time I had finished this, driven Mr. Adikai back to his home, Ben to his home, and then returned to the chapter house, I had had a full day. I was weary but eager to continue the survey, for I was finding more of interest than I had anticipated. I fixed dinner for myself and Bernadine, and we retired early so as to be ready for another long day.

My second day in the field on Black Mesa measured up fully to my new expectations. We visited six sites, recording a total of nine hogans, three corrals, a windbreak, a sweathouse, and an antelope trap. Again I was able to write unusually long and detailed descriptions of the structures. Bernadine had to translate specific tradition on the occupation of only two sites, but he also passed on from Mr. Adikai traditions regarding the use of pottery, including the first account I had heard linking a taboo on the manufacture of painted pottery and building of stone houses with the destruction of the prehistoric Anasazi people by a wind storm and attributing those prohibitions to Blessingway, the central ceremony of Navajo religion. I had long heard the story of the demise of the Anasazi as a result of wind or tornadoes, for my Navajo friends knew that as an archeologist I should be interested in the matter, but they had never explained why this happened. My collections that day included two lots of Navajo pottery, one tin can, and a *mano*—the hand stone used for grinding corn and other materials on a *metate*—plus several wood specimens. Only two of the sites were to be dated by tree-rings; both were the remains from late-nineteenth-century occupations in the

1860s and 1870s. Again it had been a long day, but a very productive one. After supper I spent what time was left before unrolling my sleeping bag checking the labels on my collections against my notes to be certain that I would catch any errors before my memory of details should fade.

On the tenth Mr. Adikai was unable to go with us. As a result, we relied on various guides to take us to sites in the upper Polacca drainage. Ben took us to the first site of the day, a single forked-pole hogan in which there was a burial. He did not know the history of the site, but it was not exceptionally old, probably dating within the present century. In deference to Navajo beliefs regarding burials, I did not make any effort to make collections of any sort, but I did record a good description and take a photograph. A second site of similar description showed evidence of even lesser age, and I noted abandoned modern artifacts, doubtless left as a result of the death that had taken place there. I felt that both sites were of far too recent an age to be of consequence in the forthcoming litigation, but did record them in as much detail as their status as burial places permitted.

We finally found an older guide, Etsitty Bitsoi, who took us to four sites, three of which predated Fort Sumner, the other dating to the late nineteenth century. Most interesting of these was W-LLC-BC-P, consisting of a cribbed-log hogan, a summer shade or ramada, a corral, a log cabin, and an area paved with stone slabs which I thought might have been a threshing floor. While the guide knew tradition for the other three sites, he could tell me only that he had first seen this one some forty-two years earlier and that the structures had already collapsed by that time. Two tree-ring specimens from the cabin later dated at 1765+G and 1798+inc. Pottery from the site included Navajo types dating both before and after 1800, as well as trade types from the Hopis. It was a site that stood out as especially interesting, one that I still feel is worthy of more intensive investigation, as much for what it might reveal of early Navajo life as for evidence of specific Navajo occupation. We were taken to one other site that day by yet another Navajo guide, Hostiin Speckled. It consisted only of a partially collapsed forked-pole hogan. By the next day Lee had joined us, along with Maxwell and Clyde. They worked primarily in the large Moenkopi Wash subarea, recording large numbers of sites, while I continued with my crew working more to the east. On that day Mr. Adikai was again free to go with us. He took us to four sites in the Upper Dinnebito and Upper Oraibi subareas. Again, these were some very interesting sites, and he provided traditional information for three which he considered to date before Fort Sumner. He could relate these sites to ceremonies which had been held there and, in one case, to a Spanish or Mexican expedition which had invaded the area, the Navajo language not making a distinction between Spaniards and Mexicans. Dates subsequently reported by the tree-ring lab helped substantiate his opinions for two of the three sites and indicated that the site for which he confessed ignorance of its history was also probably of an early date.

It was at one of these sites that I first described a hogan type which I came to consider typologically early. A cribbed-log structure with a flat roof, four walls, and a shorter fifth side formed by the entry, it appeared to be little more than a windbreak with a rather makeshift roof. In theory, at least, this variant could be an intermediate stage between the temporary shelters so common at hunting and gathering camps and the fully developed, cribbed-log hogans with domed roofs. As data accumulated on the type, I would postulate that it normally dated prior to the final treaty and found that other indications of an early date for sites with the type were in accord with that conclusion, but the suspicion that it represented a step in the evolution of the modern hogan type remained unresolved. The best explanation for its features now seems to be that it functioned as an expedient solution to the need for an enclosed shelter during the unstable conditions that so often prevailed prior to the end of the wars.

The next day Mr. Adikai was again unable to go with us. We spent considerable time looking for guides and worked with three different men, but did record seven sites. Most of these were small sites with only one or two features. One was merely a rock said to have been a marker of the western boundary of the Navajo Reservation shortly after the return from Fort Sumner, but the writing claimed to have been carved on it by white men was no longer legible and the location was more than a mile west of the true boundary. This was a dubious feature and not Navajo at all, so we did not include it in the survey. If it showed anything, it revealed some very sloppy surveying about 1878.

In addition, some of the traditional data recorded for other sites was not supported by the tree-ring dates that we later received. Two sites said to have been occupied after Fort Sumner produced dates that gave strong evidence of earlier use. One hogan at W-LLC-BC-T yielded dates of

1819+incG, 1838+incG, 1841+incG, and 1844incG. Perhaps it was occupied both before and after the exile. Site W-LLC-BC-X was especially significant, for it included a Navajo smithy. The guide said the site was occupied after Fort Sumner, certainly a possibility, and that the smith had smelted his own iron from local rocks, a most improbable claim. When we were sent the tree-ring dates, the anvil support post from the smithy dated at 1830+G, while there were two dates from one of the hogans of 1808+inc and 1846+inc.

Thus ended a very productive field trip, one that provided new insights into Navajo archeology, but which also raised important questions. I was to spend the next two weeks working in the office in Window Rock while Lee continued the field work.

While we were engaged in field work, the attorneys for the two tribes as well as for the Justice Department were also busy. The three-judge court which was to hear the boundary case had been appointed. The chief judge was Frederick G. Hamley, a circuit judge from San Francisco. Two district judges, Dane W. Ling of Phoenix and James A. Walsh of Tucson, completed the panel. In mid-March the court convened for its first session. U.S. Attorney Floyd L. France argued that the court lacked proper jurisdiction in the case and claimed that the Congress was merely eager "to toss a hot potato to the courts when it created the three-judge panel." His argument was to the effect that the Attorney General was neutral in the dispute between the two tribes. He asserted lack of jurisdiction on the basis of a claim that the dispute was political in nature and thus properly a question to be decided by the Congress.[10]

The Hopi Tribe was represented by John S. Boyden, Allan H. Tibbals, and Bryant H. Croft, but only Boyden took an active part in the presentations. Boyden replied that there was a need to get away from political pressures and to stand up for a minority, characterizing the Hopis as "poor and outnumbered." He asserted that the 1958 Act gave the Hopis title to the entire 1882 Reservation, while any Navajo rights that might have been established were not exclusive, but coextensive with those of the Hopis. He was adamant that any interests were also tribal interests, for only an allotment could establish an individual Indian interest.[11]

Attorneys present for the Navajo Tribe were Norman M. Littell, Joseph F. McPherson, and Lawrence A. Davis. Littell agreed with Boyden that only tribal interests were involved. He, however, based all rights on "the exclusive right of use and occupancy" or what he called "Indian title." He said that the Secretary of the Interior had created administrative settlement, recognizing Navajo presence through the establishment of schools, programs to improve grazing and farming, building roads, and similar actions and that the Congress had sustained him "by annually appropriating money in support of" these actions and programs.[12]

Boyden then presented arguments in favor of his motions to dismiss the Navajo Tribe's counterclaim to land, to strike certain paragraphs of the counterclaim if it should not be dismissed, and to require the counterclaim to be more "definite and certain." In view of later events, two statements made in the arguments, one by Boyden in support of his contentions and one by McPherson in defending the Navajo case, are worth noting.

Boyden raised the issue of mineral rights, saying, "The Black Mesa area, which the Hopis claim here, is reported to be one of the best oil areas in the state." McPherson, in support of tribal interest as opposed to individual interests, stated, "It is our theory that whatever rights attended settlement of an individual Indian within the Executive Order area inures to his tribe unless and until that land upon which he is settled has been allotted to him, the individual Indian."[13]

We knew little of these preliminaries to the trial for which we were preparing. By April we were all back in the field. Lee, Bernadine, Willie, and I set up housekeeping in a cabin at the homesite of John Tsosie Nez on the mesa just south of the Jeddito Wash. Nez was a tall, slim, elderly man who had been born somewhat east of the 1882 Reservation toward Steamboat Canyon. A man who had tried his hand at many things in his long lifetime, from rock art to blacksmithing and from ranching to curing, he was a well-known and respected member of his community.

He took us to several sites in the Middle Jeddito, Moqui Buttes, and Cottonwood subareas. A number of these were the large corrals with wings used to capture antelope during communal hunts. These corrals were constructed with elaborate ceremony under the direction of a hunt leader who knew the proper ritual.[14] The supernatural power inherent in the ceremony is believed to persist in these structures yet, making the wood unsuitable for use and the sites themselves dangerous places to live or even to camp. After we had recorded a few of these sites and cut wood for use in dating, Nez concluded that we all should have protection from the powerful forces residing in the structures. We were all seated in a row on the ground while he chanted and prayed for us. He dug the root of an herb growing nearby of which we all partook as a medicine. For Lee and myself it was a touching exhibition of his concern for our welfare, but for the Navajo members of our crew it was, I have no doubt, a most timely and welcome source of strength for a risky undertaking. The wood we collected was to produce a series of dates from the late eighteenth century and first half of the nineteenth century.[15]

Nez was well versed in local traditional history. He told us the names and clans of the former occupants of dwelling sites and of those who had built and used the antelope traps. He knew in detail the interrelationships of these people and could list several of the headmen who had signed the final treaty at Fort Sumner. He considered the promises made in the treaty to keep the peace and to send Navajo children to school to be important still.

With him we visited Comar Spring in the extreme southern part of the 1882 Reservation. The spring was named for a Navajo of the Tabaaha Clan whose descendants still lived in the vicinity. One of them had a letter dated 30 May 1894 and signed by Acting U.S. Indian Agent E. H. Plummer which gave notice to all concerned that the bearer was settled within the reservation. The letter had been endorsed by Constant Williams, Plummer's successor, on 1 April 1897. The continuity of the family at this location was unusually good refutation of the stereotype of Navajos as nomadic wanderers, and I took time to copy the document into my notes.

We worked on and off with Nez for a period of many months. It was while he was our guide that an incident occurred that still remains fresh in my memory. Not far from the District 6 boundary our jeep station wagon got stuck in the sandy bed of an arroyo. As we worked to get it out, two Hopi cattlemen in a pickup came by and gave us a hand. It was soon clear that their attitude toward our Navajo companions was one of superiority and disdain, such as I had previously encountered only in the South among some whites toward blacks and in Mexico among some members of the upper classes toward Indians. This overt expression of what can only be called racism by members of a society that has long been idealized in both the literature and folklore of anthropology struck too close to home for comfort. As an anthropologist I had long been familiar with the unfortunate tendency toward ethnocentrism among all peoples, but the exhibition of prejudice as strong and raw as I observed that day was to have a strong influence on my view of intertribal relations between Navajos and Hopis.[16]

It was still April when we began work out of the Pinon Chapter House with Oscar Yonnie and John Rockbridge as guides in the Wepo and Oraibi drainages. Oscar Yonnie was the same man who, as a councilman in 1953, had complained of Hopi opposition to Navajo use of the medical facilities at Keams Canyon. A forceful leader locally, he proved to be a knowledgeable guide. Few of the sites in his region produced datable wood, for this was close to the boundary of District 6 and at a rather low elevation where juniper trees were far more abundant than piñon pines.

John Rockbridge, a cheerful man in his sixties, was a guide whose intimate knowledge of his home region rivaled that of Mr. Adikai. His traditional site histories matched well the physical evidence and his willingness to work with us led me to ask for his help as often as he could spare the time from his other obligations, for he was a medicine man as well as a rancher.

My wife and I were expecting the birth of our first child and had, in fact, been anticipating that event for several weeks. Whenever there was a need to do work in the office, Lee would assign me there. I could not, in good conscience, avoid all field work, however, and having given my wife the number of the trading post in Pinon, I let the owner know the kind of message I might be receiving by telephone.

As the pressure to be ready for an imminent court appearance grew, Lee hired a second assistant, Martin A. Link. A young blond-haired, blue-eyed graduate of the University of Arizona, Marty already had some experience in Navajo country, for he had taught school at Saint Michaels Mission just west of Window Rock and had spent a summer as a seasonal ranger for the National Park Service at Canyon de Chelly. He worked with me on Black Mesa in April and with the two of us recording a site, the work went much faster.

On the fifteenth we recorded one site on the Upper Oraibi, W- LLC-UO-BB, which was of special interest. It included as one feature a fortified hogan on a high cliff, complete with loopholes and a wall blocking access, which was reminiscent of the more complex early-eighteenth-century pueblitos of the Dinetah region in New Mexico.[17] The typologically early features and a tree-ring date of 1815+incG seemed valuable substantiation for early Navajo occupation on Black Mesa.[18] A second fortified site was recorded four days later when Mr. Adikai took us to a crag in the upper Dinnebito where defensive walls lined the rim. A smaller crag nearby was said to have been used to keep captive eagles for their feathers. Two hogans, a corral, a lamb pen, and a storage chamber completed the inventory of site features. Mr. Adikai could not tell us the names of the occupants and we never received tree-ring dates for the three wood specimens collected at the site, but an early date could safely be inferred. We collected a great deal of wood from the sites located that spring, but little of it was ever processed. We located more antelope corrals in the middle Dinnebito drainage and began to write up more post–Fort Sumner sites as our guides exhausted the number of earlier sites that were relatively easy to reach.

Contrasts between the early sites and these later sites provided us with new ideas for dating. At some early sites with cribbed-log hogans we found the corrals built adjacent to the dwelling, but Lee noticed that this did not appear in the later sites. Our guides believed that the attached corrals provided greater security for livestock in the days of warfare.

Bernadine wondered why I spent so much time looking at ash heaps. We had carelessly assumed that these were middens, much as is the case in prehistoric Pueblo sites, and labeled them trash heaps. Bernadine scoffed at our naivete, explaining that trash was discarded at random. He told us of the custom of cleaning the ashes from the hearth each morning and carrying them out to the ash heap. I had to admit that I found relatively little trash in the deposits, but I had thought it merely due to the hogans being occupied for short periods. I soon learned of the custom of gathering up the sherds of a broken pot and depositing them safely under a ledge or a bush at a distance from the home. Any small sherds in the ash heap had simply been missed and were inadvertently swept up the next morning.

One morning while we awaited a guide at his hogan, we watched his granddaughter carry a bucket of ashes out to the ash heap, where she discarded it. She carried the ashes much farther from the hogan than were the ash heaps of the old abandoned structures that we were recording, a fact that first struck me because she was a small girl carrying a rather large load. We began to give greater attention to the distances of ash heaps from hogans and found that they tended to be closer to the hogans in the older sites, a difference that provided another way to estimate the age of sites.

Throughout the spring we recorded sites in the Middle and Upper Dinnebito and Oraibi subareas and in the large Moenkopi subarea. We experimented working together and as separate teams, depending on the availability of guides, the sizes of the sites we expected, and the mere stimulus that varying the routine could give our work. In the midst of all this activity, I became a father and did not know it. The message, which apparently was taken by a clerk at the trading post who did not know me, was never passed on to me.

With the approach of summer, our work in the 1882 Reservation ended. The land claims research demanded our attention, and as luck would have it, we also needed to spend more time in the office transcribing site reports, updating maps, and numbering exhibits, work that always seemed to be most needed just as better weather for working in the field began.

Max and Clyde recorded a few sites in August and early September, but the attorneys were busy in August and we expected an early court date. A pretrial conference was held in San Francisco. The makeup of the court had changed, District Judge Leon R. Yankwich of California having replaced Ling. The Attorney General was now represented by Mary Anne Reimann, who took little part in the proceedings. Boyden, Tibballs, and Croft attended on behalf of the Hopi Tribe, while Littell and McPherson represented the Navajo Tribe. It was announced by the court that the government's contention that the case was a political issue had been "ably disposed of." The court also concluded that the defendant, the Navajo Tribe, had the burden of presenting its case first, but that it did not have the sole burden of proof. All parties appeared to agree that the matter was basically a quiet title suit.

The two issues of mineral interests and individual versus tribal interests which had been raised during the hearing the previous spring were again discussed. With regard to the mineral estate, Boyden observed, "It is entirely possible to have the [Navajo] use and occupancy and still have our rights in the mineral reserved for us," meaning, of course, to the Hopi Tribe.

Judge Hamley later asked whether it would be necessary to determine whether the rights of the contestants applied just to the surface or included the subsurface. Littell replied, "That, in our opinion, is not an issue in this case. We know of no such title and no such concept. The mineral estate follows the Indian title, or whatever you may call it, on the surface. . . . That the title was cut horizontally to separate surface from mineral rights. We know of no such title in Indian law."

The persistence of the question of individual rights, tribal rights, or some-thing in between, shows that this issue was also given considerable thought by the attorneys for both tribes, and the implication that the outcome for this issue might influence the other of subsurface rights, while never explicit, seems to have been behind the reasoning on both sides.

Boyden had changed his position regarding tribal rights, at least as far as Navajos were concerned. He now asserted that if any Navajos had been settled on the disputed land, their rights were held only by those who were within the 1882 Reservation, not by the entire Navajo Tribe. He stated, "I am very loath to make any admissions . . . that a settlement in proxy for the entire Navajo Tribe could have any place here where the Secretary has set up a reservation for the Hopi Indians and such as have been settled thereon," and added, "if this Court should say that, we will take those Indians who were settled between such and such a date [sic] and their descendants, some-thing of that kind, that would do it." He came close to reducing this opinion to strict individual rights when he noted that "then the identity of those who have been settled there would become important."

Littell continued to maintain that only tribal rights were involved, and observed that he had tried unsuccessfully to agree to a stipulation to that effect with Boyden.[19]

After the August hearing, we did some additional field work on Black Mesa. In September I spent a week on the Upper Oraibi working with John Rockbridge, and another week with Mr. Adikai in the Upper Dinnebito country with Bernadine as my interpreter. By this time, Mr. Adikai felt quite at ease with us. He took us to many large sites and told detailed accounts of who had occupied the sites, of clan origins, and of interesting characters of earlier times.

Much of Mr. Adikai's tradition could be verified in the historical record. He had learned from his father that rations were issued for the first ten years after the return from Fort Sumner, a period that coincides with the ten years of annuity payments specified in the final treaty. His story of the origin of the *Nakaidine'é*, or "Mexican People," Clan told of the capture of two Spanish babies, both girls. The two babies were raised by *Tsíikehe*, herself a captive, taken when she was a child from a people living far to the southwest of Navajo country. *Tsíikehe* received her name as a contraction of *Tsídiilkehe*, "Birdfoot," given because the kind of sandals she wore when taken by the

Navajos left tracks like those of a bird. Never having children of her own to raise, she adopted the two babes. She lived at *Tó'aheedlii*, at the junction of the Pine River and the San Juan River in the Dinetah region east of Farmington, where she nursed the child who became the ancestress of the Nakaidine'é at her right breast and the other, who founded the *Tó'aheedliinii*, at her left breast. He said this happened so long ago that he could not say when. It was not until later that I read an account by the historian Frank D. Reeve which gives the names of two Spanish captives, Doña Agustina de Peralta and Doña Juana Almassán, taken at the time of the Pueblo Revolt in 1680, and after whom a Navajo settlement in 1746 was called Pueblo Españoles.[20]

Mr. Adikai seemed especially dependable in his accounts of people. Another site that we visited at this time was used before Fort Sumner by a man named *Ch'ahiini' Bik'is*, "Brother of the Late (Mr.) Hat." I did not immediately make the obvious connection that this was an uncle of the Son of Old Man Hat, whose autobiography is so well known.[21] On the other hand, Mr. Adikai could be quite imprecise regarding matters in the world of whites. He once asserted that the government had issued 4,000 wagons to the Navajos, clearly an exaggeration, unless Bernadine misspoke when he translated.

I recorded several of the small, flat-roofed hogans which appeared to be early. I collected little wood, for the backlog of specimens needing work at Tucson was large, but I did begin to collect burned pebbles from old hearths, having recently read of a new dating technique called thermoluminescence. Unfortunately, thermoluminescence dating was far from perfected, and we never were able to make use of it.

I observed that several of the hogans were built on relatively steep slopes, a siting that would help to conceal them from observation by enemies. In order to obtain a level floor, the rear of the hogan had been excavated into the slope and a small platform consisting of soil held back by rocks or logs formed the front of the floor. A number of the larger sites included structures from both before and after Fort Sumner, for often people had returned to their prior locations.

It was during this week that I recorded a second blacksmith shop, one that Mr. Adikai believed to have been used before Fort Sumner. I collected a cross-section of the post used to support the anvil, which later produced a tree-ring date of 1846incG.[22] The two dates that we obtained from the smithies on Black Mesa are the earliest evidence that we had then of Navajo blacksmithing.

The work we were doing was obviously applied research, but a great deal of basic information was needed if we were to begin to understand what we found. Little previous work had been done in Navajo archeology, and most of that published dealt with the very early sites of the Dinetah. Most had also been done with only minimal consultation with Navajos who could provide the kinds of cultural insights that helped us avoid false analogies to prehistoric archeology.

Our field notes were all-too-often too hastily written, and in the case of Lee's notes, sometimes in shorthand, so that our typists could not readily transcribe them into finished site descriptions suitable for presentation in court. In preparing our data for the typists, we found that often we had either omitted an item in a description or failed to note that no observation was possible, as when erosion had removed an ash heap or the condition of the hogan was such that we could not identify the entry. As we were trying to monitor characteristics of sites that might help us with dating, it was a real loss to find a dimension or observation lacking in an otherwise complete description. Sites with tree-ring dates, good traditional dating, and collections of potsherds or trade goods of known date became key sites for testing the relevance of ash heap distance, hogan diameter, hogan type, corral location, and similar attributes.

In order to overcome this difficulty, Lee undertook to revise our field forms. The old forms had all information on one page for each site, with separate spaces for recording site location, details of the terrain and vegetation, description of the structures, cultural associations, artifacts, pottery, tree-ring specimens, tradition, and the like. He concluded that we needed a separate form for each structure, which included a checklist for each observation that might be made. If no data could be entered under a particular heading, assuming that it was pertinent to the feature or structure being recorded, a note explaining its absence was to be included. Thus we would no longer have puzzling descriptions of hogans, for instance, which omitted all mention of the ash heap, leaving the recorder to wonder whether none was found or whether the recorder forgot to look for it.

By early 1960 we were again concentrating on the 1882 Reservation. With our new field forms in hand, we worked on and off from February through June, both in the Black Mesa country and in the low country in the southwestern part of the reservation. The attorneys had concluded that we needed evidence of Navajo occupation as late as the 1930s. As a result, we recorded a great many relatively recent sites. These more recent remains were frequently in a very good state of preservation, and we were able to gain a better understanding of changes through time in Navajo life. We knew that township surveys had been accomplished for a part of the reservation, and we obtained copies of the survey plats and field notes. In many instances when Navajo homesites were close to the section lines, they appeared in the survey data, giving a firm date for the remains. Locating the original section corners and following the section lines became a real challenge, for no use had been made of the surveys once they had been completed. We found one corner marker used to prop up the chimney of a hogan. One guide, rather than taking us to the corner posts, thought he could be more helpful by bringing them to us. Intercultural understanding could fail in either direction. Despite such complications, we were able to add many sites to our survey.

Both the Land Claim case and the boundary dispute were now coming to a head. The *Healing* v. *Jones* case was scheduled for October and the Land Claim case for April 1961. Professor Clyde Kluckhohn of Harvard University, long a student of Navajo culture, was to be the Navajos' witness on ethnology. He felt that he needed a better understanding of the archeology that we were doing. After having our site reports analyzed by a graduate student, he asked Littell to hire a recent Harvard Ph.D., David Lee De Harport, to work with us.

Dave had done his Ph.D. dissertation on the prehistoric archeology of Canyon de Chelly. Five years younger than Lee and five years older than I, he brought with him a knowledge of the latest methods and theory in American archeology current at Harvard. He was also a very talented photographer who had done an archeological photo project at the Ajanta Caves in India for UNESCO and had been retained to do a similar project in Egypt, which had been canceled as a result of war in the Near East. A slow and deliberate man, his greatest contributions as a member of our field crews came through his participation in our only excavations of Navajo sites and in a remarkably superior photographic record of our sites. On the long drives across the southwestern landscape, he also provided intellectual stimulation that our immersion in so much field work and court preparation had denied us. Something of an introvert, he did not socialize easily. I do not think that any of our Navajo crew ever learned to like him, but Lee and I found him good company and treated him as one of the gang rather than as an inspector-general come to evaluate our work.

We spent most of the summer doing survey and some excavation of Navajo sites in the southern portion of the Land Claim, coming in only when we received word on August 2 of Kluckhohn's death following a heart attack while fishing on the Pecos River. This forced us all to take time to consider not only what effect his loss might have on the cases, but just how best to prepare for them. A final pretrial conference was held in San Francisco on August 18. Most of the discussion was taken up with agreements between the attorneys for the two tribes as to exhibits, witnesses, and scheduling. Lee and I knew that our time to prepare was running out.

I had taken on the job of looking at the ceramic evidence from our sites in order to have good descriptions of the Navajo sherds we had collected and accurate identifications of the trade pottery. The project became mine somewhat by default, for neither Lee nor Dave wanted to do it and I had developed an appreciation of ceramic data, if not of the tedium of staring at broken bits of pottery. I began with a review of what was already known about Navajo and Apache pottery types.

Van Valkenburgh, in conjunction with the late Stanley Stubbs of the Museum of New Mexico, had determined that Navajo cooking ware did change through time. The earlier type, a thin-walled variant most frequently seen as medium-sized jars, they called Dinetah Utility, while later pottery with thicker walls, fillet decoration on the necks of jars, and a different mixture of clay and temper they called Navajo Utility. Little was known about the pottery made by the various Apache tribes, however, so the possibility of confusion between their pottery and that of the Navajos was very real. I spent considerable time visiting museums with collections presumed to include Apache ceramics. I also examined all of the collections from our own survey. I concluded that the later Navajo pottery from Black Mesa differed sufficiently from Navajo Utility that I could distinguish it with some confidence. I prepared descriptions of the types and thought that I might have to testify in *Healing* v. *Jones*, but realized I would almost certainly have to do so in the Land Claim case. I was unable to finish my pottery study in time for the Hopi case, however, in part because Lee needed my assistance in our preparations for the rapidly approaching date set by the court.

Lee was fully immersed in the organizing of materials for the hearings. There was a mass of exhibits to prepare—maps, site reports, tree-ring data, photos, pottery charts, and even lists of exhibits. No matter how often we checked the piles of exhibits, there seemed to be an unending series of corrections, additions, and improvements to be made. These were often simple, but very time-consuming, projects, such as a reduced copy of the large wall map of our site locations so that the judges and attorneys could each have copies for easier reference.

When we could spare the time, we assisted the attorneys with preliminary interviews of elderly Navajos who might appear as witnesses. Joseph F. McPherson, assistant general counsel who handled all the routine legal business in Window Rock, was in charge of this. McPherson was a short, stocky, and affable man of middle age who had grown up in rural Missouri. His easy manner, a pleasant contrast to Littell's often brusque and overbearing personality, hid an intensity of purpose that seldom was apparent, except as evidenced by his cigarette smoking. Although thoroughly Anglo-American culturally, he had a strong empathy for the Navajos. When he failed to understand some aspect of Navajo culture, he frequently tried to place it in analogy with facts he knew about classical Greek or Roman culture. This process as often as not distorted the Navajo meaning, but it helped him overcome any serious effects of culture shock or culture stress. He was a man who related well to people of all ethnic groups, a talent that made him the most effective courtroom lawyer on Littell's staff. He and Littell sometimes exhibited a bit of professional jealousy of each other, and it was doubtless McPherson's relaxed ways that Littell envied.

McPherson knew well all the tricks of the trade of a trial lawyer. He had had little opportunity to make use of his ability for many years, for his administrative duties were quite demanding, but he would play an important role in the Prescott hearings. He once told me that an attorney should never ask a witness a question to which he did not know the answer, but he knew also that there were exceptions to every rule and he could judge intelligently when he should take a chance.

He and his staff worked hard at learning what each potential Navajo witness could add to the case. Max was their interpreter for many of the interviews, as was Carl Beyale, the official interpreter for the Tribal Council. Beyale was more skilled at translating, but he did not know the country and the people involved as well as Max did. Lee, Dave, and I assisted with the interview process to the extent that we were able. Many of the Navajos with whom we had worked in the field were brought to Window Rock for the interviews, and others who learned of the preparations came on their own initiative to offer their services.

The interviews were taped and a second translation prepared from the tapes. The attorneys were not accustomed to working through interpreters and often failed to identify problems in the translations, problems that were not infrequently due to the great differences between Navajo and English and to the fact that the older Navajos, most of whom had lived the greater part of their lives among relatives and neighbors, often were not alert to the need to make explicit facts that they normally took for granted. Most of those interviewed, having given their answers to the lawyers' questions, thanked them for the effort they were making to protect their homes.

Lee made handwritten transcripts of the interviews as they took place, using shorthand for much of what he recorded, when he had time to do so. We both edited the transcripts of the final translations, adding notations such as map quads of places mentioned, refinements of awkward phrasings, and simple proofreading.

By the time we had to leave for Prescott we had things well in hand. This time the hearing was not postponed. The exhibits we had prepared would be the final versions. There could be no further work that would add sites to our map or additional dates from the tree-ring lab to our lists. We were about to present our case in court.

4

PRESCOTT

The Hopi by reason of living within one of the most spectacular parts of the country, which is in the direct path of the tourist, and by reason of retaining sufficient of his ancient customs to vividly illustrate a bygone age; and by reason of his picturesque community life, has a tremendous appeal to the travelling public. He is approachable, and recognizes the possible advantages to result from enlisting a sympathetic intervention of outside influence. The traveler listens, is duly impressed, and accepts as conclusive the statements thus prepared for his consumption. He has neither time nor interest to investigate them, but acting upon his unchallenged information he enlists his activities on their behalf. The Navajo does not have those Hopi characteristics. He is somewhat nomadic, self-reliant, neither seeking nor desiring sympathy. He is somewhat unapproachable and quite unresponsive to the advance of the curious. Hence he is branded by the Hopi as an aggressor, seizing his every opportunity to encroach upon the Hopi, and true to his Navajo characteristics he makes no effort to deny or to counterbalance the outside bathos which is being cleverly capitalized by the Hopi.

So wrote bia field representative H. H. Fiske in 1930.[1]

The romance of Hopi life is nowhere in the white world celebrated with greater fervor than in the town of Prescott, Arizona, where the renowned Smoki group until 1991 annually performed the Hopi snake dance with an attention to authentic representation that even some Hopis might envy. There can be no doubt as to which side had the sympathies of the local populace that September of 1960 when contingents from both sides in the land dispute arrived for a showdown in court. The Hopis were viewed as the home team.

Our crew had reservations at the Hassayampa Hotel, an old but well-maintained inn near the center of town. In addition to the attorneys and researchers, we had interpreters, tribal and BIA officials, and some support staff coming and going as needed. The hearing began on Monday, September 26. The legal professionals were to be much the same as before. Judges Frederick G. Hamley, Leon R. Yankwich, and James A. Walsh presided. Attorney Mary Anne Reimann, seated off in a corner, was basically an observer for the Justice Department, seldom taking part in the hearings. John S. Boyden, Allan H. Tibbals, and Bryant H. Croft were again there to present the Hopi case. On the Navajo side, Norman M. Littell and Joseph F. McPherson were again present, and Walter F. Wolf, Jr., a young attorney from Window Rock, joined them.

Lee Correll, Dave De Harport, and I had our exhibits well organized. Dr. Hammond's final set of three volumes of documents, mostly from the National Archives, was being sent at the time. We had been working overtime to have all in readiness, but were filled with anticipation. The night before, I had found in my hotel room not only the *Gideon Bible,* but a *Book of Mormon,* as was usual in hotel and motel rooms throughout the Southwest at that time. As the Hopis' attorneys were known to be Mormons, I attempted the traditional practice of randomly opening the Mormon volume, out of curiosity. I was rewarded with a long text berating lawyers as avaricious hypocrites and fell asleep wondering how a Mormon attorney rationalized this passage in the sacred book of his religion.

The next morning Littell was the first to present his opening statement. He reviewed briefly the history of the dispute, using a map with transparent overlays which Lee had prepared to show each of the recommended boundaries that had appeared in the documents found by the historians. Lee assisted by pointing out map locations as Littell mentioned them. Not having been involved in the pretrial conferences, neither Lee nor I were alert to the significance of the comments by Judges Yankwich and Hamley regarding joint-interest situations. Littell, in fact, virtually ignored that possibility. Rather he described five possible solutions, each involving distinct boundaries separating Navajo and Hopi lands. The first of these was based on the history, archeology, and Navajo tradition that we would be presenting; the others were based on the legal construction that might be given to the Hopi

Constitution, the 1936 and 1943 District 6 boundaries, and the Page-Rachford proposal of 1939.[2]

Boyden followed with his opening statement. He was a tall man who looked somewhat like a minister. This resemblance was perhaps based as much on his manner of speaking as on his physical appearance, however. He relied heavily on oratorical ability and had a melodramatic style in court that made me think of an old-time preacher. He worked to make the Hopis appear as impoverished saints and the Navajos as nomadic aggressors. Boyden made repeated reference to Navajo "depredations," for example, expounding on Navajo "aggression and encroachment" upon the "quiet and peaceful" Hopis. His strong appeal to emotion rather than reason aroused in me an instant dislike for the man, as I had early in my childhood learned to favor logic over rhetoric.

He sometimes outdid himself. When he piously asserted that in choosing extracts from the documents used as exhibits the Hopi side had tried to be impartial, Judge Yankwich, who could never resist an opportunity to interrupt, asked whether or not he was an advocate. Boyden replied, "I appreciate that we may unconsciously do what your honor says, but . . . we had in our hearts the idea to put in everything that was pertinent. . . ."

Boyden's opening statement continued on the following morning, Wednesday, the twenty-eighth. As Littell had done, he listed the alternatives which he believed were open to the court in making its decision. His first proposed solution, as might be expected, was that the entire 1882 Reservation be awarded to the Hopi Tribe. His second possibility was that should any Navajos be found to have been settled on the 1882 Executive Order Reservation, they would individually share co-extensively in the settlement with the Hopi Tribe because the case was a quiet title suit. His final alternative (and one he was most reluctant to make) was that if it should be found that any individual Navajos had exclusive interest in any area, then that "might be converted to a tribal interest," but he believed that this was not the case.[3]

Following the opening statements, Lee led off as the first witness for the Navajos. In his direct testimony he presented his qualifications, outlined the field work we had done, and described our results. A portion of Boyden's cross-examination was aimed at elucidating in greater detail what we had done and how we had done it, but he also tried to nit-pick where he thought he could show bias. He objected to the word "Navajo" appearing on one of our maps within the 1882 reservation, for example. Lee pointed out that it was there as the county name, not the reservation name.

Boyden also asked questions designed to insinuate that the Navajos were an immoral people. He asked how the Navajos handled divorce, something that really had little to do with the issues before the court. Lee explained the traditional Navajo custom of the woman placing her husband's belongings outside the door while he was away, an indication that he was not welcome back inside the home. We had been so busy learning about Navajo culture and archeology that we had not done enough reading on the Hopis to know that their customary divorce method was the same. Judge Yankwich, at least, was quick to understand what Boyden was doing. When Boyden asked Lee about Navajo polygamy, the judge asked about Mormon polygamy.[4]

I knew Lee well and was uncomfortably aware of the stress he endured under the lengthy cross-examination. His slightest slip was painfully apparent to me, but he made very few, and these in inconsequential matters. A friend, another archeologist who was present as an advisor for the Hopis' attorneys, later told me how impressed he was with Lee's composure on the stand. There could be little doubt that Lee had succeeded in his explanation of what we had learned and what it meant in terms of early Navajo occupancy of the contested lands.

The second witness for the Navajos was Gordon B. Page, the man who had worked on so many surveys in the region in the 1930s for the Soil Conservation Service and who had made recommendations for a boundary between the two tribes in 1939. In 1940 he had entered the army as an officer and had eventually risen to the rank of colonel in the military's nuclear power program. He had retired from the service and continued to perform the same duties as a civilian employee of the army, living in Washington, D.C. Page was gruff and hearty, a living stereotype of a competent and no-nonsense military man. He described in a straightforward way the work that he had done before World War II and supported in personal testimony the reports that he had written. Boyden did not make a strong effort to discredit Page's testimony in cross-examination, apparently relying on the Hopi contention that use and occupation of the land were irrelevant in the case.[5]

Thursday's testimony began with Terah L. Smiley of the University of Arizona, whose supervision of the tree-ring dating made him the essential witness for gaining acceptance of the procedure in court. McPherson conducted the direct examination and it went very smoothly, being a lucid scientific explanation of the theory behind the work and the way in which it was done. Smiley's presentation provided an account of the biology of tree-ring growth and the techniques used to correlate tree-rings with calendar years. Boyden did not seriously challenge the validity of Smiley's conclusions, although he did cross-examine him.[6]

A large number of the elderly Navajos who had been interviewed in Window Rock came to Prescott to give testimony concerning their own lives in the Executive Order Reservation. A camp was set up for them at a Forest Service campground south of town, and Navajo women were hired to provide the elders with the foods to which they were accustomed. All the elders were very traditional in their outlook, and several were medicine men. On the trip to Prescott they had stopped at several places to pray, and they had held a special service at the point where Prescott first came into view. In camp one night they performed a divination ritual in which a spider was to entwine an object representing the enemy. The spider was reported to have performed as desired, a favorable omen. All in all it was a great reunion for the singers, who spent much of their free time discussing religion, illustrating their points by chanting bits of the sacred songs, much as a Christian might quote a passage of scripture to support an argument.

The elders' testimony followed Boyden's cross-examination of Smiley. Ned Hatathli, a young and very bright Navajo tribal administrator, was sworn in as interpreter. A Bureau of Indian Affairs interpreter had been scheduled to do the job, but had not yet arrived. Hatathli was a veteran of World War II, spoke excellent English as well as Navajo, and had himself been born in the 1882 Reservation, but on its western edge. Maxwell Yazzie helped locate places on the map when they were named in Navajo. I assisted by writing Navajo place names and personal names according to the Young and Morgan orthography for the court reporters.[7] This was not as easy a job as it seemed, for there was seldom a chance to have a name repeated. I also discovered later that the reporters had difficulty distinguishing my bar-l symbol (ł) from a "t". Consequently, there were a number of errors in the transcript. Nevertheless, this spelling of Navajo names made them far easier to identify than they would have been if someone unfamiliar with the language had tried to write the words as they thought they sounded. The method also provided greater consistency in spelling, so that a person named by one witness could be more reliably identified in the testimony of others.

James Cook, the first Navajo witness, was seventy-seven years old and had lived all his life on the Executive Order Reservation. In response to questions by Littell, he told of being born south of Keams Canyon about three miles from the school, and of living for the past fifty-eight years at Rat Springs, north of Low Mountain.[8]

The second Navajo witness was Joe Kabinto, one of the few Navajos still living inside District 6, the Hopi land management district. Then seventy-nine years old, he had a white mustache that drooped on the ends, which gave him a slightly Oriental appearance. Living as he did on land under Hopi jurisdiction, he was obviously risking possible retaliation for his testimony, but he felt that he had good relations with his Hopi neighbors and probably did not anticipate any repercussions. He had been born at Noisy Springs, outside of District 6, but at age fifteen had begun working for Tom Pavatea, a Hopi who owned considerable livestock. Kabinto had spent much of his adult life caring for Pavatea's sheep and cattle. He named the heads of thirteen Navajo families that had been driven out of District 6, as well as several early Navajo headmen who had lived within the Executive Order Reservation.[9]

Subsequent testimony by others on Friday elaborated on the travails of Navajos who had been forced to move when District 6 was first established in 1936–1937 and then expanded in 1943. David Bitsillie told of families that had been uprooted twice.[10] David Benally and his wife both testified. Mrs. Benally told of having to relinquish her grazing permit when she had been forced to move. She had not been issued a new permit after settling in District 7 and subsequently had been jailed for "trespass," the BIA euphemism for grazing without a permit.[11] John Reed and John Tsosie Nez, both of whom had worked with us as guides, also testified that day.[12]

Several newspapers carried stories on the hearing. The *Arizona Republic* in Phoenix provided the most detailed coverage, although it was also probably the most one-sided. In the story published on Thursday, September 29, Bill Nixon wrote, "Page's testimony was about as effective as a B-B gun. He admitted that he couldn't see what effect his testimony could have on the trial."[13] Nixon was a bit more subtle in his story for Friday's paper. I took offense when I read his story for Saturday's paper, however, in which he called Nez a "skinny 82-year old" who "had to stretch his memory to recall that particular Navajo farming area near Jeddito Wash," for I had grown to like and respect the old man.[14] I hoped that Nixon's conclusions were not shared by the judges, for I recognized that my own reactions to the testimony were influenced by having worked with many of the witnesses and having come to know them on a personal level.

After the weekend recess, John Tsosie Nez's direct examination continued on Monday morning (October 3), but he had to sit waiting on the witness stand while Littell and Boyden thrashed out an agreement before the judges to omit expert testimony by historians on both sides. Dr. Hammond had been advised by his doctor not to travel to higher elevations because of a heart condition, which meant that the court would have had to convene in California close to sea level if it were to take his testimony. With Boyden's stipulation that he would not call Dr. Lyman Tyler, a historian at Brigham Young University, and that he would restrict the testimony of Dr. Harold S. Colton of the Museum of Northern Arizona to matters concerning archeology and ethnology relating to Anasazi sites, it was then possible to avoid a separate California session to accommodate Dr. Hammond.[15]

Following this, Nez testified concerning the eviction of Navajos from District 6. In view of his qualifications as a medicine man, he also testified about ceremonial use of Hopi pottery by the Navajos. Boyden, in cross-examination, dwelt on Hopi use of the Jeddito Valley and Navajo livestock trespass into District 6.[16]

Emil Kanuho of Comar Spring was the next witness. He brought the original of the 1890s document that I had copied in the field, and it was admitted as an exhibit. He was one of the younger Navajo witnesses, being only fifty-six, but as the current holder of the letter protecting his family's right to live at Comar Spring, he had solid documentation of their continuity at that place. He even brought a photograph of his father, who was mentioned in the letter.[17]

The order for the calling of Navajo witnesses, whether intentional or otherwise, followed the clockwise circuit of Navajo ritual. Comar Spring is due south of the Hopi villages. The next few witnesses were from the southwestern quarter of the disputed area. George Nells testified as to occupancy in the Tovar Mesa area.[18] He was followed by Slow Horse from Shonto Springs on the lower Oraibi Wash, who was still on the stand at the end of the day.[19] He returned to complete his testimony the next morning. On cross-examination Boyden quizzed him about a Hopi horse which Boyden was later to imply through Hopi testimony had been stolen by Slow Horse.

The next witness on Tuesday was Ashiihii Ts'osie, or Slim Salt, who had lived at Burro Spring until the 1943 expansion of District 6, when he settled at Kachina Point. He had lost a farm at Burro Spring because the new boundary cut right through it. Boyden, on cross-examination, asked how Kachina Point got its name. This, of course, was a puzzle to Slim Salt, who knew little if any English, but Judge Yankwich broke in to explain that *kachina* was the Spanish word for kitchen. Ned Hatathli was interpreting and gave the Navajo name as *Alchíndahaasnaatani*. The resulting trilingual confusion was never resolved.[20]

Boyden's sensitivity to linguistic complications was very limited despite his long service as counsel for the Hopi Tribe, perhaps because most Hopis already spoke passable English by the time he arrived on the scene. Dealing with the progressive pro-Council faction, he probably seldom had reason to converse with any Hopis who did not speak very good English. I suspect that he honestly believed that all of the old Navajos could have testified in English if they had wanted to do so. He had a Hopi who understood Navajo present to check on our interpreters. He eventually objected so strenuously to the quality of interpretation by the BIA interpreter that the Navajos' attorneys ceased using him. This actually solved a problem for us, since his interpreting was causing rampant misunderstandings, yet we had lacked firm grounds for dismissing him. On the other hand, Ned Hatathli was a superior interpreter who could bridge the great differences between English and Navajo with accuracy and artistry, often rendering complex Navajo phrases into eloquent English, and I have no doubt, turning abstruse English into good colloquial Navajo. Hatathli helped Judge Hamley as interpreter for local cases involving Navajos in the mornings before our sessions began, and the court reporters told me that he was the best interpreter from whom they had ever taken dictation.

Lester Benally followed Ashiihii Ts'osie. A mere fifty years old, he had been born on Padilla Mesa. Benally was barely into his testimony when Littell asked permission to excuse him temporarily so that a ninety-year-old woman who could not stay long in Prescott could be put on the stand. Asd-zaan Tsedeshkidni was introduced as Hatathli's grandmother, although in actuality she must have been his great-grandmother. She was born at Tona-lea, but at the age of about twenty had moved to the Howell Mesa area. Her family had ranged their sheep eastward across the Dinnebito to a place called variously Beautiful Mountain or Beautiful Mesa until, as Hatathli trans-lated it, they "heard the rumble of the Hopi hoes." When the Hopis began to farm around Beautiful Mesa, the Navajo family no longer grazed their sheep around the site and retired permanently to the west side of the Din-nebito.[21] Next, McPherson presented Asdzaan Tsedeshkidni's seventy-three-year-old daughter, Lillie Sonnie, whose testimony corroborated that of her mother.[22] Boyden declined to cross-examine either of these women.

Lester Benally then returned to the stand to complete his testimony. He described the expulsion of the Navajos from the expanded District 6 in 1943, noting that one Navajo whom he knew had been arrested for not moving on two-day's notice. A singer, he also told of shrines on Tovar Mesa, where prayers and offerings were made for building antelope traps, for dis-posing of old medicine bundles, and for making new ones.[23]

On Wednesday, October 5, Yellow Hair Bedoni, a brother of Lillie Son-nie, testified about early occupancy on Howell Mesa and conflicts with Ho-pis over a Navajo-built dam.[24] Scott Preston, vice-chairman of the Navajo Tribe, was the next witness. Littell conducted his examination. His testi-mony took up the rest of Wednesday and resumed Thursday morning. Pres-ton's father had been a white trader who had apparently taken little interest in his son, for Preston had a strong distrust of whites, bordering on an active dislike. At age sixty-one he was a well-regarded medicine man who was ex-tremely knowledgeable in Navajo traditional culture. He listed a great num-ber of Navajos by name who had lived in the 1882 Reservation, described Navajo lifeways, eagle hunting, trade for Hopi pottery, and the gathering and use of herbs. Although he could speak and understand English, his skill with the language was distinctly that of a non-native speaker, and he pre-ferred to testify in Navajo. Much of what he talked about required a good command of classical Navajo, in which he could express himself with confi-dence. Boyden, on cross-examination, challenged Preston's decision to speak through an interpreter. Preston replied that this would help them avoid ar-guing, but in that respect he was in error, for the two men were soon deep into extended quibbling over such semantic technicalities as the difference between a road and a trail. It is unfortunate that Preston allowed himself to be drawn into these petty disagreements. I do not believe that Boyden intended to undermine Preston's testimony in quite that way, but his condescending attitude, which Preston was too keen an observer to have missed, plus his lack of patience with the slow process of interpretation, led to a clash of personalities that did ultimately erode to some degree Preston's credibility.[25]

The next witness was Jacal Baadaanee, a portly and dignified medicine man, who testified in response to McPherson's questions about Navajo occupation in the Blue Canyon region.[26] He was followed by Oscar Yonnie from Hardrock, who told of having to move out of District 6 both in 1937 and 1943.[27] Hastiin Bedoni told of helping to build the Dinnebito Diversion Dam. He said that Paul Jones, then District 4 supervisor for the BIA, had told them that the dam was to be for Navajo use. He also reported that while he still planted a field inside District 6, he had to live outside.[28] The last witness of the day was Moses Dijoli from above Hardrock on the Oraibi Wash. His testimony suffered such confusion in translation that it was agreed the next day that a written statement would also be submitted.[29]

The story on Friday morning in the *Arizona Republic* emphasized the slow pace of the proceedings, observing that the "use of an interpreter has slowed the trial to a walk," and adding,

> During the trial, interpreters have been used in virtually all testimony, even from those Navajos who speak good English. The translations have consumed considerable time.[30]

At this time the attorneys for the two sides were exploring the possibility of a stipulation that would permit the introduction of written statements by other older Navajos waiting to testify. While this was being negotiated outside the courtroom, Littell began to call some of his other witnesses.

The first witness on Friday morning was Paul A. Krause, Navajo Agency range conservationist, who testified as to how the grazing regulations worked. He also qualified for admittance as exhibits copies of various grazing records, including lists of permittees and their livestock holdings, and a map showing the areas of responsibility of the different grazing committees for each grazing district which overlapped a portion of the 1882 Reservation. The grazing districts had been laid out according to natural boundaries on the landscape rather than with regard to the arbitrary boundaries created by of the various executive orders. With the assistance of the grazing committee members, Krause was able to tell how many permittees ran livestock inside the disputed area, giving his totals as 991 Navajo permittees, who were allowed to graze 71,172 sheep units and who actually owned 78,285 sheep units as of the most recent count.[31] He also explained that the grazing permits merely specified the grazing district to which they applied. Each family controlled what was called a "traditional use area," and local recognition preserved these land-use rights. Unfortunately, neither the Navajos' nor the Hopis' attorneys brought out clearly the nature of these rights. The legal theory of the Navajos' attorneys that *tribal* use and occupancy was the relevant variable prevented them from seeing the importance of this information. Boyden, for his part, was more interested in showing the limits of Krause's information and in trying to show that the Navajos were villainous people.[32]

Krause was followed by Maurice McCabe, another of the up-and-coming, young, well-educated Navajos. He held the position of Navajo tribal executive secretary, a post that ranked second only to that of chairman in terms of political power. He had overseen the tribal emergency grain-feed distribution program in 1956. He had planned to show from the records of that program where Navajos had lived within the 1882 Executive Order Reservation at that time, but Boyden successfully objected to the exhibits he had prepared.[33]

Next came Clarence Ashby, assistant general superintendent in charge of community services for the BIA at Window Rock. He was well into explaining the BIA school census when the court recessed for the weekend. On Monday, October 10, morning he resumed his description. The school census mapped Navajo home locations hogan by hogan, making it possible to predict where new schools were needed, where school bus routes should be located, and the size of the coming year's enrollments in each school. The Indian Health Service (IHS), a branch of the U.S. Public Health Service, as well as the public school districts also relied on this census data. By projecting the 1882 Reservation boundaries on the census map, it was possible for Ashby to calculate that the Navajo population of the disputed area was about 8,252, including 2,928 school-age children.[34]

Robert W. Young, assistant to the general superintendent of the Navajo Agency and the leading authority on the Navajo language, was then called to testify on his population studies of the Navajo Tribe. Young's testimony was necessary primarily to provide two figures. The first, the percentage of the population that was of school-age, he estimated as between 34.74 and 35.5 percent. The second, the annual growth rate of the tribal population, he gave as 2.25 percent.[35] These helped to put the figures given by Ashby into better context.

Next came Remi Van Compernolle, director of the administration division of the Navajo Tribe, to identify the seven trading posts within the 1882 Reservation that were operating under Navajo leases. Boyden cross-examined as to whether the trading leases specified that the posts were inside the 1882 Reservation area, which, of course, they did not. Boyden also introduced into evidence a letter requiring that all rent moneys from the disputed lands be held in escrow. Van Compernolle stated that he had never seen the letter and said that all rents went into the tribal general fund.[36]

The last witness of the day was Edward O. Plummer, youthful head of the Navajo Tribe's Land Investigations Department. He was the son of Ned Plummer, one of the more influential members of the tribal council, and son-in-law of Annie Wauneka, long the only woman on the council. He had been educated at the Methodist mission school in Farmington and was another of the more promising young Navajo leaders of that time. His testimony was necessary in order to introduce into evidence a map of the locations of the trading posts listed by Van Compernolle. He was the last to testify on behalf of the Navajos before Littell rested the Tribe's initial presentation.[37]

Following this, Littell and Boyden agreed before the judges to the introduction of a number of written statements in lieu of testimony by several Navajo elders. The statements of Moses Dijoli, Tsinnajinni Nez, John Rockbridge, Bizaholoni Bikis, and Hastiin Keshgoli Begay Adikai were admitted at this time. All were concerned with further details of Navajo use and occupancy within the 1882 Reservation.

The Hopis began the presentation of their case on Tuesday morning. We then had to begin work on materials for rebuttal, and we were much busier than before.

The first witness for the Hopis was Charles Pitrat, land operations officer for the Hopi Agency. He began by presenting a vegetation map of the disputed lands, which he used to indicate the locations of Hopi farms and wood-gathering areas.

Pitrat followed this presentation with a map of places where Hopis collected plants. As an aid to his description of Hopi plant use, he brought into court more than ninety herbarium sheets on which were mounted wild plants said to be used by the Hopis for a variety of purposes. The plant specimens were from the BIA herbarium at Keams Canyon and were not intended to be exhibits, but merely to help illustrate Pitrat's method of acquiring data. He had earlier placed the sheets all around a room to which he had invited older Hopis. They had told him which plants they recognized, to what use these were put, and from which locations they were generally gathered. Pitrat had combined this information with that found in Alfred F. Whiting's 1939 work, *Ethnobotany of the Hopi*.[38] He had then drawn a map to depict the areas from which the plants came and had written up a one-page information sheet for each species, all of which were bound together as part of one of the plaintiff's exhibits. While the overall importance of the plants collected outside of District 6 was not great in comparison to the Navajos' dependence on the land, the elaborate display was quite impressive. It addressed a kind of use we had ignored in our efforts to cover the more basic kinds of land utilization, such as residence, farming, and livestock raising. Pitrat also testified to what he called Hopi eagle shrines and ceremonial shrines, fox trapping, and grazing permits outside District 6, including a list of 105 Hopis who had requested permits in the surrounding grazing districts and whose applications had been denied.

A good deal of Littell's cross-examination of Pitrat questioned his qualifications to deal with the kinds of information to which he had testified. He could claim expertise in botany, which meant that the vegetation map and the ethnobotanical exhibits would probably carry the greatest weight in the eyes of the court. While he had shown most Hopi plant gathering in terms of very specific locales, for a few species he had colored rather wide areas on his map, and Littell quizzed him on the manner in which these were determined. Despite the doubts which were raised as to the professionalism of his ethnography, the exhibits he had prepared were accepted. During Pitrat's testimony, which extended into Wednesday, the attorneys engaged in a vigorous debate as to whether the Hopis had to show occupancy to gain land beyond District 6.[39]

Pitrat was followed by a large number of Hopi witnesses. The first was Bennett Cooka, a man of mixed Hopi and Hopi-Tewa ancestry and a member of the Hopi Tribal Council. Among the matters to which he testified, he was asked to tell what he knew about Tom Pavetea's grazing areas in order to introduce possible discrepancies with Joe Kabinto's testimony. (Kabinto, the reader will recall, was the Navajo who had spent much time in Pavatea's employ, and who had testified about his knowledge of Navajo families who had been forced out of District 6.) He also told a rather patronizing story about the origin of Kabinto's name, saying it came from the Navajo word for moccasin and the Spanish word for spotted because Kabinto had been very poor in his youth and wore patched moccasins. His manner of relating the story indicated that its purpose was clearly to disparage Kabinto as a person.[40]

Edna Sequi, the next witness, was an eighty-eight-year-old woman who had lived outside District 6 in the Jeddito Valley since 1916. She told of being challenged by local Navajos as to her family's right to settle there and described in detail a fracas with Navajos when members of her family began to plant a cornfield. According to her story, the Navajos broke her husband's planting stick, beat him up, grabbed her by the hair, and began to beat her too until they realized that she was a woman. She also accused the Navajos of killing her calves. Littell objected to this sort of testimony, maintaining that he and Boyden had agreed not to bring in the violent confrontations that had inevitably taken place in the competition for land. Although Navajo witnesses had been instructed to avoid telling about such incidents, his objection was overruled.[41]

A Pima Indian, Justin Sanderson, who had married a member of the Sequi family, next testified that he had tried three times to build a home even more distant from District 6 than the Sequi farm, but each time the structure was destroyed. He too complained of losing livestock, although he had a grazing permit for District 7 in which he was located.[42] When George Lomayesva, Sanderson's Hopi father-in-law, also testified, it became apparent that the various grazing permits claimed were all obtained from Edna Sequi's husband's permit when it was divided.[43]

The last witness of the day was Irving Pabanale, a Hopi who had worked as a surveyor's assistant during the second allotting program. He also claimed to have built a home outside District 6 only to have it destroyed.[44]

Not surprisingly, the *Arizona Republic* had a story the next day which focused on the ethnic conflict.[45]

I examined the ethnobotanical exhibits and the herbarium specimens during breaks in the hearings and felt that the impact of Pitrat's presentation had been greater than the subject deserved, but that part of this impact resulted from our failure to show that the Navajos made any use whatever of wild plants. I had also noted a number of discrepancies in the Hopis' identifications, and I felt that we could at least do as well as they did. I talked to some of the Navajos about trying to put together something of our own based on these same specimens. Both Vice Chairman Scott Preston and Clyde Peshlakai were willing to try to identify the plants in terms of their Navajo names and to tell uses that they knew for them. Max Yazzie volunteered to interpret for us. The court granted us permission to examine the specimens in a room across the hall from the courtroom after hours.

I had some concern as to how well Indians would be able to identify plants in the dried and pressed state of herbarium specimens. Ethnobotanists who had done research among the Navajos had emphasized the importance of accompanying informants into the field to identify plants in their natural habitats,[46] or at least while still "in a fresh condition."[47] Preston was a medicine man, however, and Clyde an herbalist and the son of a medicine man. I had hopes that their professional experience would give them a greater skill in recognizing dried specimens than would be the case with the average Navajo. Since the environment in which a plant was found was reported to be a factor in the recognition of species, I felt that they deserved that information from the herbarium labels as an aid in recognition, knowing that a modern scientist would take that into account in his or her own use of the collection. Moreover, the Hopis had undoubtedly been sufficiently literate to have been able to consult the labels when they did their identifications for Pitrat. As it turned out, in the few instances when Preston and Clyde did not immediately recognize a specimen and the description of the collection site was translated for them, they were sometimes able then to tell what the plant was.

I worked first with Preston. He was able to give names and uses for almost all of the plants. I got the impression that he knew more plant lore than he was willing to tell to a white man regarding some of the species, but I did not press him for information he believed improper to reveal. I was especially pleased when he correctly identified two plants that were in error in the Hopi identifications. One was a confusion between the Fremont barberry, a shrub or tree, and the holly grape, a perennial too small to produce usable wood. The Hopis had specified use of wood that could not possibly be obtained from the holly grape, to which they attributed that use—a clear sign that they had misjudged the plant. The similarity of the leaves of the two species could easily mislead, and I felt new confidence in Preston's botanical knowledge when his information correctly matched the specimen. The second error concerned a shrub that was misidentified on the herbarium label. I did not feel qualified to question the label, but Preston was adamant that he recognized the shrub even in its preserved state. I dutifully recorded his identification, as I knew that the prepared statement had to accurately present his observations, but did so with some misgivings.

Clyde was beginning to lose his eyesight and found the environmental data from the labels especially helpful. He eventually identified more of the specimens than did Preston. He did not always have the same names for the plants, however. In a few instances this was the result of a misidentification by one or the other man, but more often I could attribute the disagreement to different acceptable names for one species in Navajo, much as we use the terms "yucca" and "Spanish bayonet" interchangeably. In addition, Clyde's gentle sense of humor made the late hours more pleasant, as when he pronounced one edible plant to be "medicine for a hungry person." Clyde also corrected the Hopis' errors on his own. He recognized the holly grape for what it was and quite independently identified the misidentified shrub in the same terms as had Preston.

In the meantime, the Hopi testimony continued during the days. On Thursday, October 13, four Hopis took the stand—Preston Masha, Peter Nuvumsa, Lee Saknumptewa Thomas, and Donald Maho. Boyden, as usual, conducted the direct examination of each witness, and McPherson carried out the cross-examination. A Navajo who knew the Hopi language, Manuelito Lewis, was sworn as interpreter to check on the Hopi interpreter, much as a Hopi who understood Navajo had listened to the translations by the Navajo interpreters. Masha testified primarily regarding Hopi livestock raising.[48]

By far the most impressive of the Hopi witnesses was Nuvumsa, the village spokesman for Mishongnovi on Second Mesa. A seventy-two-year-old member of the Bear Clan, he testified in a quiet and dignified manner befitting his status in Hopi society. He seemed, in fact, somewhat out of place among the others who appeared—almost a token traditionalist for the council faction that controlled the Hopi case. He testified about wood gathering, use of shrines, plant use with reference to the herbarium specimens, alleged Navajo theft of Hopi horses, and Navajo occupation. He rather upset Boyden when the lawyer once again reiterated the assertion that Navajos were continually moving into the 1882 Reservation. Nuvumsa stated that the same Navajo families had lived within the area he knew from 1922 up to the present, and added, "I don't recall any other new ones come in since then." He also described the Hopi effort at expansion at the expense of the Navajos, mentioning a man from Bakavi who planted eight acres of corn down the Oraibi Wash near the Red Lake Store, but who after two years went "back home" due to Navajo opposition.[49]

McPherson's cross-examination soon brought out new information that disturbed Boyden even more. I had found in the published literature on the Hopis a reference to "substitute shrines" close to the villages for a few of the more distant shrines. McPherson chose Nuvumsa as the Hopi to ask about this matter, but his question caused me to hold my breath in shock; ". . . you people have substitute shrines near your villages for all of the outlying shrines that you have made mention of, is that true?" Nuvumsa not only agreed with that statement, but in reply to another question asserted that the distant shrine and its substitute had the same religious significance.

Nuvumsa had misidentified the herbarium specimen of pinyon pine as fir during direct examination by Boyden. McPherson cross-examined him at some length on this specimen and at the end of this questioning read into the record the botanical identification on the label, apparently to help in a later evaluation of the reliability of the ethnobotanical exhibit.[50] It should be noted here that McPherson did not conduct cross-examination in the aggressive and accusatory style frequently portrayed in the movies and on TV, but in a very low key manner that respected the integrity of the witness.

Lee Thomas, a Hopi who was also a Phoenix plumber, took the stand to characterize the Navajos as "renegades from the north," relating conflicts his family had as they tried to move out into territory already fully occupied by Navajos.[51]

Donald Maho's testimony was given, in part, to support an alleged Hopi farm on one of Boyden's maps. It turned out on cross-examination by McPherson that Maho was married to a Navajo woman, and there was doubt as to whether the farm was his or, in accord with the matrilineal customs of both tribes, really the property of his Navajo mother-in-law. While he also claimed that he ranged sheep outside District 6, it became clear on cross-examination that the sheep were grazed under his Navajo wife's permit and belonged to her. He also had stories to tell of Hopis who had tried to expand into traditionally Navajo territory and who had been rebuffed.[52]

Following Maho on Friday morning, T. K. Johnson took the stand. A small, thin, and lame eighty-four-year-old, he was well chosen for the role of eliciting sympathy as a Hopi David put upon by Navajo Goliaths. In 1910 Matthew Murphy, the second allotting agent, had surveyed an allotment for him well down the Dinnebito among the Navajos. With hired help, Johnson had completed a house and planted an orchard. He had then returned to his home at New Oraibi, and at the urging of an Oraibi "chief," he had taken the time to accompany a team of dancers to the Tewa village on First Mesa. On this trip his horse took a tumble in the dark, breaking Johnson's leg. He was absent from his house on the Dinnebito for over three months as a result of this injury. When he returned, the house and orchard had been destroyed. McPherson decided to forego cross-examination.[53]

Next came Earl Albert, a sixty-seven-year-old resident of Hotevila, who had attempted in the 1920s to settle at the place abandoned by Johnson. He had been a bit more fortunate than Johnson, for he had actually lived at the site for about three years, but he testified that his crops always disappeared while he went "home," so he eventually gave up. Albert tried to minimize the Navajo presence at the place, but in order to account for the loss of his corn and fruit, he was forced to acknowledge that there was nobody there except himself and the Navajos.[54]

Louis Nunkema, a Hopi from Moenkopi, also testified to resistance by Navajos when he and others had tried to establish farms at Red Lake.[55]

Kirkland Polacca, a forty-two-year-old man from First Mesa, testified that his father had built a house east of Pinon. When Kirkland had tried to expand from his father's place upon his return from the service following World War II, he found that the Navajos already there objected.[56]

The last witness for the day was Roger Quochytewa, who claimed to have grazed some 500 cattle in the vicinity of Tolani Lake. He accused several Navajos of stealing his stock.[57]

Most of these witnesses also testified regarding less intensive use of the disputed land, such as hauling firewood, gathering wild plants, religious use, and the like. The Phoenix newspaper continued to slant its stories in favor of the Hopis. This bothered me, for I was not sure whether the tone of the writing came from previous bias or from a failure on our part to adequately present the Navajo side of the story.

During the time that McPherson handled the cross-examination of Hopi witnesses, Littell and several of our crew were busy preparing for the Navajo rebuttal testimony. It had become clear that we would have to show the density and continuity of Navajo occupation and use of the land outside District 6. We worked through the weekend, for we expected Boyden to end his presentation early the next week.

On Monday, October 17, the lawyers arranged for the submission of additional exhibits that they would use during rebuttal, including a number of prepared statements by elderly Navajos that would shortcut the slow process of testimony through an interpreter.

Boyden then presented testimony by William H. Beck, a BIA range conservationist for the Hopi Agency, who told about trespass by Navajo livestock inside District 6.[58]

Dr. Fred Eggan, a professor in the Department of Anthropology at the University of Chicago, was the last witness for the Hopi Tribe. Eggan had been involved in Hopi studies since 1932. He was undoubtedly the foremost scholarly authority on the Hopis at the time, but confessed to having limited knowledge of Navajo ways. His views on Navajo-Hopi relations were of special interest, for he seemed to find them difficult to explain. He noted that the Hopis considered some Navajos to be friends and trading partners, but that they distrusted Navajos that they did not know.

He stated, "The attitude toward the stranger Navajo is pretty much one of fear and apprehension . . . he may fear for his own person; . . . he may fear for the loss of his sheep and cattle. And underlying that, I think, is a prevailing fear that somehow or other he is going to lose his whole reservation to the Navajo." Eggan continued: "I have been in the Hopi kiva when Navajos have been invited down, and they sit around and smoke with the Hopi. They are the ones that are known and are friendly . . ."

Eggan generalized about Hopi diet; "The Hopi conception of food, real foods are corn and beans and squash, the vegetable foods. Meat and some of these other things are thought of as sort of relishes, you add a little bit to give it taste, to give it flavor . . ."

Eggan also placed the Hopi shrines into a different context, testifying, "I think it has something of the same significance as, say, the Holy Land to Christians."

Because of Dr. Harold Colton's feeble health, Eggan also testified on the archeology of the 1882 Reservation. Littell's cross-examination brought out the fact that archeological sites postdating the Great Drought, which ended in A.D. 1299, are concentrated in the vicinity of the three Hopi mesas.[59]

The Navajos' rebuttal testimony began that afternoon with Lee describing how the maps used for the Navajo exhibits were made.[60] The next morning Dave De Harport began his testimony, explaining some basic archeological principles and helping to introduce the 1890 census map of the area, which showed the concentration of Hopi settlement at the mesas.[61]

De Harport was followed by Wilbur E. Morgan, supervisor of the Census Section of the Navajo Area and son of the late Jacob C. Morgan, who had been tribal chairman in the 1930s and one of the strongest opponents of government programs of that time. Morgan was short and a bit paunchy, an intense man in the office who somewhat intimidated clerical personnel, but a man whom Lee and I had always found to be very cooperative when we needed his assistance. He described in detail the census data maintained under his direction and showed how this information was used to plot on a map the homes of Navajos whose names appeared on the 1937 sheep dipping records and the 1957 school census. These maps helped to demonstrate the continuity of Navajo families within the Executive Order Reservation. The link back to 1937 was not an easy one to make, and Boyden cross-examined Morgan closely on the details. Boyden's preachy, self-righteous, and condescending approach antagonized Morgan, who replied with the unresponsive complexities of an experienced bureaucrat. Unfortunately, in the courtroom context, rather than frustrating an unwelcome interloper, his tactic meshed with Boyden's real objective, which was to discredit the link. Morgan was still on the stand at the end of the afternoon and returned the next morning for redirect and recross. Boyden and Littell clashed strongly on the propriety of the Navajo evidence. Boyden asserted that the evidence being given had no bearing on the case, while Littell expounded on Boyden's refusal to acknowledge Navajo occupancy.[62]

Two witnesses followed Morgan on Wednesday. The first was Reino R. Sarlin, who oversaw forestry operations for the Navajo Area. He explained all the details of woodcutting permits and payments for timber cut.[63]

Clifford Beck, the Navajo tribal council delegate from Pinon, next took the stand. No sooner had he been sworn to tell the truth than Boyden and Littell were again arguing as to whether the Navajo evidence was proper and relevant. Beck, a tall and distinguished middle-aged man, had to sit waiting in the witness chair while the two attorneys disputed the issue. Littell's basic contention was best summed up in an explanation he gave early in the debate, that "the purpose of this testimony is, first, to supply the missing link in the information before you from the records, how long these people lived there. Because you don't have it until 1957 in these . . . school census exhibits. And I propose to relate by these witnesses the locations of these hogans and the people who lived in them or in those communities for a considerable period of time."

Beck was not the only witness who was forced to endure seemingly endless squabbling, but I frequently wondered at the time if either attorney was serving the interests of his client. Whether each was trying to convince the court of the correctness of his views, or hoping to undermine the composure of his opponent's next witness, or merely indulging in a display of machismo, their antics at the time seemed unproductive to me. Rereading the transcripts almost thirty years later, I find these portions of the proceedings of unusual interest, however, for they do offer insights into the thinking of the competing gladiators in the courtroom spectacle. I feel that I have long since come to understand the facts of the case, but I now find a need to comprehend the dynamics of a process that applied those facts in a particular way. After what at the time seemed an interminable interlude, Beck was allowed to present his testimony.

Beck told of his experiences as a young man in his twenties working for the government in his home community. From 1928 to 1932 he was an assistant to the Navajo range riders and a census taker, along with Manuelito Lewis and Jim Cook, for a BIA census. Using the lists from the census and the dipping records, he described the locations of the various Navajo families' hogans at that time, while Lee pointed them out on a map.[64]

Beck's testimony was interrupted by questioning of Littell by the judges. Judge Yankwich then tried to sum up the purpose of the testimony:

> In view of the statement just made by the Court I think we all agree that the only purpose for which this testimony is offered is merely for the purpose of tying certain testimony here to information given about the presence of Navahos at certain times, tying them to a particular occupancy. The Court made it very clear yesterday and previous to this that there are no individual Navahos or Hopis such as were postulated in the statute for adjudication of rights. Therefore the possibility of the Court requiring a list of individuals and their ancestry must be eliminated, because no one has appeared so far and no one has asked for a right to intervene, no individual. So as of now, unless something should develop later on and this Court is asked to allow individual Hopis or others to intervene, we are adjudicating the rights of the tribes against one another. So the possibility of the situation to which Mr. Boyden— the possibility of the Court needing that must be eliminated, because we are not adjudicating the rights of individual Hopis or individual Navahos in any of this territory.[65]

Littell agreed, saying that he thought that the issue of tribal versus individual rights had already been settled.[66]

Judge Hamley pursued the purpose of the Navajo testimony further, asking, "If you have a witness here that personally says that a certain man lived in a certain place, a certain Navaho, for 30 years, 'and I know him,' that he was there all that time, what does the census record add to that?"

Littell replied, ". . . the second point, that complete recognition of the Secretary of the Interior and the constant processing of the data in regard to these people."

Judge Hamley then asked, "Are you saying that the fact that this man was enumerated and put on the census is an administrative declaration by the Secretary of the Interior that he was settled thereon?"

Littell then asserted, "Indeed I do. It's one of a series. It doesn't stand alone, but it's one of a series."[67]

Following further discussion, Judge Hamley then inquired, "Do you mean that because it is in a census, this indicates the Secretary of the Interior knew they were there all this time, therefore he has acquiesced in their settlement?"

To this Littell responded with a more inclusive explanation: "Yes, I do, and he took cognizance of their stock problems and he took cognizance of their school problems and he was recognizing their existence and treating them as settled upon this land all that time."[68]

This exchange was followed by some more testimony by Morgan on the census records and the testimony of Donald Mose, a grazing committee member from Pinon, who extended Beck's testimony on Navajos living in the Pinon area. At the end of Mose's testimony, court was recessed early, at 11:45 A.M., to allow the attorneys time to try to reach agreement on a stipulation as to the admissability of statements by local Navajo officials as to Navajo residence.[69]

The final day of testimony was Friday, October 21. Only one witness, Annie Wauneka, appeared. The only woman then a member of the Navajo Tribal Council and very influential in tribal politics, not only because she was a daughter of the late Henry Chee Dodge, but also because of her own strong personality, she had played a major role in the success of programs to improve Navajo health. She had served on the council for about nine years and was not quite fifty years old at the time of her testimony. She described the religious and emotional ties of Navajos to their place of birth.[70]

Following Mrs. Wauneka's testimony, Littell and Boyden quibbled further over the exhibits and addressed other items of business that needed attention before final arguments were to be made on Saturday. Boyden then took the initiative to clear the way for possible mineral exploration within the boundaries of the Executive Order Reservation:

Now the Court, by order of the 19th of September, 1960, approved this agreement that had been reached by us with respect to the stipulation: "The parties hereto will agree upon a joint form of geophysical permit which, when

THE NAVAJO-HOPI LAND DISPUTE

approved by the duly constituted authorities of each tribe, may be issued upon approval of applications therefore for both tribes provided, however, that no geophysical work shall be done in the Executive Order area prior to the completion of the taking of testimony in this case and the submission thereof for decision."

In order to clear that, we would like it understood that it has now been submitted for decision insofar as this stipulation is concerned so that we can proceed with geophysical permits if we so desire, . . ."[71]

The belief that mineral wealth might underlie the 1882 Reservation had been a behind-the-scenes motivation throughout the hearings. That possibility had been noted frequently in the newspaper reports during the four weeks of the trial, but it had not been dealt with in court. On October 18 *The Arizona Republic* claimed, "The land was recently evaluated as rich in oil and uranium deposits."[72] A story in the *Republic* on the twentieth quoted the Hopis as saying that "the Navajos have illegally settled on the potentially rich oil and uranium grounds,"[73] and in stories printed on both the twenty-second and the twenty-third, the country in dispute was described as "potentially oil-rich land."[74] The paper had also played up the allegations of Navajo misbehavior in their conflicts with Hopis that had been so much a part of Boyden's case, and followed this with such extraneous items as the fact that there was a Navajo named Jesse James then living near Pinon, a detail that formed the headline for their story on the 20th.[75]

On Friday night we worked late, helping the attorneys prepare for the final arguments the next day. I assisted McPherson in computing the number of Navajos who had been forced to move out of District 6 and was able to identify ninety-six or ninety-seven family heads by name. We were convinced that the actual figure must have been well over a hundred.

In the final arguments on Saturday, Littell tried to counter the repeated insinuations that the Navajos were an inherently evil people. He characterized them as "a peace loving people who would rather move and compromise than to stay and fight," but added that "they have tough fighters too, very aggressive men just like we do." He further accused the Hopis of continuing efforts to foment discord during the dispute, claiming that they "are stooping to do underhanded things against the Navahos."[76]

Littell summarized the history of the dispute and presented the five options which he believed were open to the court:

1. Division of the reservation on the basis of the "green line" on the Navajo map exhibits, which encompassed the area the Navajos asserted to be the limit of exclusive Hopi use and occupation.
2. Division on the basis of the area agreed to by the Hopi Constitution, which he construed as the 1936 District 6 boundary.
3. The District 6 line approved 16 March 1937.
4. The Page-Rachford line of 1939.
5. The 1943 District 6 boundary.[77]

The judges were interested primarily in Littell's views on legal questions. Judge Hamley asked, if the Court should find that the Navajos had been settled within the reservation, "would it be appropriate for us to consider whether or not he [the Secretary of the Interior] correctly interpreted the Law, or can we go behind his exercise of discretion for that purpose?" The judge repeated the question in another form: "Can we consider whether or not he exercised discretion under a misapprehension of the law?" To each of these questions Littell replied in the negative.[78]

Judge Yankwich phrased the issue in somewhat different terms: "In other words, it goes back to the fundamental proposition in jurisprudence that the power to make a decision includes the power to make a wrong decision provided it isn't arbitrary and capricious," to which Littell said only, "Possibly, your honor . . ."[79]

McPherson also contributed to the final arguments, emphasizing the importance of long Navajo occupation of the land and dealing with the hardships suffered by the Navajos who had been forced to move from their homes with the creation of successively larger boundaries for the Hopis. He contrasted this with the "insignificant and inconsequential" Hopi settlement and use of the land outside District 6.[80]

Boyden, of course, presented a very different history of the dispute. He contended that use and occupation were not legally decisive in the establishment of ownership. Judge Hamley had asked four questions that may have guided Boyden's thinking. These were:

1. What is meant by "settlement" in the Executive Order of 16 December 1882?

2. Does the 1958 Act require use of the reservation on 22 July 1958?

3. What is the difference between "exclusive use and occupancy" and "exclusive interest" in the reservation?

4. Is there any exclusive interest held by individual Indians or by the Navajo Tribe and why?[81]

Boyden contended that Navajo occupation within the 1882 Reservation did not constitute settlement and characterized their presence as illegal, making reference to the implications of a Navajo being named Jesse James. He maintained that "the settlement of individual Indians upon the Hopi Reservation under Indian Law would confer no exclusive interest, but only a communal interest to share coextensively with the Hopi Indians—." He went on to assert that no Navajo had ever acquired such an interest.[82]

The possible fate of Navajo families long settled on the lands in question received only passing attention. The hearings ended with no real hint as to how the court regarded the matter.

We returned to Window Rock feeling that we had done an effective job of demonstrating the importance of the land to the Navajos who resided on it and believing that no United States court could make a decision that would displace so many people from their homes.

A final note: As the long legal proceeding drew to a close, the anti-Council, Hopi traditional leaders declared that the entire lawsuit was illegal.[83]

THE LONG WAIT

A S WE CONSIDERED our experiences during the hearing at Prescott, our optimism grew. Chairman Paul Jones, in his report to the fall session of the Navajo Tribal Council, had little doubt as to the eventual outcome when he praised the performance of Littell, McPherson, and Plummer. He stated that the Navajos' attorneys had "made the Hopi counsel appear ridiculous by comparison" and asserted his faith in the tribe's legal department.[1]

I shared these expectations of a favorable decision. In November I wrote a friend that all indications were that the Navajos would get most of the land for which they had contended. In December I wrote another friend that I expected the court to draw a boundary close to the then-current District 6 line.

My expectations were based in part on the work we were soon doing for the attorneys to help analyze the data in the court record for the writing of *Defendant Navajo Tribe's Proposed Findings of Fact.*[2] This was a major undertaking. There were 22 volumes of testimony and hundreds of exhibits to consider.

One of my projects in this analysis was the extraction of all the evidence of use and occupation by identified Navajos, which was to be tabulated according to the quads on our map. While extracting the Navajo data, I also noted all information on Hopi use and occupation. The tabulation of Navajo use and occupancy became a part of Finding 7D, running for 127 pages. The attorneys decided not to include the Hopi data in the finding.[3] The two volumes of proposed findings were submitted to the court and the Hopis' attorneys in May 1961.

There were other matters requiring our attention and we could not work exclusively on the boundary dispute. The Land Claim case was also coming to a head. Testimony in that case had been taken from a number of elderly Hopis at Grand Canyon, and we were told to sit in on this in order to help the Navajos' attorneys with questions on cross-examination. We also continued field work, branching out into ethnographic interviews for the claims case. Lee hired Aubrey W. Williams, Jr., then a graduate student in anthropology at the University of Arizona, to help us with the interviews. In addition, a dispute over school sections on the portion of the Navajo Reservation in Utah required a part of our time.

When the Hopi attorneys' proposed findings were received, I again was asked to assist in an analysis of their interpretation of what the evidence in the boundary dispute case showed. This was where my file of Hopi use and occupation more than proved its worth. The Hopis' lawyers had used only their own exhibits and the testimony of their own witnesses to demonstrate the farming that they claimed had been done by Hopis outside of District 6. My file included all information on each farm from all sources, and I soon found that the Hopis attorneys had done some very sloppy work, both in creating their original map of alleged Hopi farms and in putting their data together when writing their findings.

Of nineteen supposedly abandoned Hopi farms which Boyden had placed in evidence on the map with a promise to support each location with testimony, I discovered that eleven lacked any support whatever. The remaining farms had use claimed for periods ranging from less than one growing season to twelve years and were clearly farmed either with the permission of Navajos who had close relationships with the Hopis involved or were simple trespass which the Navajos had resisted vigorously. In one case a Hopi store owner had planted a small field beside his trading post, where he sold goods to the surrounding Navajo population. An additional several farms that were claimed still to be in use by Hopis were cultivated under similar circumstances, including the one that was planted by a Hopi man married to a Navajo woman. Some farms were intermixed with Navajo fields along the edge of District 6, although the Hopi map showed the entire strip as under cultivation by Hopis.

Taken as a whole, the Hopi claims showed such poor knowledge of the geography and such poor control of location that I concluded that the attorneys were not trying to deceive us so much as that they just did not know what they were doing. One farm was shown in three different places on the map, as three different farms, for instance. It appeared almost as if they did not really care whether their asserted use data were accurate.

This apparent disdain for fact gave me additional cause to feel that the decision should favor the Navajo claim, but I had to qualify my optimistic assessment by admitting that I could not judge how well they had crafted their contentions regarding the law of the case.

The Hopi attorneys had, as anticipated in view of Boyden's statements in court, made frequent mention in their findings of presumed Navajo sins against the Hopis. The Navajos' lawyers' first exception was taken to this attempt to arouse ethnic bias. In the process they exhibited some ethnic bias of their own, quoting several derogatory descriptions of the Hopis. They did sum up the dynamics of Navajo-Hopi relations quite succinctly, however, even if they erred in considering the Hopis as a well unified tribe with only one opinion.

> Adept at passive resistance, the Hopis found it profitable to find fault with the Navajos, dwell upon Navajo misdeeds, and make them both a scapegoat and a bargaining point; they would do thus and such (maybe) if the Government would make the Navajos do such and thus.

The Navajos' attorneys added that following 1890 the government had been required to employ military force against the Hopis a number of times, but never against the Navajos.[4] While this was true for the 1882 Reservation, it showed a lack of historical knowledge on the part of the Navajos' attorneys, for on a tribal scale there were incidents among the Navajos which did require troops. Still, the issue of the Navajos as an evil people loomed so large in the Hopi attorneys' strategy that several more pages of the Navajo response were devoted to countering these charges.[5]

The Hopis' attorneys' exceptions to the Navajo proposed findings again required some of my time when they were received in July 1961. The Navajos' attorneys had omitted my explanation for consolidating the various forms of the same Navajo name in my analysis of Navajo use and occupation. The Hopis' attorneys took exception to those identifications, for they undermined the Hopis' contention of a constant stream of Navajos coming onto the disputed area. I wrote a rebuttal of the Hopi responses, but I never learned whether any use was made of it. In May 1962 we heard reports that the boundary dispute decision was being written and felt that we would hear good news within a few months.

Lee and I were keeping busy organizing data for the proposed findings in the Land Claim case. There was an even more voluminous record in that case than in *Healing* v. *Jones*, and each overlap with a neighboring tribe's claim required a separate set of findings, so that we found a great deal of our time taken up. Boyden had been threatening to reopen the case as it concerned the overlap in the land claims of the Hopis and Navajos, and that lent urgency to our work. During that summer we discovered that hospital records and death certificates gave the place of birth not only of the subjects, but of the subjects' parents, and Lee felt that this additional data should be introduced in the Land Claim case record if there were any opportunity to do so. Dave de Harport helped with the search for and microfilming of a large number of these records. Despite a limited budget, by the end of August we had amassed some 1,800 records that provided information on Navajos who were born before 1868. Most of the birthplaces were within areas still occupied by Navajos, but many were in areas where occupation at an early date was contested, including much of the overlap with the Hopi claim.

Finally we heard that the *Healing* v. *Jones* decision was written. The court asked that the two tribes stipulate agreement on a metes and bounds description for the 1943 District 6 boundary. This seemed a promising indication of what the decision might be, but we had to await publication by the Government Printing Office to learn if we were correct.

By the last week of September we heard that Boyden did plan to hold another hearing in the Land Claim case in October. Lee was pushing hard to have all of the clinical records and death certificates ready for submission at that time. Preparation for a hearing in the Utah school section case was also still under way.

Littell stopped in Window Rock on his way to meet with Boyden in California for the release of the *Healing* v. *Jones* decision on 28 September 1962. He was going by way of the Hopi mesas, and Lee gave him directions for sightseeing there. We assumed that Littell's and Boyden's meeting was nothing more than a formality.

The decision, when it came, was more than a disappointment. We felt real shock and depression when we learned that not only had the Hopis been awarded all of District 6, but they were also given "joint, undivided and equal rights and interests" with the Navajos to the remaining land in the 1882 Reservation. The specter of Navajos being driven from their homes by the military was in our imagination, and Ed Plummer predicted that an attempt to enforce the decision would lead to bloodshed, an exceptionally strong statement for a person as soft-spoken as he. The *Gallup Independent* published an Associated Press story on Friday, September 28, that claimed some 4,000 Navajos would have to move.[6] We could see little possibility of any solution other than dispossession of the Navajo residents.

The Navajo Tribal Council met in Window Rock on Friday night and authorized an appeal to the Supreme Court. Maurice McCabe, Navajo Tribal administrative officer, declared the decision "simply impossible of administration," noting that "a court action intended to establish peace and quiet for both tribes has in fact stimulated new areas of controversy." Boyden was obviously satisfied at first, for he announced that he did not intend to appeal.[7]

When we read the opinion of the three-judge court, it quickly became apparent that we had indeed proven Navajo use and occupation, but that the matter of the lives of the Indians in the disputed area was relegated to a minor role in reaching a decision. The court's words were not as clear as the result.

> We are of the opinion that neither the test as to the character of use and occupancy of "other" Indians, as suggested by defendant, nor the test as to whether the Secretary [of the Interior] acted to "settle" other Indians, as suggested by plaintiff, is alone sufficient in determining whether "other" Indians have been "settled" on the 1882 reservation. In our view, Indians other than Hopis acquired rights in the 1882 reservation under the executive order provision in question if: (1) such Indians used and occupied the reservation, in Indian fashion, as their continuing and permanent area of residence, and (2) the undertaking of such use and occupancy, or the continuance thereof, if undertaken without advance permission, was authorized by the Secretary, exercising the discretion vested in him by the executive order.[8]

The judges went on to recognize Navajo presence on the land.

> The evidence is overwhelming that Navajo Indians used and occupied parts of the 1882 reservation, in Indian fashion, as their continuing and permanent area of residence, from long prior to the creation of the reservation in 1882

to July 22, 1958, when any rights which any Indians had acquired in the reservation became vested. . . .

The use and occupancy of the reservation area for residential purposes by a constantly increasing number of Navajos, is therefore definitely established, and we have so found. But the critical question is whether such use and occupancy was by authority of the Secretary, granted in the exercise of the discretion lodged in him by the executive order to "settle" other Indians on the reservation.[9]

They did find that some Navajos had been officially settled on the reservation during the years 1909–1911.

Approximately three hundred Navajos residing on the 1882 reservation indicated a willingness to accept allotments subject to approval. In 1911 this second allotment project was abandoned, and none of the allotments to Navajos or others was approved. These three hundred Navajos must nevertheless be regarded as "settled" Indians, since the only Navajo permanent residents who were denied that status under the Commissioner's ruling of February 25, 1909, were those who were unwilling to accept allotments.

It is not ascertainable from this record who these three hundred Navajos were; which, if any, were still living on July 22, 1958, and residing in the reservation; or which of them, if any, had descendants living in the reservation on the latter date and, if so, who were such descendants. It is therefore not possible, on this record, to find that any Navajos residing in the reservation on July 22, 1958, derived rights of use and occupancy by reason of the fact that in the years 1909 to 1911, the Secretary had settled three hundred unidentified Navajos in the reservation.[10]

In this regard, the court took an extremely narrow view, ignoring possible individual rights that had not been effectively represented in the hearings. The evidence of Navajo continuity in occupation had been recognized, but the implications of this evidence for the allottees and their descendants was apparently not given consideration.

Regardless of this question, the court concluded that various actions by officials in Washington from 1931 to 1943 did settle the Navajos as a tribe within the 1882 reservation.[11]

While recognizing that there was some Hopi use outside of District 6, the judges did not consider it to be especially important.

For present purposes, however, we will assume that actual Navajo use and occupancy of the area was exclusive or was so nearly so as to render Hopi use and occupancy *de minimus*.[12]

Reasoning that the Hopis had been given rights to the entire executive order reservation at the time it was created, the court next specified that these rights continued to exist along with those assigned the Navajos unless they had been "lawfully terminated." After reviewing congressional actions, the court concluded that Congress had never extinguished this interest. Similarly, there was no evidence that the Executive Branch had ever done so, nor had the Hopis ever abandoned their interest.[13]

Throughout, there were references to Navajo "badness." The typical western scenario of the black hats versus the white hats presented by Boyden had been irresistible. The judges were apparently unaware of the power and danger of ethnic stereotypes, as they made repeated use of these characterizations to color their prose. Their disclaimers of bias seemed weak to us, as did their suggestions for the future.

The decision avoided making any detailed recommendations for the implementation of the joint interest.

It will now be for the two tribes and the Government officials to determine whether, with these basic issues resolved, the area lying outside district 6 can and should be fairly administered as a joint reservation. If this proves impracticable or undesirable, any future effort to partition the jointly-held area, by agreement, subsequently authorized suit, or otherwise, will be aided by the determination in this action of the present legal rights and interests of the respective tribes.

In the course of this opinion it has been necessary to say some unkind things about the activities of the Navajo Indians in the reservation area in years long past. We wish to make clear that the record contains nothing concerning the conduct of the Navajos in this area in recent years with which they can be reproached. They as well as the Hopis are now conduct-

ing themselves as good citizens of which the West and the nation can
be proud.[14]

The irony of the thousands of Navajo and Hopi dollars spent on litigation
which ended with the proposal that if the solution advanced by the court
should not prove to be "practicable," one way out of the difficulty might be
further litigation, did not escape us.

We were most distraught, however, at the suggestion that partition might
be the solution. It seemed clear that the judges, on narrow legalistic grounds,
had placed corporate tribal property interests above human values. Their
passing mention of the hardships suffered by Navajos forced to abandon
their homes in the past had not influenced their thinking as to future possibilities. Joe McPherson assured me that no Navajos would ever lose their
homes as a result of the decision. I could only hope that he was right. The
thought of the Navajos on Black Mesa, living immersed in a tradition that
belonged to the distant past, being uprooted was not a prospect that was
easy to contemplate. I recalled the stories of the displaced person camps that
had been one symptom of the turmoil in Europe which had led to World
War II during my childhood.

We were busy with other work, and that kept us from brooding on the
situation. Our old team was dispersing. Aubrey Williams was back in Tucson.
His experiences with the land claims research had convinced him that he
should do his doctoral dissertation on Navajo political process, and he was
visiting Navajo country from time to time. Marty Link had helped establish
a Navajo tribal museum, of which he was director. While we saw him regularly, he now had other interests and responsibilities. Dave de Harport's contract expired in November. He was about to accept a teaching position at
Arizona State University in Tempe. Lee and I remained as the only anthropologists involved in research for the tribe on land issues. More housing was
becoming available at Window Rock. Until 1963 my family and I had lived
in Gallup, but feeling more confidence in the future of my position, I rented
one of the houses built for tribal employees.

In March, not long after we moved to Window Rock, tribal elections
brought a dramatic change in the administration. Raymond Nakai, the new
tribal chairman, was a former announcer for a Navajo language radio program in Flagstaff. He had been seeking election for more than eight years.

His residence off the reservation had prevented his running in the two previous elections, but the tribal council relaxed the rules to allow his participation in 1963. He was a friend, although not a member, of the Native American Church, and many traditional Navajos who feared the effects of peyote, a hallucinogenic cactus taken as a sacrament in the services of that church, were strongly opposed to him. Most, but not all, of the Navajo political leaders, whether Christians or traditionalists, supported the tribal ban on the use of peyote. The religion had spread widely among the people, however, for it offered the promise of solutions to many of the problems they faced. In addition, many of the Navajos with whom we had worked in the field were members. They included singers or medicine men, who were able to combine a belief in the teachings of this new religion with their traditional Navajo beliefs. Even one of our interpreters, Bernadine, was a member. Littell himself was convinced that peyote was a dangerous drug that was a threat to the welfare of the tribe. Those of us who were anthropologists had been taught in our university classes that it was innocuous, at least as used by Indians in their religion, and we tried to do our work without becoming involved in the politics of its use. Lee and I viewed the matter as something the Navajos had to settle among themselves, for we both believed that as non-Navajos we should not meddle in tribal politics.

While political parties were not a formal part of tribal political life, there were many divisive issues, and the use of peyote was one of the most strongly felt at the time. The question of whether peyote, even used as a religious sacrament, could be allowed on the reservation helped polarize a people at a time they were much in need of unity. A split between the Nakai supporters and what came to be called the Old Guard engendered a factionalism more crippling of tribal government than was the endemic Hopi factionalism. At Hopi only one faction had legal standing in the eyes of the federal government, for the Hopi traditionalists refused to take any part in the tribal council set up by the BIA. The traditionalists' refusal to participate in a tribal organization that they did not recognize as legitimate limited their ability to affect the course of tribal business. In most matters the pro-Council faction could do as they wished, and this was especially true in their dealings with outside interests. The two Navajo factions, however, disputed within the organization, and each had a power base that gave it a legitimacy in the popular mind as well as in the federal view.

Nakai's long exclusion from tribal elections on technical grounds had made him bitter and suspicious. His inaugural address at the tribal fairgrounds in April 1963 pledged all the right things—the end of corruption, defense of tribal sovereignty, promotion of education, elimination of poverty—a generally liberal and uplifting agenda. It also, as reported by the *Albuquerque Journal*, "bristled with barbs." It caused Governor Jack M. Campbell of New Mexico to "wince on a couple of occasions," which he refused to identify for the reporter, but which he thought were self-evident.[15]

Nakai lacked a staff experienced in government. He was able to attract to his cause a number of well-educated Navajos from cities off the reservation, but few had the kind of skills needed to direct tribal affairs. Thus, he was dependent on many of the officials of the former administration to keep things running at all, even if not really smoothly.

There had been some distance between the Jones administration and the recently installed administration of John F. Kennedy in Washington. Nakai was apparently seen in the national capital as a possible, even natural, ally. Tribal politics—in theory, nonpartisan—soon became enmeshed in national political currents. A symbol of this alliance was the presence of Philleo Nash, the new Commissioner of Indian Affairs, as principal speaker at Nakai's inauguration, bringing official greetings from President Kennedy and Secretary of the Interior Stewart Udall.[16]

One influence in the uneasy relationship between the Navajos and the Kennedy administration was the land issue, as represented by both the Land Claim case and the boundary dispute with the Hopis. Robert Kennedy, the president's brother, had been appointed Attorney General of the United States. In that capacity he had published a popular article attacking Indian land claims against the federal government generally and singling out the Navajo Land Claim case for specific ridicule.[17] The Navajos' attorneys had taken strong offense at what they regarded as a violation of the ethics of the legal profession, for it was the Justice Department that defended the government's interests before the Indian Claims Commission.

The dispute with the Hopis was a much stronger factor in the alienation of the Navajos, however. The Udalls were an Arizona family with long and close connections with the Hopis.[18] Stewart Udall was also well known as a conservationist. Among western conservationists the image of the sheepherder as destroyer of rangelands was still strong, and the Navajos were regarded as the most destructive sheepmen of all. Thus, two strongly negative stereotypes of the Navajos, one as nomadic raiders encroaching on the peaceful little Hopis, and the other as the black-hatted despoilers of the environment, the sheep ranchers long depicted in western novels and moving pictures, were a part of Udall's intellectual and emotional baggage. Indeed, these images were current and strong throughout much of Arizona, as I had discovered once I began to work for the Navajos. With no sign of embarrassment, people let me know that I was working "on the wrong side." I could not help but feel a distrust of the government's influence in the boundary case.

On the other hand, Udall was known to be a member of the Church of Jesus Christ of Latter-day Saints, better known as the Mormon Church. The denomination had suffered persecution so recently in the past that it seemed logical to expect Udall to support Nakai's ideal of religious freedom for the Navajos, particularly as this applied to the Native American Church. In addition, there were many Mormon converts among the Navajos, so that it was possible that these religious ties might guide the Secretary to objectivity. This church affiliation was shared, however, with some members of the Hopi pro-Council faction and with John Boyden himself. In Navajo country, religious affiliations had long been extremely powerful influences in politics. How they would bear on white-Navajo relations in the modern world I could not predict.

There were also significant conflicts between the Navajo Tribe and the State of Arizona. In a case before the Supreme Court to decide the respective rights of Arizona and California to the water of the Colorado River, Littell had led the Arizona tribes in asserting their claim to a share of the water. In addition, there were conflicts over a dam proposed for the Colorado River, the right of the state to tax trading posts on the reservation, and the right of a trader to attach Navajo property on the reservation for the collection of debts.[19] The issue of Navajo voting rights would soon emerge as well, for the Kennedy administration was committed to the advancement of civil rights. Their sheer numbers made them a potent force in electoral politics. The Navajo nation, the largest Native American group in the country, possessed the votes that could decide close elections.

The stage was set for high drama. Nakai had promised during his campaign to fire Littell, but found himself confronted by a council dominated by the Old Guard.[20] I had been so immersed in the legal cases dealing with land that I evaluated many events on the basis of their effect on the Navajos' claims. Of all these cases, the Navajo-Hopi dispute was the one about which I had the strongest personal feelings. It had the awesome potential to dispossess thousands of Navajos, many of them people with whom I had worked and who I knew were so thoroughly Navajo that there could be no satisfying life for them outside their own small, traditional communities.

It has been alleged that in April 1963 Nakai met with Boyden, Udall, and representatives of the Peabody Coal Company to discuss a coal lease in the 1882 Executive Order Reservation.[21] We were outsiders in the view of the new administration, however, and were not privy to any dealings that were not public matters.

The final blow in the lawsuit came on 3 June 1963, when the Supreme Court refused to review the Prescott decision, thereby affirming it as the supreme law of the land. Boyden immediately announced that the surface of the jointly held land would probably be divided and the subsurface administered jointly by the two tribes. Littell promptly objected, stating that no Navajos could be moved without the consent of both tribes and threatening that should Navajos be evicted from their homes, Hopis would be expelled from Moenkopi, the Hopi village outside the 1882 Reservation on the Navajo Reservation.[22]

Word of the Supreme Court's decision had been leaked to the Nakai administration in advance of Littell being informed, allegedly by a rival law firm hoping to get the contract as tribal general counsel when Littell was fired. Littell reported to the tribal council on the decision on Friday, June 7, in what was a rather stormy session, but he retained his job.[23]

The Department of the Interior called a meeting for June 10 in Washington to assemble the attorneys, tribal chairmen, agency superintendents, and area directors for the two tribes to discuss the implementation of the decision.[24] The meeting was not held until July, however. Those attending, in addition to Littell and Boyden, included Fred M. Haverland, director of the BIA area office in Gallup; Navajo Superintendent Glenn Landbloom; Wade Head, who was director of the Phoenix area office; and Herman O'Hara, Hopi superintendent.[25] The tribal chairmen apparently were not present. Commissioner of Indian Affairs Nash later called the event a "first exploratory meeting," indicating that little if anything substantive was accomplished.[26]

Nakai had visited Washington briefly in June for meetings with Udall, Nash, Interior Department solicitor Frank Berry, and various congressmen. He had then held a press conference at which he announced plans to fire Littell for meddling in tribal politics. It was rumored that he intended to replace him with Richard Schifter of the Washington law firm of Strasser, Spiegelberg, Campelman, and McLaughlin. Schifter and an attorney from Globe, Arizona, accompanied him at the press conference.[27] This, of course, further inflamed the factionalism at Window Rock and may have partially explained the absence of the tribal chairmen at the July meeting.

The term *joint-use area* to designate the lands between District 6 and the exterior boundary of the 1882 Reservation came into our vocabulary sometime during this period. I first heard it used by an attorney for the Hopis and believe that it was coined by them. The implications of the term for displacement of Navajos were so strong that I objected to its use to the Navajos' attorneys, but they did not feel that its use was a threat to Navajo occupation in the joint-interest area, my preferred term, outside District 6. I suspect that they considered Boyden's pronouncements on partition and eviction of Navajos nothing but a bluff for purposes of bargaining. "Joint-use" all too soon became the standard term for describing the area.

The BIA scheduled an August meeting in Scottsdale, and Associate Commissioner of Indian Affairs James E. Officer prepared a book of briefing papers for the use of BIA officials who were to attend. It included an agenda, maps, a copy of the Prescott court's judgment, information on costs for surveys and school construction, assorted facts and figures on the administration of the joint-interest area, historical information on Moenkopi, and recommendations for dealing with the dispute over use of the lands.[28]

The recommendations of various BIA officials, which were also included in the book, are most revealing of the trend of thought in that agency.

E. Reeseman Fryer, Assistant Commissioner for Economic Development, wrote a memorandum dated 11 July 1963, which seemed to advocate a return to the stock reduction days when he had presided as the much-disliked "Goat Killer" over the Navajo Agency. He suggested first that the entire 1882 Reservation be placed under the administration of the Hopi Agency at

Keams Canyon, to be followed by intensive surveys of settlement, land use, and range carrying capacity of the area. New grazing permits would be required, and new grazing regulations to enforce conservation should be written. All this, he asserted, would give Hopi morale a boost, while showing the Navajos that they had to share surface use with the Hopis. He apparently realized overnight that he had forgotten something. He submitted a second memo the next day in an attempt to deal with the impact that his recommendations would have had on the Navajos. He fully understood the devastation that might result, for he wrote

> . . . for hundreds of Navajo families the finality of the Court's decision holds grim tragedy.
>
> There are many things that can be done and must be done, to lessen the social and economic impact of the Court's findings. The most important of these is the quickening of the construction of the Navajo [Irrigation] Project; its preparation for the resettlement of Navajo people who will be displaced by Hopi insistence on the use of one-half the surface.
>
> . . . Where Navajos will go if the Hopis move early to take that which the Court has held is theirs is immediately unanswerable. There is no place, really, in terms of grass, grass beyond the subsistence needs of the Navajo people already there, for them to go.[29]

Navajo Area Director Haverland suggested that a special jurisdiction independent of either the Navajo or Hopi agencies be set up to administer the jointly-owned area and that surveys of land-use be done. He thought that the BIA should remain neutral in disputes between the two tribes and believed that a congressionally authorized court action would be required to settle the issue of partition. He advocated that the Moenkopi problem be kept entirely separate from the 1882 Reservation dispute.[30]

On the other hand, Wade Head, the area director in Phoenix who had the Hopi Agency under his supervision, wanted the land partitioned promptly, and argued that it could be "accomplished in an orderly fashion if a proper educational program is extended to both parties involved." He hoped that the two tribes could agree on partition and that Moenkopi could be used in negotiating a settlement.[31]

An unsigned set of recommendations summed up the proposals of the various advisors. It was taken for granted that partition would be the ultimate solution but that a separate jurisdiction would be required to administer the area until this was accomplished in order to meet immediate needs.[32]

The meeting, variously referred to as the Scottsdale meeting or the Phoenix meeting, convened at the Valley Ho Hotel in Scottsdale, Arizona, on 6 August 1963. Commissioner Philleo Nash presided over the thirty participants. Nine were BIA officials—the four who had attended the Washington meeting on June 10, as well as three solicitors, Deputy Commissioner John Crow, and Associate Commissioner James Officer. The Navajos were represented by Chairman Nakai and five members of the tribal council, as well as Maurice McCabe, Ned Hatathli, Ed Plummer, Littell, and, perhaps unofficially, Mrs. Nakai. The Hopi delegation, led by Chairman Abbott Sekaquaptewa, was composed of five council delegates, governors of two of the villages, Peter Nuvumsa, Logan Koopee who was head of the Hopi Regional Committee, and Boyden.

The Commissioner, in his introductory talk, pointed out that the Department of the Interior lacked the authority to partition the land. He said that if the tribes could not settle the issue by land exchange, sale or purchase, a court would have to be set up by Congress to effect partition. He indicated that the BIA should begin to draft legislation for that purpose.[33]

Littell pointed out that the Department of the Interior had written the Supreme Court at the time of the Navajos' appeal saying that there was no basis for asking that the case be heard in terms of the department's responsibilities to the two tribes. Littell reiterated the former agreement that the tribes could cooperate for the management of the subsurface rights. With regard to the surface rights, he suggested that the Navajo Tribe either buy or lease these from the Hopi.[34]

Boyden's first request was that the Navajo Tribe remove some six "family groups" of Navajos living within District 6. He agreed with Littell that the mineral interests could be handled jointly. He then went on to say that the Hopis did not want to sell their interest in the surface; they wanted the land. He saw no solution but "a voluntary partition."

Boyden then launched into some rather dramatic rhetoric, once again dwelling on the stereotypes of the Hopis as "a passive people" and the Navajos as aggressive, and adding, rather piously, that Hopis did not want to "try to inconvenience people . . . not trying to impose on them. . . . You know, we'd like to be awful good neighbors to these Navajo people . . ." He did, at least, accede to the fencing of District 6, an agreement he was later to withdraw when some of the Hopis raised objections to it.

After further discussion, Boyden concluded that the only solution was to get legislation passed to authorize partition immediately. He justified this by saying that the Hopis knew it was impossible "to get along side by side," but that "we want to be friendly with the Navajo people."[35]

Nash polled the two chairmen as to whether either favored sale or purchase, leasing, land exchange, or partition. The only strongly worded reply was Sekaquaptewa's insistence on partition. Nash quickly picked this up as a mandate for the Secretary of the Interior to propose legislation for that purpose.[36] It soon became obvious, however, that the Navajos would oppose any legislation authorizing partition. Boyden then threatened to use Hopi control of the subsurface to garner support for partition.

> . . . if the Navajo says we are not going to do anything about the surface, we may have to take the position we will do nothing about the minerals, because the pressure is on the minerals, and the moment we give that up we lose half our political support. I am just being practical.[37]

Later in the day he reiterated this threat.

> Now, if we just go ahead and do this, then the matter of partition is of no interest to the oil companies, but if, partition was holding up the oil development the oil companies would be awfully interested in getting the legislation in.[38]

Boyden then made a series of nine demands:

1. Immediate stock reduction to protect the range, first to its original carrying capacity, then, once determined, to its current carrying capacity.
2. Payment to the Hopi Tribe by the Navajo Tribe of grazing fees dating back to 28 September 1962 and continuing until the land is partitioned.
3. Set deadlines for "relinquishment of the Hopi interest by the Navajo Tribe."
4. Partition.

5. Full accounting of all income that the Navajo Tribe has received from the 1882 Reservation and payment of half to the Hopi Tribe.
6. Removal of the area outside of District 6 from Navajo jurisdiction immediately.
7. Recognition of Hopi rights at and around Moenkopi.
8. Redefinition of the reservation boundaries and mineral rights of each Tribe by Congress.
9. Mineral development of the 1882 Reservation to be contingent on the other eight points.

Boyden then went on to claim that he did not intend "any inconvenience or great hardship upon those who must find other places," but he thought that his proposals took "all of those things" into consideration.[39]

Littell quickly attacked the proposal for stock reduction, recognizing it as a subterfuge to drive the Navajos from the land. He met Boyden's challenge on mineral development, saying that the Navajos could wait too and that the minerals were merely "money in the bank." He suggested that the government compensate the Hopis for their half-interest with public lands elsewhere in Arizona.[40]

Nakai then made an unfortunate slip. He had been advocating negotiations between committees appointed by each tribe. He went on to indicate that he believed that if the negotiations should fail, partitioning would be "the only way for us to turn."[41] Clifford Beck, however, made quite clear the unbending opposition to partition by his constituents in the Pinon area.[42]

It was agreed that negotiating committees should be appointed and that they would meet in Flagstaff on September 16. The Navajo committee would include Nakai, McCabe, Hatathli, and one other, and would have the aid of Plummer as a consultant. In the meantime, Commissioner Nash was to put into effect several administrative actions for the joint-interest area.[43] Few of those measures actually materialized, however.

At a press conference following the meeting, both Nash and Nakai discussed the possibility of partition. Partitioning would be the government's option if "joint administration and use" did not work out, according to Nash, but he equivocated when it came to removal of the Navajos, saying that "no one is prepared to say that any Navajos will have to go nor how they would be moved." Nakai was not so reticent and assured the press that the displaced Navajos "could be absorbed in industrial development and in the . . . Navajo Irrigation Project."[44] The story caused Littell to write the commissioner to protest the publicity given the partition proposal.[45]

Nash himself came to the meeting of the negotiating committees in Flagstaff that September, as did both agency superintendents. The meeting lasted two days but broke up with the negotiators deadlocked over the issue of surface rights. Rumors were that the commissioner was not particularly sympathetic to the Navajos' dilemma. Another meeting was set for October 12, suggesting that compromise was still possible.[46] The land issue was soon forgotten, however, as the feud between Nakai and Littell flared into open warfare.

In October Nakai wrote Secretary Udall wanting to know whether *Healing v. Jones* was a claims case according to Littell's contract and, if it were, could attorneys being paid for general counsel work properly take part in the case. He wanted the information for use at the tribal council meeting in November. A reply was delayed awaiting research of the answers by the departmental solicitor.[47]

On Friday, November 1, Secretary Udall suspended Littell. The departmental solicitor had apparently concluded that *Healing* v. *Jones* was not a claims case and that an amendment to Littell's contract declaring it one was invalid. The precise charge against Littell was not made public.[48] Littell immediately challenged Udall's authority to suspend him and asserted that Udall wanted to fire him so that a political friend could take the position.[49]

On Saturday the famous, or infamous, raid on Navajo tribal records by the Department of the Interior took place. The newspapers reported that the raids at Maurice McCabe's office and in the general tribal files, which were under the supervision of Angie Whipple, resulted in the seizure of tribal records, which had then been taken to Nakai's garage.[50]

Lee was in Washington at the time, writing proposed findings for the Havasupai overlap in the Land Claims case. I was at home and received a call from the Chairman's office to come open our office. I did so, not knowing what was going on at the time. None of our files were locked, and they contained only papers relating to our research in the various cases. I was extremely suspicious of the motives of the searchers, whom I did not know, but reasoned that the Chairman had the authority to authorize a search. The searchers spent some time going through the drawers reading the labels on the folders, but found nothing of interest to them and left without taking anything. I wrote Lee to have him ask Littell just who had the authority to give outsiders access to our files and whether documents containing our recommendations to the attorneys should be considered confidential, but Littell was so involved in the battle with Udall that Lee was never able to get an answer. My first reaction was to fear that the BIA was trying to get information that would give the Hopis an edge in the negotiations.

Several BIA employees assisted Stanley Zimmerman, the Interior Department investigator.[51] Zimmerman and three aides spent several days examining the files in Nakai's garage, periodically getting additional documents from the files of the reporters who kept the minutes of the tribal council. It seemed logical to conclude that the raid was a search for materials that could strengthen the case that Nakai and Udall were building against Littell.

By Friday, Nakai felt confident in informing the press that "irregularities" had been found in the seized files, but he did not explain just what they were.[52] Four days later the Interior Department's solicitor made a similar statement to the press, describing the findings as "irregularities in the handling of tribal funds," but there was the suggestion that little more than sloppy bookkeeping was involved.[53] At the end of the week Littell filed a suit in court for an injunction prohibiting Udall from firing him.[54] Nakai then issued a "white paper," reporting on the efforts to fire Littell and revealing that Littell was "charged with failing to make full disclosure to the tribe with respect to such matters as fees and using junior attorneys on the tribal pay roll for claims work."[55]

The case was sufficiently complicated that Littell secured the temporary injunction against Udall's action that same month.[56] By December Nakai had hired a personal attorney, Harold Mott of Washington, D.C., to assist him in his struggle with Littell.[57] He had also tried to have four Old Guard councilmen recalled, but they were handily re-elected by their communities.

I did not doubt Littell's charge that Udall was out to get him, but feared that it was not so much a matter of political patronage as an effort to undermine the Navajos' resistance to partition of the joint-interest area. There were rumors that Nakai's "white paper" had been written by somebody in the BIA. I reread it with this in mind and concluded that the rumors were probably true. This strengthened my concern that there was an organized effort by the Interior Department to weaken Navajo opposition to partition. I was uneasy about the charges that had been revealed, in particular those concerning the use of general counsel staff for claims work, for I had heard some of the younger attorneys on Littell's staff complaining about that very thing. While I felt myself lacking the legal knowledge necessary to judge the technicalities of the case, I knew there was reason to suspect that Littell might have left himself open to legitimate charges in a situation where the Navajos very much needed his skills for themselves. I kept my fears and doubts to myself, for I was not at all sure of my information and I did not want to do anything that might hurt the Navajos in the disputed area. In addition, I had strong feelings that outsiders, even when tribal employees, should not dabble in tribal politics. Littell had become, in effect, the attorney for one tribal faction in its dispute with another faction. As an anthropologist, I thought Littell's political meddling a worse sin than any bookkeeping problems with what might or might not be claims cases. It also seemed to me that Udall was as guilty as Littell in regard to meddling in tribal politics.

Maxwell Yazzie and Clyde Peshlakai happened to be in Window Rock one day during all this confusion, and they stopped by our office to talk a bit. Max said that he was glad that he was no longer on the council and in the midst of all the fighting. The house in Window Rock that had been occupied by the former vice-chairman, Scott Preston, remained vacant. Preston was a well-regarded medicine man, or singer as the profession is called in Navajo, and Nakai's followers, who claimed to be "businessmen, not medicinemen," refused to live in the house for fear it had been witched. The insecurities of Navajos who had grown up between two worlds were to remain a factor in the contest as long as Nakai was in office.

In the course of so much uncertainty, a great many of the tribal employees at Window Rock were looking for more secure positions. I watched for a place to jump should it become necessary, but I did not really want to leave. I felt some loyalty to the tribe as an institution, but also knew that one of the favorite political ploys in Navajo elections was to promise to get rid of all the white employees. Bernadine had once confided to me that to gain rapport for the two of us in the field he would sometimes liken my position to that of captives kept as slaves in the good old days. It was best to look at the situation without illusions. Lee and I had hoped to find support to write up the claims research for publication, and we followed several leads to possible grants or other assistance, but nothing ever came of these. The threat to jobs was not limited to non-Navajos, however, and several of our Navajo colleagues felt their employment prospects to be just as insecure.

The efforts of the Hopi Tribal Council and John Boyden to achieve partition continued unabated during the trouble at Window Rock. Whether or not Boyden had a hand in stirring up the political cauldron, he was not slow to take advantage of the fact that the Navajos and the tribal legal department were distracted by other issues. On 19 December 1963, Representative Wayne Aspinall of Colorado, at Boyden's request, introduced a bill, H.R. 9529, to authorize suits by either the Navajo or Hopi tribes to partition the joint-interest area. Another suit authorized by the bill would have determined the rights of each tribe in the land included in the Arizona Boundary Bill of 1934, which established exterior boundaries for the Navajo Reservation in that state. Still other suits were authorized to settle damages, collect rents, and share income from the joint-interest area.[58]

The Navajos' attorneys thought that a bill introduced by request this way had little chance of being enacted into law. It turned out that they were correct in this instance, but I had doubts as to their assessment at the time and made a personal attempt to oppose the bill. I asked my mother in New York to contact her congressman, which she did, sending him a copy of a critique that I wrote of the bill. I also drafted a petition for the local Plateau Science Society, asking that Congress hear both sides before taking any action, but this was never approved by the membership, some of whom worked at the Hopi Agency at Keams Canyon while there were others who subscribed to the tribal stereotypes promoted by Boyden. My concern for the people whom I knew in the disputed area led me to a partisan stand, but one that I felt was more than justified by the personal knowledge I had gained of the area and its people. It was not easy to convince others, however. Dave de Harport had returned to his home in Denver, his job in Arizona not having worked out. He wrote me in February asking for a copy of my critique of H.R. 9529, suggesting additional ways to oppose the bill, and dwelling at some length on the difficulty of overcoming anti-Navajo bias even among anthropologists. He was especially upset by some unfeeling remarks by Ruth Underhill, an ethnologist who had written extensively about the Navajos.[59]

In early February 1964, Littell was barred from reporting to the Navajo Tribal Council by Nakai, as he had been the previous December. The issue of interest to the Old Guard in February was the partition bill. Councilman Frankie Howard from Tolani Lake, who had many constituents inside the 1882 Reservation, was especially bitter.[60] Joe McPherson, whose more amiable disposition had made him such an asset to the Navajo legal department, had retired in 1963. He had emphysema and the stress of the political situation made demands that his health could not sustain. Littell's own confrontational style would help to determine the nature of the dispute as much as would Nakai's personality.

Littell quickly obtained an injunction from Judge James A. Walsh in Phoenix against Nakai to force the issue of his appearance before the council. Following this, Littell issued a strong statement to the press, asserting that the real issue was not his position but the "resources of the Navajo Tribe in oil, gas, coal, timber and other assets totalling an undetermined several hundred million dollars." He stated that the legal advisor of the tribe would control whether the benefits of these resources went to the Navajos or to outside interests.[61] Nakai then tried to delay the issue in the council until a further hearing on the restraining order. This brought about further dissension in the council chambers.[62]

On Monday, February 17, Littell was finally permitted to address the council and charged that the BIA had helped Boyden draft the partition bill. He also defended his version of the matter regarding the charges against him by Udall.[63] His success was timely, for a few days later Judge Walsh refused to make permanent his restraining order.[64]

Fortunately for the Navajos, the House Indian Affairs Subcommittee had made no progress on any bills as late as February 26 and there was little prospect that any legislation dealing with that subject would get through Congress in 1964. The Aspinall partition bill had not even gotten through committee.[65]

The threat of mineral leasing by the Hopi Tribal Council brought about an open confrontation of traditionalists and the pro-Council faction at Hopi. The traditionalists invited the Los Angeles Chapter of the Congress of Racial Equality (CORE) to assist them in the dispute. They also wrote Aspinall, asking that the partition bill be withdrawn.[66] The meeting of the CORE delegation with the Hopis led to violence; three Hopis, one a member of the tribal council, were injured in the fracas, and two opponents of the council were jailed and charged with disturbing the peace.[67] The political cartoonist for the *Navajo Times*, Claire (Tom-Tom) Thompson, who also served as an interpreter for the tribal council, drew a cartoon of a Hopi traditionalist and a Navajo shaking hands across the District 6 boundary while two dogs, representing the tribal lawyers, bared their teeth.[68]

The Hopi tribal police had been making a major effort to arrest any Navajos whose livestock strayed into District 6, impounding the sheep and collecting high bail and impoundment fees. The Navajo legal aid office was enlisted to help one young Navajo who was allegedly beaten by the police, and whose sheep, in the midst of lambing, were held for over a week without feed.

Navajo tribal politics continued to be even more unsettled than those at Hopi. A recall petition was being circulated against Nakai. Both of the court reporters who transcribed the minutes of the tribal council quit. The Navajo police laid siege to the house of one, Steve Lapropoulos, rumors being that he had tribal office equipment or documents there. Nobody seemed to know where Steve was, but our Navajo cleaning lady, whose daughter worked for Steve, said he was merely in Phoenix visiting his mother.

In the midst of all this turmoil, there was a hearing in Washington on the suit that Littell had brought against Secretary Udall. Both Annie Wauneka and Maurice McCabe testified on Littell's behalf. Judge John J. Sirica presided over the case. He ruled that Littell failed to prove that there was a conspiracy against him, but at the same time stated that there was an effort under way to fire him. He did chastise the BIA for supporting Nakai's prohibition of Littell's appearance before the tribal council.[69]

While the Hopi traditionalists arrested as a result of the fight that broke out at the meeting with the CORE representatives were still awaiting trial, two more Hopis were arrested for shooting at a crew engaged in oil exploration south of Hotevila and inside District 6.[70] While CORE had taken no further interest in Hopi affairs, the Arizona chapter of the American Civil Liberties Union (ACLU) became involved, again at the request of the traditionalists. The ACLU found no restraint on freedom of religion or speech on the Hopi Reservation, but did promise to monitor the trials of the two Hopis who had been arrested at the meeting.[71]

On May 7 the Advisory Committee of the Navajo Tribal Council approved a two-year lease for coal exploration. It also voted approval of Nakai's cooperation with Boyden in negotiations for surface rights in the joint-interest area.[72]

There were some parallels in the political unrest on both reservations. A Hopi, Caleb H. Johnson, wrote a letter to the *Navajo Times* in which he blamed most of the trouble in both places on the tribes' respective attorneys.[73] The Littell-Udall battle continued to be fought in the courts in Washington. In August the District of Columbia Court of Appeals upheld the injunction restraining Udall from firing Littell, but the apparent victory concerned only the proper methods by which he might be dismissed, did not address the substantive issues of the case, and included a dissenting opinion by one member of the court.[74]

In September Walter Wolf resigned from his position as assistant general counsel for the Navajo Tribe. He gave as his reason for leaving the fact that he had been forced to do extra work for the past year and a half due to the fact that attorneys who had previously left were not replaced, and he received no additional compensation because Udall had not approved the amendment to Littell's contract that would have provided a raise in pay. He left to practice law with David F. Cargo in Albuquerque.[75]

In October a number of Navajo families who had farms on a thirteen-acre tract inside District 6 were evicted by the Hopi Tribe.[76] While Frank Luther, a Navajo councilman, protested the eviction in the tribal newspaper, no official resistance took place, and neither the tribes nor the federal government did anything to help the families re-establish themselves elsewhere.

In the same month, the Hopi Tribe billed the Navajo Tribe for $356,375 in grazing fees plus interest for Navajo use of the joint-interest area between 1962 and 27 September 1964.[77] The Hopi Tribal Council was selectively accepting and rejecting bids for oil and gas leases in a strategy of withholding some tracts in hopes that oil strikes on those lands already leased would lead to higher bids on the others. The U.S. Geological Survey was advising the Hopis on the leases. Hopi traditionalists threatened court action to block all leasing, and when the council continued leasing, the traditionalists retained an attorney.[78] Within two months the Hopi Tribe had received $3,000,000 from oil leases and additional money from leasing coal for strip-mining. The Hopi council voted to pay Boyden an even $1,000,000 for his services.[79]

An adverse audit of the Navajo Tribe's finances added fuel to the dispute between Nakai and the Old Guard. Annie Wauneka claimed that the problems were directly due to Nakai's poor management, while Nakai asserted that the tribe had had the same sorts of difficulties all along.[80] Nakai's followers then staged a protest march of some 200 members of the Navajo Rights Association.[81] The audit convinced an overwhelming majority of the council that changes were needed, however, and they voted to take authority over the financial operations of the tribe away from the Chairman's office. A new position of Director of Administration was created, and Maurice McCabe was selected to fill the post.[82] Secretary Udall was reported to be considering having the BIA take over the management of tribal finances.[83] Charles Goodluck, acting tribal treasurer, resigned in protest as a result of the McCabe appointment.[84] Had his wife not been hired by the tribal newspaper where she became editor, the family would have lost their tribal housing, which was next door to our house.

Annie Wauneka began the new year in 1965 by sending a letter to President Lyndon B. Johnson, President Kennedy's successor, to complain of the actions of Secretary Udall and the BIA. One of the issues she raised was Nakai's reshuffling of lines of authority of the tribal organization, which led, she asserted, to the loss of checks and balances necessary for proper accounting for tribal expenditures. She also raised the question of oil and gas leases, claiming that while Littell had been giving the tribe unhindered legal advice the Navajos had received the highest payments of any tribe, but that now, due to the government's interference, leases were pushed through the council too rapidly.[85]

After the new Congress convened in January, there was again a belief that legislation would be required to settle the land dispute. While Aspinall stated that the matter should be resolved, he declined to sponsor another bill. John Crow, deputy commissioner of Indian affairs, was reported as saying that he assumed there would be a new partition bill and that the department would be required to comment on it.[86]

The hearing on the injunction forbidding Udall's interference with Littell's performance of his duties as Navajo General Counsel began before Judge Sirica on February 1. The court bowed to the Court of Appeals' decree that the merits of the case should be heard as well as the issue of whether the Secretary had acted legally. There was widely divergent testimony on behalf of the litigants.[87]

The *Healing* v. *Jones* case was a key issue, but only in regard to its status as a claims case and the potential fee that Littell might receive. Littell testified that he might be paid $1 million[88] while Frank Barry, the Interior Department solicitor, claimed Littell might demand as much as $40 million.[89] Of consequence for the day-to-day work in which Lee and I were engaged, Littell noted that three of his staff attorneys had left the tribe because of Secretary Udall's delay in acting on approval of raises.[90]

Leasing for oil drilling had been spirited. The *Navajo Times* reprinted a story from *The Oil and Gas Journal* that detailed high-priced leases accepted by both the Hopis for lands inside District 6 and the Navajos for tracts just outside the 1882 Executive Order Reservation.[91] The two tribes were still working out a procedure for leasing in the joint-interest area. The court challenge filed by the Hopi traditionalists concerning the legality of Hopi Tribal Council leasing had been dismissed, clearing the last major legal obstacle to continued leasing.

The spring session of the Navajo Tribal Council began routinely. Then a fist fight between Maurice McCabe and Allen Hill, a follower of Nakai, provided more interesting news for the papers.[92]

Toward the end of May it was reported that the three oil companies—Skelly, Ameranda, and Texaco—that had drilled wells in District 6 had capped them and their public comments were limited to saying only that the wells would provide valuable new data.[93]

On 26 May 1965 Judge Sirica's decision was released. It included a strong rebuke of Secretary Udall's interference in tribal affairs and made permanent the injunction against him.[94] While this did not settle the feud, it did clear the way for greater attention to current legal problems, including the need to defend Navajo interests in the dispute with the Hopi Tribe. All that had saved the Navajos living in the 1882 Executive Order Reservation from a concerted Hopi drive for partition had been the intensity of factionalism among the Hopis, and perhaps the fact that the Hopi Council and its attorneys had been busy with mineral leasing.

Executive Mansion.
December 16, 1882.

It is hereby ordered that the tract of country, in the territory of Arizona, lying and being within the following described boundaries, Viz: beginning on the one hundred and tenth degree of longitude west from Greenwich, at a point 36° 30' north, thence due west to the one hundred and eleventh degree of longitude west, thence due south to a point of longitude 35° 30' north; thence due east to the one hundred and tenth degree of longitude west, thence due north to place of beginning, be and

the same is hereby withdrawn from settlement and sale, and set apart for the use and occupancy of the Moqui, and such other Indians as the Secretary of the Interior may see fit to settle thereon.

Chester A. Arthur

The Executive Order of December 16, 1882. The order created the reservation occupied by both Hopis and Navajos. The *Healing* v. *Jones* decision reproduced the handwritten text signed by President Chester A. Arthur.

Above: J. Lee Correll Recording a Cribbed-Log Hogan in the Moqui Buttes Subarea in 1960. The hogan serves as the burial place of the owner and probably dates from the late nineteenth century. (Courtesy, Navajo Nation Library Systems, Navajo Nation, Window Rock.)

Above left: Hastiin Adika'i Keshgolii Biye' beside a Forked-Pole Hogan at Site W-LLC-M-E. Tree-ring dates of 1805 and 1875 were obtained from this hogan. The condition of the structure suggests a late-nineteenth-century date. (Courtesy, Navajo Nation Library Systems, Navajo Nation, Window Rock.)

Below left: Clyde Peshlakai *(left)* and Maxwell Yazzie *(right)* Examining an Old Sweathouse on the Middle Oraibi. A hogan at this site, W-LLC-MO-L, produced a tree-ring date of 1835. (Courtesy, Navajo Nation Library Systems, Navajo Nation, Window Rock.)

Above left: Norman M. Littell, Navajo Tribal Counsel, at Window Rock, Arizona, 1947. (Courtesy, Navajo Nation Museum, Window Rock.)

Below left: Norman M. Littell Visiting with Navajos outside the Tribal Council Chambers, Window Rock, Arizona, 1947
(Photograph by Milton Snow, Courtesy, Navajo Nation Museum, Window Rock.)

Below: John S. Boyden during a Visit to Window Rock, Arizona, in 1947. (Photograph by Milton Snow, Courtesy, Navajo Nation Museum, Window Rock.)

Above: Paul Jones during His Inauguration as Navajo Tribal Chairman. (Photograph by Gene Price, Courtesy, Museum of New Mexico, Neg. No. 36420.)

Above left: John S. Boyden *(right)* Talking with Chic Sandoval *(left)*, Window Rock, Arizona, 1947. (Photograph by Milton Snow, Courtesy, Navajo Nation Museum, Window Rock.)

Below left: Navajo Tribal Council Advisory Committee, 1952. *Left to right back row*: Alan G. Harper (Bureau of Indian Affairs general superintendent), Leo Parker, Billy Bicenti, Yellowman, George Hubbard, Frank Bradley, Grey Valentine, Howard Gorman, Adolph Maloney, Clifford Beck (behind Littell), and Norman M. Littell; *left to right front row*: Maurice McCabe, Sam Ahkeah (chairman), John Claw (vice-chairman), and Paul Jones (interpreter). (Photograph by Milton Snow, Courtesy, Navajo Nation Museum, Window Rock.)

Above: Paul Jones, Navajo Tribal Chairman, 1955. (Photograph by Milton Snow, Courtesy, Navajo Nation Museum, Window Rock.)

Above right: Maxwell Yazzie as a Candidate for the Navajo Tribal Council in 1955. (Photograph by Milton Snow, Courtesy, Navajo Nation Museum, Window Rock.)

Below right: Oscar Yonnie as a Candidate for the Navajo Tribal Council in 1955. (Photograph by Milton Snow, Courtesy, Navajo Nation Museum, Window Rock.)

Above: J. Maurice McCabe, 1955. (Photograph by Milton Snow, Courtesy, Navajo Nation Museum, Window Rock.)

Above left: Scott Preston, Navajo vice-chairman, Identifying Plants with David M. Brugge in the Federal Courthouse in Prescott, Arizona, October 1960. (Courtesy, David M. Brugge.)

Below left: Ned Hatathli Addressing the Navajo Tribal Council at an Unknown Date. (Concho Collection, Courtesy, Navajo Nation Museum, Window Rock.)

Above: Inauguration of Raymond Nakai, 1963. (Concho Collection, Courtesy, Navajo Nation Museum, Window Rock.)

Above right: *Navajo Times* Political Cartoon by Claire Thompson, Published March 19, 1964. (Courtesy, *The Navajo Times*, Navajo Nation, Window Rock.)

Below right: *Navajo Times* Political Cartoon Published February 10, 1972. (Courtesy *The Navajo Times*, Window Rock.)

Above: *Navajo Times* Political Cartoon Published March 23, 1972. (Courtesy, *The Navajo Times*, Navajo Nation, Window Rock.)

Navajo Times Political Cartoon Published April 13, 1972. (Courtesy, *The Navajo Times*, Navajo Nation, Window Rock.)

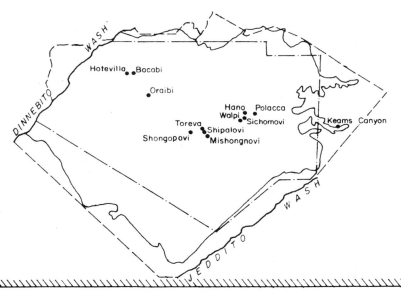

L E G E N D

⟋⟋⟋⟋ 1882 Executive Order Area: A rectangle of land approximately 70 miles north
to south and 57 miles east to west. The north boundary line is located
approximately 34 miles south of the Arizona-Utah state line and the
eastern line is 54 miles west of the Arizona-New Mexico state line.   The
northeast corner of the Executive Order Area is approximately 63 miles WSW
from the Four-Corner Monument marking the corner common to Arizona,
New Mexico, Colorado, and Utah.

— · — Boundary conceded by the Navajo to be Hopi.

———— Boundary of Land Management District 6 as originally created in 1936.

— — — Boundary of Land Management District 6 as approved April 24, 1943.

36° 30'

111° 00.'

110° 00.'

WASH

DINNEBITO

Hotevilla● ●Bacabi

●Oraibi

Hano Polacca
Walpi ●●
Toreva ●●Sichomovi
●Shipalovi
Shongopovi ●●Mishongnovi

┐Keams Canyon

JEDDITO   WASH

35° 30'

111° 00.'

110° 00.'

Note: This map represents a simplified version of one in larger scale filed in the
records of the case pursuant to stipulation of counsel for the parties dated
August 15, 1962.

Map Used in the *Healing* v. *Jones* Decision

PROGRESS (OF SORTS)

L EE AND I had not been entirely idle during the long period of stagnation brought about by the fight between Littell and Udall. We had reorganized our office as the Research Section under Ed Plummer's supervision. This would permit us, when not busy with legal issues, to work on more general research, both in order to make the results of our investigations on the claims case more widely available to the anthropological profession and the Navajo public and to try to overcome the tribe's low repute among Southwesternists. Boyden's repeated stereotyping of the Navajos as inferior and immoral people had made us all too aware of the consequences of such bias.

Our major achievement, undertaken with Marty Link and the Navajo Tribal Museum, was hosting the 27th Pecos Conference, the annual get-together of Southwestern archeologists, in 1964. We also began to publish some of our results as articles in professional journals and as popular accounts in the *Navajo Times*, the tribal newspaper.[1]

In addition, we made an effort to welcome and assist researchers in various fields who were working among the Navajos or on Navajo subjects in other locations. While we had engaged in some of this sort of cooperation earlier, it was more restricted in scope under the attorneys' supervision and largely in response to requests. It was something that both Lee and I enjoyed doing, but we found a new reason for the new emphasis. The bias that many historians and social scientists held against the Navajos was reciprocated by the Navajos themselves. This backlash led to an anti-intellectualism that was not infrequently encouraged by certain government employees, traders, and missionaries. Some Navajo politicians felt that charging a hefty fee to do research among the Navajos might be a good way to raise money for the tribe and to control unfavorable publications, while others merely resented the fact that some visitors imposed on Navajo hospitality to invade the privacy of their hosts in insensitive ways. Unfortunately, all whites wishing to learn something about Navajo ways were generally lumped together as "anthropologists," regardless of their actual professions, so that callous treatment by journalists, professional writers, and even the occasional tourist with literary ambitions was usually blamed on our colleagues.

A more serious matter was the offense that Navajos took to the large number of scholars who testified against the tribe in claims cases or who wrote accounts that either were deprecating in their attitudes toward Navajos or that set forth data or conclusions that Navajos found offensive in one way or another. Some of these writings were by partisans of other tribes or ethnic groups such as the New Mexico Hispanics, or by those who had suffered some unpleasant experience among the Navajos, ranging from a simple unfriendly encounter of some sort to genuine culture shock. Others had legitimately arrived at conclusions that were contrary to Navajo religious beliefs or that were embarrassing to them as a people. Scientific views as to Navajo origins and the relationship of the prehistoric Anasazi cultures to modern Navajos and Pueblos were prime examples of conflict with Navajo religion, while the problems arising from the use of alcohol was a prominent example of the latter.

I felt strongly that freedom of inquiry was essential if we were to overcome some of the unjustified bias that was so often expressed in writings about the tribe and its peoples, and Lee and Marty were in general agreement with me, but it was not easy to promote this view among some of the Navajos who had been offended by the writings of outsiders.

We were also busy with work on the proposed findings of fact for the Land Claim case and trying to raise grant money to assist us in doing a full scale professional report on the claims research for publication. Our increasing professional contacts kept us informed on developments in anthropology, not only in terms of current research, changing methods, and similar matters of interest within the discipline, but also in terms of what might be happening with relation to the numerous claims cases.

By March 1965 I had put together various hints that staff at the Museum of Northern Arizona, the research base for Dr. Harold S. Colton and others who had provided much of the data relied upon by Boyden in the boundary dispute and the land claims cases, were not only interested in the history of

Moenkopi and using materials from Mormon church archives in their work, but that they seemed to be avoiding any formal ties to Navajo tribal activities. I felt it likely that the museum was conducting new research for Boyden's use in the settlement of Hopi rights to land around the Moenkopi area to the west of the 1882 Reservation. I suggested to Lee that we recommend to Littell that Navajo research on that issue also begin.

New attorneys came, and sometimes went. Woodrow Sneed, a young Cherokee law school graduate who had a Navajo wife, was hired. The family moved into the other half of the duplex where we lived, and their two children, who were in the same age ranges as our own, were soon playing with ours. They did not stay long, however. The political scene at Window Rock was difficult to avoid as an employee of Littell. When Sneed was offered a job with the VISTA program in Utah, he did not hesitate to accept. Two who did last longer were William G. Lavell, who was hired to replace both McPherson and Wolf, and Theodore R. Mitchell, who took a position in the tribe's legal aid office.

In June Secretary Udall invited several Navajos to meet with him in Washington to discuss a number of economic development prospects. Among those listed were Peabody Coal Company's operations and water needs. Nakai and a number of his supporters made the trip, but the Old Guard and their allies refused to meet off the reservation. Nine members of the tribal council's Advisory Committee sent a letter telling Udall to come see them and reciting their grievances at length. A new issue surfaced in this narrative, a complaint that BIA officials had pressured the Navajos to approve a $6,000 contract with Bechtel Corporation for work that Motorola had offered to do without charge, a survey for a microwave system of communications on the reservation. After Bechtel received the contract, their engineers merely wrote a report based on data obtained from Navajo tribal files, or so it was alleged.[2]

At the 1965 summer session of the tribal council, both Lavell and Mitchell were given contracts as full-time attorneys; they had been working in law clerk status up to that time. In addition, John H. Schuelke, a Gallup lawyer, was hired to work half time. There was considerable opposition, discussion, and redrafting of the resolutions before the two factions reached a sufficient degree of accord for a vote to be taken.[3]

Work was picking up in the aftermath of *Healing* v. *Jones.* Lee and I extracted information from the *Healing* v. *Jones* record and other sources that we had in the office on the names of people who had been evicted from District 6. Ed Plummer sent Bernadine, Ned Yazzie, and Ed Raymond out with these lists in order to try to obtain information on the values of improvements left behind by the evictees.

We also began preliminary research on the Moenkopi situation in anticipation of the resumption of negotiations between the two tribes. I started a search of the literature and the documentation in the archival collections we had received from Dr. Hammond as well as in the old agency letterbooks that the BIA had in Window Rock. These letterbooks, dating from before the days of carbon paper, had been kept in two sets by each agency, one for correspondence sent to Washington and one for all other correspondence, most of which was addressed to local recipients. The Moenkopi area had been under the jurisdiction of the Fort Defiance Agency in the early years. The Fort Defiance books held scattered information on the area from about 1880 until 1902. The Tuba City Agency was established in 1902, and the letterbooks of that agency covered the period from 1902 to 1917. A search was also made of the Keams Canyon letterbooks, also in the collection at Window Rock, which spanned only the period from 1910 to 1916 and which contained an occasional reference to the Hopis at Moenkopi.

Lee had begun a search for other records that might shed light on the subject. We thought it likely that the BIA files at Keams Canyon would contain materials of historical significance, but found it impossible to get clearance to see what they had. Finally, Lee asked Allan Yazzie, who was head of the tribe's Navajo-Hopi Negotiating Committee, to make an inquiry to the bureau's Washington office. Yazzie sent a letter on May 27, but Washington did not reply until August 19. The BIA was then willing to conduct a search for us, but would not allow us to see any files.[4] We eventually did gain access to some of the material at Keams Canyon, but continued to feel that we were being given a bureaucratic runaround to delay our work.

The Littell-Udall war erupted into a new battle in October when Udall announced a plan by Peabody Coal Company to sell coal from Black Mesa to a power plant in Nevada, shipping it either by a slurry pipeline or by rail. Littell and the Old Guard immediately objected to the idea of a slurry line, which would not only deprive the tribe of a proposed railroad across the western part of the Navajo Reservation, but would require 30,000 acre-feet of water, probably from the Navajos' allotment of 50,000 acre-feet from the San Juan River.[5] When it was learned that a representative of Peabody had also suggested that San Juan County, New Mexico, and the Utah Water Conservation District might use 20,000 acre-feet of the Navajo allocation for a second slurry line, McCabe angrily charged Udall and Peabody with trying to take all of the Navajos' San Juan water.[6] Littell was able to convince Peabody that their lease needed to be renegotiated.[7] Both sides of the feud agreed that coal leases needed to be made promptly, for it was thought that nuclear generation of electricity would replace coal-operated facilities in the near future.[8]

Udall, in an effort to overcome the opposition, appointed a task force to deal with the Navajos on such economic development issues as coal leasing, electric generation, water rights, and industrial proposals. The members of this new body were Rich Allen, an assistant solicitor for the BIA, Robert L. Bennett, newly appointed deputy Indian commissioner, and Robert Vaughan, deputy assistant secretary for public land management.[9]

Bennett, himself Indian of Oneida descent, had been transferred from his position as area director for Alaska. He had served in Navajo country early in his career and had friends among both the Navajos and Hopis. His appointment to the deputy position in Washington was a result of a serious split between Secretary Udall and Commissioner Nash. According to Bennett, they were no longer on speaking terms. Bennett had become a go-between for the two, a most difficult position, but one that he managed with skill and discretion.[10]

Littell soon denounced the Secretary's task force, criticizing him for appointing "inexperienced" men.[11]

Meanwhile, exploratory drilling continued in District 6. Four companies had failed to find oil, but a fifth—Moore, Moore and Miller—leased land near Oraibi in October to put in a new well.[12] This fifth would-be oil well on Hopi land turned out to be merely another dry hole.[13]

In mid-November Representative James Haley, chairman of the House Subcommittee on Indian Affairs, visited Window Rock. He was accompanied by Graham Holmes, an assistant commissioner of Indian affairs in the legislative division, who frequently joined Haley when he made excursions to Indian reservations. Haley was quite uncommunicative with the press when questioned about his reasons for stopping at Window Rock or what people he had seen.[14]

Less than a month after Haley's unexplained visit to Window Rock, Graham Holmes was appointed to oversee Navajo affairs as area director for the BIA.[15] While there was considerable concern among people at Window Rock as to the reasons for Holmes's appointment, McCabe urged a wait-and-see attitude, noting that when Holmes had previously served at Window Rock he had had a reputation as "a square shooter."[16] Holmes had not only served among the Navajos, but had conducted a series of hearings at the Hopi villages in 1955. By the end of December there were also rumors that Robert Bennett would replace Nash as commissioner.[17]

During December Littell engaged in a series of meetings with the Peabody Coal Company, renegotiating their lease to mine coal on the joint-interest area and on a tract immediately north on the Navajo Reservation. These meetings were successfully concluded in January. A major concern with regard to the old lease agreement, which Littell had asserted to be invalid, had been that it described the land in the 1882 Reservation as "joint-use" land, thus giving the Hopi Tribe rights that had not yet been settled and "laying the foundation for possible expulsion from the area of five to six thousand Navajo families." Littell also met with representatives of the Department of the Interior and the attorneys for the Hopi Tribe in San Francisco. While the tribes were still at odds over coal leasing procedures, there was agreement on several points, including fencing the Hopi Reservation or District 6, establishing a separate office to administer the disputed area, and the need for legislation to settle land rights in the Moenkopi area.[18]

On 29 December 1965 the Hopi Tribe served eviction notices on two Navajo extended families living inside District 6 on what had now become Hopi Reservation. One was the family of Joe Kabinto, who had been described so deprecatingly by a Hopi witness during the hearings in Prescott. The other was David George's family. The Kabintos lived in Echo Canyon, where they had corn fields and a number of hogans. The Georges' homesite was above the canyon on the south. George and Kabinto were married to sisters, and the two groups cooperated in various undertakings. My impression was that Kabinto functioned somewhat as a headman for them all, which resulted in something very much like the classic Kluckhohn descrip-

tion of an outfit.[19] Kabinto was a singer, or medicine man, and his first recourse upon being served with the eviction notice was to visit some of the
Hopi religious leaders who had long been his friends. These Hopi friends
were staunch traditionalists, and they advised him from their point of view,
namely that the Hopi Tribal Council had no proper standing. He was told
that he could merely ignore the eviction notices.

Kabinto's younger relatives were more worldly and concluded that it
would be wise to consult with tribal officials at Window Rock. The tribe
took up their cause early in 1966, in part because it seemed to provide an
issue for negotiation. It was suggested that this might help to settle the
Moenkopi claim. One thought was that the Navajos should put pressure on
the Hopis living at Moenkopi. I had developed a file on every named Moenkopi Hopi that I could find in the documentary record. I even had an entry
on a Moenkopi Hopi who had purchased a stolen mule in Flagstaff some
fifty years earlier, but my main object was to extract all the information on
grazing permits, farm assignments, and other land uses.

We put Joe Colgan back to work at the National Archives. At the end of
February, Lee and I extended our search of BIA records to Phoenix. Tom
Atcitty and Melvin McKenzie, of Ed Plummer's staff, were eager to go with
us to do our microfilming. They were young Navajos, and their enthusiasm
was stimulated in part by an all-Indian basketball tournament to be held in
Phoenix during the week for which the trip was planned.

Samuel Billison, an unsuccessful candidate for tribal chairman in the 1963
primaries, was getting ready to announce his candidacy in the next election
as leader of the Old Guard faction. In a speech at Window Rock he raised
several issues. Among others, he accused Nakai of deserting the Navajos
living in the 1882 Reservation.[20]

The struggle between the Nakai faction and the Old Guard continued
with heated debate at the winter council session. Major issues were audits
of tribal finances and a resolution asking for removal of the BIA from the
Interior Department.[21]

On February 17 the agreement that Littell had worked out with Peabody
Coal Company on leasing coal rights in the joint-interest area was presented
to the tribal council. It provided for use of water by drilling wells on Black
Mesa for a slurry pipeline, should a railroad not offer competitive prices for

transporting the coal. The council approved the lease the next day by a vote of 53 to 1.[22]

Meanwhile, December rumors that Bennett would replace Nash as commissioner were revived when Udall announced that Nash would not attend a major conference on Indian education, doing so in conjunction with Representative Thomas G. Morris of New Mexico who made some very critical remarks about Nash.[23] In early March, Nash submitted his resignation and Udall quickly nominated Bennett for the post. Speculation on the reasons for Nash's departure ranged from his failure to push economic development to a rumor that he was being blamed for the administration's failure to oust Littell.[24]

The deadline given for the Hopi Tribe's eviction notices was 1 April 1966. None of the Echo Canyon people had moved. On April 4 the BIA, at the behest of the Hopi Tribal Council, served eviction notices, hoping to avoid violence. The action was announced from Washington by Assistant Secretary Harry R. Anderson. Holmes received orders in Window Rock to send a team out to help with the relocation. If the Navajos would not move, the case would be referred to the Attorney General.[25]

On April 6 the Advisory Committee met to discuss the eviction order. Graham Holmes was asked for his opinion. Holmes said that he had sent a man to contact the Navajo families, to tell them to move, and to offer help by the BIA.

Clifford Beck noted that the tribal legal staff had indicated that the Navajos should not comply with the eviction order and asked for the basis for that advice.

John Schuelke attended the committee meeting on behalf of the legal staff. He said that it was just a question of time before the Navajos would eventually have to move. The lawyers had advised stalling in hopes that the negotiating committee could work out some sort of trade or purchase, but that that had failed. The Prescott decision was the law. It would be necessary to find out what the Echo Canyon people wanted. He recommended, however, that the BIA be forced to get a court order to move them. In that way, there would be a determination as to who should compensate the evictees for their improvements. He added that the Navajo Tribe could serve eviction notices on the Hopis at Moenkopi, but that that would not alter the BIA stand on the matter, and it would probably lead to a court case over Moen-kopi before anybody was really ready for it.

Allen Yazzie next reported in detail on the last meeting of the negotiating committee with the Hopis, which he characterized as a lot of talk with little actually accomplished. On the question of fencing, he said that the Hopis did not want to complete the fencing of District 6 and that they would not give an inch. With regard to the Echo Canyon people, he claimed that the Hopis did not really have the authority to remove them. The Navajos had tried to get an extension of the deadline to the second week in July so that a crew from Ed Plummer's Land Investigations Division could do a survey and report to the Navajo Council. The Hopis refused to compromise. They also said that they thought that partition was the only way to solve the matter, and they would probably try to get another bill through Congress. Finally, the Hopis asserted that they had been impounding Navajo livestock only during the last year and a half, "but of course we know better," Yazzie stated.

At that point, Graham Holmes returned to the meeting to read a telegram he had just received informing him that the eviction proceedings had been turned over to the Attorney General "for appropriate legal action." Holmes observed that this was not an unusual procedure, but something that happens all the time when anybody is occupying Indian land without authority.

One of the committee members asked whether Navajo legal action should be taken in the name of the tribe or the individuals. He feared running a risk of contempt of court if such action were done on behalf of the tribe, but wanted to know about evaluation of the homes and farms and grazing permits that would be lost. Schuelke advised that there was no risk of contempt of court, for the action would have to be brought against the individuals and the initiative had been taken by the Secretary of the Interior. Roger Sandoval from Land Investigations reported that an evaluation of the assets that would be lost was in progress. He added that the grazing permits had been issued at Polacca. Bernadine Whitegoat identified Kabinto and George and added that some members of the families were part Hopi.

The meeting had lasted most of the morning at this point, and it was recessed for lunch. The afternoon session began with a talk by Frankie Howard, the Navajo "hawk" when it came to relations with the Hopis. He thought that since the people did not want to move, he did not see why the

Bureau should make them move. He recommended that they be told not to move until compensation was received for the losses they would suffer. The entire problem was a result of the Secretary of the Interior stopping the Supreme Court from hearing the Prescott case on appeal. The Secretary and Boyden were "buddies." He should treat the two tribes equally. Howard also complained that at the meeting in Holbrook, the Hopi negotiating committee had stated that no grazing permits were ever issued to Navajos in District 6.

Nelson Damon, the vice-chairman, observed that it would appear that removal would take place. He asked whether the BIA would allow the people to hold out for compensation.

Pete Riggs advised that it would be best to accept the suggestions of the tribal attorneys. In good Navajo fashion, however, he stated that the people themselves had their own views. He blamed the problem on the Hopis' way of not respecting individuals. He then moved that a resolution be drafted for presentation to the council. His motion was promptly seconded.

Beck added a request that the crew doing the field check also investigate the expulsion of Navajo people about three years earlier, perhaps in reference to the families evicted in 1964. He also wanted to know who was doing the field work. Bernadine explained that he was gathering information, but that the government apparently also had people working on the boundary situation. Annie Wauneka then advised that before acting on the motion, the people should be advised that they can get legal help from the tribal legal department; the motion should direct Schuelke and Plummer to send somebody to inform them that they could get help. Then the question of grazing permits was raised. What would happen to the livestock owned by the evicted people? Would the BIA compensate for loss of grazing rights?

Carl Todechine asked who should compensate for losses and what privileges under the law did squatter's rights confer. Schuelke stated that in law, squatter's rights applied to a unique situation in which, if somebody were unlawfully on property, the fact that they were there and that they had gotten there peacefully was sufficient to require that they not be removed without a court order. With specific reference to the people in District 6, this meant that they were entitled to the protection of the law, to the extent that they could not be removed forcefully without a court order.

Holmes, also a lawyer, said that he would agree with Schuelke's explanation.

Schuelke then added that if the committee wanted to stall for time, one way to do so would be to force the Secretary to bring legal action, which would have to be brought against each of the Navajos individually.

Damon then called for a vote, and Pete Riggs's motion passed without further discussion.

As the Navajo Tribal Council prepared to consider the matter in its spring session, the Hopi anti-Council faction issued a statement opposing the eviction, claiming that the village chiefs had not been informed of the action, and that the majority of the Hopis did not want the Echo Canyon people moved.[26]

The Navajo Tribal Council was scheduled to consider the dilemma of the Echo Canyon people on April 20, but the arrival of Robert Bennett, the new Commissioner of Indian Affairs, in Window Rock brought about a brief postponement. Instead, Littell and his staff met with Bennett privately and discussed the eviction issue at length. They agreed to prepare a joint memo on their talk, but the tribal legal department and the BIA ended up producing differing versions of the memo. Between the two, it is possible to learn something of what was discussed relating to the eviction order.

Bennett seems to have agreed that there might be other, more productive methods for solution of the problem. He suggested, however, that "in deference to the Hopis," there should be a six-month limit on any delay in the eviction while alternative solutions were considered. He stressed that he wanted to be impartial in his dealings with the two tribes, and promised to give reasonable notice of any further action in the eviction proceedings. The question of Graham Holmes's role as a Bureau employee who had responsibility to look out for Navajo interests was raised, but it was ultimately agreed to allow Holmes himself to decide whether he had a conflict of interest in specific situations. Littell brought up the Moenkopi question, asking whether the commissioner would be willing to give equal consideration to requests to evict Hopis illegally settled there. There was apparently no firm agreement on this last issue, there being some ambiguity as to just what was the legal standing of Hopi occupation in the 1934 Reservation area.[27]

On Friday, April 22, the council passed, by a vote of 38 to 0, a resolution asking the Echo Canyon families to remain on the land until their legal rights were settled, and authorizing the tribal legal department to spend funds in their defense.[28]

With some respite in this affair, Lee and I could turn our attention to other cases which were also in need of work. There were hearings in Utah on the school section dispute that took us away from the research on Hopi conflicts for awhile.

In the same week that the council was discussing support for the Echo Canyon people, the U.S. Court of Appeals in Washington heard final arguments on Secretary Udall's request that the injunction against him be invalidated.[29]

There developed another complication in Navajo-Hopi relations in 1966 that needs to be mentioned in passing. The BIA arranged for a meeting between the Navajo Tribe and the BVD company, a clothing manufacturer, to discuss the establishment of a plant on the Navajo Reservation. After a trial period to test the aptitude of Navajo women for the work, the company agreed to locate the plant at Fort Defiance, and the tribe agreed to expend $1.6 million for construction of the plant facility. In the interim, the city of Winslow, Arizona, some distance south of the reservation, offered free land in return for locating the new facility there. The Navajos refused to pay for the plant if it were to be off the reservation. The Department of the Interior supported the Winslow site, and next made a proposal to the Hopi Tribe that it support the construction of the plant in Winslow. There were accusations that the change in location was a political ploy by Udall to help his home state.[30]

While the Moenkopi issue had been discussed as a possible bargaining chip in settling the land-use dispute in the 1882 Reservation for some time, the fact that the Navajos raised this possibility in the Echo Canyon talks may have been sufficient to tip the scales somewhat. On July 8 the commissioner issued an order, that has since been called the "Bennett freeze," placing the same limitations on construction and development in lands directly west of the 1882 Reservation as already applied to the joint-interest lands. Any development would require the consent of both tribes, and all revenue from the land would go into a special account to be held until the respective rights of the Navajos and Hopis could be determined.[31]

According to Bennett, the freeze idea had originated with E. Reeseman Fryer and Secretary Udall. Bennett was working late on July 8 when Fryer brought him the freeze order some two hours after quitting time. Fryer told Bennett the order was something that Udall wanted him to sign and that it was needed to protect the water rights of the Moenkopi Hopis, as the Navajos had plans to shut off their water. According to Bennett, he signed the order without even reading it.[32]

The Navajo Tribal Council, in its summer session later the same month, debated a resolution condemning the order. Bennett was then quoted as saying the freeze order had been precipitated by a Navajo decision to grant a right-of-way across the disputed area without consulting with the Hopis. Boyden had objected and threatened to take legal action to block any construction by the company to which the right-of-way had been granted unless it also had an agreement with the Hopi Tribe. The Old Guard supported the resolution opposing the freeze, with Frankie Howard arguing their case most vociferously. Nakai's followers opposed the resolution, warning that Littell could lose even more of the Navajo's land. The motion charged that Udall had told Bennett to issue the freeze order as a favor to Boyden, who was characterized as an old friend of the Secretary. After two days of acrimonious debate, the motion passed by a vote of 52 to 2.[33] Within two weeks the Hopi traditionalists had also protested the order as "creating another problem for both the Hopi and Navajo people."[34]

On 6 January 1967 the Navajo-Hopi Negotiating Committee held a meeting in the Navajo Tribal Resources Building with Allen Yazzie, the chairman, presiding. In addition to the committee members, those present included Littell and Lavell, Annie Wauneka, Ed Plummer, Lee, and myself.

Littell reported on the progress in defending the Echo Canyon people. He first noted that the tribe had filed an answer to the eviction request and a motion to intervene. He claimed that the U.S. attorneys in Phoenix had been reluctant to bring the suit, but that they had been ordered to do so.

He then went on to explain the theory on which the tribe's legal position would be based. He said that *Healing v. Jones* did not adjudicate any individual rights. The Navajos were settled there legally by the Executive Order of 16 December 1882, and prior to that time they had established aboriginal occupancy. The Act of 1958 did not involve individuals. All Navajos were settled by the Act of 1934 pursuant to the 1882 Executive Order. Therefore, all Navajo individuals had rights, and if living within the area were legally resident there. In *Healing v. Jones*, the court found that as of 2 June 1937 the

Navajo Tribe was legally settled in the 1882 Reservation by virtue of the approval of grazing regulations.

At this point Frankie Howard asked if this included the area of expanded District 6, to which Littell replied in the affirmative.

Littell then brought up Section 2 of the Act of 1958, which provides that the two tribes might adjust their holdings by buying, selling or exchanging lands within their reservations with the approval of the Secretary of the Interior. He said that, at Prescott, Boyden had agreed that this provision was to adjust for people who found themselves on the wrong side of the line set by the court, but that now Boyden had changed his mind. Littell then went on to recount some of the history of the Moenkopi question. Both he and Lavell stressed that any disagreements within the tribe on the negotiations on Moenkopi should not be made public, but that the Navajos present a united front.

Lavell predicted that the Moenkopi question would end up in court. In the meantime, the tribe should establish a policy for all officials concerned. He suggested three points:

1. The tribe should do nothing in the area outside of District 6 in the 1882 Reservation.
2. The tribe should be willing to negotiate on lands in the area around Moenkopi, but not on all of the land in the Bennett freeze.
3. The people in the chapters should be told to ignore the freeze order, that they should continue to live as before, that the order was illegal in any case, that they should apply for any leases that they wanted and if the BIA held them up, they could collect damages later.[35]

Three days later the Supreme Court decided that Udall did have the authority to fire a tribal attorney. Littell soon resigned, leaving Lavell in charge of the legal department on an interim basis.[36]

Lee and I were soon deeply involved in researching the history of the Echo Canyon families. We obtained detailed genealogies and compared them with the Murphy 1911 allotment schedules. Unfortunately, the Echo Canyon area had never been surveyed during Murphy's time, and no allotments were laid out there. Aside from identifying an uncle and a second cousin of the Echo Canyon people among the allottees, we were at a dead end. Lavell suggested that we might do better trying to tie in some of the families who had been forced to move in the Jeddito area, and we were able to trace a number of descendants and even a few surviving allottees in that region, but it did little to help the Kabintos and the Georges.

We were always willing to try to help the Navajos outside of the narrow scope of our official duties. Bertha Dutton, director of the Museum of Navajo Ceremonial Art in Santa Fe, wanted to install an exhibit on Navajo pottery. I offered to help and contracted with Mrs. Kabinto to provide the specimens, including tools, pots at various stages of production, and one finished vessel. I hoped that the display might help to attract some favorable publicity to the family's situation, but the exhibit was a small one that led to no further developments.

The tribe began to send Lee and me out to chapter meetings in the joint-interest area to explain the current status of the land dispute and to gather information that would help our research. On March 11 we attended a chapter meeting at Teestoh, where we recorded some historical tradition as well as leads to people who might be allottees.[37]

Also in March, Boyden was involved in an automobile accident. He was a passenger in a car driven by Clyde Pensoneau, Hopi Agency superintendent, when the car was struck head-on by a vehicle operated by a drunk driver. Pensoneau received such severe brain damage that he was very shortly granted a permanent disability retirement. Boyden, however, was only slightly injured. According to a family account, he sustained little more than bruises. A BIA spokesman, however, said as late as mid-April that delays in negotiations on the part of the Hopis were caused by their lawyer's injuries. When we heard the news of the accident at Window Rock, our first fear was that a Navajo driver might have been involved and that Boyden would exploit the fact in his usual manner, but it turned out that the intoxicated driver had been a Hopi.[38]

About this time, or a bit earlier, Bennett had selected Wayne Pratt, a former BIA school teacher who had once been stationed among the Hopis, to work on the land problem on behalf of the BIA. Bennett had worked with him in the development of training programs on the Pima-Maricopa Reservation at Sacaton, Arizona. Pratt had developed a very successful program there for returning Indian veterans, and Bennett was impressed by his skills in working with the community. As Bennett later explained, Pratt was to learn the views of the Navajos who would have to be moved and to explain to them that it was not the BIA, but the Supreme Court, that had made partition necessary.[39]

I first encountered Pratt at a very well attended chapter meeting at Pinon on April 15. Clifford Beck, the local councilman, introduced the subject of the land dispute, describing the work of the negotiating committee and explaining a map produced by Ed Plummer to show the area of the Bennett freeze, and our map of the Murphy allotments. Milton Bluehouse, a Community Action Committee worker stationed at Pinon, translated parts of the talks made in Navajo for me. Following Beck's presentation one of the Navajos who spoke from the audience said that for a long time the Hopis had been claiming that Nakai's election ensured them the land. He wanted to know just what was the status of the land.

Beck then introduced Harold Drake, a member of the negotiating committee and councilman for the Navajo Mountain community. Drake began his talk by introducing himself in Navajo terms, saying that he was of the Salt Clan and that his family had originated at Hard Rock. His remarks were meant to illustrate that there is always hope, and his general tone was likewise optimistic.

Manuelito Lewis was the next speaker. Like Drake, he placed himself in kin terms with relation to the audience. He used an introductory story that was strictly Navajo and that carried the message that a way could be found to prevail. He also expressed confidence that if the Navajos all worked together, they would not lose their land.

Drake then introduced Pratt. Pratt began by telling the crowd that he had first worked in the area in the 1930s. He did not explain that he had worked in one of the Hopi schools at that time, but I noticed that his pronunciation of Hopi words was quite good, while he had no real familiarity with Navajo words. He began with two jokes, neither of which related to the experiences of Navajos living on the reservation.

He then began a long talk about the land dispute, starting with the fact that he had been appointed special representative of the Commissioner of Indian Affairs and saying that he was looking for a solution to the difficulty. He read from the Prescott decision the phrase "joint, undivided and equal," then wrote it on the blackboard and re-emphasized the importance of the words. He read from the decision the court's summation of what was settled, that the Navajos did have rights on the reservation, that those rights were not exclusive, and that District 6 became the Hopi Reservation. He then spoke about the concept of joint use.

While Bluehouse was translating, Pratt wrote on the blackboard:

1. Navajos residing on the reservation.
2. Negotiations involving west end.

Pratt next told about the Echo Canyon people, noting that the Hopis had ordered them to move but that the Navajos' attorneys thought they had established squatters' rights. Drake came to Bluehouse's aid in trying to explain squatters' rights in Navajo.

Pratt then went on to his second point, explaining briefly the 1934 Boundary Bill and its relation to the Hopi settlement at Moenkopi. He repeated several times that "many people" thought that if the two tribes could settle the question of the rights of the Moenkopi Hopis, they should then be able to solve the problem in the 1882 Reservation. He claimed that he was attempting to get negotiations on the "west end" moving. He noted that Boyden had been injured in an auto accident and that that was holding up progress by the Hopis in arranging for a meeting with the Navajos.

Pratt asserted that he was trying to see that work on improvements needed for conservation and range development should go ahead in the "joint-use area."

Next, he recounted the history of the negotiations held under Nash's sponsorship. He said that while Nash had wanted to allocate $6 million for administration of the "joint-use area," he (Pratt) preferred to use the money to meet the needs of the people with such things as a new school and a clinic. He noted that his office was in Holbrook and that both Navajos and Hopis had visited him there to suggest solutions. He emphasized the long-time friendship of the Navajos and Hopis, claimed that Navajo masked dancers had originated from Hopi Kachinas, also observing that while Tuba City is located in Navajo country it has a Hopi name, and concluding that the tribes had a basis for negotiation. He praised the Pinon community for their fine letter setting forth their needs. He thought that he would be able to help, but had no answers at that time.

Beck asked Pratt if he had any solution for speeding up development needs. Pratt said that he had no suggestions, but that if negotiations on the "west end" and the court case on the eviction of the Echo Canyon people could be expedited, that might help. He thought a lease agreement for the Navajos might work, but said the Navajos were opposed to leasing. Beck protested that he believed that the western part of the reservation was outside the Executive Order Reservation. Pratt replied that that was correct and that the two areas were not legally connected, but that "a great many people" were of the opinion that if the two tribes could resolve that issue by negotiations, they would be in a better position to handle the other issues as well. Drake asked Pratt why the Moenkopi question had not been a part of the suit heard at Prescott. Pratt confessed ignorance in that regard.

I was the next speaker, following a report by Bluehouse on the Community Action Committee. After describing the status of the Echo Canyon case, I explained the potential importance of the Murphy allotting program as a result of the Prescott decision and asked for help in locating people who had been included or their descendants. We then got questions from the floor as well as comments.

John Smith, a member of the Community Action Committee, spoke of how the Navajos and Hopis had shared food and a water hole in the past, that they were related by clan and had respect for one another. He pointed out that this sharing was no longer possible, and he wanted to know what could be done. He contrasted the backwardness of Pinon with the progress at Chinle, and he hoped that Pinon could receive some attention.

Clark Gilmore asked next if the 1868 Navajo Treaty were still in effect. Pratt said that he would have to ask the tribe's lawyers. Gilmore then complained that the grazing regulations and range development programs now seemed to be rescinded and he wanted something done. Pratt reassured him that he wanted the same and that he was trying to find a way to accomplish it.

Another man asked whether, if they could not get a new BIA school, it would be possible to get a public school. Pratt said he was sure that would be possible. I interjected the observation that it was as unlikely that the state would build on disputed land as it was that the BIA would do so, but that if there were free land in the area, that could probably be used.

Alexander Tsoh asked me whether there was any evidence of joint use and what were the respective surface rights of the tribes. I noted that the term joint use did not appear in the Prescott decision and that the Hopis had not made any significant use of the land for a very long time. I added that at the meeting in Scottsdale the solicitor had said that no Navajos could be moved unless there were either an agreement by both tribes or special legislation enacted by Congress to authorize partition. I added that one possible way to obtain full surface rights might be by giving the Hopis a larger share of the mineral rights, but emphasized that this was my own idea, not something that the tribal administration endorsed. Pratt later found this suggestion interesting.

Drake explained the difference between "use" and "interest," and then introduced Paul Hand, superintendent of the Chinle Agency.

Hand discussed the problem of increasing numbers of school children and said that the BIA lacked room at Pinon for more than 100 children between the ages of six and seven. He urged parents who could not enroll their children at Pinon to bring them to the school at Chinle. He commented on the need for roads to the area where there would be employment opportunities at the coal mine in about two years, on the need for a new school and a sewage disposal system at Pinon, as well as on range development, and on maintenance work for the improvements that then existed. He added that he had known Pratt for a long time and had confidence in his ability and fairness.

Jones Van Winkle, a Navajo councilman who had arrived late, asked about the freeze order and its effect on mineral development. He also asked how the surface rights might be settled. Pratt could say little in reply beyond the fact that he too was looking for the answers to those questions. Van Winkle then asserted that the Navajos had the surface rights and seconded Hand's request that all parents get their children into schools.

After Frankie Howard gave a rather long talk entirely in Navajo, a member of the audience asked how the Executive Order Reservation boundary had been established, saying that either Pratt or I might reply. Pratt merely noted that the "present boundary" was made by the Prescott court. I gave a brief history of the Hopi agent's troubles in 1882 and how they led to the Executive Order.

The same man then asked about fencing District 6, complaining that it was costing the Navajos a lot of money when the Hopis impounded livestock. Pratt said that the Hopis did not want a fence, so that would have to be settled sometime in the future.

Jack Frank, a son-in-law of Joe Kabinto, next wanted to know what progress was being made in negotiating with the Hopis. He was concerned that there had been no new information on the Echo Canyon situation. Pratt stated that the last time the tribal negotiating committees met, they could agree on only one thing, that they were not getting anywhere. Pratt claimed that he was trying to act as a go-between and expected to see some progress as a result.

Frankie Howard again gave a long talk, all in Navajo. He ended by stating that the Hopi claim that the prehistoric Anasazi people were their ancestors, thereby showing that wherever there were ruins they had lived, was not true. This evoked vigorous applause, and he was asked to translate his speech. His translation was much shorter than the original presentation, but it made it possible for me to understand better what I had inferred from the little that I could understand of his Navajo. He recapitulated a good deal of the history of the land dispute, analyzing the Prescott decision and mentioning our archeological work that showed long Navajo occupation of the land, while the Hopis could show only transient presence for taking young eagles and the like. He blamed the problems now facing the people on Secretary Udall's favoritism because he was a "buddy" of Boyden. He then told of Navajo military service in World Wars I and II, in Korea, and in Vietnam, saying he had served four years in World War II. He claimed that the Hopis did not serve in any of these wars.

Another talk by Bluehouse was followed by Frank Cowboy, a resident of District 7. While my notes may not be his exact words, they are close enough that I quote them here:

I live in District 7. I am sixty-four years old. I raised three boys. The three served in the armed services in different national conflicts. I have lost one boy, and on the day when I heard this, some official decorated with stars came to see me on the very ground where I reside. He said that "on this earth there are many valuable things and also in the earth, and people in this nation have one common goal, freedom, and you yourself were strong to raise this child," and I had mixed emotions and I remember crying. The man with stars said there will always be people and this property is yours and should anyone deny you this property all you have to do is report this to the officials in Washington, D.C. I would like you to know what he said to me. I was given a medal of honor on my son's behalf and I live in District 7.[40]

One of the women from Echo Canyon also spoke, telling of their plight and urging that they be helped soon. After the meeting, Jack Frank gave me his mailing address, asking that he be kept informed of developments in the case.

I had not been favorably impressed with Pratt. His condescending, school-teacherish manner of talking to Navajos I found offensive, and he seemed to be trying to prepare the Navajos to lose their homes. Manuelito Lewis and Pratt had agreed to attend a chapter meeting at White Cone on May 6. Lewis asked me to be present also. Several people had asked for copies of the map of the allotments surveyed by Murphy, so that when I returned to Window Rock, I had copies made to distribute at the meeting at White Cone.[41]

Lavell was to meet with Boyden on April 25. Allen Yazzie called a meeting of the negotiating committee for April 21 to advise him. Yazzie opened the meeting by listing three agenda items:

1. The eviction proceedings against the Echo Canyon people,
2. The Moenkopi problem and the Bennett freeze,
3. The lack of development in the disputed area since 1962.

He called first on Lavell to report on the eviction case.

Lavell said that Pratt would go to Washington within a couple of weeks. He intended to talk to the commissioner about getting funds to relocate the people from Echo Canyon. Lavell said that if a good enough offer were made, he would recommend to the Navajos that they accept it. He did not seem to feel that the Navajos' case was a strong one, but was not concerned that the U.S. attorneys had not replied to his brief, saying that the longer the case was delayed, the longer the people could stay. He felt that a case involving the allottee applicants was stronger, and he would prefer to go to court on that issue. He suggested that the tribal council set aside funds to help any Navajos who had planted inside District 6 and subsequently lost their crops to the Hopis.

When Frankie Howard asked whether such a fund could be used to retrieve impounded livestock, Lavell agreed that that would be a good idea. Most committee members favored the suggestion, but Beck feared that if the Hopis knew that the tribe was paying, they would go all out to collect the money. Lavell said if they went overboard that the Navajos might be able to take them to court. He noted that the sum needed would not be large, perhaps as little as $5,000. Howard moved that the committee request that sum from the council, and the motion was passed by a unanimous vote.

Lavell then brought up the neglected needs of the people living in the joint-interest area which had been discussed at the Pinon Chapter meeting. The BIA had done nothing because the Hopis refused to agree to any work in the area. He said the Navajos had been on the defensive in the matter since 1962 and that the western area was now included under the same policy as a result of the July 8 freeze order. It had gone on to the point where it was punishing the people. The time had come to go on the offensive, sending letters and requests, and to take the BIA to court if necessary. He stated that Pratt was on the Navajos' side in this issue, and it should be possible to force the BIA into action.

While Lavell's remarks were being translated into Navajo, Graham Holmes joined the group.

Howard then made a short speech critical of the BIA's lapse of activity, which was causing suffering for several thousand people. He moved that letters be sent to congressmen and that a delegation be sent to Washington to ask that something be done. He predicted that the situation might go on for another ten or twenty years, an insight that I unwisely discounted at the time as mere political bluster. Even so, we all felt that for children to be deprived of education and their families of other government services for one or two years was a serious problem. His motion carried without dissent.

Lavell next took up the Moenkopi question. He said that one reason for the committee meeting had been to discuss Boyden's reply to a letter sent by the Navajos, but that Boyden had failed to send the answer he had promised. Lavell had talked to Boyden by phone and agreed to meet him in Salt Lake City to learn just what the Hopis wanted in order to settle their claim in the 1934 area. Boyden had wanted the attorneys for both sides to get together to discuss settling all Hopi claims, but Lavell would restrict the meeting to the Moenkopi area, with the intention of defining a smaller area than that presently covered by the Bennett freeze to which the restrictions would apply. On the basis of the outcome of the meeting with Boyden, Lavell would be able to recommend whether both negotiating committees should meet. The freeze order was already beginning to hurt. The new high school had been held up, and contracts let for the new hospital had had to be canceled. In addition, a low-rent housing project and several homesite leases were involved. On the basis of what Boyden might say, one way or the other, Lavell hoped to have arguments to present to the commissioner. If Bennett did not then act, he suggested filing a law suit under the administrative procedures act.

Howard Drake moved that Lavell be instructed to discuss only the Moenkopi area and to report back on the outcome. This was seconded and passed unanimously.

Frankie Howard then questioned Holmes about the high school and hospital at Tuba City. Holmes claimed that thus far neither the school nor the hospital had been held up. Surveys were in progress, and the only delay was the result of the Public Health Service objecting to the spot selected for the hospital. He said the BIA was going ahead, with the assumption that the Hopis would give their approval. He did not want to speculate on what would happen if the Hopis should go back on their word that they would approve both projects.

Drake then brought up the joint-interest area, noting that the dispute might not be settled for twenty years. He wondered whether a separate agency to administer the area might not make it possible to continue the maintenance and development of roads, schools, and other facilities.

Holmes replied that the area outside of District 6 was owned by both tribes, which prompted Drake to query whether that meant the land or the people or both. Holmes said just the land, that the people did not make any difference. He said the land could be divided, but that the BIA had not figured out how to do it. Hopi approval was necessary to make any improvements. The bureau had built a school at Cottonwood on the edge of the area, but could not build the roads to bring the children out to it because of Hopi refusal. He said the whole problem resulted from the failure of the various Secretaries of the Interior to take any action through the years. He thought the most equitable solution would be for the United States to buy the Hopi interest.

Lavell said that when the delegation went to Washington they should try to convince the commissioner to find a way around the need for Hopi consent, possibly by way of condemnation under the powers of eminent domain. Holmes's reply was a rather uncertain "maybe."

Howard broke in to accuse the Secretary of being on the Hopi side and of preventing the Supreme Court from reviewing the Prescott decision because he was a "buddy" of Boyden. Holmes defended the Supreme Court, citing its power to act on its own, but failed to convince Howard. He did not address the question of Boyden's possible influence with Udall.

Drake then asked Holmes whether he thought the bureau should continue to develop the area. Holmes said that he did, but he did not know whether there was the legal authority to do so.

At this point, Howard took time to translate into Navajo the exchanges that had taken place. The meeting ended with Holmes comparing the act that had authorized the Prescott hearings with a bill then before Congress to authorize a suit between the Navajos and the Utes, which he felt was better as far as right of review by the Supreme Court was concerned.[42]

The Hopi disputes were being discussed at chapter meetings throughout much of the western Navajo country. A meeting of the Cameron Chapter on May 4 was one of many, but the White Cone meeting on May 6 was particularly important, as Graham Holmes made a presentation. Lee attended in my place and delivered a copy of the allotment map to the chapter officers for me.

Holmes traced the history of the reservations, giving special attention to the 1882 Executive Order area and the 1934 Boundary Bill. He then explained the impasse resulting from the Hopi council's refusal to approve any construction in the jointly owned area. The Hopis were saying that the area should be divided before any new development took place. The Hopis were insisting on their half of the land and were not willing to sell their half-interest.

Manuelito Lewis interrupted to ask if the court had said that the Hopis had half-ownership, and Holmes replied that it had. Holmes was asked about the boundary survey and could only say that since the decision the government had surveyed the District 6 boundary. The White Cone people were especially concerned about the refusal of the Hopis to approve a right-of-way for a power line so that they could have electricity. Holmes concluded his talk by noting that "we were better off before we got the decision than we are now."

Pratt was at the meeting and gave very much the same talk he had presented at Pinon.

Lee then explained the work he and I were doing in the Jeddito area. He relayed Lavell's advice that any Navajos who had been farming inside District 6 should continue to do so, for the only way individual Navajo rights there could be determined would be through a test case in court. He added that the Navajo Tribe would probably set up an indemnity fund to reimburse any Navajos who lost improvements or crops as a result of Hopi or BIA actions.[43]

The negotiating committee met again in Window Rock on May 10. Pratt was invited, and Holmes also attended. Most of the discussion centered on the developments that were being held up by the Hopi Council. Pratt reiterated his statement that he felt the government had created the problem and that it should have "a share in seeking a solution." Holmes was willing to go further; he asserted that the only solution was for the government to condemn the Hopi interest and pay the Hopis. The only improvements receiving Hopi approval were a road that would give them access to the Peabody mine and the right-of-way for the slurry pipeline. The Hopi Agency wanted to fence District 6, but the Hopi council had refused permission for even that.[44]

The next negotiating committee meeting had been scheduled for Monday, May 22, but was rescheduled for the preceding Friday. The Hopi Council was to meet on Wednesday, and the question of approval of the high school and hospital at Tuba City was said to be on their agenda. The Navajos in the Jeddito area were in the midst of a drought, and the Hopis were complaining that sheep were coming into District 6 as a result. The Navajo Council had not yet taken up the resolution to allocate $5,000 to help Navajos who incurred losses due to the land conflict.

The main purpose of the meeting, however, was to prepare for the delegation to go to Washington. I presented a map of the restricted freeze area we would be proposing to the commissioner, the new freeze line being drawn so as to exclude a power line, the business area at the road junction south of

Tuba City, and the uranium mill. The committee members studied the map. Ned Hatathli noted that a portion of the bull pasture fence on the Moenkopi Plateau was inside the line, but Lavell said that existing improvements could be maintained under the freeze order. The corridor that the Hopis wanted to link Moenkopi with their reservation was also considered. While Lavell thought it should be included in the talk with the commissioner in order to make a more suitable offer, the committee decided not to bring it up. Hatathli suggested that the Navajos invite the commissioner to Window Rock to meet with the entire committee and to see the area under discussion. It was decided to call him and try to change the plan for the meeting. On the phone it was learned that the commissioner was planning to be in Santa Fe on other business the week of June 5. A meeting was then tentatively scheduled for June 6 in Albuquerque.[45]

On May 27 I wrote Joe Colgan in Washington explaining the status of Navajo-Hopi relations in some detail. I dealt first with the Echo Canyon people, noting that they had more firearms than I had seen among any other Navajos, but expressing my faith in Joe Kabinto's ability as a leader despite the fact that conflicts over conversion of some family members to Christianity had arisen within the group. We had understood that the government might make an offer of some sort for an out-of-court settlement if the people should move voluntarily and expected Commissioner Bennett to make a proposal at the forthcoming meeting at Fort Wingate, probably to include land as well as compensation and help in moving and erecting new homes. Acceptance of the offer would require consensus among the family members, which did not seem likely to me, but I much preferred such a settlement to trusting to the uncertainties of a law suit.

I explained to Colgan just what the Bennett freeze was and what were our beliefs regarding it at that time. According to Lavell, Boyden had complained to Secretary Udall that the Navajos would not make any effort to settle the Moenkopi dispute and he wanted the government to apply a freeze order to all of the Navajo Reservation lying within Arizona so as to force the Navajos to negotiate. Bennett had been willing to issue a moratorium only on the lands directly west of the 1882 Executive Order Reservation, but even this was upsetting the course of development of services such as education and medical care for the western Navajos.

We were making an effort to have the freeze modified. I had drawn up a description of an area to which the freeze might be narrowed for purposes of discussions with the Hopis, modifying it in accordance with suggestions from the negotiating committee. Lavell believed that if the commissioner should not modify the freeze to permit construction of a new high school and hospital at Tuba City, the Navajos would have just cause to go to court over the issue. We thought that much of what Boyden was demanding was merely a bluff, including his insistence on a connection between the Hopi Reservation and any area that might be set aside for the Moenkopi Hopis. Lavell and Holmes were in agreement that the best solution would be for the government to buy out the Hopi interest under the power of eminent domain, but Holmes did not feel this would be possible until there was a change of administration in Washington.

I described our impressions of Wayne Pratt, whom we considered ineffectual and probably too biased in favor of the Hopis as a result of his former service as a teacher ar Oraibi to ever gain the Navajos' confidence. His one suggestion thus far had been a program of voluntary Navajo relocation that would clearly do little more than help relieve some of the overcrowding on the land for the Navajos.

Our most immediate concern was possible loss of legal staff. Contracts for Lavell and one other attorney were due to expire in August and we feared that they would leave then. The Navajo Tribal Council was not taking any action toward renewing the contracts, and even if they did, we had little hope that Secretary Udall would give prompt approvals. Should the tribal legal department collapse, the Navajos on the disputed lands would be at the mercy of Boyden.

The meeting with Commissioner Bennett was postponed until June 16, and was relocated to Fort Wingate School, which would save the tribe some travel expense.[46] The uncertainty of the future, both for the legal department and our field work, on top of our ego-centered feelings that all the turmoil was probably a result of a concerted effort to force several hundred, if not thousands, of Navajos from their homes to satisfy Hopi territorial ambitions, gave a sense of foreboding. Had we known what would be revealed after the fact by Kammer, Iverson, and Redhouse,[47] we might have been really paranoid in our outlook. As it was, we found little cause for hope.

FALSE HOPES

T HE BENNETT ADMINISTRATION ushered in a period of negotiation between the two tribes that makes apparent the aims and strategy of each,
as well as the strengths and weaknesses, perceived and real, faced by the two.

The planned meeting of the Navajo negotiating committee with Bennett
finally took place at Fort Wingate on 16 June 1967. The committee and
support staff arrived early and held a brief meeting of its own prior to the
commissioner's appearance. Two motions were passed, one asking the commissioner to revoke the freeze order, and the other asking the Navajo Tribal
Council to pass a resolution approving in advance all public works for which
the Hopis might give approval. The second motion also included a proposal
that the chairman provide funds to retain Lee and Bernadine and myself as
tribal employees to complete our research on the various land issues. Ed
Plummer promised support, in terms of men and equipment from his Land
Investigations Division, for our work.

Allen Yazzie then went to find Bennett, and upon his return introduced
him, explaining that Bennett could meet with us for only an hour or so.
Bennett then spoke.

He expressed confidence that if the committees would continue to meet,
progress would be made. He observed that when people and their relationships were involved, progress must necessarily be slow. He also announced
that the Hopi negotiating committee was meeting in Salt Lake City, saying
that he had visited the Hopi reservation himself to try to expedite their reply
to the Navajos' letter, but had arrived the day after the auto accident in
which Boyden and Pensoneau were injured. He said that he was aware that
a deep problem that develops over many years, as had the dispute between
the two tribes, would have to depend on changes in attitudes over time for

a resolution, and he hoped to arrange for a meeting between the two committees.

Yazzie then described the events leading to this meeting and called on Lavell to present the resolution just passed which petitioned for an end to the freeze order.

Lavell read the motion, and added that progress in meeting human needs should not be slow. He believed that the freeze order, as an administrative decision of the commissioner, could be modified in the same way, so as to permit the needed developments at Tuba City. He recalled the meeting with the commissioner at Window Rock during the tribal fair when Bennett had said that one reason for the freeze was the claim by the Hopis that the Navajos would not negotiate with them unless forced to do so. The Hopis had talked only to the commissioner, however, and never to the Navajos. The last Navajo letter to the Hopis had been sent December 19, and there was still no reply.

Lavell said he had talked with Boyden and Boyden thought that the Hopis might be willing to compromise if they could obtain title to lands they wanted at Moenkopi and to a corridor connecting the Moenkopi area with the main Hopi reservation. Boyden could not commit the Hopi Tribal Council to the proposal, however. Boyden also claimed that there was considerable ambiguity in the 1934 boundary statute; this was apparently a veiled threat of litigation if the issue were not settled by agreement between the tribes.

Lavell then explained the research done up to that time and showed the commissioner Ed Plummer's map of land status in the freeze area and the map I had prepared. He listed the various public works being delayed, as well as the desire of El Paso Natural Gas Company to let the Navajos have the housing it was no longer using at the uranium mill. He noted that the Phoenix area office had forwarded the Navajo request for approval of some public projects in the Executive Order Reservation to the Hopi council as early as November 1966, but that no action had yet been taken.

He ended his presentation with a reference to the law suit for the eviction of the Echo Canyon people. He had hoped that Wayne Pratt would come up with a commitment for some help for the Navajos that would be better than merely loading them on a truck and moving them out, but he had not done so. Lavell noted that Joe Kabinto was at the meeting.

Yazzie asked Bennett if he would like to respond to Lavell's presentation.

Bennett replied that he thought Lavell had been reasonable in what he said. The lack of an answer from the Hopis suggested that they were delaying progress. He said that during our recess he would call Boyden to see if they had taken any action at their meeting in Salt Lake City. He emphasized that his mind was always open and that the committee could always approach him with questions of this kind.

Yazzie agreed that it was important to find out what had transpired at Salt Lake City. He went on to assert that the Navajos outside of District 6 would rebel before they would move. In the Forest Lake Chapters the reservoir dams were broken and the windmills had not been maintained for four and a half years. The people had suffered long enough. He asked for an administrative decision and then recessed the meeting for lunch, repeating that he would like for Bennett to contact the Hopis.

At one o'clock the commissioner's phone call still had not been returned. While we were waiting, Ben Howell, an attorney for El Paso Natural Gas, explained that the uranium ore processed at their plant near Tuba City was depleted and that the plant had thus been closed. There were twenty houses at the plant, all with water, sewage lines, and electricity. These were movable homes, and the company could, under its contract, take them away, but the Navajo Tribe had an option to purchase them. The houses were worth more if left where they were, and El Paso could include their sale to the tribe as a part of the coal lease they were negotiating.

At this point, the commissioner was called to the phone. Graham Holmes informed us that this was the anticipated call from Salt Lake City. While Bennett was gone, Frankie Howard complained that as the houses were built long before the freeze order, he did not see why their transfer to the tribe should be held up. He asked Holmes for his opinion. Holmes said he would like to wait until the commissioner returned to discuss the issue.

Yazzie listed the specific projects in the joint-interest area that were being delayed. They included a new school at Pinon complete with modern utilities and a gym, improved roads including those in the Forest Lake area, domestic water development, medical facilities, and a solution to the sewage problem at Pinon.

Bennett returned before the list could be completed and announced that the Hopis and Boyden were still meeting. They expected to send a letter before the day was over, one that would address what Boyden and Lavell had discussed. He had hopes that it would provide a basis for negotiations. The hospital, school, and housing at Tuba City were under discussion. Bennett said that he was giving the Hopis until the anniversary date of the freeze order, July 8, to respond, and if they had not taken action by then, he would do so unilaterally. In response to a question from Howard, he stated that the Hopi response was expected to deal with all public works and the El Paso housing as well.

Clifford Beck asked if the District 6 situation would be included in the Hopis' response. Bennett said that would be subject to negotiation and that he would like to hear from any of the Navajos from District 6 who were present. Frankie Howard got the discussion off track with another question on the commissioner's intentions regarding the freeze, but James Maloney brought it back to the Echo Canyon representatives.

Joe Kabinto spoke in Navajo, with Edward McCabe translating for him. He said the eviction notices had caused his people not to sleep, not to eat well, and not to make a good livelihood. He said that his ancestors had instructed them to take care of the land and the water and not to give them away. His mother had died there, as had other relatives. His great-grandfather had died at Fort Defiance protecting their title to the land. He complained that no Hopis with any authority had ever contacted him about moving, only the federal government. He had lived there for fifty-five years and had once worked for Tom Pavetea, a Hopi, for five dollars a month. He hoped that the matter could be resolved. He talked of his troubles in a very Navajo manner, and I quietly hoped that the eloquence of his words would come through clearly to a non-Navajo. Bennett, even though he was himself Indian, might not understand all the nuances of Kabinto's plea.

Following Kabinto, Jack Frank addressed the commissioner, saying the Navajos had come to the meeting hoping that the problem would be settled, but that was apparently not the case. He said they made their living from the land where they had grazing permits, homes, and water. They had children graduating from high school and wanted better homes for them. Public works programs and welfare were just not enough to go around. They appreciated Pratt's assistance, and they wanted the commissioner to know about their difficulties.

Lavell explained that Pratt, Lee, and I had discussed relocation with the

Echo Canyon families. He thought that if it were approached correctly it might be possible, but that the people, and especially the women, did not like the idea. Ed Plummer noted that there was public domain land available for resettlement.

The discussion then turned to broader problems, with no commitment forthcoming on the part of the commissioner for the Kabintos and the Georges. Yazzie raised the question of children who were not in school and suggested that perhaps a trailer school would be alright. He then went through his list of projects.

Harold Drake brought up the need for jobs. He mentioned that there would be employment opportunities at the new coal mine and that it would be good to train some of the younger men in the operation of heavy equipment so that they could qualify for the new jobs.

Clifford Beck asked if Bennett agreed with the opinion of former Commissioner Nash that the Navajos could not be moved. Bennett said that was true outside of District 6, but if the people inside District 6 should have to be moved, every effort would be made to see that money was available so that the move could be made without hardship.[1]

I was very favorably impressed by Bennett at the Fort Wingate meeting, especially by his reasonableness and appreciation of all that seemed to stand between the Navajos and successful resistance to a concerted effort to dispossess them of their homes. I later wrote a friend that unless things improved, the Navajos might, however, find themselves with a demagogue as tribal chairman or a rebel leader in the hinterland.[2]

In the midst of these developments, the Navajo legal department disintegrated. The meeting with the commissioner occurred on Lavell's last day of work. A goodbye party had been held for him and for Woody Sneed the night before. Before he left, Lavell advised the negotiating committee that they should hire their own attorney to work only on the Hopi dispute.

A national television show presented the side of the Hopi traditionalists. The show characterized the Hopis as peaceful people. It reported that the Hopis had received $3 million for mineral leases and that $1 million of the money had been given to their attorney, but that nobody knew what had happened to the other $2 million. Public sympathy seemed to be entirely on the side of the Hopis so much so that even a television show about the Hopi traditionalists—who were friends of the Navajos—came across in an ambiguous way with regard to Navajo relations. It was unclear what effect public opinion might have on the matter at that point, but because stereotypical characterizations had been so influential in the earlier court decision, it seemed they continued to present an ominous threat, even when raised by the Navajos' sometime allies.

Lee and I had prepared a report on our work to give to the tribal advisory committee on Wednesday afternoon of the following week. Allen Yazzie also appeared before the advisory committee and reported on the progress of the negotiating committee. He began with the observation that the committee had been trying for almost a year to begin negotiations. He described the meeting with the commissioner at Fort Wingate, placing special emphasis on Bennett's promise to take action if the Hopis had not responded to the Navajos' letter by July 8, but added that Bennett had not said what that action might be.

Next, Ed Plummer presented his maps of land status in the freeze area, directing particular attention to lands that had been purchased with Navajo tribal funds or set aside by Congress explicitly for Navajo use. His discovery that these land status areas had been arbitrarily encompassed in the freeze order was the strongest argument for a modification of the order, one that made a modification imperative, at least to exclude such lands.

Yazzie then called upon me to outline the history of the area, which I did, explaining the research we had done and what still needed to be done. I described our survey of the current use of the land, noting especially the importance of recording tradition and genealogies, and the problem caused by the lack of tree-ring dates in open country where datable wood seldom remained on Navajo archeological sites. The only areas important in our research that contained extensive forested tracts were on Grey Mountain and perhaps on Preston Mesa. We had already done work for the Land Claim case on Gray Mountain. I also discussed the possible uses that might be made of our data in negotiations and in court, should the dispute lead to a law suit.

James Maloney spoke up to claim that in the early days the Hopis were restricted to thirteen plots of land, apparently with reference to the Murphy allotments, and were not allowed in Reservoir Canyon. One member of the advisory committee asked about the letter of 8 July 1966. Yazzie explained the freeze order. Annie Wauneka commented that work on the problem should continue, adding that we should ask for local help. Maloney expanded on her suggestion, advising us to contact the local leaders.

Yazzie explained that a good deal of our work thus far had been a search for records in places such as the Keams Canyon agency files. He emphasized the need for an attorney to deal with both the joint-interest area and the freeze area while the eviction proceedings against the Echo Canyon people were still pending in court in Phoenix. He urged that the council also support the negotiating committee with a resolution on the need for public works projects to continue in the two areas.

Frank Luther noted that the council had appointed a committee to deal with the need for legal representation. He expected the council to take the matter up in their next meeting. He said Lavell would remain in the area until the end of the month, and that the Echo Canyon people were retaining him to handle their interests in the eviction suit, so the council did not need to bother with that. Mrs. Wauneka thought that the temporary unavailability of tribal counsel constituted a poor excuse to abandon the Kabinto and George families. She asked that a letter from Lavell on the work that Lee and I were doing be distributed to members of the council. With that, the meeting was adjourned.[3]

Frankie Howard asked me to attend a meeting of the Tolani Lake Chapter that Saturday. Lee went with me, and we found that Pratt had also been invited. Howard began the meeting with a long talk on the history and status of the land dispute, ending by introducing the three of us.

Pratt spoke first, explaining his position and saying that in six months of trying, he had made little progress toward finding solutions. He did avoid the term "joint use," which impressed me as an indication that he was beginning to understand the problems somewhat better. He said that he was trying to find money to help the Echo Canyon people, but had thus far had no luck in Washington, so he hoped to obtain funds from the Navajo Tribe.

Pratt then went on to discuss the freeze area, suggesting that if the negotiating committees of the two tribes could settle that issue, it would help with the dispute inside the Executive Order Reservation. He had obtained, from the land operations people on both sides of the dispute, lists of all the things that needed to be done in the Executive Order area, and he had forwarded the lists to the Hopi attorney. He had also forwarded a request from the Navajos at Sand Springs for completion of the District 6 fence. He reported that the Hopis had discussed it for two weeks and then rejected it. The Hopis had wanted to take over law-and-order operations outside District 6, or have them placed under federal control, but when they found out how much it would cost, they changed their minds. He believed that the best solution would be for the Navajos to lease the Hopi interest in the surface rights. The Hopis were even opposing townsites for the employees of the new coal mine, which would be in operation within eighteen months, but some of their people would be among the employees. Overall, Pratt's summary of Hopi actions gave little reason for optimism.

When Howard called for questions from the floor, he got a strong but contentious response. Floyd Williams argued in favor of fencing District 6, for the Hopis could not be relied upon to keep their word, but always changed their minds. Joe Yazzie asked what would be the result if no agreement were possible between the two tribes. Pratt predicted that if that should come to pass, the matter would end up back in court. Yazzie responded that the BIA had been playing favorites on the Hopi side. Jerry Monroe, the chapter president, related a story told by his grandfather to the effect that the Hopis were eagle people meant to live on their mesas and get their meat from rabbits, while the Navajo religion was based on raising livestock. Kee Bahe complained that District 6 had already been extended twice, and now they were again trying to take land from the Navajos. He said the Navajos would never give up their land.

Earl Johnson asked when Pratt's appointment would expire and said he should not be wasting his time on the reservation on a job he could not do. Pratt admitted that he did not think he could settle the dispute, but he hoped to do a little good. Bahe then noted that the Navajos were increasing in number and that the District 6 line should be diminished rather than extended. Finally, Harry Bitsui, the chapter vice-president, called for a vote on fencing District 6. The "aye" vote was unanimous.

Howard then called on us. Lee described the Murphy allotments, showing where they were on a map. He explained that the lawyers believed that the Navajos who had been allotted land, even land inside District 6, still had individual rights, since the Prescott hearings had considered only tribal rights. He told of our interviews to identify the allotees and their heirs. I described the work we were doing relative to the freeze order and land rights around Moenkopi. This ended our part in the chapter meeting.[4]

The need for professional legal assistance had not gone unrecognized. Raymond Nakai had nominated Harold Mott, a Washington attorney who had done some personal legal work for the chairman, to be the new general counsel. As Mott had no experience in Indian law, Graham Holmes recommended against hiring him, but on July 20 the tribal council voted 39 to 28 to offer him a contract at $100,000 per year to cover his own salary and all expenses. Mott hired two other attorneys and a law clerk to help him.[5] Nakai insisted that Mott move to Window Rock immediately, which he did, although he still had to await approval by Secretary Udall before he could receive any pay from the tribe.

The tribal comptroller had issued a purchase order for the services of Lee and myself just before the end of the fiscal year in June; thus, we were able to continue our research on Moenkopi, but how long we might be able to work would depend on our field expenses. Toward the end of August I took the family to Tucson to visit friends, while I attended the Pecos Conference. While there, Dick Woodbury of the Smithsonian advised me to file an application with the Civil Service. Mott would inevitably have to be frugal in his expenditures, and I did not feel that I could depend on employment under his tenure.

In the meantime, the commissioner's initiative to stimulate negotiations did accomplish that at least. We were informed on rather short notice that the negotiating committee was to meet with Bennett and the Hopi committee on August 16 at the BIA area office in Albuquerque. Allen Yazzie asked Ed, Lee, and me to attend. Lee and I had been doing field surveys of current land use since May, and we felt fairly well prepared. Yazzie tried to round up as many committee members as possible. Ned Hatathli could not be contacted in time, which left only James Maloney to represent the people living inside the freeze order area, including Tuba City. We lacked other members whom we thought should also be present, but felt it was important to cooperate with the commissioner. Drake, Beck, Howard, and Ned Benally were available to make the trip, in addition to Yazzie. No attorneys were to be allowed at the meeting. Since Mott had been on the job only a few days and still did not have an approved contract, we believed that this restriction was in our favor, however.

It turned out that the meeting was to discuss the freeze order, Tuba City, and the Moenkopi problem. The Hopis appeared with a full complement of

Upper Moenkopi representatives, most from the Honanie family, but nobody from conservative Lower Moenkopi. Two of their people, Abbott and Robert Sekaquaptewa, were said to be Hopi law school students; they could and did speak legalese as well as ordinary English. Their delegation was led by their tribal chairman.

Both Graham Holmes and the acting Hopi Agency superintendent were present for the BIA, as was Richard Massey, who accompanied Bennett from Washington and who recorded most of the proceedings for him.

The morning session was largely taken up with listing all the various problems caused by the freeze order. Shortly before lunch the Hopis requested that an area to be set aside temporarily for exclusive Hopi jurisdiction. We adjourned at 11:30 so that the Hopi delegation would have time to decide just what area it was that they wanted.

In the afternoon the Hopis described the set-aside area they desired and traced it on a base map which we provided for them. They asserted that the source of their description was Roger Honanie, a Hopi stockman from Moenkopi who was present at the meeting. Although neither Lee nor I had met Honanie, we had both heard our Navajo colleagues in the Tuba City area characterize him as "mean" and as the Hopi most often involved in disputes with Navajos in that area.

Honanie claimed that three Navajos, Maxwell Yazzie, Tillman Hadley, and Billy Sawyer, had given the area to the Hopis through the mediation of a range rider named Joe O'Neal in 1937. Maxwell had recently been killed in a traffic accident, a premature death that some Navajos, probably most in the Tuba City area, attributed to Hopi witchcraft. Tillman Hadley, a former tribal judge, was in poor health, but was the only one of the four people named by Honanie who was still alive. He was not present at the meeting.

The area described stretched from Cameron on the southwest to Little White Mesa (also known as Middle Mesa) on the northeast. There was some confusion as to just where certain of the other boundary points might be. It was, however, clearly a much larger area than that which Gordon Page reported as having been set aside for the Hopis at about that time.[6] A substantial Navajo population resided within its borders. We could not imagine that Maxwell Yazzie, Hadley, and Sawyer could ever have taken it upon themselves to give away the homes of their friends, relatives, and neighbors so freely. It was clearly beyond the capacity of the Navajo negotiating committee to agree to even a temporary exclusive Hopi jurisdiction over so vast a tract, and it would obviously be political suicide for all of them even to recommend such an action to the tribal council.

Despite our misgivings, we did not want to be responsible for destroying the momentum for negotiations which Bennett had started. Some of us harbored dark thoughts that this was just what the Hopis were trying to get us to do. The Navajos finally concluded that they could safely ask the Hopis to show them the boundary points on the ground, in view of the uncertainty as to exactly where they might be located. The committee agreed to meet on August 30 and 31 so as to more precisely map out the Hopis' claim. Ed suggested that subcommittees be assigned responsibility for dealing with the three basic land uses of grazing, farming, and residential areas.

One member of the Hopi delegation stated that even if a temporary Hopi jurisdictional area should be set aside, they would not be willing to approve any of the public works needed at Tuba City. Thus, the incentive to establish such an area was greatly diminished even before the Hopis' request had been very well defined. It became less certain by far that the Hopis had made a serious proposal, even as a bargaining position.[7]

The next morning, back in Window Rock, we met with Mott to tell him about the meeting and to discuss what should be done. Mott concluded that we had been too easygoing and decided on a "get-tough" policy toward the Hopis.

Allen Yazzie and I attended a chapter meeting at Tuba City on August 20. James Maloney introduced us. Most of the discussions were in Navajo, resulting in rather sparse notes, but there was strong interest and a good turnout. Maloney began by telling about the meeting in Albuquerque. Yazzie then went into greater detail on the meeting, using maps to depict the legal status of various tracts of land, the area over which the Hopis had requested jurisdiction, and a boundary that Maxwell Yazzie had described to Ed Plummer a year previous. This last boundary received spontaneous applause. Maloney went on to tell of our plans for the mapping of the Hopi line.

A number of people made comments and suggestions. Maloney summed up the feelings of the community by stating that no Navajos would be willing to move voluntarily to make room for Hopi livestock.

Peter MacDonald was present and brought up a question that had been troubling me for some time, the possibility that if a Navajo delegation should accompany the Hopis on a tour to map the boundary the Hopis were requesting, it might be claimed years later by the Hopi Tribal Council that the expedition constituted Navajo recognition of their claim. But the commissioner had sufficiently impressed all of us with his effort to be fair. Consequently, our committee did not want to back out of their commitment to go over the Hopi proposal as promised. We could only hope that the commissioner was being given some real freedom of action by Udall, for we were all plagued by fears that Frankie Howard's allegations of collusion between Boyden and Udall might be true.

Back at the Navajo capital, I passed MacDonald's thought on to Mott, noting however that if Judge Hadley's account of the alleged 1937 events should expose Hopi duplicity, that could help overcome the disadvantages we faced in terms of tribal stereotypes.[8] I met the next day in Window Rock with Maloney, while Lee began a search for Joe O'Neal, for none of our people was aware that he was deceased. Graham Holmes provided help, asking William Fair, the area soil conservationist, to search the records of the Branch of Land Operations. This provided the names of two retired BIA officials then living in Flagstaff. We returned to Tuba City to follow up on leads obtained from the chapter meeting and from the area office.

I spent part of the morning looking for Hadley. I finally located his daughter's place in Tuba City and made an appointment to see him that afternoon. I then used the remainder of the morning to explore a portion of the surrounding country which I had not yet seen.

Lee spent the afternoon on a trip to Flagstaff where he learned that O'Neal had died some years earlier and that his widow lived in Tucson.

I had better luck. Hadley met me at his daughter's home and was willing to recount considerable local tradition and history. Hadley, who had been born about 1895, spoke good English, and could relate a good deal of the traditional history on the basis of knowledge he had received from his own ancestors. In addition, he could also tell stories he had heard from the Reverend William R. Johnston, an early missionary who had helped the western Navajos acquire title to their lands. Johnston had been known in Navajo as *Kinlichíí*, or "Red House." Hadley denied ever having helped O'Neal set a boundary, and added that even if he had been involved, he would have had no authority to grant land to the Hopis. He could recall no involvement with Maxwell Yazzie and Billy Sawyer, except about 1927 or 1928 when Governor Herbert J. Hagerman had held a meeting in Flagstaff, and he said that nothing had come of that because the Hopis claimed everything east of the San Francisco Peaks.

I was in need of an interpreter, as Paul Talker, who had worked with me earlier, now had a full-time job at Page, Arizona. Hadley recommended William Yellowhair, Sr., who lived in Kerly Valley. Following the interview, I drove to Yellowhair's home. He was not in, so I left a message that I would return and went to look at the ruins of a house near the bridge across the Moenkopi Wash, where Hadley had said an old Navajo named *Ch'iyáán Iił'íní*, "Cook," had lived when Hadley had herded sheep in the area as a child. I found the ruins easily, photographed them and then rented a motel room at Tuba City where I could write up my notes.

In the morning, I found Yellowhair at home. He was a middle-aged man with a rather affable, low-key personality that promised to go well with the kind of work we would be doing and was willing to work with me. We picked up Herbert Zonnie, a sixty-year-old man who was reported to know one of the boundaries set for the Hopis in the past. He did know a boundary, one that he said was established long ago by the Western Navajo superintendent. He had learned the landmarks from his father, and said that he had discussed them with others, including the conservative Hopis from Lower Moenkopi, who also knew of them. Of those who had helped establish the line, he said, only one was still alive, Frank Goldtooth.

We drove as much of the boundary as was accessible to our jeep, following it on a proper Navajo sunwise, or clockwise, circuit. A number of the points on or near the line were well-known landmarks with Navajo names such as *T'iis Ntsáázi Ií'áhí*, "Large Standing Cottonwood," *Tsé Dijool*, "Globular Rock," *Né'éshjaa' Ch'ah*, "Owl's Hat," and *Didzetsoh Łani*, "Many Peaches."

We next visited Johnson Etsitty, an elderly Navajo who lived at Many Peaches, to ask him about the boundary. He claimed to have learned it from his father, and said that both Joe Dale and *Tséyi'nii Tsoh* also knew it. He said that after the chapter meeting that I had recently attended, he, Joe Dale, and Emmett Tsoh had gone to various high points from which Dale had pointed out the landmarks that he knew, and that they were about the same as Johnson had learned them. He mentioned Owl's Hat and Many Peaches, but did not describe the entire boundary for us. He assured us, however, that it had been laid out a very long time ago. He described Roger Honanie as a Hopi who was against all the Navajos, and said it was only the stockmen from Upper Moenkopi who were making the large claim.

We were unable to locate *Tséyi'nii Tsoh*, but interviewed his wife, a woman in her seventies. We could estimate her age very closely, for she said that it was her maternal grandfather who had shot *Dághaa' Łichíí*, "Red Whiskers" or Lot Smith, and that she had been one month old at that time. Smith was shot in 1892 in a dispute between the Mormon settlers at Moenkopi and the Navajos.[9] She gave us considerable genealogical and historical information, but could tell us little that was specific about the boundaries. She did inform us that her father had had a farm at Large Standing Cottonwood.

Our final interview of the day was with *Chala Tsoh*, or Charlie Kisani, who lived southwest of Middle Mesa. He claimed to be 63 years old and knew only of Hopis coming to his area to trade with the Navajos. The only boundary marker to which he could attest was that at Many Peaches.

Lee had gone to interview Frank Goldtooth that morning, and from him he had obtained a detailed description of a boundary that Goldtooth had helped mark in 1937 with Maxwell Yazzie and a BIA employee whom he knew only as *Naakeeł Gaana*, "Skinny Eyes." Goldtooth narrated the boundary in a counter-clockwise circuit, or as he said, "in the whiteman's way."

This was a larger area than that shown me by Herbert Zonnie, but it dated from a later time. Only on the northeast corner at Large Standing Cottonwood and Globular Rock did it approximate the earlier boundary. On the west, *Tó Ndigishi*, "Spurting Spring," and *Tó Naalin*, "Spring Flowing Down," were the landmarks, while man-made features such as windmills, trails, and a gravel pit helped identify other points.

Herbert Goldtooth, one of Frank Goldtooth's sons, described a boundary that his grandfather had told him about. It was essentially similar to the boundary I was recording, but had somewhat different markers. It dated from the time of the Murphy allotments.

Lee also interviewed Scott Preston, the former tribal vice-chairman. Preston was recovering from a heart attack, but was able to confirm the 1937 boundary as described by Frank Goldtooth.

Both Goldtooth and Preston complained of Roger Honanie as a troublemaker for the Navajos, while Goldtooth named a few other Hopis who, in his words, "despised the Navajos," two of these also being members of the

Honanie family. He said that generally the Navajos and Hopis got along "pretty well."

The next week, Lee and I went together to see "on the ground" the Goldtooth boundaries. On August 29 we toured an early boundary, said to date from before the time of *Bila' Agodí*, "Cut Finger" or "Stump Finger", as Matthew Murphy was known. We had two four-wheel drive vehicles and were guided by Frank Goldtooth, Sr., and three of his sons. William Yellowhair was also in the party. Herbert Goldtooth said that Adolph Heavy, his mother's father, had shown him this boundary in 1941 "just in case trouble with the Hopis came up."

Both Lee and I kept notes, trying however not to duplicate each other by splitting the work. I also took photographs at the boundary points. We also recorded various bits of oral history, genealogical data, and information on land use as we went around the boundary.

That evening a meeting was held at the Tuba City Civic Center by the District 3 Grazing Committee, the District 3 Land Board, personnel from Window Rock, and several interested Navajos. Most of the discussion was held in Navajo and concerned the various traditional boundaries, the freeze order, and the Hopi claim. The proposed recording of the Hopi line was to begin the next day. Ed Plummer and his crew were to meet the Hopis at 9:00 in the morning. While they were engaged in that, Lee and I would continue our survey of the traditional boundaries.

Our group was considerably smaller on the second day. I drove the truck and Victor Sagenetso rode with me, while Lee had Frank Goldtooth, Sr., Frank, Jr., and Jerry Elwood from Ed's office in the jeep. Again Goldtooth followed a counter-clockwise circuit. The places to which he took us were those he had described to Lee the day before, and we also obtained additional Navajo place names. A dry lake bed on the western boundary was called *Tóbił Naiyoli*, "Windy Water," while a high place on a ridge on the eastern border was named *Łii' Hadit'ii'*, "Horse Lookout Point." A comparison of Sagenetso's line and that traced by Goldtooth made it clear that the two were not exactly the same. Sagenetso was describing a boundary of land set aside in 1926 or 1927 under the direction of Superintendent Chester L. Walker, known to the Navajos as *Naagaahi*, a translation of his surname, whereas the laying out of the 1937 line had been overseen by O'Neal. Still, they were similar, which may account for some of the confusion between them. They provided at least a rough idea of actual land use during the two decades before World War II.

Ed and some of his people spent the day with the Hopis. He said afterwards that even on the ground the Hopis had trouble agreeing on just where their line should go. As plotted, it differed from the line described in Albuquerque and took in somewhat less acreage. His crew was so far from us that we never saw each other during the entire day. They continued their work on the thirty-first, the same day that I revisited Johnson Etsitty to get from him a more complete description of the boundary that he knew.

With the information from this field work, I was able to define two traditional boundaries. One, an early line dating from after the turn of the century, measured some seven to eight miles east-to-west by about four and a half miles south-to-north and encompassed about twenty-seven sections. The later area was considerably larger, about seventy-six sections, the increase being on the east and south. These descriptions were adequate for negotiations, where reliance on historical precedents would not be as crucial as in a legal suit. Both were small enough to form the basis for an initial offer in hopes that bargaining would ultimately lead to agreement on an area approximating current use, as I understood it from earlier field work during the summer. I did feel that we needed more information on range use, however, for there was enough overlap that it was not easy to know just what division would be least likely to impact anybody's livelihood. The grazing and farming areas were sufficiently different that we did not try to combine the two.

Lee and I were busy preparing maps of our data and legal descriptions of our boundaries that might be used in negotiations. In the meantime, Allen Yazzie received a letter from Abbott Sekaquaptewa, the chairman of the Hopi negotiating committee. It was dated August 9, suggesting that it had been drafted even before the Albuquerque meeting. Yazzie called a meeting of the Navajo committee for September 19 at Window Rock to consider all that had transpired.

Yazzie opened the meeting by presenting the letter from Sekaquaptewa. Its language was sufficiently legalistic that we were not entirely sure just what it meant, but it seemed to imply that the Hopis were asserting a joint Hopi tribal interest in most of the Navajo Reservation in Arizona. After making this implied threat to the homes of tens of thousands of Navajos, Seka-quaptewa seemed to rather jovially invite the Navajos to negotiate, but asked them to make an offer to settle that the Hopis could consider prior to actually meeting. The letter claimed that the Navajos had illegally begun work on a low-rent housing project at Tuba City. It also asked that both committees be accompanied by their attorneys at the meeting.

Yazzie asked William McPherson, Mott's assistant, to explain just what Sekaquaptewa's letter meant. McPherson rather apologetically explained that the entire legal staff was so new that they needed time to research the law and to do a brief.

Lee and I explained the research we had done, but emphasized that we had worked on the historical, not the legal, aspects of the case. Yazzie said the advisory committee had turned down a request for funds to hire a full-time attorney to handle only this case. McPherson said he needed only a few hundred dollars to put some students to work for a few weeks. We promised to help him with as much of our data as possible, including a copy of the map that Lee had under preparation. We also offered to show him the country, and we set a date to meet at Tuba City on Friday.

At this point, Graham Holmes arrived and he was given a copy of Seka-quaptewa's letter. McPherson asked him if he thought we should negotiate or take the matter to court. Holmes replied that Congress could effect a settlement, but that negotiations were the least expensive course and that we should continue with them unless we hit a stalemate. He and McPherson agreed that the letter was merely a bluff, early sparring in an effort to place us at a disadvantage in the negotiations. Holmes suggested it was our turn to make an offer to the Hopis, and McPherson agreed.

James Maloney recited the history of the dispute with the Honanie family, adding that recently a man from the Branch of Land Operations Office at Keams Canyon had gone around with Roger Honanie, apparently to define the boundary over which Ed's people had been led.

The meeting recessed for lunch, and when we returned in the afternoon, we discussed the joint-interest area. Yazzie brought up the possibility of buying out the Hopi interest and thought that the federal government should do it.

Mott's contract still had not been approved. The eviction proceedings were on hold until the tribe should again have official legal counsel. Udall had attended the Navajo Tribal Fair, and there had promised that he would soon approve the contract.

Yazzie adjourned the meeting after deciding to try to set a date to meet with the Hopi committee, saying that he would make a report to the tribal council when they convened in October.[10]

The commissioner himself again scheduled the next meeting of the negotiating committees for October 14 in Flagstaff. Lee and I continued our research in preparation for this encounter, which we considered likely to be a crucial one.

I was back in the field the day after the committee meeting of the nineteenth, engaged primarily in interviewing older Navajos. While I encountered the usual problem of all-too-often visiting hogans when nobody was home, I was able to interview several people by the end of the week. Bill Yellowhair went with me as interpreter.

Our first interview was with *Tséyi'nii Tso*, whom we tried to find at his home and then finally located at a relative's house in Tuba City. He told us a good deal about early times in the area. Perhaps his most significant information concerned early Paiute presence nearby. He emphasized that Hopi stock did not range into his traditional use area because he returned wandering stock and got along well with the Hopis.

We then drove to Joe Dale's home in Kerley Valley. He was off herding sheep, so I spent some time identifying Navajo place names known to Bill until Dale returned. Dale also related considerable tradition. While he told a lot of family history, he could add little new to what we already knew. He did confirm some of the accounts about boundaries established for Hopi livestock. He also mentioned that the second superintendent after Murphy at Tuba City had affirmed a boundary for Hopi livestock. This superintendent was called *Naat'aanii Yazhi*, "Little Headman," and was apparently Clarence R. Jeffries. His line seemed to be quite similar to that attributed to Murphy.

We next found Alvin Nez by the side of the road and interviewed him only briefly. He was a grandson of the famous Navajo headman, Sam Bagody, so we decided it would be worth listening to him at greater length. We agreed to visit him again the next day.

In the morning, we first interviewed Tom Ferrell, a son-in-law of Alvin

Nez, primarily to learn the area in which he ranged his livestock. We also stopped at Bill Bryant's place, but only his wife and small daughter were at home. Their livestock consisted of only one horse, but Bryant was reputed to know about the Hopi boundary. We waited for him until it was time to keep our appointment with Alvin Nez and had to leave without seeing him. We spent the rest of the morning with Nez, who knew stories ranging back to the final time of the Navajo wars in the 1860s.

In the afternoon, we first visited Mrs. Maxwell Yazzie, hoping that she might still have Max's papers. She did, and allowed us to look through them, but we found nothing relating to the Moenkopi land issue. We then stopped at Cameron to interview Frank Johnson, but he was not at home, and we continued on south to talk with Clyde Peshlakai, who had assisted Max during his earlier investigation of the Moenkopi boundary. Clyde could still describe the boundary that Max had drawn on a map for Ed Plummer, but could not tell us about current use. He said that it was up to the Navajos of the Tuba City area to settle with the Hopis, a view much in accord with traditional Navajo values, reflecting the strong Navajo reluctance to interfere in another's decisions.

The next morning I met Bill McPherson. I first showed him a little of the country around the Pasture Canyon area so that he could get a feel for the terrain and settlement patterns. We then picked up Bill Yellowhair and tried, this time successfully, to locate Frank Johnson. Johnson was about seventy years old and had an exceptionally detailed memory of his family history. We spent the rest of the morning at his place. In the afternoon, I gave McPherson a short tour of some of the country southeast of Moenkopi and then took him to meet Judge Tillman Hadley, who related further traditions of Navajo life in the Tuba City area.

Lee and I continued to work on a map that would meet our needs in the negotiations, and we tried to foresee just what research would produce the most useful information. A number of the Navajos whom we had interviewed had mentioned the Paiutes who lived in the vicinity. In view of early documents that described Paiutes nearby, it seemed that we should give some attention to their occupancy. Work with the traditional Hopis of Lower Moenkopi was also considered, but we did not want to approach them without the aid of local Navajo leaders. We needed much more detailed data on the irrigated farms, especially those in Kerley Valley. Lee wanted to take on that project. We also realized that we would need a complete census of the Navajos living within the boundary of the Hopi claim for temporary jurisdiction. An initial guess was that there might be as many as 2,000 people affected, should the Hopis be allowed in that area, but we did not really know.

The Hopi threat to assert a half-interest in the entire region, while considered a bluff on the part of the Navajos' attorneys, did not appear an idle threat to us in view of the decision at Prescott and the continuing Hopi efforts to force removal of several thousand Navajos in the 1882 Reservation. The one place that we could see a possible strong bargaining stance was in the Hopi use of Navajo allotted lands near Tuba City. While Lee worked on land usage of the farm assignments, I began interviews of heirs to the allotments.

I found that the several heirs of two Navajo allotments did very much want to get their land back from the Hopis who had taken it over. They told me that the BIA was at that time in the process of doing probates for the inheritance of the allotments, which complicated the matter somewhat, but which had already aroused their interest. I could do little more than guess at what course the bureau employees might take in dealing with the rival claims, however.

Bill Yellowhair and I also played Paul Revere in a small way, going to see several people who were interested in the boundary question to let them know about the commissioner's meeting soon to be held in Flagstaff. Tillman Hadley lamented that too many Navajos did not realize how serious the matter was, but of those I visited, most said they would be there, and one family intended to send a representative even though they would be in the midst of a curing ceremony.

Three days before the Flagstaff meeting the Navajo negotiating committee held a session to plan strategy for the encounter. Mott's contract still had not been approved, and the commissioner had therefore again excluded the attorneys. Bill McPherson would be allowed to attend in the role of law clerk, but not as an attorney. From the Navajos' point of view, the emphasis of the meeting was to be Mott's new "get tough" policy, including a possible refusal to negotiate unless the freeze were lifted, rejection of the boundary requested by the Hopis, and several lesser points such as asking the commissioner to restrain "antisocial" people from intimidating the Navajos, a barb aimed especially at Roger Honanie.[11]

The negotiating sessions began at 9:00 A.M. in a conference room at the Americana Motel in Flagstaff. A Navajo effort to have representatives of Lower Moenkopi attend resulted in a refusal by the Hopi committee to meet should the Lower Moenkopi representatives be allowed in. The BIA ruled in favor of the Hopi position, and the Hopi traditionalists were excluded. The Hopi committee was chaired by Emory Sekaquaptewa and numbered eleven members, including the tribal chairman, Logan Koopee, and four members of the Honanie family. The Navajo committee, under Allen Yazzie's leadership, had eight members. Several BIA officials were present representing the Navajo and Phoenix area offices, the Hopi Agency, and the Tuba City Agency. Ed, Lee, and I were on hand, as was Bill McPherson. There was a large turnout of interested Navajos. Forty-six names appeared in the minutes, but a few more were not listed. Navajo spectators probably actually numbered well over fifty.

Commissioner Bennett chaired the meeting and gave an introductory talk. Yazzie asked that it be translated, to which Bennett agreed, and Claire Thompson, one of the interpreters for the Navajo Tribal Council, took over so that the older Navajos present might be able to follow what was said.

Bennett then called on Yazzie, who read a statement from Navajo Tribal Chairman Raymond Nakai. This was essentially a formal statement of the positions agreed upon at the planning meeting, including the reference to "antisocial individuals" who were identified only as Hopi, not by name. The statement raised the question of what would become of all the Navajos living on the land claimed if the Hopis were to get what they wanted. It also argued forcefully that the freeze order placed the Navajos at a disadvantage in the negotiations. Following this, Yazzie added on behalf of the committee the belief that unless the freeze order were revoked, or at least narrowed significantly, the Navajos really had no room to negotiate.

Bennett, rather than answer Yazzie's request immediately, called on Emory Sekaquaptewa to respond. Sekaquaptewa made a legal argument that the commissioner not only had to maintain the freeze, but that he should extend it to the entire Arizona portion of the Navajo Reservation. In retrospect, it would seem that the Navajos' legal staff should have anticipated this reply, but they were so new to the case and so overwhelmed with equally demanding problems, including whether they were even to have their contracts approved, that they had no way of predicting Hopi behavior.

Sekaquaptewa then called on the Hopi tribal chairman to make a statement. Koopee's speech was an assertion of the justice of the Hopi cause and an expression of disappointment that the Navajos refused to negotiate, a seemingly unquestioned acceptance of the finality of the Navajo opening statement. In hindsight, I suspect that he hoped the Navajos would call off the negotiations, allowing Boyden to proceed with lobbying for a bill to authorize litigation. As long as the two tribes were involved in any semblance of bargaining, such a bill stood no chance of passage. If the Navajos could be maneuvered into halting negotiations, that would give the Hopis an out for which they would not have to take the blame.

Yazzie next raised the problem of lack of approval of Mott's contract. Sekaquaptewa promptly retorted that Boyden was not present because the Hopis felt that legal matters should not be involved at that stage of the negotiations.

Bennett decided to get the discussion off that tack. He asked for reports from the leaders of the two delegations that had conducted boundary inspections of the area over which the Hopis had requested jurisdiction. He first asked Ed to tell the Navajo side.

Ed told of examining the alleged Hopi boundary on August 30 and of finding no monuments to indicate its presence. All boundary points were with reference to roads and windmills, man-made features, most of which post-dated the 1920s. He also had searched for documentation to support the line and could find none. He noted that the boundary as seen on the ground differed significantly, especially on the east and southwest, from that described in Albuquerque. He said it had been difficult to judge just what the significance might be of the farm lands claimed, in view of the absence of documentation, and he observed that the community lands were self-evident. He deferred making any statement as to the feeling of the Navajo people, saying that the negotiating committee should present that information, but he predicted that they would express those views during the meeting.

Bennett next gave the floor to Daniel Honanie to give his report on the mapping. Honanie began his talk by complaining that the Navajo delegation had been made up of people from outside the Tuba City area. He asserted flatly that the boundary shown during the inspection "was exactly what was shown and requested at Albuquerque and was no different." Following the examination of the farm land and allotted land on the second day, the two delegations had met at the community center. Minutes had been taken of that meeting, and Honanie read them. It was apparent from the minutes that James Maloney, at least, had been a member of the delegation, and thus Honanie's complaint of a lack of local representation was not really justified. The minutes also showed that Honanie had tried to get the survey delegation to engage in negotiations. This seems to have been inspired, at least in part, by reports that the Navajos intended to offer the Hopis only the area of Moenkopi village. Honanie tried to get a commitment from the Navajo mapping party that this would not be done. Both Ed and Maloney were firm in adhering to the limits of their authority and insisting that they had next to report to the full negotiating committee and to inform the local people. Honanie ended his report by asserting that the Hopis "were very sincere" in the matter and that he felt a great deal of work had been done with no result.

Yazzie then raised the issue of the freeze order again, followed by a lengthy plea by Maloney that the commissioner terminate the order, approve the Navajo legal counsel's contract, and see that Hopis not be given so many jobs in Navajo communities. He also elucidated the difference between the upper and lower villages at Moenkopi, saying that all the trouble was the fault of newcomers living in the upper village.

Following a coffee break, Bennett began alternately asking each chairman to call on a member of his committee to speak. Having begun with the Navajos for the first part of the morning, he now started with the Hopis. Sekaquaptewa named Daniel Honanie to give a prepared statement.

Honanie began by again making mention of the Hopis' sincerity, as well as their gratitude for the meeting. He then accused the Navajos of violating the freeze order by continuing work on the housing project, of not living up to their treaty, and of failing, along with the federal government, to enforce the grazing regulations. He cited a Hopi prophecy that the Navajos would have to return in exile to Fort Sumner if they did not settle the land question by negotiation.

It was then noted that the discussions were moving too slowly. In order to allow all to speak, Yazzie suggested dispensing with interpretation. He then asked Harold Drake to speak.

Drake's talk was short and addressed the commissioner's promise to do something about the freeze order. He recognized Bennett as Oneida, and in an effort to create less antagonism, if not real harmony, with the Hopis, he placed all the blame for the problem on the white man's laws.

The next Hopi speaker was Stanley K. Honanie. He also had a prepared statement. Following a recitation of his version of the history of the Moenkopi Hopis, his arguments were quite similar to those made by Daniel Honanie, but with specific references to certain Navajo Tribal Council resolutions and to the Navajo Grazing Regulations to support some of his contentions. After overt and implied accusations of wrongdoing on the part of the Navajos, he ended with a rather pious wish that the Navajos and Hopis might "be friends and neighbors together as we were meant to be."

After a recess for lunch, it was again the Navajos' turn to present a speaker. Pete Riggs, councilman for the Lechee District, took the floor. He repeated the complaints about the freeze and the lack of approval of an attorney contract. He indicated, however, that the Navajos did have some idea of what land the Hopis used, and he thought what was going on was so important that the commissioner should not be in a hurry to leave. He mentioned the Navajos who had come at their own expense to attend the meeting.

Emory Sekaquaptewa picked up on the suggestion that the Navajos could make a counteroffer, and he asked that they do so.

Bennett seemed to agree, but he first wanted somebody from the unofficial attendees from each tribe to speak. For the Navajos Tillman Hadley was recommended, and he was given an opportunity to speak first.

Judge Hadley spoke in Navajo, wondering just who was causing the controversy, for he said that he got along well with his Hopi neighbors. He disclaimed having ever given any Navajo land to the Hopis. He noted that he had been born and raised in the local area, had been a livestock owner all his adult life, and that he expected to spend the rest of his life raising stock there. He also observed that he knew only one Moenkopi Hopi among those present. He mentioned the traditional history recited by Stanley Honanie and offered to give the Navajo side. The commissioner noted, "We shouldn't have the time," whereupon Hadley thanked all concerned for the opportunity to speak.

The Hopis next called on Alton Honanie, Sr., then governor of Upper Moenkopi. He spoke in Hopi, and his talk was also translated. He accused Hadley of not knowing the history of his own people and claimed that the Navajo elders had withheld their traditions from their children, thereby causing the troubles that had arisen. He characterized the Navajos as aggressors who had come to make war on the Hopis. He said that the Navajos would have to become Hopi and cut their hair in Hopi fashion if they were to stay in the Tuba City area.

Bennett then asked for one last Navajo speaker, and Yazzie introduced Mark Begay of the Coal Mine Chapter. Begay spoke of the two areas that had been set aside for the Hopi stockmen years before, first a small area and then, as the Hopis had built up their herds, a larger tract granted because they and the Navajos were all poor people together. Now, suddenly, the Hopis were demanding a large piece of land where the Navajos lived, farmed, and grazed their own stock. He said the Navajos were willing to let the Hopis keep the area set aside for them in the past, but were not willing to allow the new claim, which he labeled absurd. He accused Roger Honanie of being behind this new claim and thought him to be "in cahoots" with the commissioner. Since he spoke through the interpreter, I suspect there was some confusion in the translation of bureaucratic offices and professional titles, concepts still alien to some tribal groups, and that he really meant to accuse the Secretary of the Interior, but this point was never questioned at the meeting.

The Hopis were also allowed one last speaker. They chose Abbott Sekaquaptewa to conclude their formal presentations. His talk was a plea for true negotiations and compromise, but in the process he held that the area the Hopis wanted for temporary jurisdiction was a compromise on the part of the Hopis and that the freeze was essential for the negotiations to continue. It was a speech equal in eloquence and guile to any argument that Boyden ever gave in court, a display of apparent reasonableness that conceded nothing.

Following this, Commissioner Bennett ended the meeting with rather extensive closing remarks. He began by announcing that the next negotiating session would be held at Casa Grande the twenty-seventh, twenty-eighth, and twenty-ninth of November, in hopes that a three-day working session would permit substantial progress. He asked Daniel Honanie and Ed Plummer to prepare recommendations regarding use areas, and hoped that the local people would be able to reach some agreements on their own which would not have to involve the negotiating committees and the tribal councils.

He went on to say that he would modify the freeze order to the extent of allowing construction to proceed on the new school and hospital. He further suggested that it might help to have a committee made up of local people to consider applications for future projects.[12]

On our return, Yazzie called a meeting of the Navajo negotiating committee to be held in Window Rock on November 15–16 to plan for the commissioner's November negotiations. Mott was in Albuquerque to see Bennett about the general counsel contract, leaving McPherson to attend the meeting. It was expected that the contract would be signed momentarily. Mc-Pherson reported that Bennett wanted the Navajos to make an offer in response to the Hopi request for an area of exclusive jurisdiction. The attorneys' advice was that the offer should be for a permanent settlement. Mc-Pherson did not expect an agreement to be reached in the upcoming meeting, but thought that we should be prepared in case the opportunity to compromise arose. During the morning session, I presented maps of the boundaries that might be used as offers in the negotiations. The critical questions for the committee were what would be the initial offer and what would be acceptable to the local Navajos as a final settlement.

In the afternoon Moe Christiansen of the Navajo Tribal Utility Authority (NTUA) joined us to explain NTUA's plans for extending electric service which were being hampered by the freeze order. These involved not only electricity for the local residents, but a possible allocation of power from the Glen Canyon Dam, a purchase of transmission facilities owned by the Arizona Public Service Company, and possible sale of electricity outside the tribe. Christiansen believed that the extent of the freeze was governed by Udall's connections with utility interests in southern Arizona, who wanted some of the same resources and customers for which NTUA was contending. He pointed out that the presidential election was approaching, but implied that the larger population in the southern part of the state would most likely be the deciding factor in how Arizona's electoral votes would go.

The next morning Ed made a presentation of his work. He asked that McPherson and the committee approve a letter he had drafted to Daniel Honanie. By this time, Ed had gone to work for the BIA. During his employment in the Nakai administration, he had found himself too often entangled in politics because of his family connections. His father was Ned Plummer and his mother-in-law Annie Wauneka, both leading figures in the Old Guard. BIA officials at Keams Canyon were already trying to force him to give them copies of work he had produced as a tribal employee in researching the land status issues of the 1934 Reservation. He had told them to go to the Navajo Tribe for that information. McPherson backed him up in his decision, saying that the material was the attorneys' "work product," and the BIA was not entitled to it.

The discussion then turned to the research Lee had done on the agricultural lands. He explained the difference between the farms on allotted land and the farmland assignments in the irrigation project, where assignees lost their rights if they failed to farm two years in succession. The Hopis had complained that they were not represented on the land board that oversaw the irrigation project. Lee had discovered that initially they did have a representative on the board, but that when the Navajo Tribal Council voted to pay Navajo representatives on land boards and the Hopi council declined to pay Hopi representatives, no Hopis were willing to serve. In response to Hopi pressures, Ned Hatathli had recommended to the board that no action be taken on Hopi land assignments. It also appeared likely that the heirs to the Navajo allotments that had been taken over by Hopis might be able to regain possession through probate. In addition, we had discovered that all the heirs to three of the Hopi allotments now lived off the reservation. We suggested that it might be possible to buy their rights to those allotments. Plans were made for the trip to Casa Grande before we adjourned.[13]

Because of a poor turnout for the first meeting, Yazzie called another for the twenty-second. A preliminary get-together was held with only three members on November 21 so that Mott could report on his discussion with Bennett in Albuquerque. Nakai had insisted that Mott's contract be for a flat $100,000 to cover all legal costs. The departmental solicitor in Washington refused to approve any contract that did not set a specific sum for Mott's salary plus expenses, in order to avoid any conflicts of interest. Thus, until the Secretary of the Interior should resolve that issue, Mott's contract remained unsigned. Mott asked those present whether they wished to go ahead with the Casa Grande meeting with only McPherson present to give legal help.

McPherson was not eager to confront Boyden, a much older and more experienced attorney, but was willing to go as the committee's advisor, if necessary.

Mott believed that a final settlement was a real possibility at the upcoming meeting and that the Navajos should have the best legal assistance possible. He recommended that if the contract were not approved by the twenty-seventh, the meeting should be postponed.

Graham Holmes joined the meeting by invitation and promised to call Bennett to tell him that if Boyden were to attend the meeting and Mott could not attend, because of his unsigned contract, they would have to hold off.[14]

The next morning the full negotiating committee convened. After a brief discussion of plans for presentations at an Agency Council meeting at Tuba City,[15] Holmes joined the meeting to report that he had talked with the commissioner and that the Casa Grande sessions had been cancelled.[16]

McPherson, Ed, and I went to Tuba City for the Agency Council meeting. McPherson and I spent that Saturday morning interviewing heirs to the Navajo allotments who had come to the Tuba City Civic Center. McPherson opened our meeting with the heirs by saying that, if necessary, the tribal legal aid service would file suit, but that he understood from the area director that if the legal department merely filed a request with the BIA for the return of the allotments, the BIA would comply. The purpose of the meeting was to determine just what the heirs wished to do. A large number of the heirs were present. They were in agreement among themselves that they did indeed want the land returned to them.

In the afternoon we attended the Agency Council meeting, along with Ed, Allen Yazzie, and Clifford Beck. Yazzie gave a talk summarizing the history of the land dispute and recent happenings such as the meetings of the negotiating committees. He then called on Ed, who presented a map to show the area affected by the freeze order, the Hopi claim, and the various land status areas. I described the work that Lee and I were doing to map present-day use and occupancy. There followed a long and spirited discussion, mostly in Navajo, with several of the speakers receiving applause.[17]

Shortly after this meeting, Lee and I began a survey with the assistance of grazing committee members to ascertain in greater detail actual land use over a much wider area. Our funds were running low, however. By the end of January we were working without any appropriation in hopes that the council would act so that we might be paid. This made family life a bit tenuous, and I resolved to take any other job I might find, for I feared the strains would affect my family's attitudes toward the Navajos. In addition, I was beginning to have doubts about Mott and felt that I did not want to work too closely with the man. His get-tough policy seemed dangerous if not informed by facts, but his personality caused me as much concern. He could change from being cordial to an all-business attitude in such an abrupt fashion that it was unsettling, making me wonder how much was real and how much mere acting. The deciding factor came when he told me that he intended to get rid of Lee and keep me on. I said nothing, but from that moment on my search for a different job took on a new urgency.

Mott's contract was finally approved, despite the reservations of the solicitor. Bennett then set a new date for the resumption of negotiations, 3–4 April 1968 in Phoenix.

In February, meanwhile, our operation was reorganized as the Research Section and was made a part of the Tribal Parks and Recreation Department. I was still planning to leave whenever I could find another position, but I felt an obligation to carry through with my part of the upcoming negotiating session. I also tried to leave much of the new Hopi research for Lee to do, as I would thus be less important for carrying on beyond that time. I hoped that something would come of the next meeting and that Lee would be able to handle any follow-up easily by himself. Our new organizational location removed us somewhat from legal work, however, and we found ourselves assigned new duties and involved in bureaucratic processes that were new to us. Long meetings during which most of the discussion concerned park issues for which we had no responsibility cut into our time for our own work.

The commissioner's April meetings were held in the conference room of the Phoenix Indian School. Harold Drake served as chairman for the Navajo committee, since Allen Yazzie could not attend due to his wife's illness. Commissioner Bennett opened the meeting by calling on Samuel P. Shing, governor of Upper Moenkopi, for an invocation. Shing was an elder in the Mormon church and gave a Christian prayer. Bennett next asked the members of the two committees to introduce themselves. He then made a brief opening statement, encouraging both sides to work toward a solution. He called first on Drake to begin the negotiations.

Drake first asked Carl Beyal to interpret the commissioner's remarks. Following this, Drake gave a short talk emphasizing friendship and the need to settle the disagreement. Emory Sekaquaptewa expressed similar sentiments. The meeting was then recessed for an hour to allow each committee to meet separately with its staff.

Mott took charge of the meeting of the Navajo committee, beginning by saying that the 1934 Reservation belonged to the Navajos and that any land conceded to the Hopis amounted to giving away Navajo land. He asserted that it was not possible to negotiate away any Navajo territory. The only offer to make was a line around the Moenkopi villages. The dispute was going to have to go to court; anything that the committee offered would be that much of an advantage for the Hopis when the question finally ended up in litigation. It was also to the government's advantage for the two tribes to draw lines as close together as possible. McPherson seconded Mott's views, agreeing that everything outside of the village should be claimed as exclusively Navajo.

Beck brought up the problem of the freeze and its effect on the people's lives. Mott advised that discussions be limited to the 1934 Reservation area, thereby avoiding any linkage to the stalemate in the joint-interest area, which could be a subject of a claims case later on. McPherson added that the only freeze order with which they should be concerned was that in the 1934 Reservation. I personally feared that such a claim—that only the village was legitimately Hopi land—was such an extreme position that it undermined the Navajos' credibility as negotiating in good faith, but the committee agreed to this as a first offer.

The Navajos had committed themselves to making an offer at Flagstaff. Bennett therefore asked Drake to begin with a Navajo proposal when we reconvened. Drake called on me to present my map of Moenkopi as it existed in 1934 and to explain how the boundary was derived. I noted four events that determined the village lines on my map. The first was the allotment program beginning in 1892 which led to the eleven Hopi and five Navajo allotments which were patented in 1905. Second was the withdrawal of the Executive Order Reservation of 1900. The third was the survey of house lots for Upper Moenkopi by Superintendent Sullivan in 1913. Finally, there was the Boundary Act of 1934. An aerial photo taken of Moenkopi in 1934 provided a clear picture of the extent of both the upper and lower villages at that time. My map took in all of the village area outside of the allotted lands, which were, of course, not tribal property. I tried to explain the Navajo position clearly by saying, "The Navajo Tribe believes that all of the land outside of the allotments and this area, is Navajo land, and that the area within is what the Hopis legitimately have a claim to on tribal rights, and that all Hopi use outside of this area is permissive use at the sufferance of the Navajos for trespass."

Sekaquaptewa asked the first question, wanting me to show how much area the Hopis were then using at the sufferance of the Navajos. I explained that we were still doing research on that question, not wanting to get prematurely into the data upon which we might base subsequent offers. A severe snowstorm had forced us to suspend our field work, and we did have considerable research yet to do if we were to be sure that our information on Hopi use was complete.

Sekaquaptewa then tried to get Ed to reveal whether local Navajos had participated in formulating the line I had described. Ed also avoided a direct answer, referring the issue to the attorneys. Sekaquaptewa then began to ask Ed questions relating to the legal interpretation of the 1934 Boundary Bill, in a manner not unlike a lawyer's cross-examination. McPherson came to Ed's rescue. He extricated us from the legalisms in which Sekaquaptewa seemed to be trying to enmesh us by emphasizing that this was basically an offer in the course of negotiating a settlement, not an action to establish what might be a legitimate claim.

Bennett chaired the session very skillfully, congratulating the Navajos on making the first concrete offer for a settlement. He asked the Hopi committee to study their copy of my map and to make a counteroffer of their own after lunch.

Mott had been called away for a telephone call during much of this exchange. He returned as I was answering a question for Sekaquaptewa regarding Navajo population figures. Sekaquaptewa suggested that we break for lunch early. Mott interjected with a demand that the Hopis also present us with an offer. Bennett explained the procedure that he had formulated for the negotiations, saying that he was allowing the Hopis time to decide upon their reply during the lunch recess.

Following lunch, Sekaquaptewa introduced John Boyden, who immediately launched into an extended statement of his legal theory as to the status of the lands in the 1934 Reservation, implying a threat to claim half of all of the reservation that was not explicitly Navajo and charging that the Navajo offer was not made in good faith. This, of course, brought a strong response from Mott, and the two engaged in legal wrangling based on a mutual lack of understanding of the facts, leaving most of us quite confused. Members of both committees were led to ask questions that were not particularly germane. James Maloney apparently took Boyden's threat personally, for it would, if carried out successfully, clearly mean that Maloney and his family would lose their homes. Maloney made such an intemperate reply that Bennett ordered major portions of it stricken from the record.

Bennett remained calm, however, and asked Drake if his committee was prepared to receive in good faith any offer made by the Hopis. Drake assured him that they were. Sekaquaptewa then began a rather self-serving statement of his own, but quickly added that he wanted a short recess. Following the recess, Sekaquaptewa proposed that the area of the freeze order, excepting only those national forest lands specifically termed Navajo reservation land by congressional acts in 1930 and 1931, be considered Hopi land. In response to a question from Mott, Sekaquaptewa added that the former railroad sections already deeded to the Navajo Tribe that were inside the freeze area were also included in the lands the Hopis wanted. Bennett then adjourned the meeting until the next day, asking the Navajo committee to prepare a counteroffer for the morning session.

As he had the previous day, Bennett began the session on the fourth with an invocation, this time calling on Maloney, who prayed in the Navajo language. Drake was then asked to present the Navajos' response to the Hopi offer. The Navajos' initial offer had encompassed some 75 acres, while the Hopis first counteroffer took in about 2,500,000 acres. We were quite far apart and Drake reported that the Navajo committee, in its turn, could not agree to the Hopi line. He questioned the sincerity of the Hopi offer and of Boyden's claims. He noted that the Navajo committee represented nine grazing districts and that the Navajos were united in their position. He observed that only Upper Moenkopi was represented on the Hopi committee, and he asked whether there was anybody who represented the lower village. Melvin Tewa raised his hand. There was immediate objection from several members of the Hopi committee and a long discussion on procedure. Ultimately, Bennett ruled in favor of the Hopi committee, refusing to recognize Tewa.

Bennett next asked Drake if there was a Navajo counteroffer. Drake asked for a short recess. After a brief discussion, the committee voted to present my second boundary proposal. The offer was subject to a number of conditions, such as exclusive Hopi use inside the boundary and exclusive Navajo use outside, preservation of existing water rights, and being subject to approval by the Navajo Tribal Council and the Hopi Tribal Council within sixty days of the Navajo council's action.

Drake presented the map and conditions to the Hopi delegation upon reconvening, and Bennett was very congratulatory on this step forward. Sekaquaptewa asked for a description of any monuments or landmarks. Drake again called on me. I read into the record a prepared description of the boundary, avoiding any additional comments that might lead to another embarrassing entanglement in discussions which properly belonged to the committee's mandate.

Sekaquaptewa was sufficiently impressed by our efforts that he immediately asked for a recess during which they could consider the offer.

Drake asked that before we recessed he be allowed to make a statement, which Bennett permitted. He again brought up the issue of the freeze order. Before there was any answer on this, Sekaquaptewa asked that Boyden be allowed to ask a legal question. Boyden wished to know if our offer excluded the 1882 Reservation in the area of exclusive Navajo use, and Mott assured him that it did. Bennett then declared a recess to last until after lunch.

I think that the very fact that we had come to the meeting prepared to make explicit offers took the Hopis by surprise. Our second offer enclosed 19,353 acres and, in my mind, constituted our first really serious offer. Even though we felt it unlikely that the Hopis would accept it, I considered it a demonstration of dealing in good faith to work toward an ultimate solution, and I believe most of the Navajo committee thought the same. The Hopis would find it very difficult to assert convincingly that the Navajos were not negotiating in good faith. I feel confident that they recognized this fact, but whether they considered it an opportunity or an obstacle is not so clear.

Bennett called the meeting to order again at 1:40 P.M. Sekaquaptewa gave every indication that he felt progress had been made. While rejecting our offer, he was ready with a counteroffer that encompassed something over half of the area included in their initial offer, or about 1,556,582 acres. The counteroffer included only lands in Grazing District 3. Other conditions included the standard provisions for exclusive Hopi use inside the line, exclusive Navajo use outside, except for the 1882 Reservation, and a requirement for further negotiation on shrines and water rights.

Bennett was pleased with this progress. He gave the Navajo committee a thirty-day period in which to submit any counteroffer and appointed a committee of three members each from the Navajo negotiating committee (Allen Yazzie, Drake, and Maloney), the Hopi committee (Emory Sekaquaptewa, Stanley Honanie, and Logan Koopee), and the BIA (Fred Massey of the Washington office, LaFollette Butler of the Phoenix Area Office, and Kent Fitzgerald of the Navajo Area Office). This committee was to convene in May. Their decision would be presented to the tribes for their comments, on the basis of which legislation would be drafted.

Bennett had to leave early, but granted a recess for the Navajo committee to discuss the situation, appointing Massey to preside over the final details after the recess. The committee met and voted 6 to 0 to reject the Hopi counteroffer, and 4 to 1 to go along with Bennett's smaller committee.

When Massey reopened the meeting, Drake gave a formal rejection of the counteroffer, but said that the Navajos would continue to negotiate and would accept Bennett's proposal for the nine-member committee. The meeting ended in mid-afternoon amid mutual congratulations on the progress made and the encouraging prospect of a final settlement.[18]

I soon attended a chapter meeting at Cameron where the outcome of the Phoenix meeting was reported by Maloney, Ned Benally, Claire Thompson, and myself. There was a large crowd present, which included representatives from several nearby chapters. The issues were discussed at length and a motion passed in support of the negotiating committee's work.

The good feelings engendered by the end of the negotiating sessions did not run deep. I confided to various colleagues shortly after the meeting that I was very upset by the theatrics of both the Hopi and Navajo attorneys, who had not done their homework before attending the meeting. I felt that the two sides should have been able to come much closer to agreement had so much time not been squandered by the attorneys' uninformed argumentation. Had Bennett not exerted considerable pressure behind the scenes, the negotiations would probably have broken down the first day. Bennett later recalled experiencing the same sort of frustration, and he blamed the lawyers for the ultimate failure of the negotiations, despite the fact that he himself was an attorney.[19] While I admired Bennett's skills as a mediator in a dispute between Indians, I had little hope of ultimate success.

One last attempt to schedule negotiations in Albuquerque while I was still at Window Rock broke down when Bennett was ordered to remain in the nation's capital during the Poor People's March on Washington. When the two delegations met in Albuquerque, the Hopis, who had advance notice that Bennett could not be present, immediately decried the commissioner's absence, but when the officials from Washington appeared, quietly let the Navajos echo the Hopi complaint and receive the blame for the failure to negotiate.

My time with the tribe was rapidly running out. In May I participated in a panel discussion on Navajo education organized by Allen Yazzie. I had developed strong opinions on how to incorporate Navajo history and culture into curricula for Navajo students and expressed some of these quite freely. Another member of the panel was Gary Witherspoon, who was working at Rough Rock Demonstration School, an innovative school run by a local Navajo board under a contract with the BIA. He said afterward that they would like for me to work at Rough Rock. Over a weekend I drove the family to Rough Rock to see the school and to discuss the offer. The job not only appeared to offer an ideal opportunity to apply some of my ideas in writing textbooks for use in Navajo schools, but it would pay a bit more than I was then earning at Window Rock, and we would probably be assigned a larger house than we had in tribal employee housing.

I submitted my resignation and talked with Shirley Sells, a Navajo woman in a master's program in anthropology at Arizona State University, about the possibility that she might be my replacement. The tribal administration, however, used my leaving as an excuse to eliminate my position.

My new job was short-lived, for I soon discovered that liberal as were my opinions, they were not as liberal as those held by the school administration. When I was asked to write Navajo religious traditions as "history," I felt compelled to resign on short notice. I was fortunate in securing a position as curator for the National Park Service at Hubbell Trading Post National Historic Site, one of the oldest trading posts in Navajo country and recently acquired by the government. This kept me among the Navajos, but I was an outsider now as to further developments in the dispute between the two tribes. One Navajo friend even asked me how I could go to work for the enemy. I had not told Lee about Mott's plan to fire him and learned much later that he felt I had deserted him. He was never to learn the full story.

CONFRONTATION

THE NEGOTIATIONS REMAINED alive, but barely so. Few people other than Bennett had faith in their potential to solve the land problems. The Hopis supported them only for advantages that might be exploited later in the courtroom and covertly tried to undermine them, while the Navajos followed Bennett's lead because he was a fellow Indian whom they wanted to trust. Nevertheless, they remained ever suspicious and ready to balk at the slightest hint of betrayal. With limited land and unlimited population growth facing both tribes, the attorneys' self-righteous posturing inevitably spawned greater ethnic discord than enlightened discourse.

There were new issues in Navajo tribal politics which took much of the attention of officials at Window Rock away from the land dispute. One that especially involved the Legal Department concerned a new legal aid service, *Dinébe'iina Nahiilna be Agaditahe* (DNA), established under the war-on-poverty programs. The first director of this agency was Theodore (Ted) R. Mitchell, a young attorney who had a law degree from Harvard. He had first come to work on the reservation in 1965 for the tribal legal aid service. He had been brought up as a Mormon, but no longer considered himself a member of the church and had very liberal views. I had initially found my new neighbor on Manuelito Drive quite interesting. My wife and his wife became friends, both having connections with the Unitarian Church. I helped introduce Ted to Navajo culture, even taking him to his first Squaw Dance at an Enemyway held near Fort Defiance. He had strong opinions on policies that might promote Navajo interests, some of which I thought quite sound, while others seemed to be based on conspiracy theories that I thought rather difficult to validate. He eventually became highly critical of Littell, and Littell apparently heard of his remarks, for he seriously considered firing Mitchel. At one point I put in a good word for him, but I doubt that I had any significant influence. Ted left tribal legal aid services in March 1966, but returned in January 1967 to head DNA.

As an activist organization, DNA and its young director quickly gained both friends and foes. Mott and Bill McPherson initially relied on the cooperation of DNA attorneys for the protection of the rights of heirs to allotments in the Tuba City area. By the time I was moving to Ganado in 1968, however, even Nakai was opposing Mitchell, and the Advisory Committee soon voted to exclude him from the reservation. This, of course, led to a bitter legal struggle which consumed a good deal of Mott's time, energy, and limited budget.

Mott's handling of the Mitchell case convinced me, long before it had run its course in the courts, that he was not up to the job and that Mitchell could prevail, as he did. Mott also immersed himself in writing a constitution for the tribe, another project that ultimately withered in the heat of tribal politics. The Hopis seem to have been forgotten in the turmoil. According to Bennett, the negotiating committees "just sort of faded."[1]

The election of 1968 brought a change of administration in Washington. Nakai's close relations with the Lyndon B. Johnson Democrats did him no good among the Richard Nixon Republicans. Bennett continued in a position that had, for him, an uncertain future. As soon as Walter Hickle was appointed Secretary of the Interior, Bennett knew that he would be replaced. Prior to coming to Washington, he had been BIA area director in Alaska. Hickle was then governor of that state. Bennett's efforts to protect the land rights of the native peoples had brought him into conflict with the governor. Rather than wait for Hickle to fire him, Bennett submitted his resignation to the President and took retirement.[2]

Shortly before Bennett left, a Navajo delegation made up of the negotiating committee and another committee seeking support for education of Navajo children visited him in Washington. They made one last plea that he relax the freeze order. Bennett was reported later to have stated that the Moenkopi land question would have to go to Congress.[3]

Bennett did attempt to adjust the Moenkopi boundary, at least, writing Nakai in May to propose that some 105,000 acres be set aside for the Moenkopi Hopis. His proposal was based largely on the Page line of 1939.[4]

Lee was fully occupied with other projects in Window Rock. Research for both the 1882 and 1934 Reservation areas was in abeyance.

In September the negotiating committee flew again to Washington. The U.S. attorney in Arizona had filed for eviction of the Echo Canyon people, and one of the committee's objectives was to ask for dismissal of that suit. There were rumors that they also intended to propose a land exchange with the Hopi Tribe, but if they did, nothing came of it.[5]

In October the Economic Development Administration canceled a multi-million dollar grant for a road on Black Mesa due to the impasse on the land.[6]

Toward the end of January 1970, another Navajo delegation left for Washington to make yet another effort to gain federal recognition of the increasingly difficult situation of their people living in the joint-interest area. The *Gallup Independent* published such an anti-Navajo characterization of their mission that I felt obliged to respond with a letter to the editor.[7] This may have had some slight effect on the paper's report of the results of the trip, which, while not so strongly worded against the Navajos' cause, was not really sympathetic either.[8]

The delegation, having concluded that negotiations between the two tribes had failed, had suggested that the Hopis' interest in the 1882 Reservation outside of District 6 be purchased. The Arizona representatives, Morris Udall, John Rhodes, and Sam Steiger, advocated, despite party differences, that the area should remain jointly owned, with authority over development controlled by a commission on which the Navajos, Hopis, and BIA were equally represented. Senators Barry Goldwater and Paul Fannin, both Arizona Republicans, refused to make any commitment without consulting with others. Goldwater wanted to ask the Hopis their opinion, and Fannin wanted to consult with other Arizonans in Congress. Only Senator Clinton P. Anderson of New Mexico was won over. Joseph M. Montoya, the other senator from New Mexico, said that he might back the idea of a purchase should Anderson, Goldwater, and Fannin all agree to it.[9]

In February Harrison Loesch, Assistant Secretary of the Interior, wrote to Nakai affirming Bennett's suggestion for an administrative area to be set aside for the Moenkopi Hopis subject to subsequent legislative resolution.[10] Proposals for legislation would soon appear.

The Hopi Tribe had not been idle. On March 16 the tribe petitioned in federal court in Tucson for a writ of assistance or order of compliance "to enforce its rights as co-tenants."[11] In April at a hearing on this petition, Boyden was at his best with his overblown rhetoric, asserting that, as soon as the Hopis had been awarded a joint interest in the lands outside District 6, Navajos had begun to stream onto the land, increasing their numbers "to overgraze, damage and destroy" the resources of the area. He characterized the situation as "one of the most flagrant examples of total disregard of minority rights now in existence in the United States." The *Gallup Independent*, in reporting the court action, quoted and paraphrased extensively from Boyden's statements, but any defense raised by Mott was ignored. Presiding was Judge James A. Walsh, who had been a member of the three-judge court in Prescott. He heard both sides and ordered that briefs be submitted.[12] It would appear that Mott's defense was based on the question of jurisdiction, for that was the basis of the decision. Walsh concluded that joint-interest lands were reserved for further action by Congress.[13]

In the meantime, the eviction suit against the Echo Canyon people was also slowly moving through the federal courts. On April 13, District Court Judge Walter E. Craig postponed a ruling on a U.S. attorney's request for a summary judgement while denying a motion for dismissal by the Navajo defendant's attorney.[14] On April 27 Craig ruled against the Navajos, but stayed the eviction order for sixty days to allow an appeal to be filed.[15] The case finally was appealed to the Ninth Circuit Court in San Francisco.[16]

The big news for the Navajos in July, however, was the decision by the Indian Claims Commission in the Navajo Land Claim case, declaring that the tribe had originally had aboriginal title to some 38 million acres. Mott had said that as tribal attorney he would stay out of tribal politics, but he claimed major credit for himself and Nakai in this decision. His dismissal of Littell's role in the case as almost inconsequential struck me as being as politically slanted as any of Littell's dabbling in tribal politics.[17]

Politics obscured all else as Navajo tribal election time approached. The nominating convention in August made the race for the Chairman's position a contest between Nakai and Peter MacDonald. In November MacDonald won by a decisive majority. Mott resigned as tribal general counsel following Nakai's defeat.[18] Mott had been an issue in MacDonald's attacks on Nakai, much as Littell had been one of Nakai's campaign issues in his victory over Paul Jones. MacDonald was more fortunate in being able to bring in his own choice of attorney in the March following his election. George P. Vlassis of the Phoenix firm of Brown, Vlassis and Bain became the key attorney, although the general counsel contract was with the firm. Vlassis brought with him Lawrence Ruzow, a younger man, as an assistant.[19] Once again, a change in tribal administration brought a complete change in attorneys and a need for them to learn about the pending cases.

Opponents of the Navajos were quick to take advantage of this lack of continuity. One long-time politician who seemed especially eager to do so was Representative Sam Steiger. In 1969 he had managed to entice the Navajo Tribal Council into waiving their Winters Doctrine water rights in the Colorado River for only 750 acres of land.[20] Toward the end of the 91st Congress late in 1970 he made an initial effort to partition the surface rights of the joint-interest area, prompting the Navajo council to pass a resolution opposing partition in its first session in 1971.[21]

Undeterred by this Navajo action, Steiger introduced two bills in the House of Representatives in February. The first, H.R. 4753, was entitled "A Bill to Authorize the Partition of the Surface Rights of the Hopi and Navajo Indian Tribes in Undivided Trust Lands, and for Other Purposes." The second, H.R. 4754, was intended to partition the 1934 Navajo Reservation, setting aside a large tract for the Hopi Tribe, and to authorize allotments for Paiutes living within the 1934 Reservation.[22] Then, in October, Steiger introduced H.R. 11128, a revision that combined the two earlier bills into one.[23]

In 1970 the Hopi council had passed a new ordinance making Navajo livestock inside District 6 subject to impoundment by the Hopi Tribe. Enforcement of the regulation became more vigorous as the movement for partition grew, apparently in hopes of provoking Navajos to violence in order to arouse public sympathy for the Hopi council faction.[24] Certainly, the Hopis managed to gain attention from the press, and they made accusations against the Navajos, alleging intentional trespass when horses and cattle on open range crossed the unfenced boundary. Some Navajos attempted to release impounded horses from a corral one night in early November, and the Hopis drove them away with gunfire.[25]

Navajo Chairman MacDonald met with Hopi Chairman Clarence Hamilton, hoping to persuade him to call off an auction of about sixty Navajo horses and to get an agreement to fence the boundary. Hamilton rejected both proposals.[26] Two people had been injured in disputes over straying livestock, and the federal government was about to take over law enforcement in the area. Following the legal advice of Vlassis, the Navajo Tribal Council authorized funds to fence the exterior boundary of the Hopi Reservation (District 6) and passed a resolution asking that the federal government not intervene.[27] Abbott Sekaquaptewa promptly challenged the Navajos' right to build the fence, proclaiming that it would create "a concentration camp of Hopis." He also opposed the use of Navajo police and supported the government plan for a separate police force and court in the joint-interest area.[28]

The Hopis then hired an Anglo cowboy to patrol their boundary, a man described by Kammer as a "feisty former rodeo cowboy who liked to throw his weight around."[29] The Hopis repeated their charge that the Navajos deliberately drove their stock across the line. By the end of November the cowboy, Elmer Randolph, had already fired his gun at a Navajo whom he accused of drawing a gun.[30]

The Navajo Tribe had begun construction of their fence, but at the request of Commissioner of Indian Affairs Louis Bruce, MacDonald halted the work for two weeks to allow time for the two tribes to reach some kind of agreement.[31]

The *Gallup Independent* on December 3 published an editorial strongly supporting the Hopi position, but urging that the two tribes resolve the dispute by negotiation.[32] Florence Holmes, a Navajo, the granddaughter of an army scout, wrote objecting to the obvious prejudice in the editorial and to complain that her family had already been evicted from long-held lands by the Hopis.[33]

In the midst of this dispute, the Ninth Circuit Court of Appeals reversed Judge Walsh's decision and ordered that he hold another hearing to determine how to assist the Hopis in asserting their interest in the disputed land.[34]

The *Gallup Independent* published on its editorial page an account of the Hopi side of the dispute. The paper promised to follow this later with the Navajo side and an analysis of the Steiger bill.[35] The disparate views of participants saw further expression in the *Navajo Times* in letters by David Monongye, a traditional Hopi religious leader at Hotevilla who claimed the land for all Indians including the Navajos;[36] by Joanne Yazzie, who urged that the two tribes maintain harmony;[37] and by the Reverend Caleb H. Johnson, a Hopi who began to take an interest in the matter as an advocate of the views of the anti-Council faction.[38]

The contest for support in Congress was rapidly escalating. The Indian

Inter-Tribal Council of Arizona, toward the end of January 1972, endorsed the Steiger bill, a major coup for the Hopis.[39]

A decision by the Ninth Circuit Court, in a second appeal by the Navajo Tribe in which a request for a new hearing was denied, became the occasion for another major news story in Gallup presenting the Hopi case and advocating passage of the Steiger bill.[40]

The contest was proceeding on several fronts. While the lawyers argued in the courts, and many partisans tried to influence public and congressional opinion, the people on the land found themselves increasingly locked into more serious clashes. The Hopis' range rider, Elmer Randolph, had begun to shoot at Navajos when they crossed into District 6 to retrieve strayed livestock, and on occasion to arrest them for trespass. The numbers of animals impounded increased dramatically. Apparently successful Navajo efforts to release their stock from the Hopi corrals led to the construction of a steel corral that would be more difficult to penetrate. MacDonald feared that more violent encounters were in the offing, but he found the Hopis unwilling to help lessen the growing antagonisms.[41]

Environmentalists were beginning to take a part in the debate also. A Los Angeles TV station, KABC-TV, produced a five-part series on the problems raised by stripmining coal on Black Mesa. Following this, the Hopi tribal chairman, Clarence Hamilton, issued a statement attacking the series for failing to present the views of the Hopi tribal government. Al Wiman, reporter for the station, responded with a letter noting that Hamilton had refused to be interviewed and charging that his statement had actually been prepared by a Salt Lake City public relations firm, "West Associates," which represented a consortium of twenty-three utilities.[42] The full name of "West Associates" was actually Western Energy Supply and Transmission Associates, or WEST, its preferred acronym; the public relations firm was actually David W. Evans and Associates.[43] The environmentalists, for a while at least, by siding with the Hopi traditionalists, were also indirectly siding with the Navajos.

Thomas Banyacya, interpreter for the Hopi traditionalists, spoke to the Governor's Advisory Commission on the Arizona Environment, relaying the decision of a group of Hopi elders that Hamilton should no longer be considered a Hopi because he "had joined a white man's church, had taken a Navajo wife and recently was found intoxicated." Banyacya then stated the religious leaders' opposition to the coal leases on Black Mesa in terms of Hopi belief and prophecy. Wiman also addressed the commission to defend his TV series, repeating his charges that the utility companies were putting words into the mouth of the Hopi Chairman.[44]

The next day Hamilton and a delegation of his followers met with Arizona Governor Jack Williams. The Sekaquaptewas had torn down a fence built by Navajos to keep their stock out of District 6, inviting a TV station from Phoenix to film the action. The Hopi council faction now wanted the governor to call out the Arizona national guard to intervene in the dispute. Evans and Associates was deeply involved in helping foment hostile encounters between Navajos and Hopis along the District 6 boundary and in publicizing them widely in the media.[45]

There followed a resolution by the Hopi Tribal Council calling for the resignation of Commissioner Bruce for failure to defend their interests. In rhetoric typical of Boyden's style, the resolution asserted, "We continue to feel the hot breath of the unchecked advancing Navajo."[46]

Delegates from both tribes journeyed to Washington to present their cases for and against the Steiger bill.[47] Hopis picketed the BIA offices and met with members of the Arizona delegation to urge support for the bill. Bruce announced his endorsement of the bill.[48]

Chet MacRorie of the *Navajo Times* wrote his weekly editorial in the form of an open letter to Steiger, pleading that he withdraw his bill.[49] An opposition Navajo paper, *Diné Baa-Hané*, criticized MacDonald for failing to solve the problem, and reported that the Hopis now had two armed white Anglos who were impounding livestock and abusing and arresting Navajos, with support from the Hopi police. The two Anglos denied that they were beating up Navajos.[50]

MacDonald was not ignoring the situation, however. He issued a statement defending the Navajos' rights in the joint-interest area and opposing the Steiger bill. The statement was a well-reasoned appeal that lacked the wild exaggeration and highly emotional tone of those issued by the Hopis.[51] His restraint may have worked against him; at least it had no effect on the editorial writer for the *Arizona Republic*, who published a slyly biased argument for passage of the bill, purporting to be ignorant of what the solution should be, but claiming that if Congress should fail to act, an intertribal war was likely.[52]

Conflicting statements seemed to flood the media. Steiger claimed that the Navajos had refused to negotiate the dispute until his bill was introduced, but that now they were eager to do so, for which he took credit.[53]

Donald Mose, councilman from Pinon, accused Boyden, Assistant Secretary of the Interior Loesch, the BIA, and the Arizona congressional delegation of trying to divide and conquer, so as to deprive the Indians of their Winters Doctrine rights to Colorado River water. He asserted that if the partition bill had been drafted with Navajo help, and had included lands to which the displaced Navajos could relocate, he thought that matters could be worked out. He further stated that until the recent trouble, MacDonald and Hamilton had been discussing the issue, but that any possibility that the two tribes might join peacefully to solve their problems scared those who wanted to exploit the situation.[54]

The Hopi traditional leaders also wrote Steiger, asking that he withdraw H.R. 11128 and challenging the right of Hamilton and the Hopi Tribal Council to speak for the Hopi people. They released copies of their letter to the papers.[55]

The confrontation along the District 6 line also continued. On the last day of March, a ninety-seven-year-old Navajo man, Tsinijinnie Yazzie, was yanked from his horse and arrested by Randolph, who charged him not only with trespass but with resisting arrest. The case was dismissed, apparently in the face of the adverse publicity which made it apparent that an elderly and partially deaf Navajo with limited understanding of English would not be likely to put up much of a fight against eight armed Hopis and Anglos. A suit for illegal arrest was promptly filed.[56]

The exchanges in the papers continued. MacDonald wrote a letter to the editor of the *Arizona Republic* contesting the assertions made in their editorial, blaming the threat of an Indian war on the activities of Boyden's public relations firm in Salt Lake City, and attacking the Steiger bill as a grave injustice to some 10,000 Navajos whose homes and livelihood were threatened.[57] Again his tone was moderate, especially in comparison with that of the Hopi tribal officials and their attorney. Hamilton's reply to MacRorie's editorial proclaimed that the Navajos "continue to maraud and steal," "have stripped the grass" from the reservation, and they "rape the range land."[58] The release, which bore an Oraibi return address, had been mailed from Salt Lake City.[59]

MacDonald publicly lamented the Hopi Tribe's campaign to brand the

Navajos as "a ruthless band of marauders" opposed to "this innocent and peaceful Hopi," but his complaint had little effect on public opinion, which seemed to perceive the Navajos as bullies. He repeated his accusation that the propaganda was designed ultimately by powerful whites who wanted to exploit the resources of both tribes.[60] I was frankly puzzled when visiting relatives in Phoenix to learn that people there really believed that a war between the two tribes was likely, for the whole idea seemed preposterous to me. Those with little direct knowledge of the two tribes were all too easily led to accept such claims when they were dramatized in the news media, especially when it was possible to add the spice of actual small-scale violence promoted by militant enforcement of grazing regulations.

Hamilton's reply to MacDonald was the old claim that the Navajos negotiated in bad faith. He accused them of even refusing to meet at one of the last efforts to get together.[61] This was probably a reference to the last meeting I had attended in Albuquerque, when the Hopi delegation had loudly objected to meeting if the commissioner were not present, but once the BIA officials arrived, had quietly let the Navajos repeat the objections that they had originally raised.

More serious news came to light when Anthony Lincoln, the first Navajo to be appointed area director for the BIA Navajo Area Office, announced that a decision to support the Steiger bill had been made in Washington and that the matter "was not open to debate" in the BIA. He courageously stood up for his people, saying, "In this case, I must be a Navajo first and a bureaucrat second." There seemed little left to do but try to lessen the impact of relocation.[62]

Hearings were set on the bill for April 17–18. A congressional aide estimated that relocation would cost about $19 million. Navajos who were removed from their homes would be resettled on the Navajo Indian Irrigation Project in New Mexico and on public domain lands adjacent to the project.[63]

For three weeks a Navajo crew, financed by their local community, had been building a fence along their portion of the District 6 boundary. Just three days before the hearings were to begin, a large force of Hopi and BIA police appeared with a television crew in tow. They set to work tearing up the fence and burning the fence posts. The Navajos refrained from violence, and the television crew got a relatively tame view of the "range war."[64]

The Hopis may have overplayed their hand, for the Nixon administration suddenly reversed its position, at least to the extent of promoting further negotiations and trying to defuse the tension along the District 6 line. The BIA called a meeting in Commissioner Bruce's office attended by Bruce, Loesch, Hamilton, and Navajo Vice-Chairman Wilson Skeet. Skeet relayed MacDonald's proposal for a jointly manned patrol to watch the boundary, none of the officers to be armed. Hamilton rejected this idea and said he would agree only to stock reduction. The position of the administration on the Steiger bill remained unclear, but MacDonald had been in direct contact with the White House and apparently had had some influence there.[65]

Delegations were on their way to Washington to testify at the hearings on the Steiger bill. The official Navajo delegation was made up of Donald Mose, Raymond Pete, Dudley Yazzie, Carl Todacheenie, Charlie Billie, Glen George, William Yellowhair, Marlin Scott, and Annie Wauneka. In addition, Harold Drake was to lead a delegation of Paiutes from the Navajo Mountain area, and several Hopi traditionalists would attend to lend support to the Navajo cause.[66] Testimony began on April 17 as scheduled. Loesch appeared for the administration and gave the bill his full support, but he suggested that some amendments might be proposed. MacDonald led off the Navajo testimony with a strongly worded attack on the bill, calling it an "evil, unfair, biased, wrong, unconstitutional monstrosity."[67]

Despite his strong words, MacDonald's statement was a reasonable argument that the two tribes should be allowed to settle the matter themselves, with an obligation to go to arbitration if they could not reach an agreement within a reasonable period of time.[68]

Testimony continued on the eighteenth, with Annie Wauneka, John Smith, and Bahozonie Begay presenting the Navajo side, while Boyden and Hamilton argued the Hopi case.

Annie Wauneka addressed the issue of land shortage. She suggested that vacant federal lands be used to settle the dispute, asking that the Navajos be given back lands they had lost and that the Hopis be given other lands beyond their present reservation boundaries.

Richard Schifter, an attorney for the Navajo Tribe, presented the case for a more liberal interpretation of the Prescott decision, one that did not distort its meaning with the term "joint-use area" with its implication that the Navajos living on half of the land in dispute should be driven from their homes.

Vice-Chairman Skeet described the Navajo Tribe's plans for the Navajo

Indian Irrigation Project in New Mexico and explained why resettling evictees from the Executive Order Reservation would be a disaster for both the
people and the project.

Mina Lansa, Kikmongwi of Old Oraibi, testified on behalf of the Hopi
traditionalists. She described the bill as a threat to the Hopi way of life and
pleaded that it not be passed.

Commissioner Bruce testified in some detail on the administrative problems of the joint-use area.[69]

Back on the reservation, MacDonald's proposed joint Navajo-Hopi un-
armed patrol of the District 6 line began on April 26 with three vehicles in
use. Lacking police powers, the effort was called a courtesy patrol. In addition, water was hauled to four storage tanks located at critical places along
the boundary so that Navajos nearby would not have to depend on springs
within the Hopi area for stock water.[70] Bruce, along with Loesch and the
Phoenix area director, appeared before the Hopi Tribal Council on the
twenty-eighth. Loesch assured the Hopis of his support of the Steiger bill
and announced that the Department of the Interior was working on plans to
reduce Navajo livestock in the 1882 Reservation. When Hamilton objected
to the courtesy patrol as a scheme "to stall passage" of the Steiger bill, Bruce
defended it as a way of reducing tensions and was able to quiet Hopi objections, although he could not convince them that it should continue.[71]

Loesch and Bruce met with the Navajo Tribal Council on May 2. Loesch
urged renewed negotiations and brought up the old idea that if the Moenkopi issue could be resolved by negotiation, it would be easier to reach
agreement on the joint-interest area.[72]

Despite the Nixon administration's lack of sympathy for the Navajo families living within the Executive Order Reservation, the Navajos were not
ready to give up their opposition to the Steiger bill. MacRorie wrote an
editorial outlining the many steps at which a bill could be opposed in Congress, but he lamented that as long as the bill had a chance of passing the
Hopi officials would be unlikely to negotiate.[73] George Vlassis, however,
came up with a series of amendments for the bill which would allow partition, but only if every displaced stockowner were to be be resettled with
enough land to graze his or her animals, in essence, four acres for every acre
used in the joint-interest area. The council approved the proposal, but with
several abstentions.[74]

MacDonald was able to claim success for the courtesy patrol and the hauling of feed and water for Navajo cattle after only a few weeks. Hamilton was "not available" for comment, however.[75]

With trespass under control by peaceful means, at least temporarily, Hamilton found a different cause for complaint. He charged that Navajos were building new homes at three different locations within the joint-interest area and criticized Bruce for allowing this to take place.[76] Although the freeze on construction and development in the area had long been observed with regard to government projects, it does not appear to have been applied to private undertakings up to that time. The Hopi council's objections exerted new pressure on the Navajo occupants, for growing families and the normal deterioration of old hogans and small cabins led to continual need for building and repair.

The Navajos suffered a setback when the Supreme Court in May refused to hear their appeal in the case of the Hopi petition for a writ of assistance.[77]

In addition, the Anglo range riders and their Hopi police assistants continued to seek opportunities to confront Navajos over livestock trespass. The courtesy patrols could not be everywhere. Toward the end of May some Navajo children carelessly herding sheep lost some that wandered across the line into District 6. Hopi rangers were quick to confiscate the animals. Sam Maize, in his seventies and too ill to herd his flock, still made an effort to protest their action. He was arrested and hauled off to jail at Keams Canyon. MacDonald spoke out against the Hopi council's tactics, but with little effect.[78] Robert Hilgendorf, an attorney with DNA, branded the Hopi procedures unconstitutional.[79] A few days later DNA filed suit for Tsinijinnie Yazzie, asking $20,000 in punitive damages for his arrest by Elmer Randolph.[80] The next day the Navajo Tribal Council passed a resolution rescinding a 1954 resolution which prevented Navajo police from arresting Hopis.[81]

In the meantime, the Hopis destroyed what was described as "a Navajo meeting hall" near Low Mountain. The Hopi officials claimed the structure was illegally built, while the Navajos charged that the Hopi action was in violation of a court order.[82] While the news account described the incident as having taken place inside District 6, the location of the meeting hall was never very precisely specified.

About a week later the *Arizona Republic* ran a full-page feature story on the dismantling of a Navajo hogan at the Kabinto homesite in Echo Canyon, with a dramatic account of a stand-off between armed Navajos and Hopi tribal and agency employees.[83] Photographs showed the hogan being torn down and Elmer Randolph on his horse supervising the operation. Although threats were exchanged, there was no shooting, and again there was disagreement as to whether the destruction was legal. The Hopi council did seem to be engaging in increasingly provocative actions, however, seeking to instigate a violent encounter that would discredit the courtesy patrols, and inviting a reporter and a photographer from the *Republic* to be present to publicize some of the encounters.

The *Republic* had begun a series of articles that helped sensationalize the grazing conflict. The following Monday there was another story, this one dealing with Navajo livestock trespass. One photo, captioned "Navajo sheep," actually showed a small herd of angora goats.[84] A few days later a story appeared that blamed the Navajos for the intensity of Hopi factionalism, again with several photographs.[85] On Sunday the story was about an interview with Peter MacDonald, but two of the pictures were of confiscated Navajo livestock, again with a small flock of goats mislabeled as sheep.[86] The next day there was a rather neutral story which recounted a day spent with one of the courtesy patrol teams.[87] The development of the series seemed to suggest that the reporter was beginning to realize that there were two sides to the dispute.

Finally, on Thursday, June 24, an incident took place which gave the media ample material to claim that a range war was in progress. It began with sheep belonging to Hoskie and Joann Yonnie entering District 6 along the northern border. The Hopis claimed that the Navajos had deliberately allowed the sheep to trespass, while the Navajos asserted that the sheep had been induced to wander over the line by Elmer Randolph. In either case, Mrs. Yonnie was arrested when she tried to bring them back and was jailed at Keams Canyon. While Randolph and several Hopi and BIA police were rounding up the sheep, over thirty Navajo men appeared and attempted to retrieve the herd, which consisted of about 200 head. Fighting broke out, leaving the Hopi police with some injured and in possession of only thirty-five to fifty of the sheep. Accounts of just what happened differed considerably, but Mrs. Yonnie was found bruised and battered in a jail cell at Keams

Canyon by a DNA attorney. Hoskie Yonnie, who journeyed to Keams Canyon to pay the impoundment costs for the release of his sheep, had also been arrested. Both were released on bond. Tribal leaders on each side blamed the other tribe, Hamilton charging that the courtesy patrol was a failure, while MacDonald threatened to place a "human wall" around District 6 to protect Navajo women, children, and elders from mistreatment by Randolph and the Hopi police.[88] A Ute judge was brought to hear the cases. Hoskie Yonnie was found guilty of trespass; the cases against Joann Yonnie and the others were postponed.[89]

The eruption of serious violence was timely for the Hopi cause. Five days later the House Interior Committee approved the Steiger bill. The press release from Washington cited "rising tensions and bloodshed" in the area to be partitioned.[90]

The violence having accomplished the Hopi council's purpose, Hamilton was willing to place into effect a two-week moratorium on "strict enforcement" of the tribe's trespass ordinances while the BIA began an air patrol of the District 6 border. Hamilton claimed to be shocked by the "human wall" suggestion, asserting that he had "to protect our Hopi Reservation from being overrun by Navajos."[91]

As reported out by the House committee, the Steiger bill included several amendments which the Navajos had not seen. These included a prohibition on fencing District 6; a reduction by $3 million in the amount to be authorized for relocation, leaving only $16 million; a cutting in half of the time allowed for Navajo removal to five years; allowing both tribes to purchase extra lands for resettlement purposes; requiring immediate stock reduction in the joint-interest area; allowing only one court action, that by the Hopi Tribe to sue for its share of the revenues collected by the Navajo Tribe from the Executive Order Reservation; and giving the Hopis some 208,000 acres around Moenkopi. MacDonald was reported to have proposed amendments to the bill, to be made when the full House took it under consideration.[92]

The Navajo amendment proposals came as a real blow to my own hopes, and they suggested that MacDonald had been forced to give in to political pressures and to agree to relocation. Information in the various newspapers was contradictory as to the status of the bill. Lee was poorly informed and could tell me only that MacDonald wanted to handle the matter without interference from Anglos and Hispanics. Lee had a copy of the bill that he thought was the version being sent to the House floor, but it differed from what was being reported by the press. I found no reports that the bill had passed in the House, but there was a news story concerning a bill in the Senate. Whether that was the Steiger bill or something newly introduced was uncertain. I wrote letters to both Arizona senators opposing partition and asked several colleagues who had been involved in Navajo studies to write the congressional delegations of their states.

The *Gallup Independent* reported that MacDonald had proposed that new land be provided for the resettlement of any Navajos or Hopis displaced by boundary changes.[93] The front-page headline that day, however, was about twenty-seven Navajo sheep trespassing on the Ute Mountain Ute Reservation. Why so trivial an incident should receive such prominence in the paper at any time, much less at this critical moment, was not a question in my mind. I took it for granted that it was just another display of the animus against the Navajos in Gallup. I did not realize that Boyden was attorney for the Utes as well as for the Hopis.

Loesch was busy trying to establish an administrative system for the joint-interest area that would allow a relaxation of the freezes on development in both the Executive Order and the 1934 reservations. Both MacDonald and Hamilton were involved in negotiating this "thaw," as the press described it.[94] Once again, it appeared to me, MacDonald was yielding to pressures from the administration, but in this case the picture was not as clear. Before discussions had progressed very far, however, the Hopi council rejected the plan unanimously.[95] The Hopi council faction was determined to maintain the pressure of the freeze order and to approach solutions through the courts and through Congress. Despite the Hopi action, Loesch announced that the Department of the Interior would appoint a special administrator for the joint-interest area to put into place new grazing regulations so as to force stock reduction.[96] A court hearing of a suit brought by the Hopis was in progress in Tucson before Judge Walsh, where the first issue raised was overgrazing.[97]

Navajos were sending letters to the editors of the *Navajo Times*. Lonnie Hosteen of Black Mesa protested the entire boundary case, with special emphasis on the hardships that stock reduction would bring.[98] The *Times* also published a copy of a letter Daniel Peaches of the Navajo Tribal Public Affairs Office had addressed to Sam Steiger disputing the accusation that great numbers of Navajos had recently moved onto the joint-interest area.[99]

In July the Navajo Tribe opened an office in Washington to lobby against the Steiger bill.[100] The bill was still being considered in the House, and the fight against it there soon became so critical that MacDonald himself led another delegation to rally opposition on the House floor. Rash accusations in the committee hearings, such as the claim that people "are being killed every day," had brought a fast and decisive vote with no consideration of the amendments suggested by the Navajos, but with approval of several amendments favorable to the Hopis. Despite spirited opposition to the bill by New Mexico Representative Manuel Lujan, Steiger's insistence that a "crisis" existed on the reservation led to passage by the House the day following approval by the committee. Even Arizona Representative Morris Udall, brother of the former Secretary of the Interior, had opposed passage. The bill had aroused such controversy that there was little likelihood that it would get through the Senate. MacDonald claimed to have the support of the Arizona senators, Barry Goldwater and Paul Fannin, both Republicans.[101]

MacDonald bitterly accused the House of accepting falsehoods in passing the bill, characterizing Steiger's argument in favor of his bill as "completely a lie."[102] The Department of the Interior's claim, echoed by the committee, that partition would prevent violence, MacDonald believed, was totally untrue. The *Navajo Times* on August 3 carried a similarly strongly worded account written by MacRorie.[103]

The Navajos felt the need for bipartisan support of their position in the Senate. George McGovern, chairman of the Senate Subcommittee on Indian Affairs, was a key figure. He was also the Democratic candidate in the presidential election that year. MacDonald succeeded in gaining his sympathy. Following a personal meeting, McGovern wrote a letter pledging his opposition to any action that would bring about a needless eviction of people from their homes.[104] Democratic opposition to the bill soon included Senator Fred Harris of Oklahoma, Senator Joseph Montoya of New Mexico, and Senator Henry Jackson of Washington, who was chairman of the full Senate Interior Committee. It was, by this time, clear that the bill would die in the Senate. There were rumors that the "pro-Steiger bill forces," apparently the Hopi council, Boyden, and their allies, were trying to defeat a Republican Party plan to invite MacDonald to help nominate Richard Nixon for re-election at the upcoming Republican convention. They were also said to be trying to enlist former chairman Nakai, MacDonald's defeated political rival, to revive charges against MacDonald that Nakai had originally raised during the race for the Chairman's office. It is noteworthy that neither Goldwater nor Fannin had made any public statement of opposition to the Steiger bill, despite MacDonald's repeated announcements that he had their support. When MacDonald, frustrated and realizing that his political future was in jeopardy, finally suggested that he might support McGovern for president, Goldwater turned openly against him, followed by a faithful Fannin.[105] There was almost certainly a movement afoot by the Hopi council and Boyden to gain wider support within Republican ranks, one that had probably gained the covert allegiance of the Arizona senators long before they revealed their positions on partition.

More openly, Hopi tribal officials visited Washington to lobby for hearings on the bill in the Senate.[106]

The Senate subcommittee was inclined to let the bill die without a hearing, but the full committee went ahead without a subcommittee report. Assistant Secretary Loesch and Commissioner Bruce supported partition, but when questioned closely by the senators, they had to admit to several deficiencies in the bill, including inadequate funding and lack of provision for the people who would be displaced.[107] The committee also allowed the Navajos' witnesses a fair opportunity to testify, in contrast to the situation in the House. The Nixon White House was strangely noncommittal on the bill, allowing the belief that it did not have support there.[108]

The Navajos continued to gain support. Pete Domenici, Republican candidate for the Senate from New Mexico, opposed forced partition in a campaign speech at Shiprock.[109] The bill soon was bogged down after Interior Committee Chairman Jackson named a special committee to study it, a move that effectively delayed any action during that session of Congress.[110]

In the meantime, the Hopis won the court battle in Tucson with a decision by Judge Walsh that they were being deprived of their rights in the joint-interest area.[111] Walsh postponed issuing his written order until October 14, when he produced a writ of assistance requiring the Navajo Tribe to reduce their people's livestock to one-half of the current carrying capacity of the range and ordering that there be no new construction of any sort in the joint-interest area. This was the first of thirteen such orders, all of which the Navajos appealed in U.S. District Court.[112] Walsh also ordered that the BIA draft a plan to halt the overgrazing, allowing sixty days for it to be submitted. When the time ran out in mid-December, the plan still was not ready.[113]

Another court decision went against the Navajos in October. Both the federal district court and the Ninth Circuit U.S. Court of Appeals had ruled against the Echo Canyon people, and the Supreme Court refused to review the case. There was nothing in the court decisions to help compensate the Kabintos and the Georges for their loss. The Hopi Tribal Council renewed its eviction notice, giving the Navajos thirty days to get out. The BIA did no more than send trucks to move the two families to temporary quarters in tents and trailers at the Navajo tribal fairgrounds in Window Rock. The evictees took all that they could carry, burning their hogans and corrals to prevent the Hopis from making any use of them. An unprepared tribal administration was still struggling at year's end to find permanent homes for about forty displaced persons who had been unable to extricate themselves from their dilemma on their own.[114] Joe Kabinto's death at age ninety-three shortly afterward would be attributed by the Navajos to the loss of his home and by the Hopis to simple old age. Whether either or both were right, the tragedy of a Navajo family caught in a legal quandary that they could not understand would long remain a symbol of the entire dispute. An old man dispossessed at the end of his life gave a human face to the results of the contest that thousands of nameless evictees could not provide.

The Navajos' legal staff drafted a bill to counter the partition proposals. It would have authorized a plan previously put forward that a commission be created of three Navajos, three Hopis, and three neutral members to arrive at a solution. The commission would also have the power to divide both surface and subsurface resources, and thus to balance interests by giving the Hopis a greater share of the mineral rights should the Navajos receive more of the surface rights.[115]

The failure of the Steiger bill had not been entirely due to opposition to partition and relocation, despite the surface appearance that this was the case. The bill was fatally flawed in its lack of any pretense of doing more than forcing the Navajos from the land, with woefully inadequate provisions for moving costs or resettlement, so much so that it reflected the fervor for retribution so frequently heard in the rhetoric of the Hopi council faction and their attorney. Worse was yet to come, but the sheer inhumanity of the punitive bills would lead Congress to regard less extreme proposals as harmless.

THE END OF THE LINE

A N OCCUPATION of the BIA offices in Washington by members of the American Indian Movement (AIM) led to the firing of Harrison Loesch,[1] a plus for the Navajos, but the new Congress began 1973 with a determination to settle the dispute between the Navajos and Hopis. Three bills went into the hopper in the House. Steiger's effort was recycled, Manuel Lujan joined John Conlan of Arizona to support a purchase of the Hopi interest for the Navajos, and Lloyd Meeds of Washington drafted an authorization for a mandatory arbitration process. Goldwater and Fannin went for blood, and on the Senate side their bill, written by Boyden, would evict the Navajos without any sort of compensation.[2]

Hearings were soon being scheduled and witnesses lined up. Aubrey Williams, then teaching at the University of Maryland, had been approached by the Senate Interior and Insular Affairs Committee as a possible witness. He asked whether Lee or I could give any advice. My suggestion was that a bill that would not allow any actions without the full consent of both tribes seemed essential, preferably one that would allow the tribes all the time they might need to work out a compromise that both could live with. I had seen too many Indian decisions forced by pressures to do things on short deadlines and had seen time limits in the negotiations work regularly to the disadvantage of the Navajos. I noted that almost any just solution, even a partition that might treat the evictees as human beings, would cost a lot of money. An approach that would balance mineral rights to compensate for surface rights was my personal preference, for I could not bring myself to accept the idea of uprooting so many people.

The Senate held a hearing 7 March 1973 in Winslow, Arizona, just south of the Navajo and Hopi reservations. Senator James Abourezk of South Dakota, who was chair of the Subcommittee on Indian Affairs, presided. The only other senator of the seven members of the subcommittee present was Fannin.[3]

The hearing was directed toward the Steiger bill, reintroduced in the new congress as H.R. 1193. Although the bill had not yet been approved by the House in the 93rd Congress, the Senate undertook the hearing to honor a pledge made in the 92nd Congress.[4] Thus, the bill was not actually before the Senate at that time and would not be a matter for Senate consideration unless either introduced as a Senate bill, which had not been done, or passed by the newly elected House. It was apparently Senator Jackson, still chair of the Committee on Interior and Insular Affairs, who decided that the subcommittee should hear testimony prior to there being a bill under consideration. While there is nothing irregular in a hearing on any subject deemed appropriate, the fact that the agenda was slanted toward one of several potential solutions and done so in this manner would seem to indicate some bias or political pressure behind the scenes. It also gave Steiger himself an additional platform from which to advocate partition, in a presentation outside of the equal blocks of time allotted the two tribes at the hearing.

I felt that the hearing was important enough that I took annual leave in order to drive to Winslow and hear what was said. I thought myself inadequately informed by the news accounts, and Lee could tell me little more. The hearing was held at the Winslow Civic Center where a large crowd, mostly Navajo, gathered. I quietly took a seat among the spectators, realizing that I was no longer a real participant, just an outsider, albeit one with greater-than-average knowledge and interest in the issues to be discussed.

The hearing opened with an introduction and brief statement by Abourezk, who introduced Fannin. Fannin made a similarly short statement. He made one claim which I felt was incorrect: "It might be well to stress that the problem we are examining here is a dispute between two Indian tribes. It does not involve relations between Indians and non-Indians."[5] In the complex world of the twentieth century, it would be remarkable if any dispute of this magnitude should involve only Indians. There would soon be statements to the contrary.

The first speaker, who was not considered technically to be a witness, was Steiger. He spoke at first largely in generalities, and Abourezk questioned him for specifics. How much money, for instance, would be needed for removal, and what was the social cost of dispossessing the Navajos. Steiger claimed ignorance of any possible solution but partition, but confessed later to being aware of other proposals during a very friendly questioning by Fannin.[6]

The Navajo witnesses appeared first, and MacDonald led off. He vigorously defended the rights of the Navajos within the joint-interest area and submitted the text of a bill which he asserted would "fully respect the human rights and property rights of the Navajo and Hopi Tribes."[7] He read a prepared statement for the greater part of his presentation, which did not appear improper in view of the importance of his cause, although it did not enhance the force of his talk. His proposed bill set forth a method of compensating the Hopis for their interest in the disputed area. Under questioning by Abourezk, MacDonald provided the rationale for settling the dispute in this manner, relying strongly on the needs of the Navajos living on the land.[8]

Fannin then began questioning MacDonald, approaching the issue much as would a lawyer cross-examining a hostile witness. MacDonald tried to refer the questions to the Navajo general counsel. Abourezk decided that although only Navajos might testify, the tribal attorney would be allowed to submit a written reply, but no such reply appears in the published record of the hearing. Fannin then went on to a different question in which he misstated the solution proposed in the Navajos' draft bill and entered into a discussion of the merits of compensation for land. It was clear that he and MacDonald were talking past one another, neither really comprehending what the other was saying.[9]

After a short recess to set up more chairs to accommodate a much larger crowd of spectators than had been expected, the hearing resumed with testimony by Dandy George, speaking through interpreter Carl Beyal who read a prepared statement. George very briefly described his suffering as a result of being evicted from Echo Canyon.[10]

The next witness was Chester Yellowhair, judge for the Navajo tribal court at Tuba City, who made an eloquent plea that no Navajos be thrown out of their homes, again reading from a prepared text.[11]

He was followed by Mary Lou White of White Cone. Although she was only thirty-seven years old, she based her testimony on the lives of her grandparents who had lived on lands in the joint-interest area. Like Yellowhair, she was able to testify quite effectively in English, although, like the others, she read from a prepared text. She also submitted a resolution passed by the White Cone Chapter opposing the Steiger bill.[12]

The fifth witness was Peterson Zah, then head of the war-on-poverty legal aid service, DNA. He testified both on behalf of his own community of Low Mountain and to present his observations of the problems he saw as a result of administering legal services for individual Navajos. While he referred to a written text, much of his testimony was not read, but given spontaneously. His comments on DNA's experiences in defending Navajos charged in Hopi courts were especially revealing:

> I say this because I hear and see it everyday at work. You see I am employed by a legal aid services program where we receive all these problems from clients. Ironically, we receive some of these complaints from Hopi people, as we also represent them in both tribal and state courts.
>
> Where the DNA program becomes involved is where individual Navajos are being prosecuted in Hopi courts for livestock trespass. The Hopi Tribe passed a law providing for forfeiture of livestock seized on Hopi lands. Their law did not allow any hearing on whether the animals were legally seized, and we had complaints of Hopi policemen coming across the line into Navajo lands to seize animals. So we challenged the Hopi law in court, and the Hopis amended the law, so now a hearing is provided in the Hopi courts.
>
> But even the amended livestock laws make the animal trespass a crime, not only for the herdsman, but for the livestock owner as well. It is not enough to seize the livestock and obtain its forfeiture; the Navajos go to jail as well.
>
> Based on all the cases we have had in Hopi tribal court, we think the overall purpose of the Hopi livestock trespass laws is harassment, rather than legitimate law enforcement. The Hopi chairman wasn't satisfied with the aggressiveness of his own police and courts, so now he has an Anglo policeman, an Anglo prosecutor; and an Anglo judge. The policeman is the most serious problem. We have report after report that he has provoked confrontations and has come across the line to seize animals. He arrested a very old man, whom federal records show will be 100 years old this year, and roughed him up so much as to require medical treatment. He justified this treatment because the old man didn't obey his order—although the old man is so hard of hearing he couldn't hear any order.
>
> Just last week this same policeman arrested a twelve-year-old girl, who had

custody of three goats that had crossed the line. He then came across the line and seized her entire flock of sheep, which had not trespassed.

It is clear to us that these tactics are pure harassment, to gain publicity for the Hopi chairman. He has so little support for these tactics from his own people that he must use hired Anglos to carry out such policies.

Zah spoke by far the best English of any of the Navajo witnesses, and his statements were clear and direct. His words came across with a strong dislike of whites, however—so strong that I feared that he would lose much of the sympathy that his facts should have generated. This anti-white bias was, I was sure, in part a result of his working with Ted Mitchell at DNA, for Mitchell was much given to conspiracy theories.

Zah made an unfortunate mistake as well, perhaps because he already saw MacDonald as a political rival. He tried to deal with a question by Fannin regarding Walsh's stock reduction decision on the basis of recent news accounts and some second-hand information. Fannin challenged him on this, saying that he had a copy of the decision with him. Zah felt compelled to back down, which may have further weakened the force of his testimony.[13] His was still the statement that was, I believe, best understood by the congressional audience, for none of the participants, not even those who claimed expertise in Indian affairs, as did Fannin and Steiger, really knew much about Navajo ways or how to comprehend Navajo thinking expressed in English as a second language.

Donald Mose, councilman from Pinon, gave an important presentation in that he had a far more realistic view of Navajo-Hopi relations than was evident in the statements of most of the Navajo witnesses. While he, like many others, emphasized the good relations that existed between the two peoples and placed much of the blame for discord on the current Hopi leadership, he also admitted that good relations had not existed at all times going back hundreds of years, as the Navajo politicians had portrayed them. He placed historic differences between the two tribes within a reasonable context of neighbors who "had our differences like all people," rather than within the traditional enemy paradigm so popular with the Hopi council faction and their attorney.[14]

Other Navajos who spoke included Marlin Scott, who explained the Navajo relation to the land in terms of their religion, and Glen C. George who addressed the Moenkopi issue in some detail. He also submitted as an exhibit a copy of a report that Lee and I had prepared, "Historic Use and Occupancy of the Tuba City–Moenkopi Area," which became an appendix to the hearing report. Sam Wilson discussed the importance of sheep to the Navajos, while William K. Wilson described the investments of the Navajo Tribe and the federal government in improvements in the joint-interest area. Joe Yazzie objected to being displaced to the Navajo Irrigation Project in New Mexico.[15] Again, most of the testimony was read from prepared texts, which resulted in considerable loss of spontaneity. While the method seemed to express well the thoughts of the witnesses, it lost some of the force that it might otherwise have had. Nobody even bothered to ask most of the Navajos any questions about their prepared statements.

Six other Navajos were scheduled to testify when the allotted time ran out. Abouzezk promised to include any written statements, and these were inserted into the record. They told of the suffering endured by earlier removals at the time District 6 was enlarged, of their attachment to the land as well as their dependence upon it, and of their good relations with the Hopi people.[16]

Before the morning session was recessed for lunch, Fannin raised an objection to some of Zah's prepared remarks, saying that Zah had been "antagonistic and incredible." Fannin quoted an especially strong passage from Zah's statement:

He [Zah] said that, "Congressman Steiger with this bill was trying to create hatred and hostility between two different tribes that have peacefully lived side by side for centuries. In my view there were some reasons for this. Mr. Steiger wanted the two tribes to fight over the joint use area controversy, to distract both sides from Black Mesa and what the big power companies are doing there. One only wishes that the two tribes would put their differences aside and fight the common enemies—the white man's disease: graft, discrimination and dishonesty and so forth."

Fannin then accepted MacDonald's suggestion that he call Zah back to explain his statement. Zah's explanation was as naively honest as his earlier statement had been.

Senator Fannin, as I sit back there, you know, I went to school and I read a lot of books, and I have a college education, and it just sort of kills me and gives me an uneasy feeling for the two tribes at this time to be fighting over a little piece of land.

While I like to think ideally that the two tribes will really combine their efforts and be able to work together, perhaps to take some of the land back away from the white man, that's really my feeling.

Fannin found no satisfaction in this response, took no time to learn from it, and could only proclaim his resentment, while the several hundred Navajo listeners applauded Zah enthusiastically.[17]

The afternoon session gave equal time to the Hopi council's witnesses, with Hopi Chairman Clarence Hamilton called to speak first. He began with a litany of accusations against the Navajos. He rejected negotiation, explaining, "From 1963 up to 1969, we have not negotiated between the two tribes," and he added that he had been unsuccessful in getting MacDonald to engage in negotiations.[18] He later mentioned that he had read the minutes of the 1968 negotiating session in Phoenix and claimed that the Navajos offered the Hopis no more than the village of Moenkopi.[19]

Hamilton then became involved in an extended discussion with the two senators as to how many Hopis might move into lands partitioned to his tribe, suggesting that it might be as high as eighty families. Although Fannin tried mightily to encourage him to enlarge the figure without appearing to be impartial, he was not very successful in that endeavor.[20]

Nevertheless, Hamilton did manage to paint a pitiful picture of Hopi desires and frustrations in their dealings with the aggressive and merciless Navajos, thereby setting the tone for the testimony to come. Hamilton's most dramatic moment came when he introduced a Hopi police officer who had been injured in the fracas with the Yonnies. The officer showed off his scars, which Hamilton labeled a "Navajo trade mark."[21]

He was followed by Logan Koopee, Hopi vice-chairman, who introduced himself as a traditionalist from First Mesa. He characterized the Hopis as "peaceful people," claimed their past sufferings had caused many Hopis to die "of a broken heart," and complained of "Navajo depredations which have plagued us for over 100 years." He dwelt on the history of the Navajo wars, emphasizing that the Navajos "murdered, raped, and plundered," that they broke treaties, and that they later resorted to stealing Hopi cattle and destroying Hopi houses. He denied that Joe Kabinto's death was due to his being evicted and pleaded for help from the government.[22]

The next speaker for the Hopis was Abbott Sekaquaptewa, chairman of the Hopi negotiating committee. He began by asserting flatly that it is "impossible for us to entertain the idea of ever living in harmony with the Navajo Tribe" and by accusing the Navajos of lying in their dealings with the Hopis—taking their land, killing Hopis, and refusing to negotiate in good faith. He followed this with an eloquently stated argument for Hopi justice, laying the blame for the dispute on both the Navajos and the United States government. Under questioning by Fannin, Sekaquaptewa backed off from his proclamation of eternal enmity with the Navajos, opining that partition of the land would allow the two tribes to live in harmony.[23]

Phillip Talas followed Sekaquaptewa, saying that he represented the people of Moenkopi. He laid claim to half of the 1934 Reservation on the basis of the division of the joint-interest area. He not only echoed Sekaquaptewa in blaming the U.S. government for the Hopi travails, but placed all the blame there, completely exonerating the Navajos. Following his oral testimony, a written statement was also inserted into the record; the written statement did indeed attack the Navajos.[24] Perhaps he did not want to say these accusations in front of Navajos he recognized in the audience.

Hamilton introduced the next witness, Donald Antona, chairman of the Intertribal Council of Arizona. Antona explained that the council represented all Arizona tribes except the Navajo. He said that the council did not want to take sides, but he then introduced into the record the resolution that the council had passed in favor of the Steiger bill.[25]

Hamilton next called on Theodore M. Vaughn, a member of the Yavapai Tribe, who was a pilot for the BIA at Keams Canyon. Vaughn testified that his assignment was to fly over the District 6 boundary to direct the courtesy patrol to places where trespass was taking place. He said that on the basis of his observations, he believed that Navajo trespass was intentional and that it was clear from the air that the country outside of District 6 was badly overgrazed by the Navajos, while the range on the Hopi side of the fence was in good condition.[26]

The last to testify on behalf of the Hopi council was Viets Lomahaftewa. He related a family tradition about the kidnapping of his grandfather by the

Navajos and how the grandfather's parents had ransomed him. He then told a version of the Hopi origin story in which the Hopis were portrayed as people who lived "in accord with law and peace" and the Navajos were depicted as inherently evil, "roaming about as nomads with the benefits of the pleasures of the flesh, [and] stealing," and in which it was said that the Navajos' destiny is to "continue depredations against the Hopi people."[27]

The Hopis also officially submitted for the record eight typed statements, all of which emphasized Hopi disputes with Navajos when the Hopis tried to expand their use of the land beyond District 6.[28]

The committee then allowed Major Caleb H. Johnson, a Hopi serving as chaplain in the army, to appear as an "interpreter of Hopi traditional chiefs" for two of the chiefs who were present. Johnson stated the chiefs' opposition to the Steiger bill and their belief that the Navajos should continue to live with the Hopis as they had before, "side by side for generations." He explained:

> The Hopi traditional people do not see this as a problem. It is the Hopi council who have created this so-called problem among the Navajo and Hopi people. It is they and their servants who have been impounding the sheep of the Navajo people. It is they who have painted such distorted pictures of the Navajo people in the press. It is they who are trying to divide the traditional Hopi land area and reduce it for their own reasons.

Johnson was asked by Abourezk what proportion of the Hopis supported the position of the traditional leaders. According to the published hearing transcript, Johnson is supposed to have replied "very few." But Abourezk's next question does not logically follow from this answer: Abourzek wondered why the Hopi traditionalists could not "control the tribal government if they have that much support."[29] My own notes on Johnson's testimony reveal that the transcript must have been in error, since he actually claimed about 50 percent support for the anti-Council faction. A news report of the hearings also quoted the 50 percent figure.[30]

Following Johnson's testimony the hearings were adjourned.[31]

I left the Winslow Civic Center more aware than ever of my current status as an outsider, but feeling strongly that I had an obligation to use my knowledge somehow to help prevent partition and the expulsion of large numbers of Navajos from their homes. I had vivid memories of my teenage years, when the news had been full of stories of the growing numbers of "displaced persons" living in refugee camps, as rising ethnic hatreds led to World War II. The passions aroused by the Hopi tribal government and its attorney struck me as being of the same order, differing only in the matter of scale. It was rapidly becoming ever more apparent that Joe McPherson's prediction that no Navajos would lose their homes as a result of the Prescott decision had been based on a very poor understanding of what was at stake. While I was very much in sympathy with the Navajo plight, I thought that the testimony presented by the Hopis had been more effective in terms of its emotional impact. I could see how well Anglo and Hispanic listeners had been led to believe what the Hopis wanted them to believe. My overall impression was that at best the Navajos had held their own, but it was far more likely that they had lost a round.

One more effort at negotiation began in April. At the Hopis' invitation, MacDonald agreed to meet in Salt Lake City on April 2.[32] The initial session on Monday focused on procedural matters, in particular the extent of participation by the tribal attorneys. The decision was to allow them to attend the sessions, but they should speak only when asked for advice on legal points. By the end of the second day, the two tribes were reported to be discussing the division of the land and what the new boundaries should be.[33] The sessions ended on the third day, with MacDonald saying that progress had been encouraging, while Hamilton accused the Navajos of stalling. According to MacDonald the Navajos were to prepare a written proposal on lands south of the reservation in Arizona that might be given to the Hopis, while Hamilton continued to oppose any settlement other than moving the Navajo residents off half of the joint-interest lands.[34]

Shortly after this meeting, Boyden sent a long letter to Abourezk. In it, he excerpted statements by MacDonald and Hamilton, as reported in a story in the *Arizona Republic*, but placing Hamilton's words as if they were replies to MacDonald's claims. He then went on to quote Commissioner Nash's pronouncements at the 1963 Scottsdale meeting and a part of Walsh's findings of fact in the ongoing litigation in Tucson. Taken all together and out of context in this way, Boyden used these remarks to assert Hopi ownership of the surface rights of half of the joint-interest area.[35]

A second negotiating session was held in May at the Ramada Inn in Phoenix. Bruce Perry, who was head of the Utah State Division of Indian Affairs, presided. MacDonald again headed the Navajo delegation, while Abbott Sekaquaptewa lead the Hopi contingent. The Navajos presented in writing, apparently as requested by the Hopis at the Salt Lake City meeting, two specific proposals for new lands for the Hopis outside the reservation but connected to District 6 by a corridor, and an alternate proposal that the Hopis be compensated with a portion of the Navajos' royalties from oil and mineral income from the joint-interest area until the Hopi interest had been purchased. The Hopis quickly rejected the Navajo proposals, and the meeting lasted only two hours. Sekaquaptewa asserted that the Hopis would accept nothing but getting their half of the surface area. MacDonald bitterly blamed the failure of the negotiations on Boyden. He also anticipated another meeting in which the Navajos would make an offer of a partition boundary that would affect the smallest number of Navajos.[36]

Repeated news reports that MacDonald was about to accept some sort of partition left me feeling that there was no longer any hope of avoiding the eviction of large numbers of Navajos from their homes.

There were soon two rays of hope, however. Two new bills offering alternatives to partition were introduced in the House of Representatives. Manuel Lujan jointly sponsored a bill with John Conlan of Arizona that would authorize the Navajo tribe to pay the Hopis for their half-interest in the Reservation lands with interest-free money borrowed from the federal government. And Lloyd Meeds, a Democrat from Washington, introduced a bill to settle the matter by binding arbitration.[37]

The battle quickly shifted to the nation's capital, where Congress was again assuming the responsibility for deciding what was to be done. At hearings held in the House there was testimony for the Navajos by MacDonald, Howard Gorman, Glen George, Samuel Pete, Mary Lou White, and Dr. David F. Aberle.

Aberle, an anthropologist at the University of British Columbia who had spent many years in research among the Navajos, submitted a report which documented that Navajo population increase within the 1882 Reservation was a result of normal population growth, not of large in-migration, as the Hopi attorney so often proclaimed. Appearing for the Hopis were Boyden,

Abbott Sekaquaptewa, Steiger, and Goldwater, who alleged himself to be neutral and a friend of both tribes, but who could see no solution but removal of all Navajos from half of the disputed lands.[38] The administration produced two witnesses from the BIA, who provided only weak testimony. They favored letting Walsh's court decide the issue through stock reduction and a rather far-fetched scheme for a joint stock-raising business to be operated by the two tribes.[39] It appeared to me that the bureau was doing little more than playing with the lives of the people who would have to live with anything that agency might decide. Then, in July, Secretary of the Interior Rogers C. Morton came out publicly in favor of the Steiger bill.[40]

The court hearings in Tucson went consistently against the Navajos, further restricting their right to build or repair homes or to graze in the joint-interest area.

Additional bills were being introduced, complicating the debate. A new partition bill, more punitive toward the Navajos than the Steiger bill, was co-sponsored by Goldwater and Fannin. It had been drafted by Boyden, who was alert to the advantage that an extreme measure of this sort provided. It made the Steiger plan appear to be a reasonable compromise. Boyden also persuaded Representative Wayne Owens, a Utah Democrat, to submit a bill that would authorize partition by the courts.[41]

In the summer of 1973, I was transferred from Ganado to a position with the Chaco Center, a joint National Park Service–University of New Mexico research unit devoted to investigating the archeology of what was then Chaco Canyon National Monument. The project was headquartered on the university campus in Albuquerque, which placed me in Congressman Lujan's district.

New Mexico has long had a reputation of greater sympathy for minority peoples than Arizona. Indians gained the right to vote far more easily in New Mexico, and had even had the support of some Hispanic and Anglo politicians in McKinley County in their effort to get their people registered and to elect Navajos to the state legislature. In Arizona, there had been stubborn resistance to Indian rights during the civil rights movement. In fact, Arizona had been the only state outside the South to be targeted for special attention by the federal government for enforcement of voting rights, largely due to the state's use of literacy requirements, and to challenges to interpret the state constitution so as to keep Navajos and other Indians from registering. Lujan's advocacy of the Navajo cause gave me hope that my letters might have more influence. Although I no longer had ready access to some of the newspapers that I saw on the reservation, I continued to follow the course of events as closely as I was able, even subscribing by mail to the *Navajo Times* and picking up Arizona and Gallup papers whenever my travels took me in that direction.

The House Indian Affairs Subcommittee voted to consider the Owens bill in November, leaving the other bills in abeyance.[42] Debate on the bill was spirited, so much so that Steiger was quoted as saying, "I would warn my friend from Ohio not to use logical reasoning too much in this."[43] Lujan proposed several amendments which would have lessened the impact of the bill on the Navajos, all of which were defeated. The bill was approved and sent to the full House Interior Committee in December.[44] Before the end of the year, the Steiger bill and the Owens bill had been combined, and was variously referred to as the Steiger-Owens bill, or merely as the Owens bill.[45]

Richard Schifter, a Washington attorney, had been retained by the Navajo Tribe to lead a lobbying effort against partition. It was clear that 1974 was shaping up to be a critical year. In the House the Steiger-Owens bill was expected to be considered by the Interior Committee in late January. Schifter felt that Representative Morris Udall, an Arizona Democrat and brother of former Secretary of the Interior Stewart Udall, would be a key player. Although Udall's staff was said to be sensitive to the havoc that an eviction of thousands of Navajos would create, Udall himself feared the political repercussions of siding with the Navajos. According to Schifter, the Navajos might prevail in the Interior Committee with Udall's help; without it, they had no chance whatever. Schifter urged MacDonald and Vlassis to assure Udall of Navajo political support should he take up their cause.[46]

The situation in the Senate was even more ominous, for Goldwater and Fannin were reported trying to move their bill through both the Indian Affairs Subcommittee and the Interior Committee without hearings.[47]

The predicted schedule did not hold, allowing more time for lobbying on both sides. Schifter and an assistant were busy talking with members of the House Interior Committee and their staff people, relying on help from Sergeant Schriver, a member of the same law firm as Schifter, and Representative Udall. Hope that Lujan's bill might pass faded rapidly, but the Meeds bill proposing arbitration became a fall-back position for which Schifter was able to enlist considerable support.[48]

The votes in the House Interior Committee came on February 20. The critical vote was on a motion to replace the Owens bill with the Meeds bill. In a tie vote, only the Owens bill was left under consideration. Voting in favor of the Meeds bill were sixteen Democrats, including Udall, and four Republicans, including Lujan. Against were six Democrats and fourteen Republicans. Haley, the committee chairman, did not vote, but favored the Owens bill. The failure of some congressmen who had Navajos in their districts to support these constituents led Schifter to express resentment in his report on the vote.[49]

I was, of course, unaware of much that was happening in Window Rock and Washington, aside from what I learned from the newspapers, but on February 23 I sat down to write Lujan, for the crucial last stand would soon come on the House floor. The only copy of the Owens bill that I had dated from the previous September, and I knew that there had been some changes, but on the basis of this and a story in the *Albuquerque Tribune*,[50] I posed several questions to Congressman Lujan:

> . . . The bill "provides from $15,000 to $20,000 per Navajo family for their relocation." I am curious to know how this money is to be disbursed. Will the Bureau of Indian Affairs deduct from each family's share their administrative expenses, thereby decreasing the amount available to families? How will a Navajo family be defined, as a nuclear family or as the traditional Navajo extended family? Will there be any pro-rating of the amount due a family on the basis of actual losses suffered in terms of improvements, grazing lands and farms? . . . Does Section 17 of the bill prevent Navajos from trying to recover personal losses not fairly compensated by the payments? In the event of an accident causing injury or loss of life during the removal, for instance if a child should be struck by a government truck removing Navajos from the area, would Section 17 further prevent any court action for damages? Does the bill make any provision for the approximately 3,000 children who will be deposited in other school districts?
>
> The last question leads to the most critical one of all. Where are the people

to go? Unless the bill has been changed quite a lot, there is no provision for resettlement of these people. There is certainly no available land within the Navajo Reservation and the amounts to be paid do not appear likely to be enough to allow the people to buy new lands outside the reservation should they be available. Of the people to be affected, only a small minority of those over 25 years of age have sufficient education in English to be able to adapt to life outside a Navajo community. Unless the Congress is willing to provide from the public domain in Arizona an equivalent reservation adjacent to the present Navajo reservation for the resettlement of these Navajos, we are failing completely in our duty to recognize our obligations in a situation that is in part a creation of government actions, and lack of action, over the years. Should removal be inevitable, and I hope it is not, the just and most essential requirement of any bill so authorizing should be that lands on which the people may resettle be provided before anyone is dispossessed of his or her home.

The land described for the Hopis in Section 7 is excessive and extends far beyond any area that the Hopis have claim to in the area west of the Executive Order Reservation of 1882. A rough estimate shows that it embraces about 400 square miles. On the basis of my own investigations when I was employed by the Navajo Tribe some years ago I calculated that the most the Hopis might legitimately expect in the region to be about 60 to 70 square miles. . . . A . . . serious matter is the giving of total control of the irrigation water in the Tuba City area to the Hopis.

Sections 12 through 16 appear to me devised primarily to authorize a Hopi raid on the Navajo Treasury of devastating proportions. Section 17, removing any responsibility on the part of the United States, makes this all the more ominous. . . . Only part A of Section 15 appears to be really justified and the rest is merely adding insult to injury if it is not a scheme to enrich sundry lawyers and Hopis at Navajo expense. The other lawsuits authorized by these sections add a self-righteous punitive quality to the bill that is hardly in keeping with the historic nature of the problem. Indeed, the entire bill appears to have been based on the assumption that the Navajos should be punished and made to suffer for something their ancestors allegedly did many generations ago. I do not believe that this is a proper way to treat any American citizens and it is particularly reprehensible when applied against a group identified on the basis of race, language and culture.

Navajo efforts were not limited to lobbying in Washington. A booklet, *The Navajos: An Indian Struggle For Land and Heritage*, was published for distribution both to members of Congress and to the press.[51] Howard Bryan, a columnist for the *Albuquerque Tribune*, was given a tour of the joint-interest area accompanied, by tribal interpreter Claire M. Thompson, which he described in the paper.[52]

On March 18 there was an effort made to bring the Owens bill to the House floor under a suspension of the rules, a move that would require a two-thirds vote but that would not allow amendments. The proponents of the Hopi tribal cause must have felt that they had an unusually strong position. Manuel Lujan, however, fought back vigorously, being the only speaker to oppose the motion, but assisted by Harold Runnels, Democratic representative from New Mexico, and John Conlan of Arizona, who "worked the floor" in his support. While Lujan quoted those who predicted violence and bloodshed if the Navajos were dispossessed, he also pointed out that the bill lacked any means for implementing the eviction or any provision for land for resettlement. The maneuver was defeated by a vote of 199 opposed to 133 in favor. The strong opposing vote raised hopes that the support necessary to authorize partition was lacking.[53]

Lujan replied to my letter shortly afterward, thanking me for the "excellent material" I had sent. He said that my questions had given him "ammunition" for the floor fight.[54]

Owens and Steiger were far from ready to give up, however, and began working to move the bill through the Rules Committee to the floor once again.[55]

Schifter, in reviewing the status of the various House bills in April, thought the Owens bill bogged down in the Rules Committee. If it should be reported out, he predicted that a motion by Lujan to substitute his bill would be opposed by Meeds, and that the Meeds bill would appeal most to the majority. He felt that with a few amendments the Meeds bill would be a satisfactory solution.[56]

At the beginning of May, Lujan informed Schifter that it would not be possible to keep the issue from returning to the House floor. He wanted a bill that would have a chance of passing and asked Schifter to draft one for him. Schifter wanted to write amendments to the Meeds bill, but Lujan insisted that an amended Owens bill would be required. His preference was that it defer a specific solution pending a court decision, and that any monetary compensation to the Hopis should come from the Navajo Tribal Treasury rather than from the federal government. Schifter decided to do two drafts, reworking each bill, and send them to MacDonald for his decision.[57]

Lujan proved to be correct in his estimate of the prospects for the Owens bill, which was soon on the House Docket for another vote about the end of May.[58]

Lujan and Meeds promptly agreed on a compromise bill based on Meeds's original draft, which they could both support as an alternative to the Owens proposal.[59]

Their optimism for this strategy was misplaced, however. Following the first floor defeat of the Owens bill, the Hopi council had sent two delegations to Washington to visit congressmen in their offices. Owens, Steiger, Goldwater, and Fannin all sent letters to the representatives, and Owens and Steiger manned the entries to urge that congressmen entering the House vote for their bill because the committee had recommended it. The result was that the Meeds-Lujan bill was rejected by a vote of 129 "for" and 199 "against," and the Owens bill, now including an amendment to provide 250,000 acres for Navajo resettlement, passed by a vote of 290 to 38.[60]

Attention then shifted to the Senate. Fannin sent a letter to Edward M. Kennedy, Democrat from Massachusetts, offering to provide all the background information he might need to make up his mind on the issue.[61] It is probable that he made this offer to other senators as well.

Others were also soon writing to senators. Robert W. Young, who had spent twenty years of his career as an anthropologist and linguist among the Navajos, wrote Abourezk to support the proposal that the Hopis be paid for their half-interest. There was a scrambling for support by both sides. The Hopis gained the backing of the All-Indian Pueblo Council, while a meeting of 1,000 Hopi traditionalists and Navajos endorsed a resolution opposing the Goldwater-Fannin bill. The Navajo Tribe enlisted a powerful ally in the AFL-CIO labor lobby.[62]

Senator Abourezk drafted a "compromise" bill of his own, which authorized partition, but which also provided for life estates for Navajos born within the disputed area. It also allowed occupancy to continue for those who had moved into the area for a period equal to that which they had already spent on the land[63] As nearly as I could judge from the news story, the plan would have been a bureaucratic nightmare, if it were possible to administer it at all. I wrote a long letter to Abourezk to explain why it appeared to me that his scheme would merely prolong the agony of the dispute.[64] Had I realized that the life-estate idea entailed forcing elderly people to live alone on small, isolated homesites, separated from their kin and all other fellow Navajos, I would have been even more vehement. The Navajos themselves soon figured out what the life estates really were and began to call them "death estates." Well-meaning whites with little concept of the importance of family and community in Navajo society continued to advocate the life estate as a palliative for relocation, however, and as a feature that made the partition alternative more acceptable in Congress.

The strength of the growing sentiment in Washington favoring partition was met by renewed Navajo lobbying and public presentation of their case. Vlassis himself wrote a letter to the editor of the *Arizona Republic*.[65] He pointed out the injustice of denying the Havasupais an enlargement of their tiny reservation by paying a mere ten cents an acre for traditional land, taken away long ago, in order not to have to evict whites. In the same letter, Vlassis was also critical of dispossessing thousands of Navajos who had long been established on their traditional use lands. On July 14 I sent letters to several senators expressing my opposition to the Owens bill, which seemed the one most likely to be passed.[66]

Soon, a caravan of buses was under way to Washington, with 120 Navajos from the disputed areas, including people from Pinon, Coal Mine Mesa, White Cone, Jeddito, Low Mountain, and Chilchinbito, all of whom had homes in the joint-interest area, and from Tuba City in the area claimed by the Hopis of Upper Moenkopi. They planned to stop at several cities on their way east and to reach Washington in time to begin lobbying prior to the Senate Interior and Insular Affairs Committee hearings.[67]

The two tribal chairmen, MacDonald and Sekaquaptewa, held a debate before the Albuquerque Press Club on July 17. Neither could claim victory in the confrontation, but each had the opportunity to air his side of the case before representatives of the local papers. As the debate ended, the Navajo caravan arrived in Albuquerque, and it also received favorable publicity, including special mention of the quandary in which families of Navajo-Hopi intermarriages found themselves.[68]

On the following Sunday, the *Albuquerque Journal* ran a long feature story that was a serious effort to present impartially the arguments on both sides.[69] The article noted that three bills were before the Senate: the Owens bill, H.R. 10337; S.B. 3220, sponsored by Domenici and Montoya of New Mexico and Frank Moss of Utah, which would authorize a federal loan to the Navajo Tribe for the purchase from the Hopi Tribe of lands used by Navajos; and Abourezk's S.B. 3724, with its life estates and provision for payment of rent to the Hopi Tribe until there should be no more Navajos on the half of the land which was to be Hopi.

On the first day of the committee hearings, Wednesday, July 24, the Nixon administration announced its support for the Owens bill via a letter delivered to the committee by Commissioner of Indian Affairs Morris Thompson. Domenici held firm in his support of the purchase plan despite the conflict he faced with his party, thus preserving a bipartisan backing for a purchase of the Hopi interest. Goldwater and Fannin gave their endorsement to the Owens bill. The "Owens-Steiger" bill was favored by most of those who testified on Wednesday. MacDonald spoke toward the end of the day, and again asked that the two tribes be allowed to settle the matter themselves, but he also stated that if congressional action were deemed necessary, he would prefer to see the Montoya-Domenici-Moss bill approved.[70]

The emotion-laden rhetoric of the past dominated these hearings, too. MacDonald noted that he could not promise that there would be "peace and resignation" if the Navajos were forced to move, and he characterized the Owens-Steiger bill as "a deliberate attempt to make all Navajo people pay for a century of government neglect and tragedy." Sekaquaptewa went even further, proclaiming that, "The tears of the children of Hopi herders and farmers slain by Navajo marauders for a hundred years have never been wiped away."[71]

As the hearings went on, even the traditional anti-Council Hopis were allowed to speak. Mina Lansa, their leader, made a request that the Hopis, Navajos, and Paiutes be allowed to work out their own problems. She based her reasoning on Hopi religious beliefs, which were probably poorly understood by the senators and probably even discounted as "heathen superstition" by some. Still, the sincerity of her plea must have affected the views of some of the less hardened of the politicians.[72]

Perhaps the most authoritative reasoning was that presented by David Aberle, in both his testimony and his written report. The report was a restrained and scholarly piece of work that was in sharp contrast to the exaggerated claims of those caught up in the politicized atmosphere created by partisans of the two sides. Aberle first established the continuity of Navajo occupation over several generations, based both on his own independent research and on the investigations that Lee Correll had headed. He next emphasized the urgent circumstances under which the 1882 Reservation had been created, which had prevented any careful investigation of use and occupation at that time. He then concisely summarized the history of federal procrastination as the crisis slowly developed. He listed the various estimates of Navajo population from 1882 to 1970 within the Executive Order Reservation and plotted them on a graph for comparison with overall Navajo population growth, showing that the two followed very similar curves. This led to his conclusion that "the entire increase in [Navajo] population from 1882 to the present can be accounted for by natural reproduction, with immigration and emigration balancing one another." He followed this by explaining the matrilocal settlement system, which Boyden had distorted into a system for stealing land. The Hopis, he pointed out, practiced the same matrilocal system as the Navajos. He ably refuted the charges that Navajos were flocking into the disputed area.

Aberle went on to describe the Navajo population within the disputed area as among the most traditional of the tribe, living in an area with poor roads and very limited access to "administrative centers, hospitals, high schools, towns and jobs." The freeze brought about by the Prescott decision in 1962 had halted all improvements, resulting in a continuing low literacy rate, lack of public services and jobs, worse roads for getting to what jobs there were, and high unemployability. The freeze had prevented any implementation of modern methods for the increase of forage to relieve overgrazing, causing continued deterioration of the range.

He characterized the Owens-Steiger bill as a measure that evaded federal responsibilities, one that placed all blame for the dispute on the Navajos and forced them to suffer all the costs of solving the problem. He further characterized the proposal for the Moenkopi question as being based on no justifying data whatever.

Aberle then applied the results of studies of other compulsory relocation endeavors throughout the world to predict the effects such a program might have on the Navajos. He first predicted that antagonisms and conflict would result "between Navajos, between Navajos and Hopis, and between Navajos and the Federal Government." As a conclusion to this section, he wrote:

> There is a sense in which one need not know anything about past relocation efforts, nor anything about Navajo culture, kinship or economy, to be able to anticipate the outcome of the relocation. If 8,000 inter-related human beings, living where their ancestors have lived for centuries, are thrust from their homeland under these conditions, it can be expected that they will resist relocation. Such a reaction has nothing specific to do with Navajo culture or personality; it is an expectable human response. Deprived of livestock, crowded onto the reservation, moved into new territory that lacks what is needed to render it habitable, the relocatees will be impoverished, dislocated, disorganized and dependent. Those whom they crowd will be resentful and will also be economically impaired. The relocatees will lose faith in their tribal government and be alienated from the Federal Government. Years of economic dependency, administrative problems, and waste of human potential can be foreseen. These are the results of relocation with which the Congress of the United States will ultimately have to cope.

Aberle also described the court-ordered stock reduction as punitive rather than constructive, showing the pervasive importance of livestock in Navajo society, far beyond even economic need or the use for status that the Hopi Tribe's spokesmen had made to seem so preeminent, but as a source of family stability that had enabled the Navajos to escape the demoralizing conditions that had affected so many Indian peoples.

Aberle then laid to rest some other erroneous assumptions that had dominated earlier hearings and debates on the Owens bill. He noted that Hopi occupancy in the disputed area had lapsed at least a century and a half before the United States had obtained sovereignty within the Southwest. He attacked the characterization of the Navajos as nomads constantly moving onto Hopi land, and the inference that because Navajos fought the whites in past centuries that their descendants today should be punished, or that because the Hopis avoided war with the whites in the same distant past that their descendants deserved favored treatment today.

He also attacked the "David and Goliath" image so cultivated by the Hopi side, noting that

> the groups immediately affected by the conflict are 5,000 impoverished on-reservation Hopis and 8,000 even more impoverished Navajos in the disputed territory and the Moenkopi corridor. The question is whether the Navajos shall be displaced from their homes, their farms, and their pastures for the advantage of a smaller number of Hopis who wish to use the land for range. The size of the Tribes, their treasuries, and their total territories is irrelevant.

Next, he disputed the assertion that the issue of the joint-interest area and the Moenkopi issue should be linked.

> The disputed territory and the Moenkopi issue are linked by the Hopi Tribe's eagerness to expand their holdings, by the Hopi Tribe's view that it has an undivided if undefined interest in the entire Navajo reservation, and by the Hopi Tribe's apprehension that if it displaces so large a number of Navajos, it must have a corridor from Moenkopi to the edge of Hopi land in the Executive Order territory to protect it from Navajo hostility. If Navajo relocation is not attempted in the disputed territory, the rationale for the corridor disappears, and with it the need for still further Navajo relocation.

He further showed that the issue of Paiute land needed considerably more study and thought before any action should be taken.

In conclusion, Aberle advocated that the government work to provide for the needs of both tribes without the disruptions and traumas of relocation. He suggested dividing the land and fencing firmly established boundaries on the basis of current settlement and allocating additional lands beyond the reservation for Hopi range lands. He estimated that the ultimate costs of H.R. 10337, the Owens-Steiger bill, would far exceed those of any of the possible alternatives.

In his conclusions Aberle not only reiterated his previous findings, but inferred that the Prescott court case was primarily premised on the need for definition of ownership for the leasing of subsurface rights, and that the

Prescott decision had ignored the problems of the residents of the lands. He again branded the partition proposal as punitive toward the Navajos, as far more costly than the alternatives, and as devastating in its effects on the relocatees. He urged Congress to find a less drastic solution.[73]

After all the contention and adrenalin, after all the extreme claims and the ethnic slurs, the fact that one of the parties to the dispute could submit a reasoned and balanced statement advocating a fair settlement may have influenced a few members of the committee, but the effect was less than was needed. After considerable thought and discussion, the committee rejected the bills under consideration by a vote of 8 to 6 and adopted MacDonald's suggestion for further negotiations.[74] This proviso, however, was grafted onto the Owens-Steiger bill, so that the net result was another negotiating session under the pressure of certain partition should the talks fail—a sure sign to the Hopis that they had only to stall for another six months to get their way in the end.

Still to come was the final round, the floor battle. I wrote to friends in other states asking that they write their senators, hoping to help broaden opposition to partition. The Navajos made their major effort in the floor fight merely to eliminate the Moenkopi issue, and succeeded to that extent against determined opposition from Goldwater and his allies. Having won this battle, however, they lost the war. The Senate took their victory on Moenkopi as a reasonable compromise and passed the bill by a vote of 72 to 0. The House acceded to the changes in the Senate, and the bill was quickly passed on to President Gerald Ford, who signed it into law. The lawyers for the Navajos claimed victory due to their success in regaining a mandate for negotiations and to the elimination of Moenkopi as a bargaining point. The Hopis complained about the delay that negotiating sessions would entail, and about the bill's restricting negotiations to the joint-interest area. But the Hopis knew they had clearly won and had only to wait for negotiations and mediation to end in order to make partition a reality.[75]

The Navajos knew who their enemies were. In the 1976 general election, they turned out in large numbers to vote against all Republicans. Goldwater was too popular in southern Arizona to be defeated by so small a block of votes, but I rejoiced to learn that the Navajos had supplied the winning margin for Raul Castro, the first Hispanic governor of Arizona. Goldwater was reported to be furious, and to have accused the Navajos of being lured to vote by offers of beer, a charge I knew to be ridiculous. My greatest resentment, however, was that none of the senators who had worked so hard to help the Navajos had voted against partition that one last time. Passage of the bill without opposition seemed to doom all hope for any future modification in the sentence of exile which had been pronounced, albeit in roundabout and evasive language, in the final bill.

FINAL THOUGHTS

THE PREDICTIONS of certain partition as a result of the new law were as accurate as they were gloomy. Negotiations led nowhere and a line was soon drawn. Once the required court order set the new boundary, a three-person relocation commission headquartered in Flagstaff began the process by planning methods to be followed. Despite delays as a result of a penurious Congress, bureaucratic red tape, Anglo opposition to Navajo land selections, and Navajo resistance, relocation has proceeded rather steadily. Even so, the Hopis have continued to harass even those law-abiding Navajos who registered for relocation and patiently awaited their turn for the commissioners' attention. The Hopi council denied almost every request by the Navajos for leniency to make life under the freeze more endurable and even lobbied for more punitive measures and for less aid to those who bowed to the move. As a result, many Navajos were forced to abandon their homes before the commission was able to provide them new places to live. These refugees provided yet another problem—one that the social scientists had not foreseen. One of the most important tests of the good faith of the Congress will be whether these refugees receive the aid to which they are entitled once everybody has been removed from the land.

As of this writing, almost three decades after the *Healing* v. *Jones* decision and half a decade after the date set for completion of relocation, about 70 percent of the Navajo residents in the Reservation area have been resettled. There is no agreement on the total number of refugees, or on the numbers of Navajos still living on the land, some of whom have still not registered with the commission and who continue to fight for repeal of the legislation requiring relocation.

The failures and problems encountered by the program have been amply documented by Kammer in *The Second Long Walk: The Navajo-Hopi Land Dispute*[1];

by Scudder, et al. in *No Place to Go: Effects of Compulsory Relocation on Navajos*[2]; by Wood, Vannette, and Andrews in *"Sheep is Life": An Assessment of Livestock Reduction in the Former Navajo-Hopi Joint Use Area*[3]; by Topper in *Mental Health Effects on Navajo Area Mental Health Patients from the Former Navajo-Hopi Joint Use Area*[4]; by Parlow in *Cry, Sacred Ground*[5]; by Benedek in *The Wind Won't Know Me: A History of the Navajo-Hopi Land Dispute*[6]; by Tamir in *"Relocation of Navajo from Hopi Partitioned Land in Pinon,"*[7] and *"Some Consequences of Compulsory Relocation on Navajo Socioeconomy"*[8]; by Shaw-Serder and Yazzie in *"The Navajo-Hopi Land Dispute: Sale of Replacement Homes by Navajo Public Law 93-531 Relocatees"*[9]; by Brennan in *"Navajo Perceptions of the Psychological and Sociocultural Meaning of Forced Relocation"*[10]; and even in the reports of the Navajo and Hopi Indian Relocation Commission itself.[11] Only the slow pace of the relocation has averted serious violence in the area, although two Navajos have died in Window Rock in political turmoil that can be considered at least partially an outgrowth of the disruptions occasioned by relocation. The Navajo tribal government has narrowly survived near collapse, while political divisions among the Hopis appear to be fully as bitter as ever.

The question remains, why was a course of action that was so predictably destined to result in such misery for so many American citizens so readily set in motion by our Congress? The answers, as I see them, are not pleasant ones, but they are not quite those that have been predicated by others.

First in priority are the internal dynamics of the two tribes. The centralized political structure of the Navajo Tribe at the time of *Healing* v. *Jones*, and that structure's general acceptance by the Navajo people, have been well described.[12] Less evident has been the fact that the tribal government sometimes asserted authority beyond what Navajo customary views of individual liberty would sanction, all too often under pressure from the dominant society. I have frequently made allusion to the influence of the tribal attorneys in tribal-level politics among the Navajos. What often were well-meant attempts by tribal attorneys to steer Navajo government in directions and toward goals prevailing among Euro-Americans were sometimes perceived by Navajos as actions that conflicted with traditional values. This was true, to an even greater degree, with respect to the BIA and other branches of the federal government. Neither should the private business sector be omitted from this list, for it could wield a carrot fully as powerful as the stick available to government for persuading or tempting tribal officials to act in ways they might find hard to explain to their people. While others in mainstream society—educators, scientists, the clergy, journalists, tourists, and even personal friends—have also affected tribal policies and decisions, in the Navajo-Hopi dispute the big three were lawyers, government officials, and businessmen.

Most dramatically foreign to Navajo ways has been the decision-making process itself. Whereas in large-scale societies, a few make far-reaching decisions on behalf of many others, in traditional Navajo society decisions are not made until consensus has been achieved. The respect for the individual's opinions that is so integral to all Navajo social action has been so freely overridden by outsiders that the Navajo stereotype of all whites as bossy continues to persist. All too often what an Anglo American considers to be no more than mild persuasion is regarded by a Navajo as an impertinent command. High-pressure tactics common in Anglo society are seen by Navajos as far beyond the limits of permissible behavior. The restraint so typical of Navajo dealings with those who are not relatives is more than just shyness or even etiquette, for it is based on a deeply held belief in individual rights. Less obvious conventions are equally important in interactions among close associates.

Thus, the tribe as a whole did not rise up en masse to defend the Navajos within the disputed area, for it was the business of the affected people themselves. Only when those affected requested support might it be given. Boyden's frequent ranting against supposed large numbers of Navajos taking up the cause to oppress the Hopis was simply wrong, whether based on his misconception of how Navajo society functioned or on malice. One of the great weaknesses of the tribe in handling relations with non-Indians has been this reluctance to take concerted action except in cases of threats that are clearly against all Navajos. The people in the disputed area brought their pleas only to the tribal government, and there with varying success, for they constituted no more than about 10 percent of the Navajo population, while they knew that the tribe as a whole suffered a great many other difficulties. Even the overwhelming Navajo vote against Goldwater was not so much in defense of the rights of the people of the joint-interest area as it was in opposition to a candidate who was seen as a threat to all Navajos as a result of the manner in which he had treated some of them. The people of the disputed land never were able to make a tribal cause of their dilemma. Ultimately those who resisted relocation, claiming to be a sovereign nation apart from their fellows, went not to other Navajos for help, but to whites.

The dispute did have a major impact on Navajo tribal politics, for the Hopi claim in the 1934 Reservation brought many other Navajos under the threat of Hopi expansionism, enough to carry the vote in tribalwide elections for Chairman. The land issue was a decisive factor in at least two elections, giving Peterson Zah his first victory and MacDonald his fourth.

Zah's promise to settle the matter on the basis of his personal friendship with Ivan Sidney, then the Hopi chairman, was far too optimistic an appraisal of the potential of that relationship. The western Navajo vote was his, and it helped carry him into office, but when he had nothing to show for his promise four years later, he was seen as having been badly taken in by the Hopis. MacDonald easily captured the same vote to return to office. He was able to recount his battles all along the way, including twice risking imprisonment by standing up for the people of the Hopi-partitioned lands. Despite the fact that he had lost in court, his claim to steadfast loyalty to their interests was sufficient to return him to power.

Did the irresponsible handling of truth among white politicians in their fever to throw Navajos out of their homes encourage the MacDonald administration in the extremes of corruption that finally brought it down? There had been rumors of corruption as early as MacDonald's first term, but nothing sufficient to cause a real scandal within the tribe until his fourth term. Nor were any of the early rumors ever substantiated; in 1977 MacDonald was indicted for fraud, but eventually acquitted of the charges.[13] Having witnessed the magnitude of the misrepresentations made in the Congress and in the courts could have done little to enhance belief in the value of honesty in the national society.

This does not in any way excuse the corruption of the last MacDonald administration. It is important to show, however, how the hopeless situation of the Navajo people on the lands from which the Hopi Council wanted them removed, contributed to corruption within the Navajo Tribe. MacDonald had a ready constituency for whom he could grandstand, followers ready to reach for any straw that the reprieve held out. He firmly believed, I do not doubt, that the Arizona politicians were reaping immense pecuniary gain from the energy companies as a result of their unbending support of the Hopi Council. For a person perhaps already engaged in minor graft, but certainly susceptible to the lure of wealth and power, the temptation was more than he could resist.

When MacDonald was in trouble, much of his unbending support came from the people of the west, for he had been the last strong advocate for their cause. The Navajo government has weathered the recent storm and appears to be stronger than ever, but those who would destroy it may yet find opportunities in continuing disputes over land, both in the separate issue of the Moenkopi land rights and the opposition of the resisters within the Hopi partitioned lands.

Among the Hopis the factional split is older, deeper, and less amenable to healing. The traditionalist faction, perhaps better termed the conservative faction, and the council or progressive faction are so far apart that each refuses to recognize the legitimacy of the other. The beginnings of real differentiation in Hopi society may go all the way back to the twelfth through the fifteenth centuries when the Hopis experienced an influx of peoples, as the Anasazi abandoned the entire San Juan drainage and various other prehistoric groups left broad regions within the Little Colorado drainage, apparently due to severe droughts. By the seventeenth century, a progressive Hopi faction saw the opportunities presented by the recently arrived Spaniards primarily in terms of economic potential and political alliance. New ways of making a living from livestock and trade were joined with a possibility of dominance over the conservatives. The conservatives, on the other hand, saw mainly the threats inherent in Spanish rule—the loss of autonomy and the undermining of their religion. The Spanish assault on the Kachina cult, so vital in the old Hopi way of life, was especially threatening. If the ceremonies were not performed as ordained by the gods, the rains would not fall, the corn would not grow, and their villages would meet the fate of those whose ruins were found over the land in all directions from the small surviving cluster at Hopi.

For the conservatives, the Navajos became a buffer between themselves and the Spaniards. As long as the Navajos were at war with the intruders, few whites would make their way across the arid lands between Hopi and the Rio Grande, and those who did would find it difficult to summon support. In time, this faction would actively foment war between the Navajos and the

Spaniards. In addition, Navajo presence may also have functioned to keep all the members of a village close to home where they could be easily recruited to do their duties in the kivas and the dances.

The opposite applied to the progressives, who wanted ready access to the European goods available from the settlers in the east and freedom to travel to profit from their trade. They may also have wished to try their hand at ranching with the newly introduced Old World domestic animals, which would require that they be able to range far afield for pasturage. A final desire may well have been evading the demands of the native priesthood that they participate in religious retreats and dances.

One thing is certain. Changes did come about, changes that led to the extreme polarization of the present day. The policies of the United States differed from those of the early Spanish, but the end results were much the same. A progressive, anti-Navajo faction allied with the Americans and encouraged movement away from the villages and opposition to certain of the old religious practices, while the conservatives were routinely marginalized and alienated. The stalemate led to the collapse of the first organized tribal government. Boyden had personally revived the moribund tribal council.[14] The federal government continued to insist that the only legitimate governing body was the council, and it made little or no effort to reconcile the two factions. The friends of the Navajos were thus shut out of the government by the depth of the split between themselves and the progressives. Polarization in colonial times had led to the Pueblo Revolt and the destruction of Awatobi. The new polarization brought about the dispossession of the Hopis' Navajo neighbors and a degree of resentment among the Navajos that will not end soon.

I have made allusion to the pitfalls of intercultural communication and interaction, and I believe that some specific examples with regard to Southwestern Indian-Euro-American relations are now required. I draw here on my own observations, especially in the context of tribal government and legal disputes.

Language differences are central to the miscommunication between peoples, and have played a major role in Navajo-Anglo-American relationships. Navajo language relies strongly on vowel tone and length to distinguish meaning. These are features that in English function primarily to express the emotional content and the connotation of a statement, along with an intonation pattern of which we are generally unaware, but which tells us whether what is said is a question or an assertion of fact. English spoken with a Navajo accent appears deficient in the clues we expect to provide us subtle and emotionally reassuring portions of the message. This can lead to miscommunication with regard to whether the speaker is serious or joking, sincere or evasive, even whether the statement is casual or of great importance to the speaker. In Navajo, the verb carries a greater part of the meaning in any statement. Translations into English often result in circumlocutions that sound stilted or simply awkward, again often causing an English-speaking listener to remain in doubt as to the implications and feelings underlying the literal meaning of a statement. Anglo-Americans unused to Navajo-accented speech sometimes feel that Navajos lack emotion. This obvious deficit in understanding can contribute to a feeling of uneasiness, usually labeled "culture shock," although the less dramatic term "culture stress" probably describes the situation much better. Altogether, these barriers to easy conversation can also lead a listener to doubt the truthfulness of a Navajo speaker. I recall Clyde Kluckhohn once revealing that even he had on more than one occasion suspected that a Navajo was telling a made-up story, only to learn later that what he had heard was accurate information.

A Hopi accent, on the other hand, is very different. The Hopi language is totally unrelated to Navajo. The sound system has some similarities to Navajo, but is such that it contributes to a manner of speaking in English that is much more expressive to the ear of a native English-speaker, most often giving an open, friendly, or even ingratiating quality to speech. Furthermore, grammatical construction does not lead to translations that appear to express thoughts in roundabout, stilted ways. The overall effect is an appearance of easier communication and of greater sincerity on the part of Hopi speakers.

These linguistic phenomena probably have similar effects in the translation of Navajo and Hopi speech into Spanish. Navajo speech translated into Spanish and then into English, as quoted in mid-nineteenth century documents, seems to have some of the same qualities as Navajo translated into English. In any case, the effects of characteristics of the two languages have undoubtedly colored Euro-American views of the two peoples for a very long time. I suspect that they also had at least some effect on the perceptions of Navajo and Hopi testimony in court and before Congress, as well as in dealings with federal administrative officials, representatives of the press, and others. It must be recognized that the level of English proficiency was also much higher among the Hopis than among the Navajos due to the fact that their village settlement pattern led to universal school enrollment at an earlier date. Despite an appearance of better communication on the part of the Hopis, there were errors of perception and understanding for them as well as for the Navajos, although these were due less to linguistic factors than to cultural differences.

There are two other aspects of working with a tribe that need mention here. First is what I like to think of as "the bicultural scapegoat." Any healthy society feels that it is superior to others in at least some ways, and conversely, that neighboring peoples suffer at least some kinds of inferiority. Other peoples may also be thought to excel in certain respects, and these beliefs can be manipulated in dealing with outsiders to cement relationships or to arouse antagonism as a particular situation might require. When dealing with people from outside the tribe, there is a tendency to encourage sharing of negative stereotypes of third parties. This is especially true where people are involved together in a competitive endeavor. During the various claims research projects in which I took part, I soon became aware that the Navajos with whom I worked were not reluctant to engage in ethnic remarks about the competitors for land they claimed. Thus, in the east, jokes about Hispanics, once the Navajos were sure that I was not Hispanic, were to be heard, while in the north a similar situation existed regarding Mormons. Remarks about other Indian tribes were more variable, but negative as well as positive remarks were not uncommon, ranging from complaints that an Apache dialect, mutually intelligible to those Navajos who wanted to converse with its speakers, could not be understood, to complaints about Hopi witchcraft. Having similar negative feelings about the opposition seemed both a way of making it easier to work with an outsider and to feel assurance as to the outsider's loyalty to the tribal cause.

Second, I also observed that tribal and federal employees often felt a compulsion to be stronger advocates of a tribal cause than were the Indian people themselves, or even to promote causes that tribal members did not actually consider significant. In part, this would certainly have been an attempt to show that one did indeed support tribal interests, but it not infrequently went beyond a demonstration of being on the tribe's side to become an effort in one-upmanship among non-tribal individuals who had dealings with tribal members.

Both of these tendencies could easily go beyond reasonable limits to inspire bias, stereotypical thinking, and grossly exaggerated claims. I suspect that in addition to the professional obligation that attorneys have to represent the interests of their clients, these two factors in intercultural relations could easily lead them into a kind of advocacy they might otherwise find distasteful. I personally believe that Boyden did, in fact, succumb to these kinds of pressures, although I suspect there are lawyers who would defend his methods. I also believe that he was fully aware of what he was doing. Mott, in what seemed to me to be excessive legalistic posturing during negotiations with the Hopis, may also have been influenced by similar factors, although I suspect that he, having less experience in Indian law, was less cognizant of what was happening. Those of us who served as witnesses in the various claims cases certainly felt the same pressures and dealt with them as best we could. I think we all had moments of success, when we felt we had resisted the temptation to go beyond our evidence and had perhaps even pointed out where our data may have fallen short of demonstrating some of the claims made by the attorneys. We probably had other moments, when, looking back now, we wonder whether we tried to push our conclusions beyond what the evidence showed.

Any evaluation of the role of tribal attorneys must go beyond what is simply a matter of the proper limits of advocacy, to the question of whether, or to what extent, tribal attorneys created the disputes which they litigated, or prolonged litigation when delay favored their own interests over those of the tribe they represented. As already mentioned, I did not find most lawyers inclined to confide in others in ways that would reveal their innermost feelings. I did conclude that the profession appeals most to those of a competitive and contentious nature.

In view of how our society functions, Indian tribes and nations are as much in need of legal representation to defend their interests as other organized entities. Because much tribal litigation must be authorized through individual acts of Congress, legal representation is often necessary to insure that proper language is used in the drafting of the bills that would enable court actions. Courts are bound by the wording of the legislation. A far-sighted attorney can do much to influence the outcome of a case by ensuring that the terms under which a suit is tried are favorable, or at least not unfair, to his client. Thus, the participation of a tribal attorney in the legislative beginnings of a lawsuit is not necessarily indicative of improper activity.

It is clear that Navajo-Hopi relations had their rough spots from an early date, but whether they really required a court case for settlement is a question worth asking. The answer depends largely on values and priorities. Development of mineral wealth required a legal determination that only Congress, or actions authorized by Congress, could provide. Security in their homes and way of life for many Navajos and some Hopis also rested on a determination of this sort. Congress appeared unable to make a final determination, being essentially unwilling to do so if that determination should go against the wishes of either tribe. It is not entirely clear that if there had been no pressure for mineral development, a solution would actually have been necessary at the time. If the government had been willing to refrain from periodically altering the boundary that then existed and arbitrarily moving families as a result, I do not know whether most of the Indians themselves would have felt any urgency in the matter, but there were educated tribal leaders on both sides who did want their tribes to benefit from the monies and jobs expected from mineral development.

There were alternatives, however. Congress could have established a boundary or authorized negotiations between the two tribes to settle the dispute. The tribal attorneys on both sides favored a law suit. It would be of interest to know whether the mining interests also promoted a solution at this time, and whether they favored one method over another. Litigation was probably the natural choice of members of the legal profession, however. Once the law was passed, the litigation appears to have progressed at a rather steady pace. Since the attorneys for both tribes were working on a contingency basis, there was, of course, no advantage in delaying the process.

I feel less easy about the attorneys actions during negotiations. Neither side seemed to try to ease the way to an agreement. Failure of negotiations was always a factor that worked to the Hopis' advantage, however, so that Boyden's bluster can fairly be judged as representing his clients' interest. Just the opposite was true for the Navajos. I was inclined to feel that it was necessary for the Navajos to show up the Hopis by demonstrating that they were negotiating in good faith, thereby avoiding excessive recriminations.

Also to be considered is the charge that energy and mining interests were behind the entire fiasco, controlling what happened in the shadowy background. This charge was put forth most explicitly by Kammer,[15] vigorously argued by Redhouse,[16] and picked up uncritically by Weyler.[17] There was certainly sufficient smoke that there can be no doubt that there was a fire, but the question still remains as to whose fire it might have been. Boyden let it be known in his meetings with Littell and others that he had made both offers and threats regarding leases to oil, gas, and coal companies. The companies' involvement may well have been no more than an opportunistic response to Boyden's machinations. Their retainers to Boyden's law firm were perhaps their own way of entwining Boyden so deeply in his own plot that he could not double-cross them later. It almost appears to have been a game of two cats, each treating the other as the mouse.

Most perplexing is the fact that industry risked alienating the Navajos so thoroughly as to place any future prospects of leases in jeopardy, some probably even gambling with leases they already held. They may have felt that there were political and economic constraints on the Navajos sufficient to negate such an outcome, should their support of the Hopi council be revealed. It is strange, however, that when there was uncovered good cause for the Navajos to suspect them, nothing ensued that would seriously undermine their operations. Their influence in Navajo government seems to have survived the questions raised by several Navajos, including officials of stature in the MacDonald administration.

There is no doubt that the aid the mining interests gave Boyden had a substantial impact on the course of the contest over partition, but who played Machiavelli upon whom remains a murky matter. It is clear that mineral resources were the root cause of the original litigation, but as much at the behest of the tribes themselves as from any outside source. While the tribal attorneys on both sides were obviously interested in mineral development, the degree to which they may have manipulated corporate interests for their own purposes, and possibly at their own peril, is poorly understood.

It is almost certain that energy companies would also have tried to influence legislators and administration officials, but nothing to document their efforts has turned up. Influence could have flowed through devious channels, and the identities of stockholders, board members, and corporate interrelationships must be traced before firm conclusions can be reached.

I do not feel personally equipped to provide definitive answers to these questions. They are, without doubt, critical questions in terms of white-Indian relations, but competence of a different sort than I possess is required for a thorough investigation. The complexity of the economic forces and their possible interaction with the political power structure would make a fascinating study.

The political power structure is more easily perceived. Votes counted. A cause that could be widely dramatized in the media, with little need to pay for the publicity had strong appeal. In Arizona, where there was already acceptance of stereotypes of the Hopis as peaceful farmers and of the Navajos as nomadic raiders, it took little to arouse public passions. No matter that this required such cheap shots as portraying an ethnic minority in pejorative terms not true at the time and of dubious validity even for the distant past, and contrasting this portrayal with a wildly romanticized picture of the people on the other side. Racism disguised as realism is always a potent weapon in politics. The public, eager for a new version of the popular Western myth of the white hats versus the black hats, could easily be led to read into the boundary dispute all the old Zane Grey plots pitting noble cowboys against evil sheepherders. Goldwater and Steiger seemed especially to revel in their roles as protectors of the oppressed and as authoritative friends of the Indians, ignoring the critical distinction between the individual rights of citizens and the corporate rights of tribes. Behind this show of paternalistic concern, they were undoubtedly counting votes and calculating the effect of it all on their chances in the next election.

The role of prejudice as a political weapon derives, of course, from its potency in society at large. A negative stereotype of Navajos, particularly in their relation with the Pueblos, has a long history in the Southwest. In Spanish colonial times, the Navajos and their Apachean cousins were routinely viewed as the common enemy in wars between Christian empire builders and the natives of the land. In the present century, in the reservation bordertowns, such stereotypes are especially pervasive, but they are also found throughout much of the four-corners states of New Mexico, Arizona, Utah, and Colorado. Stereotypical images also appeared in the writings of the early Anglo-American intellectuals, such as Lummis and Bancroft, which were then picked up and gained wide currency across the land. Finally, these same stereotypes appeared in the media coverage of Navajo affairs, including the stories on the dispute between the Navajos and Hopis. It showed up in the reports of journalists who would never think of making similar attacks on other minorities, many of whom, indeed, would voice strenuous criticism of anybody who wrote in a similar fashion about African-American, Hispanic, or Jewish peoples.

The opposite side of the coin, the idealization of the Hopis, may seem innocuous or even beneficial out of context, but when it is understood as another weapon in the attack on a second minority, its true nature as a form of racism can be recognized. It is ultimately as destructive of the seemingly favored minority as it is of the derogated minority. In the long run, a positive stereotype becomes as limiting a constraint on individual potential as one that is negative. In times of tensions between peoples, positive characteristics which have been applied stereotypically may even be twisted in such a fashion as to be given negative connotations. This did, in fact, happen on the Navajo side, on the part of some whites who derided Hopi pacifism as cowardice.

The definition of group differences which we find so important can all too easily be corrupted, for the line between objective observations of what is often true, or sometimes true, or what might have been true in the past, and the application of stereotypes as something always true is not a solid demarcation on a firm and level foundation, but is better thought of as a dotted line drawn on a sandy slope. Such subtle but important distinctions are too frequently lost in the popular media and in casual discourse. While ethnic bias may not have been the cause of relocation, its employment was clearly the method by which relocation was brought about.

This animus against Navajos as opposed to Pueblos permeates even the social sciences. A favorite song of student archeologists at the University of Arizona field schools in the mid-twentieth century was about the "Athabaskan bastards" who were said to have brought about the downfall of the Pueblos. Those of us who stood up for the Navajos' rights were constantly made aware of the stigma that attached to our beliefs. Van Valkenburgh, toward the end of his life, felt ready to disown the field of anthropology entirely. Even at present I feel it necessary to be attuned to the attitudes of colleagues and to mute my feelings, on occasion, in order to maintain some sort of working relations with people who I know are doing important research that I must draw on. I am aware that my own reputation is one of being excessively biased in favor of Navajo interests. It has not been very long since a fellow Southwesternist asked me how I could be on the "wrong side." The questioner is a decent person who would be strongly offended if anyone were to make racist remarks or ethnic slurs about Pueblo Indians or Hispanics similar to those that are so often acceptable by those speaking unthinkingly regarding Navajos.

Most persuasive of all arguments suggesting that it was ethnic bias that ultimately decided the course of the affair in Congress, and perhaps in the courts as well, is the strong element of racism in the one book written by an apologist for the Hopi tribal position. Catherine Feher-Elston, in her *Children of Sacred Ground: America's Last Indian War*, portrays the Hopis in terms that would make them appear an Indian master race. On the other hand, her characterization of the Navajos is all too reminiscent of the stereotypes used by the Nazis to arouse hatred of Jews and Gypsies in the 1930s and 1940s.[18]

While her view of the Hopis is little more than an extension of the romantic image so pervasive in all of the popular literature, and to a degree, even in some of the professional works dealing with that tribe, my reading of her characterization of the Navajos has not been shared by others who have read her writings. A review of Feher-Elston's book by Richard Clemmer fails to mention anything resembling my reaction.[19] As others who have commented to me on the book have been of the same generation as Clemmer, I can only surmise that they are too young to know about Nazism and its tenets regarding race.

The racist and eugenist concepts that underlie Feher-Elston's thinking in contrasting the two peoples are most evident in the remarks she has chosen from her sources to describe the genetic heritage of the two tribes. She writes with obvious approval of the alleged Navajo aboriginal custom of abandoning "deformed, abnormal, or retarded children" to die, and with equally obvious disapproval of the restrictions of missionaries and modern laws that allow such children to grow to adulthood and reproduce, resulting in "abnormal gene pools."[20] Regarding the Hopis, she asserts enigmatically that just as the best seeds are selected for their crops, "similar concepts" are used "to control population." She further notes, however, that the Hopis did use herbs in native birth control.[21] Feher-Elston fails to observe that the Navajos also used plants for contraception, a fact easily learned from the published literature.[22] The overall effect is approval of a people who keep themselves genetically "pure," as was the aim of Hitler for his "Aryan race," and disapproval of a people who allow themselves to be influenced by U.S. law requiring humane treatment of children with birth defects, a portion of the German population that Hitler tried to eliminate in his death camps.

Feher-Elston's[23] claim to impartiality is undermined in other ways as well, as she provides a "tilt" toward the Hopis, sometimes in a vague and subtle way and sometimes quite openly—a bias evident even to as friendly a reviewer as Clemmer.[24]

If a writer such as Feher-Elston can unwittingly convince herself that she is impartial and objective in a work that edges frighteningly close to Nazism, and if a handful of liberal Ph.D.s in the 30–40-year-old age range can miss that fact, what chance is there for the average citizen, dulled by information overload, to escape the quagmire of intolerance of those who are different? This is especially problematic in the case of the always entertaining spectacle of an "Indian war." A more important question may be one that asks whether ethnic bias is inherent in our species.

Ethnocentric attitudes are certainly universal. We alternately pride ourselves on having learned to overcome them and bewail the perception that we are worse than any other society. The world news regularly informs us that racism, religious prejudice, ethnic hatreds, and other varieties of dislike of those outside the bounds of conformity can appear anywhere. Perhaps we feel a need for a flesh-and-blood bogeyman to keep ourselves in line, one that we can attack when frustrations pile too heavy a load on our psyches. At best, we are not alone in our depravity. Inhumanity toward our conspecifics is all too human.

It is thus not greed alone that is the source of injustice. Pejorative stereotypes of the "other" are pervasive, and they all too easily provide a rationale for those who desire something for a selfish end, whether it be material gain, a smug feeling of self-righteous satisfaction, vindication of belief, or sheer power over others. Stereotypes supply a rationale that can be manipulated to mobilize support, sometimes enhanced by the lure of wealth, sometimes without that particular silver lining.

In the case of partition of the joint-interest area and the relocation of thousands of Navajos, prejudice was very obviously a major factor. It provided those with hidden agendas an easy method for swaying public opinion, and the feedback from public sentiment aroused by their propaganda allowed them to rationalize their actions. Thus they could ignore the suffering their actions brought about, because those who suffered were deemed to deserve nothing else. This rather inverted reasoning allowed both the public and politicians to side completely with a tribal faction that preached total nonviolence, in order to accommodate that faction's desire to do violence to its neighbors. It allowed the public and the politicians to place corporate rights above individual rights and property rights above human rights. The Navajo-Hopi land dispute provides insights into the complexities of motivation in our species that defy casual assessment and call for continuing investigation if we hope to understand ourselves as we exist in all our diversity throughout the world.

We already know that we are creatures of emotion as well as of reason. An illogical reply given with fervor can silence a well-thought-out question and gain the followers needed to decide an issue. Strong rhetoric, whether rehearsed or spontaneous, too often carries the day, and it does so more easily when it can travel on wheels of prejudice, already in people's minds, of stereotypes that lump together in all respects those who share but a few things in common.

I recently listened to a proposal for world peace propounded by an engineer whose comprehension of the humanities and social sciences was patently deficient. By lumping together all those of any one nationality, his plan would quickly eliminate just those people and groups within a society who might best oppose a totalitarian ruler, leaving only the demagogue to direct his or her subjects without opposition. To treat any society as a single, indivisible organism is to enforce conformity upon its members.

We know that to regard all the people of any nation or tribe or race or ethnic group or class as evil, and to use this belief to justify vengeful treatment of the entire population, is wrong. We have known this for generations, yet we still do it in war and all too often in somewhat less drastic, but no less unjust, actions. The internment during World War II of all peoples of Japanese descent living along the West Coast is a classic example of this phenomenon.

The lessons of the destruction of Carthage, the rampage of the First Crusade, the Inquisition, and the Holocaust remain too often mere abstractions that we ignore when our passions are aroused. The displacement from their homes of all Navajos in half of the joint-interest area is yet another example of our tendency to be distracted from principles when a self-righteous trumpet is sounded. It will not be the last and it is a less violent event than many before, but perhaps it can provide one more reason for people to be more deliberate when they hear a call to arms.

Regrettably, we still need to learn to apply what we have long known about human relations.

NOTES

....

INTRODUCTION

1. Jerry Kammer, *The Second Long Walk: The Navajo-Hopi Land Dispute* (Albuquerque, NM: University of New Mexico Press, 1980).

CHAPTER 1

1. David M. Brugge, "Comments on Athabaskans and Sumas," in *The Protohistoric Period in the North American Southwest, AD 1450–1700*, eds. David R. Wilcox and W. Bruce Masse, Anthropological Research Papers No. 24 (Tempe: Arizona State University, 1981), 286–87.

2. Alfred Vincent Kidder, *Pecos, New Mexico: Archaeological Notes*, Papers of the Robert S. Peabody Foundation for Archaeology, Vol. 5 (Andover, Mass.: Phillips Academy, 1958), 310.

3. Ibid., 315–17; John L. Kessell, *Kiva, Cross, and Crown: The Pecos Indians and New Mexico, 1540–1840* (Washington, D.C.: National Park Service, 1979), viii, 7, 12, 110–12, 132, 229–30, 288–92, 295–97, 455).

4. David M. Brugge, "Pueblo Factionalism and External Relations," *Ethnohistory* 16 (Spring 1969): 191–200.

5. Jack D. Forbes, *Apache, Navaho, and Spaniard* (Norman: University of Oklahoma Press, 1960), 58–59.

6. Ibid., 62–63.

7. George P. Hammond and Agapito Rey, eds., *Don Juan de Oñate: Colonizer of New Mexico, 1595–1628*, Pts. 1–2, Coronado Cuarto Centennial Publications, 1540–1940, vols. 5–6 (Albuquerque: University of New Mexico Press, 1953), 1027–28.

8. Frederick Webb Hodge, George P. Hammond, and Agapito Rey, trans. and eds., *Fray Alonso de Benavides' Revised Memorial of 1634*, Coronado Cuarto Centennial Publications, 1540–1940, vol. 4 (Albuquerque: University of New Mexico Press, 1945), 216–18.

9. Ibid., 76–77, 79.

10. David M. Brugge, "Pueblo Factionalism," 191–200.

11. J. O. Brew, "The History of Awatobi," in Ross Gordon Montgomery, Watson Smith, and John Otis Brew, *Franciscan Awatovi: The Excavation and Conjectural Reconstruction of a 17th-Century Spanish Mission Establishment at a Hopi Indian Town in Northeastern Arizona*, Papers of the Peabody Museum of American Archaeology and Ethnology, vol. 36 (Cambridge, Mass.: Harvard University, 1949), 16.

12. Frank McNitt, *Navajo Wars: Military Campaigns, Slave Raids and Reprisals* (Albuquerque: University of New Mexico Press, 1972), 16.

13. Ibid., 18; J. O. Brew, "Hopi Prehistory and History to 1850," in *Handbook of North American Indians, Southwest*, vol. 9, ed. Alfonso Ortiz (Washington, D.C.: Smithsonian Institution, 1979), 521–22.

14. J. Manuel Espinosa, *First Expedition of Vargas into New Mexico, 1692*, Coronado Cuarto Centennial Publications, 1540–1940, vol. 10 (Albuquerque: University of New Mexico Press, 1940), 145–55, 254.

15. Ibid., 208–28.

16. Brew, "Awatovi," 20.

17. J. Manuel Espinosa, ed. and trans., *The Pueblo Indian Revolt of 1696 and the Franciscan Missions of New Mexico: Letters of the Missionaries and Related Documents* (Norman: University of Oklahoma Press, 1988).

18. Harry C. James, *Pages from Hopi History* (Tucson: University of Arizona Press, 1974), 61–64; Albert Yava, *Big Falling Snow: A Tewa-Hopi Indian's Life and Times and the History and Traditions of His People*, ed. Harold Courlander (Albuquerque: University of New Mexico Press, 1978), 91–96; Brew, "Awatovi," 20–26; Christy G. Turner and Nancy T. Morris, "A Massacre at Hopi," *American Antiquity* 35 (July 1970), 320–31; Peter Whiteley, *Bacavi: Journey to Reed Springs* (Flagstaff, Ariz.: Northland Press, 1988), 21–22.

19. James, *Pages*, 61–64; Yava, *Big Falling Snow*, 91–96; Brew, "Awatovi," 20–26; Whitely, *Bacavi*, 21–22.

20. Yava, *Big Falling Snow*, 147, n. 42.

21. In ibid.

22. Gladys A. Reichard, *Social Life of the Navajo Indians with Some Attention to Minor Ceremonies*, Columbia University Contributions to Anthropology, vol. 7 (New York: Columbia University Press), 16.

23. Yava, *Big Falling Snow*, 94; Verna Clinton-Tullie, "Research of the Navajo-Hopi Tobacco Clan of Finger Point-Star Mountain of Tessto Chapter Community and Polacca, Awatovi and Sichomovi of First Mesa" (unpublished manuscript prepared for the Navajo-Hopi Land Dispute Commission and the Navajo-Hopi Land Dispute Task Force, Window Rock, Ariz., 1981), 10, 35. In addition to these sources, I have relied on Navajo oral tradition that I heard when working in the Jeddito area in the 1960s.

24. Frank D. Reeve, "Navajo Spanish Wars, 1680–1720," *New Mexico Historical Review* 33 (July 1958): 215.

25. David M. Brugge, "Early 18th Century Spanish-Apachean Relations," in *Collected Papers in Honor of Bertha Pauline Dutton*, ed. Albert H. Schroeder, Papers of the Archaeological Society of New Mexico, vol. 4 (Albuquerque Archaeological Society Press, 1979), 106–7.

26. Ibid., 110–15.

27. David M. Brugge, *Navajos in the Catholic Church Records of New Mexico, 1694–1875*, rev. ed. (Tsaile, Ariz.: Navajo Community College Press, 1985), 29.

28. Alfred Barnaby Thomas, *Forgotten Frontiers: A Study of the Spanish Indian Policy of Don Juan Bautista de Anza, Governor of New Mexico, 1777–1787, from The Original Documents in the Archives of Spain, Mexico, and New Mexico* (Norman: University of Oklahoma Press, 1932), 28.

29. Brew, "Awatovi," 29–30.

30. Brugge, *Catholic Church Records*, 24–25.

31. Brew, "Awatovi," 31–33.

32. This may have been the village of Payupki, now a ruin at Second Mesa. Albert H. Schroeder, "Pueblos Abandoned in Historic Times," in *Handbook of North American Indians*, Vol. 9: *Southwest*, ed. Alfonso Ortiz (Washington, D.C.: Smithsonian Institution, 1979), 239; Elizabeth A. Brandt, "Sandia Pueblo," in ibid., 345.

33. Thomas, *Forgotten Frontiers*, 159–60.

34. Ibid., 153; Brew, "Awatovi," 33–34; Padre Ignacio Lizasoin, "Noticia de la Visita General de P. Ignacio Lizasoin Visitador General, de las Missiones de esta Prova. de Nueva España, q comenzó dia quatro de Abril De 1761 ad. y se concluyó a fines de Henero de 1763 con algunas notas y addiciones qu. pueden servir pa. el conocimiento de dhas Missiones y Provincias de ellas," (copy in Bancroft Library, University of California, Berkeley, Calif.), 38.

35. Reeve, "Wars," 12–28; Brugge, *Catholic Church Records*, 45–46.

36. Eleanor B. Adams, "Fray Silvestre and the Obstinate Hopi," *New Mexico Historical Review* 38 (April 1963): 123–24.

37. Ibid., 136–37.

38. Elliott Coues, ed., *On the Trail of a Spanish Pioneer: The Diary and Itinerary of Francisco Garcés (Missionary Priest) in His Travels Through Sonora, Arizona, and California, 1775–1776* (New York: Francis P. Harper, 1900), 351–52.

39. Fray Angélico Chávez, trans., and Ted J. Warner, ed., *The Domínguez-Escalante Journal: Their Expedition Through Colorado, Utah, Arizona, and New Mexico in 1776* (Provo, Utah: Brigham Young University Press, 1976), 109–14.

40. Father Juan Agustín de Morfí, *Account of Disorders in New Mexico, 1778*, trans. and ed. Marc Simmons (Isleta Pueblo, New Mexico: St. Augustine Church, 1977), 26.

41. Thomas, *Forgotten Frontiers*, 145–46.

42. Kessell, *Kiva, Cross, and Crown*, 367.

43. Thomas, *Forgotten Frontiers*, 145–46.

44. Ibid., 166.

45. Ibid., 168.

46. Frank D. Reeve, "Navajo-Spanish Diplomacy, 1770–1790," *New Mexico Historical Review* 35 (July 1960): 214–16.

47. Ibid., 216; Brew, *Awatovi*, 36–37; James, *Pages*, 69; Thomas, *Forgotten Frontiers*, 228–29; Alfred Barnaby Thomas, trans. and ed., *Teodoro de Croix and the Northern Frontier of New Spain, 1776–1783* (Norman: University of Oklahoma Press, 1941), 109–10; Hubert Howe Bancroft, *History of Arizona and New Mexico, 1530–1888* (San Francisco, Calif.: The History Company, Publishers, 1889; reprinted by Horn & Wallace, Publishers: Albuquerque, New Mexico, 1962), 265–66.

48. Brew, "Awatovi," 36–40.

49. M. A. Stokes and T. L. Smiley, "Tree-Ring Dates from the Navajo Land Claim II. The Western Sector," *Tree-Ring Bulletin* 26 (June 1964): 25–26; Linda G. Drew, ed., *Tree-Ring Chronologies of Western America II. Arizona, New Mexico, Texas* (Tucson: Laboratory of Tree-Ring Research, 1972), 10–11, 15–16.

50. Thomas, *Forgotten Frontiers*, 230.

51. Brugge, *Catholic Church Records*, 26–29.

52. Thomas, *Forgotten Frontiers*, 237.

53. McNitt, *Navajo Wars*, 433.

54. Melgares to García Conde, 18 December 1818, Estado 33 (Mexico 14), Archivo General de Indias, Sevilla (copy, Chapman 6180, p. 39, Bancroft Library, Berkeley).

55. Melgares to Cordero, 18 March 1819, Nos. 1 & 2, and Cordero to Interim-governor, 13 April 1819, Estado 33 (Mexico 14), Archivo General de Indias, Sevilla (copy, Chapman 6183, pp. 5–7, Berkeley); Fray Angélico Chávez, *Archives of the Archdiocese of Santa Fe, 1678–1900* (Washington, D.C.: Academy of American Franciscan History, 1957), 82.

56. David M. Brugge and J. Lee Correll, *The Story of the Navajo Treaties*, Navajo Historical Publication, Documentary Series 1 (Window Rock, Ariz.: The Navajo Tribe), 48.

57. David M. Brugge, "Vizcarra's Navajo Campaign of 1823," *Arizona and the West* 6 (Autumn 1964), 225–26, 232–39.

58. Drew, *Tree-Ring Chronologies*, 10–11; Stokes and Smiley, *Western Sector*, 23–27; M. A. Stokes and T. L. Smiley, "Tree-Ring Dates from the Navajo Land Claim. I. The Northern Sector," *Tree-Ring Bulletin* 25 (June 1963), 14–18; M. A. Stokes and T. L. Smiley, "Tree-Ring Dates from the Navajo Land Claim III. The Southern Sector," *Tree-Ring Bulletin* 27 (September 1966), 8–11; M. A. Stokes and T. L. Smiley, "Tree-Ring Dates from the Navajo Land Claim. IV. The Eastern Sector," *Tree-Ring Bulletin* 29 (March 1969), 13–15.

59. Franc Johnson Newcomb, *Hosteen Klah, Navaho Medicine Man and Sand Painter* (Norman, Okla.: University of Oklahoma Press, 1964), 11–12; Virginia Hoffman, *Navajo Biographies*, Vol. 1 (Phoenix, Ariz.: Navajo Curriculum Center Press), 15–16.

60. Alexander M. Stephen, *Hopi Journal*, Vol. 2, in Columbia Contributions to Anthropology, Vol. 23 (New York: Columbia University Press, 1936) 1016–17. It is worth noting that the name Djasjini corresponds well with Navajo phonology. It may translate as "Black Legs" or "Black Ears" if of Navajo origin.

61. Hoffman, *Navajo Biographies*, 84; Richard F. Van Valkenburgh, *A Short History of the Navajo People* (Window Rock, Ariz.: Navajo Service, U.S. Dept. of the Interior, 1938), 7.

62. James, *Pages*, 72.

63. Frank Waters, *Book of the Hopi* (New York: Ballantine Books, 1963), 313–14.

64. Bancroft, *History*, 407, n. 54.

65. James, *Pages*, 148–49.

66. Bent to Medill, 10 November 1846, Record Group 98, Department of New Mexico, Letters Sent, [hereafter RG 98, DNM, LS], Old Book 1 (bound as 5), pp. 25–33, National Archives, Washington, D.C.

67. Annie Heloise Abel, ed., *The Official Correspondence of James S. Calhoun* (Washington, D.C.: Office of Indian Affairs, 1915), 45.

68. Ibid., 262–65.

69. Chandler to McLaws, 24 April 1851, Record Group 98, Department of New Mexico, Letters Received [hereafter RG 98, DNM, LR], C-38/1851, National Archives, Washington, D.C.

70. Dodge to Monroe, 12 May 1851, RG 98, DNM, LR, D-1/1851, National Archives, Washington, D.C.

71. Craig to Scott, 4 September 1851, RG 98, DNM, LR, unentered 1851, National Archives, Washington, D.C.; Bartlett to Stuart, 13 August 1851, S. E. Doc. 119 (Ser. 626), 32d Cong., 1st sess., pp. 440–48.

72. Abel, *Official Correspondence*, 415.

73. Backus to Acting Assistant Adjutant General [hereafter AAAG], 5 November 1851, Record group 98, Department of New Mexico, Miscellaneous Letters Received [hereafter RG 98, DNM, Misc. LR], Box 94, National Archives, Washington, D.C.

74. Norman M. Littell and Leland O. Graham, *Proposed Findings of Fact in Behalf of the Navajo Tribe of Indians in Area of Hopi Overlap (Docket No. 196)*, Vol. 1 (Washington, D.C., 1964), 51.

75. Kendrick to Meriwether, 12 June 1856, Record Group 75, New Mexico Superintendancy, Letters Received [hereafter RG 75, NM Supt., LR], K-44/1856 encl., National Archives, Washington, D.C.

76. Littell and Graham, *Proposed Findings*, Vol. 1, 52–53.

77. Ibid., 77.

78. Miles to Bucknam, 15 October 1858, RG 98, DNM, LR, M-73/1858 encl., National Archives, Washington, D.C.

79. McNitt, *Navajo Wars*, 390–92, 398–99.

80. Ward to Steck, 21 April 1865, Hs. Ex. Doc. 1 (Serial 1248), 39th Cong., 1st sess., pp. 355–57.

81. Canby to Assistant Adjutant General [hereafter AAG], 18 March 1861, RG 98, DNM, LR, C-42/1861, National Archives, Washington, D.C.

82. Steele to Smith, 8 January 1863, Manuscript Collection, Latter-day Saints Church Historian's Office, Salt Lake City, Utah.

83. Carson to Cutler, 19 August 1863, RG 98, DNM, LS, Old Book 124 (bound as 76), pp. 8–12, National Archives, Washington, D.C.

84. Lawrence Kelly, *Navajo Roundup, Selected Correspondence of Kit Carson's Expedition Against the Navajo, 1863–1865* (Boulder, Colo.: The Pruitt Publishing Company), 75–76.

85. Ibid., 162.

86. Dane Coolidge and Mary Roberts Coolidge, *The Navajo Indians* (Boston and New York: Houghton Mifflin Company, 1930), 25; Ruth M. Underhill, *The Navajos* (Norman, Okla.: University of Oklahoma Press, 1956), 117, 122; Van Valkenburgh, *Short History*, 23.

87. Kelly, *Navajo Roundup*, 167.

88. Littell and Graham, *Proposed Findings*, 56A–57.

89. Lynn R. Bailey, *Bosque Redondo: An American Concentration Camp* (Pasadena, Calif.: Socio-Technical Publications, 1970).

CHAPTER 2

1. There is considerable debate as to the nature of Navajo political institutions prior to their final defeat. The author is of the opinion that there was a loose, but formal means through the *Naach'id* ceremony to achieve consensus. See Gladys A. Reichard, *Social Life of the Navajo Indians with Some attention to Minor Ceremonies*, Columbia University Contributions to Anthropology, Vol. 7 (New York: Columbia University Press, 1928), 108–11; and David M. Brugge, "Documentary Reference to a Navajo Naach'id in 1840," *Ethnohistory* 10 (Spring 1963).

2. Jones to Marcy, 21 July 1969, Hs. Ex. Doc. 1 (Serial 1414), 656–67.

3. Norman M. Littell and Leland O. Graham, *Proposed Findings of Fact in Behalf of the Navajo Tribe of Indians in Area of Hopi Overlap (Docket No. 196)*, Vol. 1 (Washington, D.C., 1964), 61.

4. Crothers to Clum, 15 November 1871, 42d Cong., 2d sess., Hs. Ex. Doc. 1 (Serial 1505), 1119–22.

5. Arny to Parker, 31 May 1871, Record Group 75, New Mexico Field Papers [hereafter RG 75, NM Field Papers], National archives, Washington, D.C.

6. Defrees to Smith, 26 February 1874, Record Group 75, Arizona Superintendancy, Letters Received [hereafter RG 75, Ariz. Supt., LR], D-274/1874, National Archives, Washington, D.C.; Littell and Graham, *Proposed Findings*, 64–66.

7. U.S. Congress, Senate, Committee on Indian Affairs, *Partition of the Surface Rights of Navajo-Hopi Indian Land*, 93d Cong., 1st sess., 7 March 1973 [hereafter Senate committee, *Partition*], 320.

8. Littell and Graham, *Proposed Findings*, 65.

9. Harry C. James, *Pages from Hopi History* (Tucson, Ariz.: University of arizona Press, 1974) 131.

10. Senate Committee, *Partition*, 321.

11. Jerry Kammer, *The Second Long Walk: The Navajo-Hopi Land Dispute* (Albuquerque, N.M.: University of New Mexico Press, 1980), 27–28.

12. Ibid., xiii.

13. Senate Committee, *Partition*, 327.

14. Ibid., 328–32.

15. Ibid., 332.

16. Ibid., 333–37; James, *Pages*, 111.

17. Senate Committee, *Partition*, 338–41.

18. Don C. Talayesva, *Sun Chief, The Autobiography of a Hopi Indian*, ed. Leo W. Simmons (New Haven, Conn.: Yale University Press, 1942), 64.

19. Senate Committee, *Partition*, 341–42.

20. James, *Pages*, 125.

21. Ibid., 139.

22. David M. Brugge, "Pueblo Factionalism and External Relations," *Ethnohistory* 16: 198. The breakup of Old Oraibi was a major event in Hopi history, one that has had long-lasting effects on Hopi politics and relations with the federal government. For contrasting views of this event, see Mischa Titiev, *Old Oraibi: A Study of the Hopi Indians of Third Mesa*, Papers of the Peabody Museum of American Archaeology and Ethnology, Vol. 2, No. 1 (Cambridge, Mass.: Harvard University, 1944), and Peter Whiteley, *Bacavi: Journey to Reed Springs* (Flagstaff, Ariz.: Northland Press, 1988).

23. Senate Committee, *Partition*, 343–46.

24. Ibid., 337–51.

25. Ibid., 352.

26. Ibid., 353–56.

27. Ibid., 357–60.

28. Ibid., 361–63.

29. Ibid., 361–62.

30. Ibid., 363.

31. Ibid., 364.

32. Ibid., 364–65.

33. Ibid., 366.

34. Ibid., 367.

35. Ibid., 367–68.

36. Ibid., 368–69.

37. Ibid., 369–70.

38. Ibid., 371–74.

39. Ibid., 376.

40. Ibid., 378–81.

41. Ibid., 383–84.

42. Ibid., 384–85.

43. Ibid., 388–401.

44. Ibid., 401.

45. Edward Everett Dale, *The Indians of the Southwest: A Century of Development under the United States* (San Marino, Calif.: The Huntington Library, and Norman, Okla.: University of Oklahoma Press, 1949); T. Mitchell Prudden, *On The Great American Plateau: Wanderings Among Canyons and Buttes, in the Land of the Cliff-Dweller, and the Indian of Today* (New York and London: G. P. Putnam's Sons, 1907); James, *Pages.*

46. Dale, *Indians*, 251–52.

47. Ibid., 171; 131n. 59.

48. Ibid., 12–13.

49. Ibid., 15, 17–18.

50. Ibid., 21–22.

51. Navajo Tribal Council, *Minutes* (mimeograph), Window Rock, Ariz., 5–23 January 1953, 70.

52. Ibid., 75.

53. Ibid., 77.

54. Ibid., 76–77. A Hopi tribal council, formed under the Indian Reorganization Act in the 1930s, had lapsed as a result of severe internal tribal discord and a boycott of the meetings by the traditionalist faction. The Hopi council was revived in the 1950s. See James, *Pages*, 203–5.

55. Navajo Tribal Council, *Minutes* (mimeograph), 5–23 January 1953, 79.

56. Ibid., 79

57. Ibid., 17–27 January 1956, 89–91.

58. Ibid., 92–95.

59. Ibid., 97–99.

60. Ibid., 99–100.

61. Ibid., 16–20 July 1956, 197.

62. Ibid., 22 October–2 November 1956, 32.

63. Ibid., 28 January–16 February 1957, 213–24.

64. Untitled manuscript, MSS BC 442, Box 1, Folder 7, pp. 2–8, Special Collections, Zimmerman Library, University of New Mexico, Albuquerque.

65. Kammer, *Second Long Walk*, 46.

66. Senate Committee, *Partition*, 414.

67. Ibid.

CHAPTER 3

1. Peshlakai Etsedi and Sallie Pierce Brewer, "The Long Walk to Bosque Redondo," *Navajo Customs*, Reprint Series 6 (Flagstaff, Ariz.: Museum of Northern Arizona, 1951), 6–13; Philip Johnston, "Peshlakai Atsidi," *Plateau* 12 (October 1939): 2.

2. Navajo Land Claims Site Reports, Laboratory of Anthropology Library, Museum of New Mexico, Santa Fe. Much of what follows is derived from these site reports.

3. Typology, or the study of types, as used to date archeological sites, depends on changes in form and style in both architecture and portable artifacts that can be traced through time. In Navajo archeology, only details of hogan structure and location, pottery types, and trade objects from Hispanic and Anglo sources were known as indicators of time periods in the early 1950s.

4. Stokes and Smiley, "Tree-Ring Dates from the Navajo Land Claim II. The Western Sector," *Tree-Ring Bulletin* 26: 13–27.

5. Richard F. Van Valkenburgh, *Report of Archeological Survey of the Navajo-Hopi Contact Area*, unpublished manuscript, Navajo Land Claim files, The Navajo Nation, Window Rock, Ariz., 1956.

6. J. Lee Correll and David M. Brugge, "Navajo Agriculture," unpublished manuscript, Navajo Land Claim files, The Navajo Nation, Window Rock, Ariz., 1958.

7. Richard F. Van Valkenburgh and Clyde Kluckhohn, "Navajo Sacred Places," *Navajo Indians III*, Garland American Indian Ethnohistory Series (New York: Garland Publishing Inc., 1974), 9–199.

8. U.S. Congress, Senate, Committee on Indian Affairs, *Partition of the Surface Rights of Navajo-Hopi Indian Land*, 93d Cong., 1st sess., 7 March 1973, 208–10.

9. David M. Brugge, *Navajo Pottery and Ethnohistory*, Navajoland Publications Series 2 (Window Rock, Ariz.: Navajo Tribal Museum, 1963).

10. Bruce Kipp, "3 U.S. Judges Study Motions in Navajo-Hopi Land Dispute," newspaper clipping, 17 March 1959, MSS BC 442, Box 2, Folder 3, Item 3, Special Collections, Coronado Room, Zimmerman Library, University of New Mexico; Roger Lewis, "Indian Legal Battle Begins," newspaper clipping, 17 March 1959, MSS 442, Box 2, Folder 3, Item 2, Special Collections, Coronado Room, Zimmerman Library, University of New Mexico; *Healing* v. *Jones* transcript, 16 March 1959: 8–15.

11. *Healing* v. *Jones* transcript, 16 March 1959: 22–38.

12. Ibid., 40–55.

13. Ibid., 62–84.

14. W. W. Hill, *The Agricultural and Hunting Methods of the Navajo Indians*, Yale University Publications in Anthropology 18 (New Haven: Yale University Press, 1938), 145–56.

15. Stokes and Smiley, "Tree-Ring Dates from . . . the Western Sector," 19–20.

16. Ethnic prejudice worked both ways, of course. In working in the contact zones of the Navajos with various other peoples, I encountered Navajo expressions of superiority toward a number of non-Navajo groups, from Hopis and Utes to Mormons and Hispanics. Navajos did not voice these thoughts until they were sure that I was not a member of the opposing population. I was obviously not Indian, of course, and my pipe-smoking showed that I was not Mormon, but my dark brown hair and ability to speak some Spanish made them reticent in their comments regarding Hispanics, and I never heard pejorative opinions of Anglo-Americans (those identified as *Bilagáana* in Navajo). Most generally they expressed these feelings in the form of jokes and in a manner calculated to cement their relationship to Lee and me, as an assumption or suggestion that we shared a common bi-ethnic stereotype. On occasion there would be mention of fears of witchcraft by other Indian groups, but never did they exhibit the

kind of sheer disdain that I heard in the voices of the two Hopis that day. See Chapter 10 for additional mention of this phenomenon.

17. Margaret A. Powers and Byron P. Johnson, *Defensive Sites of Dinetah*, Cultural Resources Series No. 2 (Albuquerque, N.M.: Bureau of Land Management, 1987).

18. Stokes and Smiley, "Tree-Ring Dates from . . . the Western Sector," 22.

19. *Healing v. Jones*, Pretrial Conference Transcript, 20 August 1959.

20. Frank D. Reeve, "The Navajo-Spanish Peace: 1720s–1770s," *New Mexico Historical Review* 33 (January 1959): 17, n. 17.

21. *Son of Old Man Hat, A Navajo Autobiography*, recorded by Walter Dyk (Lincoln: University of Nebraska Press, 1938).

22. Stokes and Smiley, "Tree-Ring Dates from . . . the Western Sector," 22.

CHAPTER 4

1. Terry E. Fenzl, Craig W. Soland, and John w. Rogers, *Navajo Tribe's Responses to Hopi Tribe's Proposed Findings of Fact and Conclusions of Law, Vernon Masayesva, etc., Plaintiff, v. Leonard Haskie, etc., Defendant, v. Evelyn James, etc., Intervenors, No. CIV 74-842; PHX-EHC, United States District Court for the District of Arizona* (Phoenix, Ariz.: Brown and Bain, P.A., 1990), 30–31, n. 40.

2. *Healing v. Jones*, No. Civil 579 Prescott in the U.S. District Court for the District of Arizona, Transcript, Prescott Hearings [hereafter cited as *Healing v. Jones*], 1960, 5–65.

3. Ibid., Vols. 1–2, 96–144.

4. Ibid., Vols. 2–3, 156–340.

5. Ibid., Vol. 3, 341ff.

6. Ibid., Vol. 4, 410ff.

7. Robert W. Young and William Morgan, *The Navaho Language: The Elements of Navaho Grammer with a Dictionary in Two Parts Containing Basic Vocabularies of Navaho and English* (Phoenix, Ariz.: Education Division, United States Indian Service, 1943).

8. *Healing v. Jones*, Vol. 4, 475ff.

9. Ibid., Vol. 4, 502ff.

10. Ibid., Vol. 5, 538ff.

11. Ibid., Vol. 5, 560ff.

12. Ibid., Vol. 5, 584ff.

13. Bill Nixon, "Atom Boss Testifies in Indian Dispute," *Arizona Republic*, 29 September 1960.

14. Bill Nixon, "Navajos Cite 1882 Order in Defense," *Arizona Republic*, 1 October 1960.

15. *Healing v. Jones*, Vol. 6, 609–15.

16. Ibid., Vol. 6, 615ff.

17. Ibid., Vol. 6, 640ff.

18. Ibid., Vol. 6, 673ff.

19. Ibid., Vol. 6, 690ff.

20. Ibid., Vol. 7, 733ff.

21. Ibid., Vol. 7, 750ff.

22. Ibid., Vol. 7, 766ff.

23. Ibid., Vol. 7, 773ff.

24. Ibid., Vol. 8, 791ff.

25. Ibid., Vol. 8, 814ff.

26. Ibid., Vol. 9, 890ff.

27. Ibid., Vol. 9, 909ff.

28. Ibid., Vol. 9, 933ff.

29. Ibid., Vol. 9, 947ff.

30. Bill Nixon, "Language Barriers Slow Navajo-Hopi Suit to Crawl," *Arizona Republic,* 7 October 1960.

31. One adult sheep year-long equals one sheep unit, as does one goat, whereas one cow equals four sheep units, and one horse, mule, or burro equals five sheep units.

32. *Healing* v. *Jones,* Vol. 9, 954ff.

33. Ibid., Vol. 10, 1059ff.

34. Ibid., Vols. 10–11, 1083ff.

35. Ibid., Vol. 11, 1158ff.

36. Ibid., Vol. 11, 1167ff.

37. Ibid., Vol. 11, 1215ff.

38. Alfred F. Whiting, *Ethnobotany of the Hopi,* Museum of Northern Arizona Bulletin 15 (Flagstaff, Ariz.: Museum of Northern Arizona Press, 1939).

39. *Healing* v. *Jones,* Vol. 12, 1265ff.

40. Ibid., Vol. 13, 1428ff.

41. Ibid., Vol. 13, 1501ff.

42. Ibid., Vol. 13, 1512ff.

43. Ibid., Vol. 13, 1521ff.

44. Ibid., Vol. 13, 1524ff.

45. "88-Year-Old Hopi Woman Tells Of Jeddito Residence," *Arizona Republic,* 13 October 1960.

46. Francis H. Elmore, *Ethnobotany of the Navajo,* Monographs of the School of American Research, No. 8 (Santa Fe, N.M.: School of American Research; Albuquerque, N.M.: University of New Mexico Press, 1944), 9; Leland C. Wyman and Stuart K. Harris, *Navajo Indian Medical Ethnobotany,* The University of New Mexico Bulletin, Anthropological Series, Vol. 3, No. 5 (Albuquerque, N.M.: University of New Mexico Press, 1941), 6.

47. Paul A. Vestal, *Ethnobotany of the Ramah Navaho,* Papers of the Peabody Museum of American Archaeology and Ethnology, Vol. 40, No. 4 (Cambridge, Mass.: Harvard University, 1952), 5.

48. *Healing* v. *Jones,* Vol. 14, 1560ff.

49. Ibid., Vol. 14, 1571ff.

50. Ibid., Vol. 14, 1623ff.

51. Ibid., Vol. 14, 1661ff.

52. Ibid., Vol. 14, 1680ff.

53. Ibid., Vol. 15, 1726ff.

54. Ibid., Vol. 15, 1739ff.

55. Ibid., Vol. 15, 1761ff.

56. Ibid., Vol. 15, 1793ff.

57. Ibid., Vols. 15–16, 1815ff.

58. Ibid., Vol. 16, 1875ff.

59. Ibid., Vol. 16, 1914ff.

60. Ibid., Vol. 16, 1963ff.

61. Ibid., Vol. 17, 2001ff.

62. Ibid., Vol. 17, 2036ff.

63. Ibid., Vol. 18, 2157ff.

64. Ibid., Vols. 18–19, 2221ff.

65. Ibid., Vol. 19, 2290.

66. Ibid., Vol. 19, 2292.

67. Ibid., Vol. 19, 2293.

68. Ibid., Vol. 19, 2294.

69. Ibid., Vol. 19, 2306–22.

70. Ibid., Vol. 20, 2347ff.

71. Ibid., Vol. 20, 2370–71.

72. Bill Nixon, "Expert Holds Court Spellbound With Knowledge Of Hopi's Life," *Arizona Republic,* 18 October 1960.

73. Bill Nixon, "Navajo Jesse James Found," *Arizona Republic,* 20 October 1960.

74. "Navajo-Hopi Land Trial Testimony Has Ended," *Arizona Republic,* 22 October 1960; "Final Arguments . . . Land Hearing Nears Finish," *Arizona Republic,* 23 October 1960.

75. Nixon, "Navajo Jesse James."

76. *Healing* v. *Jones,* Vol. 21, 23–24.

77. Ibid., Vol. 21, 43–46.

78. Ibid., Vol. 21, 41–42.

79. Ibid., Vol. 21, 43.

80. Ibid., Vol. 21, 65–69.

81. Ibid., Vol. 21, 62–63.

82. Ibid., 3152ff.

83. "Land Hearing Nears Finish," *Gallup Independent,* 23 October 1960.

CHAPTER 5

1. "Chairman Reports To Navajo Tribal Council," *Navajo Times,* November 1960.

2. Norman M. Littell and Joseph F. McPherson, *Defendant Navajo Tribe's Proposed Findings of Fact, No. CIVIL 579 Prescott, United States District Court for the District of Arizona* (Washington, D.C.: Norman M. Littell, 1961). In a civil case of this sort, the attorneys for both sides submit to the court as "Proposed Findings of Fact" what they contend was shown by the courtroom hearings and the exhibits received into evidence. The judge or judges take these contentions into account in making the decision, but are in no way bound by them, for the findings proposed by attorneys on opposite sides of a case agree on very few points.

3. Ibid., 155–281.

4. Norman M. Littell and Joseph F. McPherson, *Defendant Navajo Tribe's Exceptions to Plaintiffs' Proposed Findings of Fact, No. CIVIL 579 Prescott, United States District Court for the District of Arizona* (Washington, D.C.: Norman M. Littell, 1961), 1–10.

5. Ibid., 11, 13–17, 20–27, 32–39, 41–45, 47–55, 58–66, 84–86, 89.

6. "Hopis Gain Land Verdict," *Gallup Independent,* 28 September 1962.

7. "Court's Decision Could Lengthen Navajo-Hopi Rift," *Albuquerque Journal*, 29 September 1962.

8. Frederick G. Hamley, Leon R. Yankwich, and James A. Walsh, *In the United States District Court for the District of Arizona, No. Civil 579 Prescott, Opinion of the Court, Appendix to Opinion—Chronological Account of Hopi-Navajo Controversy, Findings of Fact, and Conclusions of Law, Judgment.* (San Francisco, Calif.: Pernau-Walsh Printing Co., 1962), 26.

9. Ibid., 26–27.

10. Ibid., 35–36.

11. Ibid., 46–62.

12. Ibid., 75.

13. Ibid., 76–77, 79, 83–84, 99.

14. Ibid., 105–6.

15. "Nakai Pledges Independence For His Tribe," *Albuquerque Journal*, 14 April 1963.

16. Ibid.

17. Robert F. Kennedy, "Buying It Back From the Indians," *Life*, 23 March 1962, pp. 17, 19.

18. Jerry Kammer, *The Second Long Walk: The Navajo-Hopi Land Dispute* (Albuquerque, N.M.: University of New Mexico Press, 1980).

19. Norman M. Littell, *Report of the General Counsel to the Navajo Tribal Council at Council Meeting Commencing Monday, April 15, 1963,* unpublished manuscript, The Navajo Nation, Window Rock, Ariz.

20. Peter Iverson, *The Navajo Nation* (Westport, Conn.: Greenwood Press, 1981), 84–85.

21. John Redhouse, *Geopolitics of the Navajo-Hopi Land Dispute* (Albuquerque, N.M.: Redhouse/Wright Publications), 16.

22. "Navajo Lawyer Hits Contention of Hopi Counsel," *Albuquerque Journal*, 6 June 1963.

23. "Littell Reports To the Council," *Navajo Times*, 13 June 1963.

24. Ibid.

25. "Area BIA Officials In Washington," *Gallup Independent*, 14 July 1963.

26. United States Bureau of Indian Affairs, *Navajo-Hopi Conference, August 6–7, 1963, Valley Ho Hotel, 350 W. Main Street, Scottsdale, Arizona* [hereafter cited as United States, *Navajo-Hopi Conference*], transcript, Anderson Room, Zimmerman Library, University of New Mexico, Albuquerque, 12.

27. Paul R. Weick, "Tribal Chairman Plans Firing of General Counsel," *Navajo Times*, 27 June 1963.

28. James E. Officer, *Navajo-Hopi Conference, August 6–7, 1963*, manuscript, copy in possession of Robert W. Young, Department of Linguistics, University of New Mexico, Albuquerque.

29. Ibid., 14-b.

30. Ibid., 14-c.

31. Ibid., 14-d.

32. Ibid., 14.

33. United States, *Navajo-Hopi Conference*, 4.

34. Ibid., 17, 34–36.

35. Ibid., 41–58.

36. Ibid., 71–76.

37. Ibid., 84.

38. Ibid., 143.

39. Ibid., 160–66.

40. Ibid., 170–72.

41. Ibid., 174.

42. Ibid., 179–80.

43. Ibid., 195–205.

44. *Phoenix Gazette*, 8 August 1963.

45. Helene C. Monberg, "Littell-BIA Differ on Land," *Gallup Independent*, 16 September 1963.

46. "Indians Renew Talks," *Gallup Independent*, 17 September 1963.

47. Helene C. Monbert, "Udall Gets Questions," *Gallup Independent*, 28 October 1963.

48. Paul R. Wieck, "Littell Out As Navajo Legal Counsel," *Albuquerque Journal*, 2 November 1963.

49. "Question Removal, Littell Queries Legal Authority," *Gallup Independent*, 3 November 1963.

50. Ben Cole, "Littell Charges U.S. 'Raids' on Navajo Files," *Arizona Republic*, 4 November 1963; "Navajo Fight Taken Into Nakai's Garage," *Gallup Independent*, 4 November 1963; William Steif, "Navajo Records Seized in Raid, Faction Charges," *Albuquerque Tribune*, 4 November 1963.

51. "Navajo Fight," *Gallup Independent*, 4 November 1963.

52. Ted Hulbert, "Irregularities Found In Seized Records, Chairman Nakai Says," *Albuquerque Journal*, 9 November 1963.

53. Helene C. Monberg, "Irregularities Said Discovered in Files," *Gallup Independent*, 13 November 1963.

54. Paul R. Wieck, "Littell Files Court Action Against Udall In Contract Dispute," *Albuquerque Journal*, 16 November 1963.

55. "White Paper Statement of Raymond Nakai, Chairman, Navajo Tribal Council," *Navajo Times*, 28 November 1963.

56. "Navajo Counsel Wins Injunction Against Udall," *Albuquerque Journal*, 28 November 1963.

57. "Navajo Official Hurls Charges At Interior Aide," *Albuquerque Journal*, 12 December 1963.

58. "Navajo-Hopi Land Bill Introduced in Congress," *Navajo Times*, 23 January 1964.

59. Ruth Underhill, *Here Come the Navaho!* (Washington, D.C.: U.S. Indian Service, 1953); *The Navajos* (Norman: University of Oklahoma Press, 1956).

60. "Navajo Tribe's Council [sic] Ejected From Session," *Albuquerque Journal*, 4 February 1964; Dick Hardwick, "Agenda Changed by Council Vote," *Gallup Independent*, 5 February 1964.

61. Dick Hardwick, "Littell Secures Injunction Order," *Gallup Independent*, 13 February 1964.

62. Dick Hardwick, "Tribal Session at Fever Pitch," *Gallup Independent*, 16 February 1964.

63. Dick Hardwick, "Littell Wins One Round In Tribal Session Battle," *Gallup Independent*, 18 February 1964.

64. "Nakai Wins Court Round," *Gallup Independent*, 25 February 1964.

65. Helene C. Monberg, "Little Action Taken On Indian Bills in Congress," *Gallup Independent*, 26 February 1964.

66. Bill Nixon, "CORE Enters Factional Fight Among Hopis," *Arizona Republic*, 10 March 1964.

67. Lucile Peterson, "Fight Erupts During Hopi, CORE Meet," *Arizona Republic,* 12 March 1964; "Violence At Hopi Agency Brings Charges For Two," *Navajo Times,* 26 March 1964.

68. "Tom-Tom" cartoon, *Navajo Times,* 19 March 1964.

69. Helene C. Monbert, "Zimmerman, BIA Said In Chairman's Corner," *Gallup Independent,* 26 March 1964; *Littell v. Udall,* Civil Action No. 2779-63, U.S. District Court for the District of Columbia, 24 March 1964.

70. Lucile Peterson, "2 Hopi Men Plead Guilty To Charges," *Arizona Republic,* 28 March 1964.

71. "Civil Liberties Union Pulls Out of Hopi Fight," *Arizona Republic,* 13 May 1964.

72. Redhouse, *Geopolitics,* 16.

73. Caleb H. Johnson (letter to the editor), *Navajo Times,* 30 July 1964.

74. *Udall v. Littell,* No. 18338, U.S. Court of Appeals for the District of Columbia Circuit, decided 13 August 1964.

75. "Tribe Counsel Wolf Gives Resignation," *Gallup Independent,* 15 September 1964.

76. "Navajo-Hopi On Boundary Dispute," *Navajo Times,* 22 October 1964.

77. "Navajos Receive Big Grazing Bill," *Albuquerque Journal,* 14 October 1964.

78. "Hopis Reject Oil Lease Bids," *Navajo Times,* 22 October 1964.

79. "Lawyer Gets $1 Million Fee in Hopi-Navajo Case," *Gallup Independent,* 5 December 1964.

80. "CPA Audit Shows Navajos' Internal Operation Chaotic," *Gallup Independent,* 10 December 1964.

81. "Navajo 'March' Protests Tribe's Legal Counsel," *Albuquerque Journal,* 16 December 1964. The Navajo Rights Association was a political activist group organized in 1940 to oppose federal programs and the positions of Jacob Morgan, then tribal chairman. See Donald L. Parman, *The Navajos and the New Deal* (New Haven, Conn.: Yale University Press, 1976), 272–74.

82. Cort Klein, Jr., "Nakai Stripped Of Power by Council," *Gallup Independent,* 19 December 1964.

83. Helene C. Monberg, "Interior Said Concerned," *Gallup Independent,* 21 December 1964.

84. "Tribe Treasurer In Resignation," *Gallup Independent,* 30 December 1964.

85. "Mrs. Wauneka Makes Charges," *Gallup Independent,* 8 January 1965.

86. "Indians' Land Dispute Might Go to Congress," *Albuquerque Journal,* 22 January 1965.

87. Paul R. Wieck, "Nakai Testifies Littell Oust-Try A Campaign Vow," *Albuquerque Journal,* 2 February 1965; Wieck, "Both Sides Score In Udall-Littell Legal Quarrel," Ibid., 3 February 1965; Wieck, "Littell on Stand Brings Flareups In Federal Court," Ibid., 5 February 1965; Wieck, "Talks With Nakai Described by Littell," Ibid., 6 February 1965; Wieck, "Secretary Udall Due to Testify in Navajo Case," Ibid., 9 February 1965; Wieck, "Udall Maintains Action of Littell Was 'Misconduct,'" Ibid., 10 February 1965; Wieck, "Council Unaware of Block in Littell's Pay, Says Barry," Ibid., 11 February 1965; Wieck, "Sporadic Clashes Mark Ninth Day Of Littell's Trial," Ibid., 12 February 1965; Wieck, "Hearing in Littell, Udall Battle Ends," Ibid., 13 February 1965; Helene C. Monberg, "Government Wins First Round in Legal Battle," *Gallup Independent,* 4 February 1965.

88. "Littell Testifies Fee May be Million," *Gallup Independent,* 9 February 1965.

89. Wieck, "Sporadic Clashes."

90. "Navajo Attorney Denies Extra Fees," *Arizona Republic,* 5 February 1965.

91. "Black Mesa May Finally Feel the Bit," *Navajo Times*, 4 February 1965.

92. "McCabe Charged In Assault Case," *Gallup Independent*, 4 March 1965.

93. "Wells Plugged On Hopi Land," *Gallup Independent*, 26 May 1965.

94. "Udall Restrained By Court Order," *Gallup Independent*, 27 May 1965.

CHAPTER 6

1. J. Lee Correll, Editha L. Watson, and David M. Brugge, *Navajo Bibliography with Subject Index*, rev. ed., Research Report 2 (Window Rock, Ariz.: The Navajo Tribe, 1969), 50–51, 78.

2. "Navajo Group Renews Feud With Udall," *Albuquerque Journal*, 13 June 1965.

3. "Navajo Tribal Council Decisions August 16–20," *Navajo Times*, 26 August 1965; "Tribal Power Fight Topped in Vote on Attorney," *Gallup Independent*, 27 August 1965; "Schuelke Hired As Legal Aide To Navajo Tribe," *Albuquerque Journal*, 31 August 1965.

4. Officer to Yazzie, 19 August 1965, Navajo Tribal Files, Window Rock, Ariz.

5. "Tribe Coal Fight Draws Udall Denial," *Gallup Independent*, 6 October 1965; Glenn McCasland, "McCabe Charges Udall 'Evading Issue' on Coal," Ibid., 8 October 1965; Paul R. Wieck, "Udall Denies Interior Dept. Had Role in Firm's Talks For Use of Reservation Coal," *Albuquerque Journal*, 6 October 1965; "Water Big Issue In Coal Proposal, Asserts McCabe," *Albuquerque Journal*, 9 October 1965.

6. Glenn McCasland, "Joint City-Tribe Water Drive Urged by McCabe," *Gallup Independent*, 9 October 1965.

7. John Redhouse, *Geopolitics of the Navajo-Hopi Land Dispute* (Albuquerque, N.M.: Redhouse/Wright Publications, 1985), 17.

8. Peter Iverson, *The Navajo Nation* (Westport, Conn.: Greenwood Press, 1981), 105.

9. "Secretary Tells Plan," *Gallup Independent*, 29 October 1965.

10. Robert L. Bennett, interview with the author [hereafter cited as Bennett interview], Albuquerque, N.M., 9 November 1989.

11. "Littell Blasts Udall's Peace Keeping Trio," *Gallup Independent*, 9 November 1965.

12. "Hopis Lease Land To Oil Well Drillers," *Albuquerque Journal*, 14 October 1965.

13. Burke Johnson, "The Time Has Not Yet Come," *Arizona Days and Ways Magazine*, 12 December 1965, p. 9.

14. Eric McCrossen, "Surprise Visit Is Paid Reservation by Congressman," *Gallup Independent*, 17 November 1965; Bennett interview.

15. Eric McCrossen, "Gallup Poll," *Gallup Independent*, 13 December 1965.

16. "McCabe Urges 'Wait-See' Attitude on BIA Change," *Gallup Independent*, 15 December 1965.

17. "Gallup BIA Is Waiting," *Gallup Independent*, 29 December 1965.

18. "Norman M. Littell, General Counsel For The Navajo Tribe Makes Statement On Conflicting Claims Of Navajo and Hopi Tribes," *Navajo Times*, 6 January 1966; Ted Hulbert, "Coal Lease Would Give $30 Million to Navajos," *Albuquerque Journal*, 15 January 1966.

19. Clyde Kluckhohn and Dorothea Leighton, *The Navajo*, rev. ed. (New York: American Museum of Natural History and Garden City, N.Y.: Doubleday & Company, 1962), 109–11.

20. John K. Zollinger, "Billison Outlines Several Charges," *Gallup Independent*, 14 February 1966.

21. "Navajo Council Resolution Raps Udall," *Gallup Independent*, 29 January 1966; Glenn McCasland, "Nakai Blames Council For Navajo Problems," *Gallup Independent*, 5 February 1966.

22. "Tribal Council Debates Black Mesa Coal Issue," *Gallup Independent*, 18 February 1966; "Tribal Council Approves Contract for Coal Field," Ibid., 19 February 1966.

23. "Nash Draws New Attack by Morris," *Albuquerque Journal*, 20 February 1966.

24. James E. Cook, "BIA Shakeup Stirs Speculation," *Arizona Republic*, 17 March 1966; "Udall Will Meet With BIA Men," *Gallup Independent*, 23 March 1966.

25. "35 Navajos Get Notice to Leave Hopi Reservation," *Albuquerque Journal*, 5 April 1966.

26. "Navajos Being Evicted May Get Free Legal Aid," *Albuquerque Journal*, 16 April 1966.

27. Littell to Navajo Tribal Council and enclosure, 21 April 1966, copy in author's possession.

28. "Stay on Hopi Land, Navajos Hear," *Albuquerque Journal*, 23 April 1966; "Evicted Navajos Told to Await Court Action," *Gallup Independent*, 23 April 1966; "Navajo Aid Is Planned," *Gallup Independent*, 23 April 1966.

29. Paul R. Wieck, "Official Brutality Charged In Udall Appeal Hearing," *Albuquerque Journal*, 19 April 1966.

30. "BVD Negotiates With Hopis for Site of Factory," *Gallup Independent*, 8 July 1966; "BVD, the Navajos and Hopis," *Gallup Independent*, 9 July 1966.

31. James E. Cook, "Navajos May Fight Land Freeze Order," *Arizona Republic*, 27 July 1966. As initially implemented, this freeze affected only official actions by the federal government and the Navajo Tribe, not those by individual Navajos. It was later extended to restrict private activities also.

32. Bennett interview.

33. "Bennett Tries to Grab Navajo Land for Hopis," *Gallup Independent*, 27 July 1966; James E. Cook, "Navajos Say Udall Aids Hopis," *Arizona Republic*, 28 July 1966.

34. "Land Tiff Hones Tribal Split," *Arizona Republic*, 17 August 1966.

35. Author's notes, 6 January 1967.

36. Iverson, *Navajo Nation*, 88; Redhouse, *Geopolitics*, 20. The decision by the Supreme Court left Littell with no further legal recourse. Rather than allow Udall to dismiss him, he withdrew of his own accord.

37. Author's notes, 11 March 1967. Much of the information provided in this section is derived from notes that I made and from copies of my personal correspondence with friends during the period, as well as from my memory of events, where I feel that my unaided recall is fully reliable. Hereafter, citations will be provided only for meeting notes.

38. Orpha Sweeten Boyden, *John S. Boyden: Three Score and Ten in Retrospect* (Cedar City, Utah: Southern Utah State College Press, 1986), 198–200.

39. Bennett interview.

40. Some allowance must be made for Cowboy's limited understanding of this event. What he interpreted as "stars" may have been any of a number of insignia of various sorts on the visitor's uniform; it is not likely that the man had the rank of general. The term "medal of honor" is obviously a general gloss and does not necessarily indicate the Congressional Medal of Honor. The link in Navajo thinking between military service and their individual rights is clear, even should Cowboy's memory or comprehension of what he was told by the military officer not be accurate in all respects.

41. Author's notes, 15 April 1967.

42. Author's notes, 21 April 1967.

43. Correll's notes, 6 May 1967, copy in possession of author.

44. Author's notes, 10 May 1967.

45. Author's notes, 19 May 1967; Correll's notes, 19 May 1967, copy in possession of author.

46. Author's notes, 16 June 1967.

47. Jerry Kammer, *The Second Long Walk: The Navajo-Hopi Land Dispute* (Albuquerque: University of new Mexico Press, 1980); Redhouse, *Geopolitics*; Iverson, *Navajo Nation*.

CHAPTER 7

1. Author's notes, 16 June 1967.

2. That both predictions should come to pass, although in a more muted form than my colorful prose indicated, is a story beyond the scope of the present work. Peter MacDonald's use of the relocation issue in his defeat of Peterson Zah's bid for re-election did border on demagoguery, while the separatism of the Big Mountain resistance to relocation indicated a loss of faith in tribal leadership but action far short of guerrilla warfare. Both MacDonald's last term and the resistance movement have led to violence, however.

3. Author's notes, 21 June 1967.

4. Author's notes, 24 June 1967.

5. Peter Iverson, *The Navajo Nation* (Westport, Conn.: Greenwood Press, 1981), 88–89.

6. Gordon B. Page, *Hopi Land Management Unit, Hopi-Navajo Boundary Report, Report of the Human Dependency Survey*, National Archives, Bureau of Indian Affairs, Record Group 75, Classified Files, 1907—File Mark 24705-40-304.3 General Service, 1939.

7. Brugge to Mott, 17 August 1967, copy in author's possession.

8. Brugge to Mott, 21 August 1967, copy in author's possession.

9. Charles S. Peterson, *Take Up Your Mission: Mormon Colonizing Along the Little Colorado River, 1870–1900* (Tucson, Ariz.: University of Arizona Press, 1973), 77, 203.

10. Author's notes, 19 September 1967.

11. Correll's notes, 14 October 1967.

12. *Transcript of Proceedings, Navajo-Hopi Negotiating Conference, Flagstaff, Arizona, October 17, 1967*, copy in author's possession; author's notes, 17 October 1967.

13. Author's notes, 15–16 November 1967.

14. Author's notes, 21 November 1967; Correll's notes, 21 November 1967.

15. Each agency on the Navajo Reservation has its own council, which meets at regular intervals. These councils have little real power, but are important for the formulation of policy and opinion on an intermediate level.

16. Correll's notes, 22 November 1967.

17. Author's notes, 25 November 1967.

18. *Hopi-Navajo Negotiating Committee Conference, Phoenix, Arizona, April 3 and 4, 1968* (transcript), copy in author's possession; author's notes, 3–4 April 1968.

19. Robert L. Bennett, interview with the author, Albuquerque, N.M., 9 November 1989.

CHAPTER 8

1. Robert L. Bennett, interview with the author, Albuquerque, N.M., 3–4 April 1968.

2. Ibid.

3. "Navajo-Hopi Land Dispute May Land in Congress' Lap," *Navajo Times*, 27 February 1969.

4. Bennett to Nakai, 13 May 1969, copy in possession of the author.

5. "Navajo-Hopi Group Flies to Washington," *Navajo Times*, 11 September 1969.

6. "Navajo Request for Hopi Land Gets Cool Washington Reception," *Gallup Independent*, 3 February 1970.

7. Brugge (letter to the editor), *Gallup Independent*, 2 February 1970.

8. "Navajo Request," *Gallup Independent*, 3 February 1970.

9. Ibid.

10. Loesch to Nakai, 20 February 1970, copy in possession of author.

11. Jerry Kammer, *The Second Long Walk: The Navajo-Hopi Land Dispute* (Albuquerque: University of New Mexico Press, 1980), 80; Eric D. Eberhard, "Outline of Presentation for JUA Training," MSS BC 442, Box 1, Folder 2, Coronado Room, Zimmerman Library, University of New Mexico, Albuquerque.

12. "Hopis Consider Force to Eject Navajos," *Gallup Independent*, 17 April 1970.

13. Kammer, *Second Long Walk*, 8; MMS BC 442, Box 2, Folder 17, Coronado Room, Zimmerman Library, University of New Mexico, Albuquerque.

14. "Navajo Eviction Asked by Hopi Tribal Attorneys," *Gallup Independent*, 13 April 1970; "Decision on Navajo Eviction Delayed," *Arizona Republic*, 14 April 1970; "Hopis Consider Force to Eject Navajos," *Gallup Independent*, 17 April 1970.

15. Jesus A. Barker, "Hopis Gain District Court Order to Evict Navajo Indian Families," *Arizona Republic*, 28 April 1970.

16. "Hopi Land Claim Set at 4.4 Million Acres," *Gallup Independent*, 6 July 1970.

17. "Navajos Win Land Claim," *Gallup Independent*, 30 June 1970; Bill Schneider, "Nakai Asks Action to Determine Value of Land," *Gallup Independent*, 1 July 1970; "Ruling on Claim May Mean Several Million to Tribe," *Navajo Times*, 2 July 1970; Peter Iverson, *The Navajo Nation* (Westport, Conn.: Greenwood Press, 1981), 89.

18. Iverson, *Navajo Nation*, 128–29.

19. Ibid., 132.

20. Ibid., 112.

21. Dick Hardwick, "Council Moves at Fast Pace to Reorganize Itself," *Navajo Times*, 21 January 1971; "Council Studied Industrial Park, Land Dispute, Before Adjourning," ibid., 28 January 1971; Jon Bartel, "Nakai Pay Questioned," *Gallup Independent*, 14 January 1971; Jon Bartel, "Navajos Fight Partition," ibid., 21 January 1971.

22. H.R. 4753, "A Bill to Authorize the Partition of the Surface Rights of the Hopi and Navajo Indian Tribes in Undivided Trust Lands, and for Other Purposes," 92d Congress, 1st sess., 22 February 1971; H.R. 4754, "A Bill to Authorize the Partition of the 1934 Navajo Reservation, and for Other Purposes," 92d Congress, 1st sess., 22 February 1971.

23. H.R. 11128, "A Bill to Authorize the Partition of the Surface Rights in the Joint Use Area of the 1882 Executive Order Hopi Reservation and the Surface and Subsurface Rights of the 1934 Navajo Reservation between the Hopi and Navajo Tribes, to Provide for Allotments for Certain Paiute Indians, and for Other Purposes," 92d Congress, 1st sess., 6 October 1971.

24. Kammer, *Second Long Walk,* 92.

25. Bill Donovan, "Hopis Impound Navajo Livestock," *Gallup Independent,* 15 November 1971.

26. "Navajo, Hopi Leaders Discuss Range Dispute," *Gallup Independent,* 16 November 1971.

27. Bill Donovan, "Hopis Seek End to Dispute," *Gallup Independent,* 19 November 1971.

28. Bill Donovan, "Hopis Oppose Navajo Fence," *Gallup Independent,* 24 November 1971.

29. Kammer, *Second Long Walk,* 92.

30. "Hopis Hire Rider to Patrol Borders," *Gallup Independent,* 1 December 1971.

31. "Navajos Stop Building Fence," *Gallup Independent,* 2 December 1971.

32. "An Editorial: The Navajo-Hopi Confrontation," *Gallup Independent,* 3 December 1971.

33. Florence Holmes (letter to the editor), *Gallup Independent,* 11 December 1971.

34. Kammer, *Second Long Walk,* 80–81.

35. *Gallup Independent,* 21 December 1971.

36. David Monongye (letter to the editor), *Navajo Times,* 30 December 1971.

37. Joanne Yazzie (letter to the editor), ibid.

38. Rev. Caleb H. Johnson (letter to the editor), ibid.

39. "Navajo-Hopi Dispute Aid is Sought," *Arizona Republic,* 28 January 1972.

40. "Navajo Denied Land Hearing," *Gallup Independent,* 1 February 1972.

41. "Indian Range Fight Feared," *Gallup Independent,* 1 March 1972; "Hopis Tighten Corrals in Feud with Navajos," *Phoenix Republic,* 2 March 1972.

42. Al Wiman (letter to the editor), *Gallup Independent,* 1 March 1972.

43. Kammer, *Second Long Walk,* 87–88.

44. Grant E. Smith, "Hopi Group Claims Chairman is no Longer a Tribe Member," *Arizona Republic,* 25 March 1972; Grant Smith, "Elders Demand Hopi Chairman Quit," *Gallup Independent,* 25 March 1971; Kammer, *Second Long Walk,* 88.

45. "Hopis Will Ask Governor to Call Out National Guard," *Arizona Republic,* 25 March 1971; "Hopis Are Told Land Fight is Out of State Jurisdiction," *Arizona Republic,* 26 March 1971; Kammer, *Second Long Walk,* 89.

46. "Hopis Demand Bruce Resign As BIA Leader," *Albuquerque Journal,* 26 March 1972.

47. "Tribes Take Squabble to DC," *Gallup Independent,* 27 March 1972.

48. "Hopis Picket BIA," *Gallup Independent,* 29 March 1972.

49. Chet MacRorie, "Open Letter to Rep. Sam Steiger," *Navajo Times,* 30 March 1972.

50. "Hopi Nation Splits," *Diné Baa-Hané,* 30 March 1972.

51. "Dividing Hopi-Navajo Joint Use Area No Solution: MacDonald," *Gallup Independent,* 31 March 1972; "'What's Right' Appeal Made," *Navajo Times,* 6 April 1972.

52. "Congress Should Act," *Arizona Republic,* 3 April 1972.

53. Sam Steiger, "Joint Use Hearings Spur Offer By Navajos To Talk With Hopis," *Gallup Independent,* 6 April 1972.

54. "Outsiders Split Navajo, Hopi," *Gallup Independent,* 6 April 1972; "Water Issue Raised In Land Dispute," *Navajo Times,* 6 April 1972.

55. Thomas Banyacya, Mina Lansa, Starlie Lomayaktewa, Claude Kewanyama, Ned Nayatewa, and David Monongye, "Hopi Traditionalists Oppose Steiger Proposal," *Navajo Times,* 6 April 1972.

56. "Navajo, 97, Arrested," *Gallup Independent,* 6 April 1972; Neil Mazurek, "Suit Charges Hopis Seized Herds Illegally," *Arizona Republic,* 8 June 1972.

57. Peter MacDonald (letter to the editor), *Arizona Republic*, 8 April 1972.

58. "'Simple Justice' Cry Of Navajo Ires Hopi," *Gallup Independent*, 11 April 1972.

59. "Hamilton Attacks Editorial," *Navajo Times*, 13 April 1972.

60. "Navajo Claims Outside 'Smokescreen' Scheme," *Gallup Independent*, 12 April 1972.

61. "Hopis' Chairman Issues Challenge," *Gallup Independent*, 13 April 1972.

62. "BIA Area Director Says US Has Decided To Relocate 5,000 Navajos," *Gallup Independent*, 13 April 1972.

63. Richard LaCourse, "Land Use Crisis," *Navajo Times*, 13 April 1972.

64. U.S. Congress, Senate, Committee on Indian Affairs of the Committee on Interior and Insular Affairs, *Partition of the Surface Rights of Navajo-Hopi Indian Land, Hearing . . . on H.R. 1193*, 93d Cong., 1st sess., 7 March 1973, 92.

65. "Hopis Propose Reduction Of Stock on Joint Land," *Gallup Independent*, 15 April 1972; "BIA Negotiates Range Dispute Between Hopi, Navajo Officials," *Albuquerque Journal*, 15 April 1972; "BIA Calls in Hopi, Navajo to Relieve Tensions," *Arizona Republic*, 15 April 1972.

66. Bill Donovan, "Nixon Abandoning Land Split," *Gallup Independent*, 14 April 1972.

67. "Navajo Relocation Endorsed," *Gallup Independent*, 18 April 1972; "Joint Effort to End Dispute Of Hopis, Navajos Is Urged," *Albuquerque Journal*, 18 April 1972; "Steiger Plan Invites War, Navajo Says," *Arizona Republic*, 18 April 1972.

68. "MacDonald Tells Hearing Bill Is Wrong! Madness!" *Navajo Times*, 27 April 1972.

69. "Navajo-Hopi Violence Predicted if Land Dispute Lingers On," *Arizona Republic*, 19 April 1972; "Hopis Seek Protection by Legislation," *Albuquerque Journal*, 19 April 1972; "Partition Only Way: Hamilton," *Gallup Independent*, 19 April 1972.

70. "Range Riders to Patrol Hopi, Navajo Border," *Arizona Republic*, 25 April 1972; "Hopi-Navajo Patrol Begins Today," *Gallup Independent*, 26 April 1972.

71. "BIA Told to Cut Grazing on Indian Joint-Use Land," *Arizona Republic*, 29 April 1972; "Navajo Grazing To Be Cut," *Gallup Independent*, 29 April 1972.

72. Bill Donovan, "Two Tribes Told 'Door Still Open,'" *Gallup Independent*, 3 May 1972.

73. Chet MacRorie, "Battle Only Begun," *Navajo Times*, 4 May 1972.

74. Bill Donovan, "Navajos Concede Hopis Half," *Gallup Independent*, 4 May 1972.

75. "Range Riders Have 'Lessened Tensions,'" *Gallup Independent*, 19 May 1972.

76. "Hopis Claim Navajo Still Build on Disputed Land," *Gallup Independent*, 24 May 1972.

77. "High Court Rejects Navajo Land Claim," *Gallup Independent*, 23 May 1972; "Legal Summary, CIV 479 PCT-JAW," MSS BC 442, Navajo-Hopi Land Dispute, Box 2, Folder 15, Coronado Room, Zimmerman Library, University of New Mexico, Albuquerque.

78. "Arrest Near Border Cost Navajo $224," *Gallup Independent*, 1 June 1972.

79. "Hopi Actions Called Unconstitutional," *Gallup Independent*, 2 June 1972.

80. "Suit Charges Hopis Seized Herds Illegally," *Arizona Republic*, 8 June 1972; "Hopi 'Range Rider' Is Sued," *Gallup Independent*, 9 June 1972.

81. "Navajo Police Are Now Authorized to Arrest Hopis on Reservation," *Gallup Independent*, 9 June 1972.

82. "Hopis Tear Down Navajo Meeting Place," *Gallup Independent*, 3 June 1972.

83. Robert L. Thomas, "Navajo Trespassers Face Hopi Eviction," *Arizona Republic*, 11 June 1972.

84. Robert L. Thomas, "Hopis Charge Navajos Overgraze Joint-Use Range," *Arizona Republic*, 12 June 1972.

85. Robert L. Thomas, "Intrusion of Navajo Heightens Conflicts within Hopi's Culture," *Arizona Republic*, 15 June 1972.

86. Robert L. Thomas, "A Navajo's Version of Hopi Dispute," *Arizona Republic*, 18 June 1972.

87. Robert L. Thomas, "Hopi-Navajo Border Patrol Attempts to Avoid Incidents," *Arizona Republic*, 19 June 1972.

88. Robert L. Thomas, "Hopi-Navajo Land Dispute Brawl Erupts," *Arizona Republic*, 24 June 1972; "Indian Border Dispute Erupts Into Violence," *Albuquerque Journal*, 24 June 1972; "Range War Erupts," *Gallup Independent*, 24 June 1972.

89. "Hopi Court Begins Navajo Trial Today," *Gallup Independent*, 1 July 1972; "One of 5 Navajos Found Guilty in Tribal Land Trespass Case," *Arizona Republic*, 1 July 1972.

90. "Navajo Official Opposes Bill," *Albuquerque Journal*, 1 July 1972.

91. "Hopis Declare Moratorium," *Gallup Independent*, 1 July 1972.

92. "Steiger Bill Amendments Approved by Navajo Tribe," *Gallup Independent*, 6 July 1972.

93. "MacDonald Speaks on Navajo Land Split Proposals," *Gallup Independent*, 7 July 1972.

94. "Navajo-Hopi Accord Written," *Gallup Independent*, 8 July 1972.

95. "Hopis Turn Down Joint Plan," *Gallup Independent*, 11 July 1972.

96. Bill Donovan, "Despite Hopi Rejection, Interior Dept. To Name Joint-Use Overseer," *Gallup Independent*, 13 July 1972.

97. Ibid.; "Hopi Suit Hearing Opens," *Albuquerque Journal*, 13 July 1972.

98. Lonnie Hosteen (letter to the editor), *Navajo Times*, 13 July 1972.

99. Daniel Peaches to "Sam", *Navajo Times*, 13 July 1972.

100. "Navajos to Open Office to Fight Land Division," *Albuquerque Journal*, 19 July 1972.

101. "Navajos Fight Steiger Bill in Capital," *Gallup Independent*, 26 July 1972; "Steiger Bill Goes to Senate," *Gallup Independent*, 27 July 1972.

102. "Steiger Bill Goes to Senate," *Gallup Independent*, 27 July 1972; "'Steiger Bill May Cause Bloodshed'—MacDonald," *Gallup Independent*, 29 July 1972.

103. Chet MacRorie, "The Steiger Bill: Commentary . . . ," *Navajo Times*, 3 August 1972.

104. "McGovern pledges Aid in Navajo-Hopi Dispute," *Arizona Republic*, 4 August 1972.

105. Kammer, *Second Long Walk*, 98; Chet MacRorie, "Dispute Bill Stopped?" *Navajo Times*, 10 August 1972.

106. "Hopis Ask Senate Unit To Set Hearing Dates," *Albuquerque Journal*, 11 August 1972.

107. "President Endorses Steiger Partition Bill," *Albuquerque Journal*, 15 September 1972; "'Merits, Not Politics' Is Hopi Plea to Senate," *Gallup Independent*, 15 August 1972; Kammer, *Second Long Walk*, 99.

108. Ralph Casteel, "Nixon Has Taken No Stand Upon Steiger Bill," *Navajo Times*, 21 September 1972.

109. "'Sit Down Together'—Domenici," *Gallup Independent*, 25 September 1972.

110. "Steiger Bill May Be Dead," *Gallup Independent*, 29 September 1972.

111. "Hopi Leader Calls Court Order Triumph for Justice," *Gallup Independent*, 12 September 1972.

112. "Short History of Land Dispute," MSS 442, Box 1, Folder 7, Coronado Room, Zimmerman Library, University of New Mexico, Albuquerque.

113. "Hopi-Navajo Plan Is Late," *Gallup Independent*, 14 October 1972.

114. "Navajo Families Driven from Homes on Hopi Land," *Gallup Independent*, 28 October 1972; "Hopi-Evicted Navajos Camp At Window Rock," *Gallup Independent*, 17 November 1972; "Displaced Navajos Still Need Home on the Range," *Gallup Independent*, 13 December 1972; Ralph Casteel, *New Navajo Tears* (Window Rock, Ariz.: The Navajo Tribe, n.d. [1973?]), 28–30.

115. "Navajos Draft Steiger Bill Alternative," *Gallup Independent*, 27 November 1972.

CHAPTER 9

1. "Fired Indian Official Gets Post on Hill," *Washington Post*, 16 January 1973.

2. Jerry Kammer, *The Second Long Walk: The Navajo-Hopi Land Dispute* (Albuquerque: University of New Mexico Press, 1980), 104, 108.

3. U.S., Congress, Senate, Committee on Indian Affairs of the Committee on Interior and Insular Affairs, *Partition of the Surface Rights of Navajo-Hopi Indian Land, Hearing . . . on H.R. 1193*, 93rd Cong., 1st sess., 7 March 1973 [hereafter cited as U.S. Senate, Committee Report on *Partition*], ii.

4. "Senate Hearing Due on Hopi-Navajo Feud," *Arizona Republic*, 10 February 1973; "Senators to Consider Hopi-Navajo Land Claims," *Arizona Republic*, 25 February 1973; "Hopi Land Hearings Scheduled," *Gallup Independent*, 9 February 1973.

5. U.S. Senate Committee Report on *Partition*, 19.

6. Ibid., 20–27.

7. Ibid., 28–36.

8. Ibid., 37–49.

9. Ibid., 49–51.

10. Ibid., 51–53.

11. Ibid., 53–55.

12. Ibid., 55–56.

13. Ibid., 57–61.

14. Ibid., 61–62.

15. Ibid., 63–75, 177–204.

16. Ibid., 77–94.

17. Ibid., 75–76.

18. Ibid., 95–102.

19. Ibid., 106–8.

20. Ibid., 104–6, 109–10.

21. Ibid., 98–99.

22. Ibid., 111–15.

23. Ibid., 116–23.

24. Ibid., 123–26.

25. Ibid., 126–29.

26. Ibid., 129–30.

27. Ibid., 130–33.

28. Ibid., 136–44, 148–61.

29. Ibid., 145–47.

30. Caroline Davis, "Hopi-Navajo Case Is Aired," *Gallup Independent*, 8 March 1973.

31. U.S. Senate Committee Report on *Partition*, 145–47.

32. "Navajo-Hopi Talks To Resume April 2," *Gallup Independent*, 21 March 1973.

33. "Hopi-Navajo Talks Enter Third Day," *Gallup Independent*, 4 April 1973.

34. "Navajo-Hopi Utah Talks Cut Short," *Gallup Independent*, 5 April 1973.

35. Boyden to Abourezk, 11 April 1973, MSS 442, Box 1, Folder 17, Coronado Room, Zimmerman Library, University of New Mexico, Albuquerque.

36. "Navajos Offer Two Solutions," *Gallup Independent*, 4 May 1973; Bill Donovan, "Navajo Settlement Plan Is Rejected," *Gallup Independent*, 5 May 1973; "Land Dispute Proposals Unveiled At Phoenix Meeting," *Winslow Mail*, 10 May 1973. The story in the Winslow paper includes maps of the area outside the two reservations that MacDonald proposed be given to the Hopis.

37. "Navajo Land Bills Introduced," *Gallup Independent*, 11 May 1973.

38. "MacDonald Warns Bluecoats," *Gallup Independent*, 15 May 1973; Ben Cole, "Navajo Chief Warns of Forcing People from Disputed Land," *Arizona Republic*, 15 May 1973.

39. "Navajo-Hopi Livestock Sharing Proposal Draws Laugh in Capital," *Gallup Independent*, 16 May 1973; "Court Ruling Suggested in Land Dispute," *Albuquerque Journal*, 16 May 1973.

40. "Morton Calls For Fairness In Navajo-Hopi Dispute But—Favors Steiger Bill," *Navajo Times*, 26 July 1973.

41. Kammer, *Second Long Walk*, 108–9.

42. Gene Goldenberg, "Navajo-Hopi Bill Chosen," *Albuquerque Tribune*, 30 November 1973.

43. Ben Cole, "The Arizona Republic Telecopies File No. 400 from Washington, 27 November 1973," MSS BC 442, Box 2, Folder 6, Item 20, Coronado Room, Zimmerman Library, University of New Mexico, Albuquerque.

44. "Indian Land Bill Approved," *Albuquerque Tribune*, 12 December 1973; "Navajo-Hopi Bill," *Navajo Times*, 10 January 1974.

45. Schifter to MacDonald, 11 January 1974, MSS BC 442, Box 1, Folder 17, Coronado Room, Zimmerman Library, University of New Mexico, Albuquerque.

46. Ibid.

47. W. Richard West, Jr. to "Dick," 18 January [1974], MSS BC 442, Box 1, Folder 17, Coronado Room, Zimmerman Library, University of New Mexico, Albuquerque.

48. "WRW" to "The Files," 23 January 1974, MSS BC 442, Box 1, Folder 17, Coronado Room, Zimmerman Library, University of New Mexico, Albuquerque; "WRW" to "The Files," 25 January 1974, ibid.; "WRW" to "RS," 30 January 1974, ibid.; Schifter to Vlassis, 7 February 1974, ibid.

49. Schifter to MacDonald, 20 February 1974; MSS BC 442, Box 1, Folder 17, Coronado Room, Zimmerman Library, University of New Mexico, Albuquerque; Gene Goldenberg, "Partition in Indian Dispute," *Albuquerque Tribune*, 21 February 1974; "Hopis Win Round in Dispute On Land Division," *Phoenix Gazette*, 20 February 1974.

50. "Hopis Win Round in Dispute On Land Division," *Phoenix Gazette*, 20 February 1974; Brugge to Lujan, 23 February 1974, copy in author's files.

51. *The Navajos: An Indian Struggle for Land and Heritage* (Window Rock, Ariz.: The Navajo Tribe, n.d. [ca. 1974]).

52. Howard Bryan, "'I won't move from here if it costs me my life,'" *Albuquerque Tribune*, 6 March 1973; Howard Bryan, "Navajo-Hopi Dispute Over Land—Is There a Solution?" *Albuquerque* Tribune, 8 March 1973.

53. Paul R. Wieck, "Navajo-Hopi Bill Passage Bid Beaten," *Albuquerque Journal*, 19 March 1974; Gene Goldenberg, "Navajos, Hopis On Own Again in Land Battle," *Albuquerque Tribune*, 19 March 1974; "Land Division Bill Defeated," *Navajo Times*, 21 March 1974.

54. Lujan to Brugge, 29 March 1974, copy in author's files.

55. Meeds to MacDonald, 25 March 1974, MSS BC 442, Box 1, Folder 17, Coronado Room, Zimmerman Library, University of New Mexico, Albuquerque.

56. Schifter to Vlassis, 12 April 1974, MSS BC 442, Box 1, Folder 18, Coronado Room, Zimmerman Library, University of New Mexico, Albuquerque.

57. Schifter to MacDonald, 2 May 1974, MSS BC 442, Box 1, Folder 18, Coronado Room, Zimmerman Library, University of New Mexico, Albuquerque.

58. Howard Bryan, "Tribal Chairman Blasts Bill to Move Navajos," *Albuquerque Tribune*, 25 May 1974.

59. Paul R. Wieck, "Navajo-Hopi Compromise Drafted by Lujan, Meeds," *Albuquerque Journal*, 29 May 1974; Gene Goldenberg, "Navajo-Hopi Land Compromise Seen," *Albuquerque Tribune*, 29 May 1974.

60. Gene Goldenberg, "Navajos to Fight House Legislation on Disputed Land," *Albuquerque Tribune*, 30 May 1974; "House Backs Hopis," *Albuquerque Journal*, 30 May 1974.

61. Fannin to Kennedy, 5 June 1974, MSS BC 442, Box 1, Folder 18, Coronado Room, Zimmerman Library, Albuquerque.

62. "U Professor Suggests Hopi-Navajo Plan," *Albuquerque Tribune*, 7 June 1974; Ken Sekaquaptewa, "All-Indian Pueblo Council Supports Hopi Land Division," *Qua Toqti*, 13 June 1974; "US 'Unwilling To Admit Mistake,' Says Hanle [sic]," *Gallup Independent*, 19 June 1974; "Navajo-Hopi Group Fights Land Split," *Gallup Independent*, 20 June 1974; Kammer, *Second Long Walk*, 110.

63. Paul R. Wieck, "Another Indian Proposal," *Albuquerque Journal*, 25 June 1974.

64. Brugge to Abourezk, 29 June 1974, copy in author's files.

65. George P. Vlassis (letter to the editor), *Arizona Republic*, 11 July 1974.

66. Brugge to [several United States Senators], 14 July 1974, with replies by Henry M. Jackson, Birch Bayh, and J. Bennett Johnston, copies in author's files.

67. "Navajos Plan Caravan to Washington," *Albuquerque Journal*, 16 July 1974.

68. Phil Nicklaus, "Hopis, Navajos Say U.S. 'Bad Guy,'" *Albuquerque Journal*, 18 July 1974; Michele Weith, "Navajo Caravan Fights Hopi Bill," *Albuquerque Tribune*, 18 July 1974.

69. Phil Nicklaus, "1882 Order Sparked Indian Land Rift," *Albuquerque Journal*, 21 July 1974.

70. Gene Goldenberg, "White House Backs Partition," *Albuquerque Tribune*, 24 July 1974; Paul R. Wieck, "Bill Favoring Hopis Is Favored," *Albuquerque Journal*, 25 July 1974.

71. "Navajos and Hopis Issue Warnings," *Albuquerque Tribune*, 25 July 1974.

72. Eric McCrossen, "Hopi Traditionalist Offers Plan," *Albuquerque Journal*, 29 July 1974.

73. David F. Aberle, *Statement of David F. Aberle for Submission to the Senate Committee on Indian and Insular Affairs*, 1974, copy in possession of author.

74. Bill Donavan, "Senators Reject Partitioning," *Gallup Independent*, 7 August 1974; "New Hopi, Navajo Land Talks Asked," *Albuquerque Journal*, 22 August 1974.

75. Kammer, *Second Long Walk*, 123–30; "Senate Passes Navajo- Hopi Bill," *Albuquerque Jour-*

nal, 3 December 1974; Bob Duke, "Land Bill Pleases Navajos," *Albuquerque Tribune,* 3 December 1974; "Can Live With Bill, Hopi Leader Says," *Albuquerque Tribune,* 6 December 1974.

CHAPTER 10

1. Jerry Kammer, *The Second Long Walk: The Navajo-Hopi Land Dispute* (Albuquerque: University of New Mexico Press, 1980).

2. Thayer Scudder, *No Place to Go: Effects of Compulsory Relocation on Navajos* (Philadelphia, Pa.: Institute for the Study of Human Issues, 1982).

3. John J. Wood, Walter M. Vannette, and Michael J. Andrews, *"Sheep is Life": An Assessment of Livestock Reduction in the Former Navajo-Hopi Joint Use Area,* Northern Arizona University Anthropological Paper No. 1 (Flagstaff, Ariz.: Northern Arizona University, 1982).

4. Martin D. Topper, *Mental Health Effects on Navajo Area Mental Health Patients from the Former Navajo-Hopi Joint Use Area.* (Gallup, N.M.: Mental Health Branch, Navajo Area Office, Indian Health Service, 1980).

5. Anita Parlowe, *Cry, Sacred Ground* (Washington, D.C.: Christic Institute, 1988).

6. Emily Benedek, *The Wind Won't Know Me: A History of the Navajo-Hopi Land Dispute* (New York: Alfred A. Knopf, 1992).

7. Orit Tamir, "Relocation of Navajo from Hopi Partitioned Land in Pinon," *Human Organization* 59 (Summer 1991):173–78.

8. Orit Tamir, "Some Consequences of Compulsory Relocation on Navajo Socioeconomy." (Unpublished Master's thesis, Arizona State University, 1986).

9. David Shaw-Serder and Eugene Yazzie, "The Navajo-Hopi Land Dispute: Sale of Replacement Homes by Navajo Public Law 93-531 Relocatees" (Unpublished Master's thesis, Arizona State University, 1986).

10. Tamara Brennan, "Navajo Perceptions of the Psychological and Sociological Meaning of Forced Relocation (Unpublished Master's thesis, University of Colorado, 1991).

11. David M. Brugge, "The Relocation of Navajos from the Hopi Partitioned Lands (HPL) in Relation to the World Bank Standards for Involuntary Resettlement," paper presented at the Fourth Annual Navajo Studies Conference, Gallup, N.M., October 1989).

12. Mary Shepardson, *Navajo Ways in Government: A Study in Political Process,* American Anthropological Association Memoir 96 (Menasha, Wisc.: American Anthropological Association, 1963).; Aubrey W. Williams, Jr., *Navajo Political Process,* Smithsonian Contributions to Anthropology, Vol. 9 (Washington, D.C.: Smithsonian Institution Press, 1970).

13. Iverson, *Navajo Nation,* 208.

14. Orpha Sweeten Boyden, *John S. Boyden: Three score and Ten in Retrospect* (Cedar city, Utah: Southern Utah State College Press, 1986).

15. Kammer, *Second Long Walk,* 77–79, 85–90, 133–37.

16. John Redhouse, *Geopolitics of the Navajo-Hopi Land Dispute* (Albuquerque, N.M.: Redhouse/Wright Publications, 1958).

17. Roy Weyler, *Blood on the Land: The Government and Corporate War Against the American Indian Movement* (New York: Vantage Books, 1982).

18. Catherine Feher-Elston, *Children of Sacred Ground: America's Last Indian War* (Flagstaff, Ariz.: Northland Publishing, 1988).

19. Richard O. Clemmer, "Crying for the Children of Sacred Ground: A Review Article on the Hopi-Navajo Land Dispute," *American Indian Quarterly* 17 (Spring 1991): 225–30.

20. Feher-Elston, *Children*, 33.

21. Ibid., 36

22. Paul A. Vestal, *Ethnobotany of the Ramah Navaho*, Papers of the Peabody Museum of American Archaeology and Ethnology, Vol. 40, No. 4 (Cambridge, Mass.: Harvard University, 1952); Leland C. Wyman and Stuart K. Harris, *Navajo Indian Medical Ethnobotany*, The University of New Mexico Bulletin, Anthropological Series, Vol. 3, No. 5 (Albuquerque, N.M.: University of New Mexico Press, 1941).

23. Feher-Elston, *Children*, x–xiii.

24. Clemmer, "Crying for the Children," 225–26, 230.

SOURCES

....

ARCHIVES CONSULTED

Archivo General de Los Indias, Sevilla; at Bancroft Library, Berkeley
Laboratory of Anthropology, Museum of New Mexico, Santa Fe
Latter-day Saints Church Historian's Office, Salt Lake City, UT. Manuscript Collection
National Archives, Washington, DC
Zimmerman Library, University of New Mexico, Albuquerque
    Coronado Room
    Anderson Room

NEWSPAPERS CITED

Albuquerque Journal (Albuquerque, NM)
Albuquerque Tribune (Albuquerque, NM)
Arizona Republic (Phoenix, AZ)
Diné Baa-Hané (Fort Defiance, AZ)
Gallup Independent (Gallup, NM)
Navajo Times (Window Rock, AZ)
Phoenix Gazette (Phoenix, AZ)
Qua' Toqti (Oraibi, AZ)
Washington Post (Washington, DC)
Winslow Mail (Winslow, AZ)

PERSONAL INTERVIEWS

Robert L. Bennett, Albuquerque, NM, 9 November 1989.
Robert W. Young, Albuquerque, NM, 9 February 1990.

BIBLIOGRAPHY

Abel, Annie Heloise
    1915 *The Official Correspondence of James S. Calhoun.* Washington, DC: Office of Indian Affairs.

Aberle, David F.
    1974 *Statement of David F. Aberle for Submission to the Senate Committee on Indian and Insular Affairs.* Manuscript, copy in possession of author.

Adams, Eleanor B.
    1963 "Fray Silvestre and the Obstinate Hopi," *New Mexico Historical Review* 38: 97–138.

Bailey, Lynn R.

Sources

1970 *Bosque Redondo: An American Concentration Camp.* Pasadena, CA: Socio-Technical Publications.

Bancroft, Herbert Howe
1962 *History of Arizona and New Mexico, 1530–1888.* Albuquerque, NM: Horn and wallace, Publishers.

Benedek, Emily
1992 *The Wind Won't Know Me: A History of the Navajo-Hopi Land Dispute.* New York: Alfred A. Knopf.

Boyden, Orpha Sweeten
1986 *John S. Boyden: Three Score and Ten in Retrospect.* Cedar City, UT: Southern Utah State College Press.

Brandt, Elizabeth A.
1979 "Sandia Pueblo." In *Handbook of North American Indians, Southwest,* Vol. 9, ed. Alfonso Ortiz, 343–50. Washington, DC: Smithsonian Institution.

Brennan, Tamara
1991 "Navajo Perceptions of the Psychological and Sociological Meaning of Forced Relocation," Master's Thesis, University of Colorado, Boulder.

Brew, J. O.
1949 "The History of Awatovi." In Ross Gordon Montgomery, Watson Smith, and John Otis Brew, *Franciscan Awatovi: The Excavation and Conjectural Reconstruction of a 17th-Century Spanish Mission Establishment at a Hopi Indian Town in Northeastern Arizona.* Papers of the Peabody Museum of American Archaeology and Ethnology, Vol. 36, 1–43. Cambridge, MA: Harvard University. 1979 "Hopi Prehistory and History to 1850." In *Handbook of North American Indians, Southwest,* Vol. 9, ed. Alfonso Ortiz, 514–23. Washington, DC: Smithsonian Institution.

Brugge, David M.
1963 "Documentary Reference to a Navajo Naach'id in 1840," *Ethnohistory* 10: 186–87. 1963 *Navajo Pottery and Ethnohistory,* Navajoland Publications Series 2. Window Rock, AZ: Navajo Tribal Museum. (Rev. ed., Navajo Nation Cultural Resource Management Program, 1951). 1964 "Vizcarra's Navajo Campaign of 1823," *Arizona and the West* 6: 223–44. 1969 "Pueblo Factionalism and External Relations," *Ethnohistory* 16: 191–200. 1979 "Early 18th Century Spanish-Apachean Relations." In *Collected Papers in Honor of Bertha Pauline Dutton,* ed. Albert H. Schroeder, Papers of the Archaeological Society of New Mexico 4: 103–21. 1981 "Comments on Athabaskans and Sumas," in *The Protohistoric Period in the North american Southwest, AD 1450–1700,* ed. David R. Wilcox and W. Bruce Massey, Anthropological Research Papers No. 24, 282–90. Tempe: Arizona State University. 1982 "Western Navajo Ethnobotanical

Notes." In *Navajo Religion and Culture: Selected Views, Papers in Honor of Leland C. Wyman*, ed. David M. Brugge and Charlotte J. Frisbie, 89–97. Santa Fe, NM: Museum of New Mexico. 1985 *Navajos in the Catholic Church Records of New Mexico, 1694–1875*, rev. ed. Tsaile, AZ: Navajo Community College Press. (Window Rock, AZ: The Navajo Tribe, 1968). 1989 "The Relocation of Navajos from the Hopi Partitioned Lands (HPL) in Relation to the World Bank Standards for Involuntary Resettlement." Paper presented at the Fourth Annual Navajo Studies Conference, Gallup, NM, October 1989.

Brugge, David M., and J. Lee Correll
1971 *The Story of the Navajo Treaties.* Navajo Historical Publications, Documentary Series 1. Window Rock, AZ: The Navajo Tribe.

Casteel, Ralph
1973 *New Navajo Tears.* Window Rock, AZ: The Navajo Tribe.

Chávez, Fray Angélico
1952 *Archives of the Archdiocese of Santa Fe, 1678–1900.* Washington, DC: Academy of American Franciscan History.

Chávez, Fray Angélico, trans., and Ted J. Warner, ed.
1976 *The Domínguez-Escalante Journal: Their Expedition Through Colorado, Utah, Arizona, and New Mexico in 1776.* Provo, UT: Brigham Young University Press.

Clemmer, Richard O.
1991 "Crying for the Children of Sacred Ground: A Review Article on the Hopi-Navajo Land Dispute," *American Indian Quarterly* 17: 225–30.

Clinton-Tullie, Verna
1981 "Research of the Navajo-Hopi Tobacco Clan of Finger Point-Star Mountain of Teesto Chapter Community and Polacca, Awatovi and Sichomovi of First Mesa," Unpublished Manuscript prepared for the Navajo-Hopi Land Dispute Commission and the Navajo-Hopi Land Dispute Task Force, Window Rock, AZ. Copy in possession of author.

Coolidge, Dane, and Mary Roberts Coolidge
1930 *The Navajo Indians.* Boston: Houghton Mifflin Company.

Correll, J. Lee, and David M. Brugge
1958 "Navajo Agriculture." Unpublished Manuscript. Navajo Land Claim files, The Navajo Nation, Window Rock, AZ. Copy in possession of author.

Correll, J. Lee, Editha L. Watson, and David M. Brugge
1969 *Navajo Bibliography with Subject Index*, rev. ed. Research Report 2. Window Rock, AZ: The Navajo Tribe.

Sources

Coues, Elliott, ed.
 1900 *On the Trail of a Spanish Pioneer: The Diary and Itinerary of Francisco Garcés (Missionary Priest) in His Travels Through Sonora, Arizona, and California, 1775–1776*. New York: Francis P. Harper.

Dale, Edward Everett
 1949 *The Indians of the Southwest: A Century of Development under the United States*. San Marino, CA: The Huntington Library; Norman: University of Oklahoma Press.

Drew, Linda G., ed.
 1972 *Tree-Ring Chronologies of Western America II: Arizona, New Mexico, Texas*. Chronology Series I. Tucson, AZ: Laboratory of Tree-Ring Research.

Elmore, Francis H.
 1944 *Ethnobotany of the Navajo*. Monographs of the School of American Research, No. 8. Santa Fe, NM: School of American Research; Albuquerque, NM: University of New Mexico Press.

Espinosa, J. Manuel
 1940 *First Expedition of Vargas into New Mexico, 1692*. Albuquerque: University of New Mexico Press.

Espinosa, J. Manuel, ed. and trans.
 1988 *The Pueblo Indian Revolt of 1696 and the Franciscan Missions of New Mexico: Letters of the Missionaries and Related Documents*. Norman: University of Oklahoma Press.

Etsedi, Peshlakai, and Sallie Pierce Brewer
 1954 "The Long Walk to Bosque Redondo," *Navaho Customs*, Reprint Series No. 6: 6–13. Flagstaff, AZ: Museum of Northern Arizona.

Feher-Elston, Catherine
 1988 *Children of Sacred Ground: America's Last Indian War*. Flagstaff, AZ: Northland Publishing.

Fenzl, Terry E., Craig W. Soland, and John W. Rogers
 1990 *Navajo Tribe's Responses to Hopi Tribe's Proposed Findings of Fact and Conclusions of Law, Vernon Masayesva, etc., Plaintiff, v. Leonard Haskie, etc., Defendant, v. Evelyn James, etc., Intervenors*, No. CIV 74-842, PHX-EHC, United States District Court for the District of Arizona. Phoenix, AZ: Brown and Bain, P.A.

Forbes, Jack O.
 1960 *Apache, Navaho and Spaniard*. Norman: University of Oklahoma Press.

Hamley, Frederick G., Leon R. Yankwich, and James A. Walsh
 1962 *In the United States District Court for the District of Arizona, No. Civil 579 Prescott, Opinion of the*

Court, Appendix to Opinion—Chronological Account of Hopi-Navajo Controversy, Findings of Fact, and Conclusions of Law, Judgment. San Francisco, CA: Pernau-Walsh Printing Co.

Hammond, George P., and Agapito Rey, eds.
1953 *Don Juan de Oñate: Colonizer of New Mexico.* Coronado Cuarto Centennial Series, Vols. 5–6. Albuquerque: University of New Mexico Press.

Hill, W. W.
1938 *The Agricultural and Hunting Methods of the Navaho Indians.* Publications in Anthropology No. 18. New Haven, CT: Yale University Press.

Hodge, Frederick Webb, George P. Hammond, and Agapito Rey
1945 *Fray Alonso de Benavides' Revised Memorial of 1634, with Numerous Supplementary Documents, Elaborately Annotated.* Albuquerque: University of New Mexico Press.

Hoffman, Virginia
1974 *Navajo Biographies,* Vol. 1. Phoenix, AZ: Navajo Curriculum Center Press.

Iverson, Peter
1981 *The Navajo Nation.* Westport, CT: Greenwood Press.

James, H. C.
1956 *The Hopi Indians: Their History and Their Culture.* Caldwell, IA: Caxton Printers.

James, Harry C.
1974 *Pages from Hopi History.* Tucson: University of Arizona Press.

James, Thomas
1962 *Three Years Among the Mexicans and the Indians.* Chicago, IL: Rio Grande Press.

Johnson, Burke
1965 "The Time Has Not Yet Come," *Arizona Days and Ways Magazine,* 12 December, 7–9.

Johnston, Philip
1939 "Peshlakai Atsidi," *Plateau* 12: 2.

Kammer, Jerry
1980 *The Second Long Walk: The Navajo-Hopi Land Dispute.* Albuquerque: University of New Mexico Press.

Kelly, Lawrence
1970 *Navajo Roundup, Selected Correspondence of Kit Carson's Expedition Against the Navajo, 1863– 1865.* Boulder, CO: The Pruitt Publishing Company.

Sources

Kessell, John L.

1979 *Kiva, Cross, and Crown: The Pecos Indians and New Mexico, 1540–1840.* Washington, DC: National Park Service.

Kidder, Alfred Vincent

1958 *Pecos, New Mexico: Archaeological Notes.* Papers of the Robert S. Peabody Foundation for Archaeology, Vol. 5. Andover, MA: Phillips Academy.

Kluckhohn, Clyde, and Dorothea Leighton

1962 *The Navajo* (rev. ed.). New York: American Museum of Natural History; Garden City, NY: Doubleday & Company.

Littell, Norman M.

1963 *Report of the General Counsel to the Navajo Tribal Council at Council Meeting Commencing Monday, April 15, 1963.* Unpublished Manuscript. The Navajo Nation, Window Rock, AZ. Copy in possession of author.

Littell, Norman M., and Leland O. Graham

1964 *Proposed Findings of Fact in Behalf of the Navajo Tribe of Indians in Area of Hopi Overlap (Docket No. 196),* 3 vols. Washington, DC: Norman M. Littell.

Littell, Norman M., and Joseph F. McPherson

1961a *Defendant Navajo Tribe's Proposed Findings of Fact, No. Civil 579 Prescott, United States District Court for the District of Arizona.* Washington, DC: Norman M. Littell.
1961b *Defendant Navajo Tribe's Exceptions to Plaintiffs' Proposed Findings of Fact, No. CIVIL 579 Prescott, United States District Court for the District of Arizona.* Washington, DC: Norman M. Littell.

McNitt, Frank

1972 *Navajo Wars: Military Campaigns, Slave Raids and Reprisals.* Albuquerque: University of New Mexico Press.

Morfí, Father Juan Agustín de

1977 *Account of Disorders in New Mexico, 1778.* Trans. and ed. Marc Simmons. Isleta Pueblo, NM: St. Augustine Church.

Navajo Tribe

n.d. *The Navajos: An Indian Struggle for Land and Heritage.* Window Rock, AZ ca. 1974.

Navajo Tribal Council

1953–1957 Minutes, mimeographed, Window Rock, AZ. Copy in Zimmerman Library, University of New Mexico, Albuquerque.

Newcomb, Franc Johnson
1964 *Hosteen Klah, Navaho Medicine Man and Sand Painter.* Norman: University of Oklahoma Press.

Officer, James E.
1963 *Navajo-Hopi Conference, August 6–7, 1963,* manuscript, copy in possession of Robert W. Young, Department of Linguistics, University of New Mexico, Albuquerque.

Page, Gordon B.
1939 *Hopi Land Management Unit, Hopi-Navajo Boundary Report, Report of the Human Dependency Survey.* National Archives, Bureau of Indian Affairs, Record Group 75, "Classified Files, 1907"—File Mark 24705-40-304.3 General Service.

Parlowe, Anita
1988 *Cry, Sacred Ground.* Washington, DC: Christic Institute.

Parman, Donald L.
1976 *The Navajos and the New Deal.* New Haven, CT: Yale University Press.

Peterson, Charles S.
1973 *Take Up Your Mission: Mormon Colonizing Along the Little Colorado River, 1870–1900.* Tucson: University of Arizona Press.

Powers, Margaret A., and Byron P. Johnson
1987 *Defensive Sites of Dinetah.* Cultural Resources Series No. 2. Albuquerque, NM: Bureau of Land Management.

Prudden, T. Mitchell
1907 *On The Great American Plateau: Wanderings Among Canyons and Buttes, in the Land of the Cliff-Dweller, and the Indian of Today.* New York: G. P. Putnam's Sons.

Redhouse, John
1985 *Geopolitics of the Navajo-Hopi Land Dispute.* Albuquerque, NM: Redhouse/Wright Publications.

Reeve, Frank D.
1958 "Navaho-Spanish Wars, 1680–1720," *New Mexico Historical Review* 33: 204–31. 1959 "The Navaho-Spanish Peace: 1720s–1770s," *New Mexico Historical Review* 33: 205–31. 1960 "Navaho-Spanish Diplomacy, 1770–1790," *New Mexico Historical Review* Vol. 35: 200–235.

Reichard, Gladys A.
1928 *Social Life of the Navajo Indians with Some Attention to Minor Ceremonies.* Columbia University Contributions to Anthropology, Vol. 7. New York: Columbia University Press.

Schroeder, Albert H.
1979 "Pueblos Abandoned in Historic Times." In *Handbook of North American Indians, Southwest*, Vol. 9, ed. Alfonso Ortiz, 234–54. Washington, DC: Smithsonian Institution.

Scudder, Thayer
1982 *No Place to Go: Effects of Compulsory Relocation on Navajos*. Philadelphia, PA: Institute for the Study of Human Issues.

Shaw-Serder, David, and Eugene Yazzie
1986 "The Navajo-Hopi Land Dispute: Sale of Replacement Homes by Navajo Public Law 93-531 Relocatees," Master's Thesis, Arizona State University, Tempe.

Shepardson, Mary
1963 *Navajo Ways in Government: A Study in Political Process*. American Anthropological Association Memoir 96. Menasha, WI: American Anthropological Association.

Son of Old Man Hat
1938 *Son of Old Man Hat: A Navajo Autobiography*. Walter Dyk, ed. Lincoln: University of Nebraska Press.

Stephen, Alexander M.
1936 *Hopi Journal*, 2 vols. Contributions to Anthropology, Vol. 23. New York: Columbia University Press.

Stokes, M. A. and T. L. Smiley
1963 "Tree-Ring Dates From the Navajo Land Claim I. The Northern Sector." *Tree-Ring Bulletin* 25: 8–18. 1964 "Tree-Ring Dates from the Navajo Land Claim II. The Western Sector," *Tree-Ring Bulletin* 26: 13–27. 1966 "Tree-Ring Dates from the Navajo Land Claim III. The Southern Sector," *Tree-Ring Bulletin* 27: 2–11. 1969 "Tree-Ring Dates from the Navajo Land Claim IV. The Eastern Sector." *Tree-Ring Bulletin* 29: 2–15.

Talayesva, Don C.
1942 *Sun Chief, the Autobiography of a Hopi Indian*, ed. Leo W. Simmons. New Haven, CT: Yale University Press.

Tamir, Orit
1985 *The City of Winslow, Arizona, Navajo and Hopi Relocatees Needs Assessment, Phase One—Final Report*. Flagstaff, AZ: Navajo and Hopi Indian Relocation Commission. 1986 "Some Consequences of Compulsory Relocation on Navajo Socioeconomy." Master's Thesis, Arizona State University, Tempe. 1991 "Relocation of Navajo from Hopi Partitioned Land in Pinon," *Human Organization* 59: 173–78.

Thomas, Alfred Barnaby

1932 *Forgotten Frontiers: A Study of the Spanish Indian Policy of Don Juan Bautista de Anza, Governor of New Mexico, 1777–1787, from the Original Documents in the Archives of Spain, Mexico, and New Mexico.* Norman: University of Oklahoma Press.

Thomas, Alfred Barnaby, trans. and ed.

1941 *Teodoro de Croix and the Northern Frontier of New Spain, 1776–1783.* Norman: University of Oklahoma Press.

Titiev, Mischa

1944 *Old Oraibi: A Study of the Hopi Indians of the Third Mesa.* Papers of the Peabody Museum of American Archaeology and Ethnology Vol. 2, No. 1. Cambridge, MA: Harvard University.

Topper, Martin D.

1980 *Mental Health Effects on Navajo Area Mental Health Patients from the Former Navajo-Hopi Joint Use Area.* Gallup, NM: Mental Health Branch, Navajo Area Office, Indian Health Service.

Turner, Christy G., II, and Nancy T. Morris

1970 "A Massacre at Hopi," *American Antiquity* 35: 320–31.

Underhill, Ruth M.

1953 *Here Come the Navaho!* Indian Life and Customs No. 8. Washington, DC: U.S. Indian Service. 1956 *The Navajos.* Norman: University of Oklahoma Press.

United States Bureau of Indian Affairs

1963 *Navajo-Hopi Conference, August 6–7, 1963, Valley Ho Hotel, 350 W. Main Street,* Scottsdale, AZ. Transcript, Anderson Room, Zimmerman Library, University of New Mexico, Albuquerque.

United States Senate

1973 *Partition of the Surface Rights of Navajo-Hopi Indian Land, Hearing Before the Committee on Indian Affairs of the Committee on Interior and Insular Affairs, Ninety-Third Congress, First Session on H.R. 1193.* Washington, DC: U.S. Government Printing Office. United States Court of Appeals for the District of Columbia Circuit. 1964 No. 18338. *Stewart L. Udall, Secretary of the Interior, Appellant, v. Norman M. Littell, Appellee, Appeal from the United States District Court for the District of Columbia, Decided August 13, 1964.* Washington, DC.

Van Valkenburgh, Richard F.

1938 *A Short History of the Navajo People.* Window Rock, AZ: Navajo Service, U.S. Department of the Interior. 1956 *Report of Archeological Survey of the Navajo-Hopi Contact Area.* Unpublished Manuscript. Navajo Land Claim files, The Navajo Nation, Window Rock, AZ.

Sources

Van Valkenburgh, Richard F., and Clyde Kluckhohn
1974 "Navajo Sacred Places," *Navajo Indians III*. Garland American Indian Ethnohistory Series, 9–199. New York: Garland Publishing, Inc.

Vestal, Paul A.
1952 *Ethnobotany of the Ramah Navaho*. Papers of the Peabody Museum of American Archaeology and Ethnology, Vol. 40, No. 4. Cambridge, MA: Harvard University.

Waters, Frank
1963 *Book of the Hopi*. New York: Ballantine Books.

Weyler, Roy
1982 *Blood on the Land: The Government and Corporate War Against the American Indian Movement*. New York: Vantage Books.

Whiteley, Peter
1988 *Bacavi: Journey to Reed Springs*. Flagstaff, AZ: Northland Press.

Whiting, Alfred F.
1939 *Ethnobotany of the Hopi*. Museum of Northern Arizona Bulletin 15. Flagstaff: Museum of Northern Arizona Press.

Williams, Aubrey W., Jr.
1970 *Navajo Political Process*. Smithsonian Contributions to Anthropology, Vol. 9. Washington, DC: Smithsonian Institution Press.

Wood, John J., Walter M. Vannette, and Michael J. Andrews
1982 *"Sheep is Life": An Assessment of Livestock Reduction in the Former Navajo-Hopi Joint Use Area*. Anthropological Paper No. 1. Flagstaff: Northern Arizona University.

Wyman, Leland C., and Stuart K. Harris
1941 *Navajo Indian Medical Ethnobotany*. The University of New Mexico Bulletin, Anthropological Series, Vol. 3, No. 5. Albuquerque: University of New Mexico Press.

Yava, Albert
1978 *Big Falling Snow: A Tewa-Hopi Indian's Life and Times and the History and Traditions of His People*, ed. and annot. Harold Courlander. Albuquerque: University of New Mexico Press.

Young, Robert W., and William Morgan
1943 *The Navaho Language: The Elements of Navaho Grammar with a dictionary in Two Parts Containing Basic Vocabularies of Navaho and English*. Phoenix, AZ: Education Division, United States Indian Service. 1987 *The Navajo Language: A Grammar and Colloquial Dictionary*. Albuquerque: University of New Mexico Press.

INDEX

Index

Prescott decision, 141, 149, 151, 153, 157–58, 180, 207, 226, 236, 239
Prescott hearings/case/suit, 54, 65, 67–92, 105-6, 144, 151-52, 157, 168, 238
Preston Mesa, AZ, 166
Preston, Scott, 37, 75, 81–82, 112, 128–29, 174
Price, Gene, 125
property rights, 218, 256
proposed findings of fact, 93, 96, 269n.2
Public Law 85–547, 47. See also Hopi Boundary Bill.
Public Law 93–531, 242. See also partition; relocation.

quiet title (legal concept), 59, 69
Quochytewa, Roger, 85

Rachford, C. E., 33
Randolph, Elmer, 202–3, 205, 209–11
Rat Springs, AZ, 72
Raymond, Ed, 137
rebuttal testimony, 85
recall elections, 111
recall petitions, 115
Reconquest of New Mexico, 7–8, 18
red flannel, 20
Redhouse, John, 160, 251
Red Lake, AZ, 84
Red Lake Store, AZ, 83
Reed, John, 72
refugees (Navajo), 241
Reimann, Mary Anne, 59, 68
religious prejudice, 255
relocation, 160, 205–6, 211, 215, 234, 236–38, 242–44, 255, 275n.2. relocation commission, 241, 253
Republican Party, 198-99, 213-14, 230, 239
Reservoir Canyon, AZ, 166
resettlement, 216, 231–33. See also: new lands; relocation.

resisters (to relocation), 241, 244–45, 275n.2
Rhodes, John, 37, 199
Riggs, Pete, 143–44, 184
Rockbridge, John, 57, 60, 78
Rough Rock, AZ, 195
Runnels, Harold, 232
Ruzow, Lawrence, 201

Sagenetso, Victor, 175
Salt Lake City, UT, 155, 161, 163, 203, 205
Sanderson, Justin, 80
Sandoval, Chic, 124–25
Sandoval, Roger, 142
Sand Springs, AZ, 167
San Francisco Peaks, AZ, 9, 173
San Juan drainage, 245
San Juan River, 61, 138
Santa Fe, NM, 12, 20, 148, 159
Sarlin Reino R., 87
Sawyer, Billy, 170, 173
Schifter, Richard, 105, 207, 229–30, 232–33
Schriver, Sergeant, 229
Schuelke, John H., 136, 141–44
Scott, Marlin, 207, 221–22
Scottsdale, AZ, 105-10, 152, 226
Scudder, Thayer, 242
Second Mesa, AZ, 7, 12, 32, 82
Sekaquaptewa, Abbott, 107–8, 170, 176–77, 185, 202, 224, 227–28, 234–35
Sekaquaptewa, Emory, 181–84, 189, 191–95
Sekaquaptewa, Robert, 170
Sekaquaptewas, 204
Sequi, Edna, 80
settle (legal concept), 27, 55, 60, 88–90, 92, 97–98. See also U. S. Secretary of the Interior.
Shaw–Serder, David, 242
Shing, Samuel P., 189
Shongpavi, AZ, 11–12
Shonto Springs, AZ, 74
Sidney, Ivan, 244
Silver, Ben, 47–48, 51–52

304

Index

Udalls (family), 102
Udall, Stewart, 38, 102, 104–5, 110–12,
    115–18, 134, 136–38, 141, 145–47, 153,
    157, 159–60, 169, 172, 186, 229,
    274n.31; appoints task force on economic
    development, 138; injunction restraining,
    114, 116–18, 145, 147. See also U. S. Sec-
    retary of the Interior.
United States, ix, 46, 157, 200, 231, 237,
    246
U. S. Attorneys, 54, 59, 102, 141–42, 148,
    154, 200
U. S. Bureau of Indian Affairs (BIA), xi–xiv,
    37–38, 68, 71–72, 74, 76–77, 85, 101,
    105–7, 111, 114–15, 117, 136–38, 140–
    45, 147–49, 151–52, 155, 168, 181, 186–
    88, 195, 198–99, 204–7, 211, 215, 217,
    224, 228, 230, 242; area offices, 104, 169;
    Branch of Land Operations, 167, 172,
    177; census, 77-78, 88–89; herbarium, 79;
    police, 206, 210; probates of allottees,
    180; retired officials, 172
U. S. Commissioner of Indian Affairs, 31–
    33, 98, 102, 110, 144, 149, 154, 156–57,
    159, 169, 172, 178, 180, 194, 206; special
    representative of, 149; U. S. Congress, xi,
    24, 32, 36–39, 54–55, 99, 106–7, 109,
    113, 117, 142, 152, 157, 166, 177, 198–
    202, 204, 208, 212, 214, 216, 217, 227,
    231–32, 234, 237–39, 241–42, 244, 247,
    249–50, 254; 92nd Congress, 218; 93d
    Congress, 218
U. S. courts, 92, 244, 247, 254
U. S. Department of justice, 37, 54, 68, 102
U. S. Department of the Interior, xi, 36–38,
    104, 107, 110, 139–40, 145, 208, 212–13;
    solicitor, 111, 118, 187
U. S. District Court for the District of Ari-
    zona, 39
U. S. District Courts, 200
U. S. District of Columbia Court of Appeals,
    116–18, 145
U. S. government, ix, xii, 20, 61, 87, 95, 99,
    101, 159, 164, 177, 183, 201–2, 222, 224,
    227, 233, 237, 242–43, 246, 274n.31; U.
    S. House of Representatives, 37–38, 201,
    211–14, 232–33; Interior Committee,
    211, 229–30; Rules Committee, 232–33;
    Subcommittee on Indian Affairs, 114,
    138, 229
U. S. Indian Claims Commission, 36, 40, 45,
    102, 200
U. S. Ninth Circuit Court of Appeals, 200,
    202–3, 215
U. S. Secretary of the Interior, 27, 32, 55,
    88–89, 91, 97, 102–3, 108, 142–44, 147,
    156–57, 185, 187, 198, 213
U. S. Senate, 37, 212–13, 217–18, 233, 239;
    Committee on Indian Affairs, 32; Interior
    Committee, 213–14, 229, 235–39; Inte-
    rior and Insular Affairs Committee, 217–
    18, 234; Subcommittee on Indian Affairs,
    213–14, 229; Winslow hearings, 217–26
U. S. Supreme Court, 97, 103–4, 107, 144,
    147, 149, 157, 209, 215, 274n.36
Upper Moenkopi, AZ, 170, 183, 190, 192,
    234; governor of, 184, 189
uranium, 90, 159, 162-63
use and occupancy (legal concept), 55, 59,
    70, 77, 79, 87–92, 93–95, 97–99, 152,
    153, 188
Utes, 14, 20, 34, 50, 157, 211–12, 266n.16

Valentine, Gray, 124–25
Van Compernolle, Remi, 78
Vannette, Walter M., 242
Van Valkenburagh, Richard F., xiii, 36, 40,
    43, 45–48, 64, 253;
Van Winkle, Jones, 152
Vaughan, Robert, 138
Vaughn, Theodore M., 224
Vizcarra, José Antonio, 16–17
Vlassis, George P., 200–201, 208, 229, 234

Walker, Chester L., 175
Walpi, AZ, 7, 11